Developing Verbal Talent

Ideas and Strategies for Teachers of Elementary and Middle School Students

Joyce VanTassel-Baska
Dana T. Johnson
Linda Neal Boyce

Editors

The College of William and Mary
Center for Gifted Education

Allyn and Bacon

Boston • London • Toronto • Sydney • Tokyo • Singapore

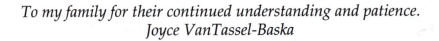

To my family for their continued understanding and patience.
Joyce VanTassel-Baska

To the sisters of the Convent of the Visitation in St. Paul for the
excellent education they have provided me.
Dana T. Johnson

To the Panama City Beach Revelers for everything you mean to
me as individuals and as a group.
Linda Neal Boyce

Library of Congress Cataloging-in-Publication Data

Developing verbal talent / edited by Joyce VanTassel-Baska, Dana T.
   Johnson, Linda Neal Boyce.
      p. cm.
   "The College of William and Mary, Center for Gifted Education."
   Includes bibliographical references and index.
   ISBN 0-205-15945-1
   1. Gifted children--Education--United States--Language arts.
   2. Gifted children--Education--United States--English language.
   3. Language arts--United States--Curricula.   4. Verbal learning.
   I. VanTassel-Baska, Joyce.   II. Johnson, Dana T.   III. Boyce, Linda
   Neal.   IV. College of William and Mary.   Center for Gifted
   Education.
   LC3993.27.D48   1996   95-16597
   371.95'3--dc20   CIP

Credits: (continued on page 386, which constitutes a continuation of the copyright page)

Printed in the United States of America

10 9 8 7 6 5 4 3 2 1   99 98 97 96 95

Contents

PART IV   Teacher Reflections and Model Lesson Plans   289

Foreword

The field of gifted education is experiencing a paradigm shift from the old conception of giftedness as a single IQ score or a singular trait of global ability to a new orientation that conceptualizes human ability as consisting of specific talents, aptitudes, or factors such as persistence and curiosity that, in combination, facilitate high-level, creative achievement. This new view of human ability was heralded by Thurstone, Guilford, and many others. The Differential Aptitude Test and the Scholastic Aptitude Test paved the way further for this differential view of human abilities. Howard Gardner's seven intelligences model reminded us again of basic differences among human abilities. In the field of gifted education, new theoretical work by Francoys Gagne and Jane Piirto have elaborated on the conception of talents as emerging specific abilities in youth that coalesce in adult careers to make expertise and creative achievement possible. In my writing, I have referred to this paradigm shift as TIDE, an acronym for Talent Identification and Development in Education.

This talent orientation calls for recognition and nurturance of talents in specific academic areas such as language arts or science, artistic realms such as in drama or music, vocational domains such as business or home economics, and interpersonal activities such as teaching or leadership. Programs for talented youth must be directed to youths' specific needs that are not being met in regular classrooms.

The 1994 report from the United States Office of Education, *National Excellence, Developing America's Talent*, sounds a clarion call for this new orientation when it says: "The term gifted connotes a mature power rather than a developing ability and, therefore, is antithetical to recent research findings about children" (p. 26). The report goes on to urge schools to look throughout the range of disciplines and fields to identify youth with diverse talents.

This important volume on verbal talent stands as a testimony to this newer conception of giftedness. It is undoubtedly the best treatise ever written on the subject of verbal talent, how to recognize or identify it, and how to nurture or develop it. In an age of declining verbal competence in the general population, rapid change in the modes of interpersonal communication, and pervasive inarticulateness of students, it is encouraging to find educators proposing solutions that might at least salvage a cadre of verbally talented youth—youth who can provide leadership in government, business, the arts, and technology.

Precocious youth need curricula and instruction at a level and pace that is far above that for students of average ability. The authors correctly note, and cite supporting research, that in an inclusion classroom where all levels of verbal readiness are represented, the teacher would be hard-pressed to use the same curriculum materials and methods of instruction appropriate for verbally precocious youth in the same way at the same time. Some of the ideas and guidelines presented in this book might be useful in teaching youth of low and average ability, but the major emphasis is on the recognition and development of talent among verbally precocious students.

The curriculum advocated in this book assumes curricular depth and content well beyond age-grade placement. It also assumes precocious levels and complexity of thought as well as the challenge of interdisciplinarity and thematic orientation. All of these assumptions clearly call for reflective, knowledgeable, disciplined teachers. Furthermore, the whole process of instruction and learning anticipates lofty personal goals, commitment, and intrinsic motivation on the part of teachers.

The authors of this book embrace the Integrated Curriculum Model (ICM) that is already well accepted in the field based on the work of the lead author. The teaching methods and curricular material presented in this book illustrate well that ICM model. The authors have all had abundant experience in what they preach so this book represents no "pie in the sky" speculation. It is sound theory, sound curriculum, and sound practice.

The authors wisely acknowledge that developing verbal talents calls for specific curricula and instruction that focus on youth's verbal precocity in specific domains. The task is immense for parents and schools. Potentially talented youth who get the benefits of the sound curricula and instruction advocated in this book will find their chances of high-level creative achievements enhanced immeasurably.

The authors of this book embrace the thematic conception of "change" as one undergirding framework for their curriculum. Alas, until schools and their leaders see the wisdom of change to using new approaches in the education of youth with special talents, many talented youth will achieve far below their potential. This book tells us clearly how we could provide education for youth who are verbally talented and motivated to the full development of their abilities.

John F. Feldhusen
Purdue University

Preface

This book grew out of the editors' intensive involvement with a nationally funded curriculum development project in the language arts. Funded through the Jacob Javits Act, the project had two interrelated goals: (1) to review existing language arts materials to ascertain their appropriateness of use with high-ability learners; and (2) to develop new language arts curricula consonant with new curriculum standards and tailored for use with high-ability learners. The nature of this curriculum challenge, coming when it did at the beginning of a major national curriculum reform effort, posed special problems and issues. It expanded our understanding and our vision of what language arts for students with talent might be in classrooms around the country. Also emerging during this time of conceptualization was the new *National Excellence: A Case for Developing America's Talent* (1993), a document that captures the abysmal state of schooling for our brightest youngsters and advocates strong recommendations for high-powered learning opportunities coupled with appropriately high standards in all curriculum areas. The timing of this report was crucial to our efforts to convert the language arts curriculum for high-ability learners to a national model of appropriate-level opportunities within a set of challenging standards.

Through work with the national project, we had opportunities to develop a curriculum framework that specified what talented students should be learning at the K–8 levels in school. Decisions were made for emphasis in some areas and not others. For example, we chose to focus on the development of analytical and interpretive reading skills rather than other reading behaviors, because high-ability learners in the language arts are good readers already. They have mastered the fundamental skills of reading at an early age, many times before entry to school. Moreover, the National Assessment of Educational Progress (NAEP) (National Center for Educational Statistics, 1992) approach to the assessment of reading behaviors has highlighted an emphasis on understanding and interpretation of literature. Thus, outcomes that focused on critical reading seemed most appropriate.

By the same token, we were careful to recommend literature that was challenging to good readers and worthy of their spending time not only reading it but also discussing it. We included in our teaching units only literature that met the test of rich language, openness of interpretation, and depth of idea. We also wanted talented students to be reading literature that was advanced for their age and grade, thus more in line with their reading level.

The curriculum framework also took a stand on what to emphasize in writing programs for the talented. We were very influenced by the 1992 National Assessment of Educational Progress Writing Portfolio study and its results showing the limited samples of persuasive writing being submitted by teachers at grades 4 and 8. Thus, we chose to emphasize this form of writing in our units and to establish outcomes related to it in the framework. This emphasis on persuasion also allowed a natural tie to the oral communication section of the framework by allowing emphasis on debate. Since we viewed writing as an extension of thinking, we also emphasized various writing response approaches, including webs, journals, and embedded assessments.

Unlike many language arts projects, we chose to emphasize oral communication as a key emphasis in the framework. Both evaluative listening skills and oral communication skills were explored in each of the teaching units developed around the framework.

We also felt that linguistic competency and vocabulary development were important emphases within the overall framework for talented learners. Given these learners' natural interest in words and word relationships, the infusion of emphasis in this area appeared warranted. But it was also necessary because of its importance in building sensitivity to language for writing and for interpreting literature.

Thus, the curriculum framework provides a set of learner outcomes for talented students in reading, literature, writing, oral communication, grammar, and vocabulary. The underlying treatment of these strands of the language arts is interdisciplinary—connecting each of the strands to the others through integrated lessons.

Another key feature of the curriculum framework is its employment of a central concept—the concept of change—for development within the units of study. By developing a set of generalizations about change and translating them into the lesson plans for discussion, writing, and oral activities, the project also supports a strong interdisciplinary emphasis.

Last, the framework of the project emphasizes thinking. Through the adaptation of Paul's (1992) reasoning model, we have infused all strands of the language arts with an emphasis on reasoning about what we read, what we write and what we say.

However, the editors did not all at once and of one unit recognize the ways in which these emphases could be realized in practice. We worked with wonderful classroom teachers who developed and taught lessons based on the framework. We designed assessments to gauge student learning in each of the key areas. We even organized a Saturday class of fourth- to sixth-graders that we taught in order to gain greater insights into the translation of these ideas at the classroom level. Through these means, we also have come to appreciate how difficult it is to deliver a curriculum as planned.

Because we valued the interaction of ideas to be derived from conversations between classroom practitioners and those of us who focus primarily on research and development in the language arts, we sponsored a symposium and follow-up discussion day with prospective authors to engage in the language of ideas and their translation into practice. Out of this conversation emerged the outline for this book—one that we believe renders theory, research, and practice in equal measure on the pages that follow. We have tried to honor their equal importance as well in choice of authors. We have teacher authors who work with talented students at all levels of the learning enterprise, from primary grades to high school. We have authors who bring special expertise in gifted and talented education, in constructivism in language arts, and in library science. We also involved authors from the university communities of English and speech, as well as education. Through such collaboration, we hoped to foster a more integrative way of seeing language arts instruction in schools. Consequently, diversity in authors' style was preserved throughout the book. Individual chapters within sections may be more interesting or appropriate for particular readers but not others because of the blend of authorship and perspective we have deliberately included.

Who should read this book? We firmly believe educators and parents who want guidance in developing verbal talent need to select from these chapters the elements that will augment current approaches or perhaps change the vision of what might be done for such students at elementary and secondary levels. This book is not, however, for the classroom teacher looking for an easy recipe to plug into lesson plans on Monday morning. It is for the thoughtful and reflective practitioner who wishes to improve classrooms for bright learners. It is also for the building and district administrator eager to implement national reform work into classroom practice in one key area of the curriculum. It is definitely for the administrator interested in affecting student learning but not for the administrator interested in reforming only the shell of schooling. Moreover, it is certainly not for the blasé educator who believes, contrary to current national and international data, that talented students need no support from schools. Certainly, this book is also for the concerned parent who senses untapped verbal ability in his or her child and wants to do something about it. Practical ideas for encouraging students in home as well as school contexts are interlaced throughout the volume.

The purpose of *Developing Verbal Talent* is to provide these various audiences with some specific tools and strategies for enhancing language arts and English classrooms in such a way as to optimize opportunities for verbal talent to emerge and be nurtured. Some of the techniques advocated in the book come directly from the general curriculum reform literature; others come from the language arts reform literature, especially reading and writing; still others come from the literature of gifted education. Taken together, they constitute a rich base on which to build powerful programs that promote talent development in the verbal arts.

As editors and authors, we take some strong stands on issues in teaching and learning in the language arts. Among them are the following:

- Basal texts are inadequate for use with talented learners in schools. Heavy emphasis on readability indices, watered-down stories, and low-level activities and questions all contribute to the dismal state of commercial texts for classroom use in language arts. At secondary levels, the choice of a good anthology may still be warranted, but more preferable is the selection of separate genre anthologies and a good writing model anthology.
- Reading selections to develop talent in the language arts must be slightly above the tested reading level of the student, not at or below it. Too many classroom sets of literature, as well as basals, are pitched too low to be a reading challenge for bright students. By fourth grade, talented readers are already at or beyond sixth-grade reading level, which is the stage considered adult reader by the larger society, as seen by the readability levels of most newspapers and magazines.
- Heavy emphasis on so-called creative writing will not improve talented students' writing habits. In order for talented writers to develop, they must write every day, receive feedback for their work, and revise and strengthen what they have produced. This rigorous process will ultimately improve one's writing, not a 30-minute assignment to create a haiku for display in a nonassessed writing portfolio.
- Direct teaching of challenging and interesting vocabulary words can enhance language arts instruction for talented learners. More than spelling, vocabulary forces students to attend to meaning, nuance, and word choice in what they read and write. Therefore, emphasis in this area will cause more growth in language than more traditional strategies.

- Direct teaching of the syntax of English in a self-study mode can allow talented learners the freedom to apply their understanding at early stages of development. Unlike the piecemeal model of teaching grammar advocated by basal texts, this approach recognizes talented learners' capacity to grasp understanding of syntactic structures holistically.
- Thinking can best be taught embedded in a general model of reasoning and applied systematically to all areas of language arts instruction rather than as isolated skills. Reasoning in literature, in writing, in oral communication, and in language study deepens student understanding for the reciprocal processes involved and helps develop both critical reading and writing behaviors.
- Interdisciplinary connections within the language arts need to be articulated and illustrated coherently. Whole language theorists have contributed much to the importance of integrated learning but have not tracked the implications down to the level of classroom practice to ensure faithful translation of those ideas. Consequently, we have teachers using literature as a basis for writing without a clue as to the meaning of reflective reading, the demands of writing, or the implications of developing critical behaviors. Talented students need a framework for discovering the natural linkages among the language arts so that each act, whether it be reading or writing or speaking or listening, is viewed in its relationship to all others. This cannot happen unless each lesson incorporates these acts in a holistic way.
- Incorporating interdisciplinarity is not the most pressing problem of upgrading good language arts instruction in schools. Making curriculum interdisciplinary may be desirable in the long run, but more emphasis needs to be placed on bringing basic language arts instruction up to a reasonable standard first. Although this book demonstrates how to develop interdisciplinary connections in language arts, it does not see this movement as central to improving verbal learning for talented students.

A central theme of this book is creating meaning through inquiry, an enterprise equally important for student and teacher. Teaching and learning the language arts is a quest, a search for understanding self in relationship to others. Thus, language arts classrooms must honor this concept by organizing searches for knowledge through research, quests for interpretation through literary discussions, and journeys to communicate through writing, speaking, and listening. We have tried to stress the importance of these approaches to construct meaning in an active way throughout the text, including questions to the reader at the end of each chapter and samples of exemplary lessons in language arts that stress student engagement with text in an active way.

Many educators believe, evidence to the contrary, that good teaching strategies applied to all learners will create a talented learner. Others believe that gifted education is only applying these excellent strategies. Thus, if we can appropriate from gifted education these successful tools and use them with all learners, how much better the world of education will be. Quite the contrary! Good gifted education is not a bag of tricks, a little creative thinking here, a dash of critical thinking there, or a dose of projects to be completed with a piece of string and chicken wire. Like all good education, gifted education has evolved from a thoughtful look at the characteristics and needs of a special population of learners who come to school already displaying advanced development in key areas. Their abilities necessitate a beginning point of learning that is more advanced and complex. And that learning must be perceived as basic and ongoing to the curriculum experiences of such learners. This book attempts to dispel the myth of gifted education as only teaching strategies. It demonstrates the cohesiveness of various aspects of nurturing talented learners in a fully developed curriculum plan.

We believe that many of the ideas in this book can be applied to all language arts learners, but we know from our project experiences that not all learners can benefit from being provided advanced literature and vocabulary or complex writing and research activities. How much what works with gifted students can be translated for all learners remains to be seen and hopefully done to some extent by the readers of this book. Yet the integrity of what was developed for talented learners should first and foremost be used with them in classrooms around the country. If larger groups of learners can profit, all the better. The only rationale for withholding the proposed curriculum ideas would be because it is not in the best interests of a child at a particular time to be focusing his or her learning in this way.

The issue of prerequisite skills is also relevant to consider here. Students who cannot read a short story cannot adequately discuss its meaning. Students who cannot write paragraphs cannot write argumentative essays. Students who cannot use a library source correctly cannot handle multiple sources well. All of these examples underscore the need to recognize that different learners have different thresholds for learning at a given stage of development and that talented learners in the language arts typically have higher thresholds from school entry until graduation.

The concept of talent development is also central to this book. The editors believe that educators should be nurturing all learners in fundamental ways that will enhance their talent in the language arts. Since the skills of language arts are lifelong and learners develop them at different rates, it is important to ensure that all students are given early and sufficient practice with them. It is particularly important to ensure that talented language arts students have opportunities to advance in aspects of language arts learning commensurate with their knowledge and skills. Books selected according to individual reading level, vocabulary chosen from these books, writing based on understanding what one has read, and oral presentations based on such books provide a way to ensure that individual differences are accommodated within an overall model of talent development in teaching the language arts. Teaching for reasoning and teaching to an overarching theme are all features of good language arts instruction for all. The use of literature groups to discuss and reflect on reading is also critical to such a program. We have found the Junior Great Books model of inquiry especially useful to teachers in incorporating small group literature discussion.

This book is organized into four broad sections, each meant to convey important ideas for teaching and learning in the language arts. Part I provides a theoretical backdrop to the book, raising important issues and questions about the fundamental philosophy of teaching for talent development in this subject area. The authors in Part I focus on general ideas about talent and development, specific issues of verbal talent and constructivism, the role of classics, and the study of literature as a reflection of life.

In Part II, various approaches to teaching the language arts in each of their manifestations are explored. Chapters focus specifically on issues of literacy development, oral communication, writing, language study, foreign language, and the need for honoring diversity in the language arts classroom.

Part III provides specific ideas for classroom practice derived from the work of the National Curriculum Project for High Ability Learners in Language Arts. Three of these chapters were written by pilot teachers and others by project staff. They provide important guidance in using both existing language arts materials and the newly developed units.

Part IV addresses issues in the development and implementation of exemplary language arts curriculum. This part features model lesson plans and framework examples that underscore important issues in keeping curriculum faithful in translation but also dynamic and changing.

Taken as a whole, *Developing Verbal Talent* represents a coherent way of responding to the concern for excellence in our schools. From the setting of high standards in language arts instruction to the corresponding translation of these standards in classroom practice, this book offers a set of unique perspectives on the development of verbal talent. More than that, it provides educators an important basis for meaningful change through offering research-based goals and a model for new practices built upon them.

Acknowledgments

I would like to thank the College of William and Mary Research Program that allowed me time to work on important ideas for this volume during the fall of 1993 as a visiting fellow to Cambridge University, Cambridge, England.

—Joyce VanTassel-Baska

All of the editors would like to thank the staff of the Center for Gifted Education at the College of William and Mary—Katie Hall, Claire Hughes, Chris Keene, Tori Moss, Amy Muraca, Cathy Wrightson, Chwee Geok Quek, and Evan Silver—for their assistance in various stages of manuscript preparation.

References

National Center for Educational Statistics. (1992). *NAEP writing portfolio study.* Washington, DC: U.S. Department of Education.

National excellence: A case for developing America's talent (1993). Washington, DC: Office of Educational Research and Improvement, United States Department of Education.

Paul, R. W. (1992). *Critical thinking.* Santa Rosa, CA: The Foundation for Critical Thinking.

Note: Some of the research for this book was supported under the Javits Act Program, a subcontract funding from Saratoga Springs BOCES, Saratoga Springs, New York, and administered by the Office of Educational Research and Improvement, United States Department of Education. Grantees undertaking such projects are encouraged to express freely their professional judgment. The contents of this book, therefore, do not necessarily represent positions or policies of the government and official endorsement should not be inferred.

Part I

Talent Development in the Language Arts

Part I of this book provides a general background to understanding the relationship between the process of talent development in general and the specific application of it to language learning and literary understanding. Authors in this section address theoretical considerations underlying practical applications of programs that may promote talent development in the language arts.

Chapter 1, written by Joyce VanTassel-Baska, presents a historical view of the process of talent development, citing the collection of factors that influence talent development, including institutions, individuals such as parents, and intrapersonal influences such as perseverance and commitment to an area. VanTassel-Baska reviews the various types of program responses schools have made to talented learners and provides commentary on the variables necessary to consider. A. Harry Passow, the author of Chapter 2 on talent development in the language arts, explores various conceptions of talent identification in this area and the processes that might be most facilitative to nurture it. Passow also examines the development of linguistic, oral, written, and communication talents as they have been studied. Chapter 3 focuses on the new view of learning language and its related skills. Nancy Nelson Spivey presents the case for constructivism from the vantage point of a researcher in the field, citing the role of text and intertext in helping students to create meaning. Michael Clay Thompson, author of Chapter 4, argues for cleaving to the classical traditions in the teaching of the language arts. Thompson provides a rationale for using classical literature as the founda-

1

tion for language arts programs. Chapter 5, written by Barbara Allen Taylor, explores the process of literary understanding, noting the evolution of learners from naive reader to sophisticated participant in the rich interplay of written language.

As a whole, the chapters tie together the important threads of talent development with teaching and learning in the language arts. Underlying this fusion is the recognition that all students should be taught language arts based on a talent development model, and that for students gifted in verbal areas, opportunities should be responsive to their needs for advanced work and in-depth exploration.

1

<hr>

The Process of
Talent Development

JOYCE VANTASSEL-BASKA
College of William and Mary

The development of talent in any area of human endeavor represents a concerted effort to mobilize personal and societal resources toward maximal performance and achievement in that area. The talents of the individual and the needs of society must converge on the areas in which development is likely to occur in order to assure resources to nurture optimal development. Some areas of talent development—such as dramatic performance talent, chess talent, or talent in the arts—are frequently viewed as the domain of the home or as extracurricular and not primarily the responsibility of schools. Other areas—such as writing and linguistic talent—are areas for which schools can and do influence the process. Regardless of the talent area, however, what is the process for talent development and how can we nurture it?

The development of any talent is a complex process involving the interweaving of many factors (e.g., Bloom, 1985; Feldman, 1991; Kulieke & Olszewski-Kubilius, 1989; Tannenbaum, 1983). Of all the possible influences on talent development, the role of parents has been studied in the most depth. Research on children who are gifted and have less than optimal family situations suggests that siblings, grandparents, adults in the community, teachers, and others, rather than parents, often serve as the primary influence in the development of talent (Goertzel & Goertzel, 1962; VanTassel-Baska, 1989;

VanTassel-Baska & Olszewski-Kubilius, 1989). Institutional, individual, and intrapersonal forces all appear to shape individual talent development over the lifespan (VanTassel-Baska & Olszewski-Kubilius, 1989).

Research on talent development has focused on the lives of eminent individuals from various domains as a way to understand the talent development process (Bloom, 1985). The factors that influence creativity and discriminate between a creative contributor and a competent technician have also been explored (Amabile, 1983; Getzels & Csikszentmihalyi, 1976). And the role that adversity plays in enhancing achievement motivation, performance, and resultant eminence have been addressed (Albert, 1993; Goertzel, Goertzel, & Goertzel, 1978; Ochse, 1990). Some work has been done on factors associated with talent development in specific fields. Several studies have been conducted on eminent scientists (Roe, 1953; Zuckerman, 1977), architects (McKinnon, 1962), and eminent writers and artists (Piirto, 1992).

The process of talent development in an individual may be characterized as slow and deliberate or quick and serendipitous. Bloom (1985) chronicled retrospectively the lives of 35 eminent individuals developing their talent to the highest level in middle adulthood who followed a fairly distinct pattern at stages of development along the way. He found that the pattern consisted of several variables. Initially, there was a nurturing and supportive family, the right teacher at the right time, and the opportunity to fall in love with a talent area. Later, competition was available in order to develop to the appropriate level or standard in the talent field. Considerable practice time in the area also characterized this later period.

Feldman (1991) studied talent development from the perspective of youth. By understanding prodigies, he observed other talent development processes at work. Early exposure and opportunity to develop in a given field that is socially accepted and available was an important tenet of prodigious development. A support network—including parents, peers, teachers, and mentors—that encourage the prodigy in the talent area was also seen as a prerequisite. Finally, an outlet for the talent through publication, performance, or exhibition was viewed as necessary. Moreover, regardless of age, the internal characteristics of commitment to hard work, perseverance, and the need to create for both prodigies and successful adults form a valuable part of the talent development puzzle. How people develop talent, then, has been credited to a combination of influences related to home, schooling and special training, and personality variables that facilitate the process (VanTassel-Baska & Olszewski-Kubilius, 1989). These influences can be seen in the life of Darwin, for example, who made a remarkable breakthrough in science because of a careful organization of intent and intellect brought to bear in a constrained environment (Gruber, 1976).

Case Histories of Writers: The Talent Development Process at Work

One approach to understanding the talent development process is to study intensely the lives of eminent individuals who, by their work, clearly exemplify talent that has developed to a very high level. In a recent study of Charlotte Bronte and Virginia Woolf, eight common themes were found that impacted on their process of talent development as writers (VanTassel-Baska, 1995). These themes, emerging from studies of their lives and works, were characterized as adversity, autodidacticism, practice of the craft, need for emotional support, a defined philosophy of being, influence of place, loneliness, and search for a mother figure (Batchelor, 1991; Berg, 1987; Bloom, 1987; Gordon, 1984).

While these themes defined the lives of Bronte and Woolf, there also could be discerned through studying their lives a unique developmental path for talented writers—one that transcended time, place, and circumstance. This path may be characterized by four stages (see Figure 1–1). Each stage may overlap with either the preceding or following stage. For example, work in early literacy development would suggest that preschool-age children engage in active experimentation with various writing forms (Farr, 1985; Strickland & Morrow, 1989). Evidence from Bronte's and Woolf's lives suggests this led to more formalized practice with specific forms.

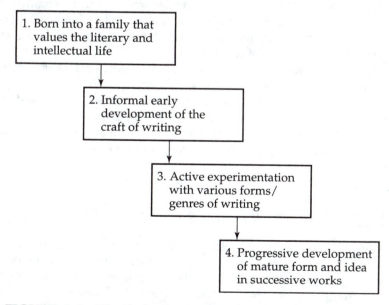

FIGURE 1–1   The Path of Talent Development for Writers

At stage 1, where the critical variable is the family into which a writer is born, a value system that promotes a life of the mind through intellectual and literary pursuits seems of primary importance. Within the family structure, it is important to have family members interested in talking about the world of ideas and encouraging self-study. In such a family, there also needs to be freedom to spend time alone reading and writing, suggesting a more isolated and unstructured childhood than the norm. Both Bronte and Woolf had families that provided the rich base for the development of their individual writing talents.

At stage 2, the path of writing talent may be characterized as informal. The child engages in imaginative play, using words, images, and self-crafted skits and plays. A key component at this stage is the use of audience to provide feedback to the young writer. Both Bronte and Woolf used their siblings and other family members for such exercises on a regular basis. Both the imaginative nature of creating stories and the shared knowledge about their creation are important aspects at this stage of development.

Stage 3 may be characterized as a period of active experimentation with form. The writer indulges in trying out new genres and seeking reactions to the results with a circle of friends who also create in artistic forms. This period may be seen in Bronte and Woolf as they matured as writers. For Bronte, the formalization of her little books with appropriate illustrations to be read by Branwell, Emily, and Anne exemplified this period of development as a writer. For Woolf, the creation of Bloomsbury and its ready coterie of intellectuals provided the stimulus for this period of her work and the leavening process necessary for further development. Continued self-study also characterizes this stage of the process.

Finally, stage 4 involves the progressive growth of a writer within a genre and within one's body of work. Charlotte Bronte's (1924) greatest novel was undoubtedly *Villette*, which was also her last. Theme and narrative voice had reached new levels not seen in the earlier novels. For Woolf (1976), *The Waves* represents a mastery of form and idea only hinted at in earlier works. If a writer is to have lasting impact in literature, it is at this stage that such genius emerges.

Educational Implications

In the lives of both Bronte and Woolf lie the seeds of understanding better the talent development process for writers. Moreover, their lives point to some practical considerations for parents and educators in facilitating writing talent throughout the school years. As an avenue for helping verbally talented learners gain control and mastery over self and a sense of self-esteem that emerges from meaningful intellectual activity, writing offers an ideal intervention. Specific considerations include the following:

1. *Encourage early writing behaviors.* Since writing can be developed early, it would appear important to have it encouraged in children even at preschool levels. Given the degree of pleasure it provided both Bronte and Woolf between the ages of 4 and 12, it might be seen as a strategy for enriching childhood.

2. *Provide a supportive network of young writers to test out ideas.* Just as Bronte and Woolf had their families to react to and consult with in their early literary attempts, so too do today's young writers need access to others with similar interests and abilities. Literary clubs or a literary journal project provide venues for such relationships to develop.

3. *Encourage reflection and writing on the student's own life experiences.* Both Bronte and Woolf reworked their lives through their writing, transforming them into high-level art. Young writers need to understand the power contained in the material of their own lives and be encouraged to write about it.

4. *Encourage bookmaking, the phenomenon of product.* Words and images are the material of writers, but until that material finds an outlet in a finished product, it has little form or meaning to anyone, including the writer. Thus, it is important to engage young writers in the act of producing books. For Charlotte Bronte and her siblings, this act of book production was an ongoing important task for most of their childhood and early adulthood.

5. *Develop artistic interest as an analogue to literary talent.* Charlotte Bronte and her siblings engaged in artistic development alongside verbal talent development. While art fed their imaginations as well as literature, it also provided a context for careful observation and analysis and the development of the important habits of precision and patience. All of these qualities were highly desirable for a life of writing. Moreover, writing and drawing at an imaginative level are reciprocal activities. Writing illustrates graphically one way the writer sees the world. Such illustrations lend assistance to crafting words to describe a unique vision. By writing, an author creates worlds that can be brought to life through illustration.

6. *Provide emotional support for the writing process.* Just as Bronte and Woolf experienced various difficulties in being able to write, so most people find writing emotionally difficult. We need to provide support for students in the writing process by establishing a climate of trust, of mutual sharing, and of understanding.

These case studies exemplify how the factors of temperament, life experiences, intrinsic talent and interest, and influences from a close literary community account for talent development in writers. Bronte and Woolf used their solitary pursuit of writing as a way to create meaning and make sense of their lives, thus bringing their talent to its optimal development.

Educational Approaches to Talent Development

The development of talent has been deliberately planned for centuries by thoughtful parents from Mozart's father to Frank Lloyd Wright's mother. Schools have been much slower to respond to the idea, however, except in specialized areas such as the arts, mathematics, and science. Occasionally, liberal arts-minded schools for the gifted were created to ensure appropriate programming in all subjects. Many of these schools, however, did not consider themselves developers of individual specialized talent (Subotnik, Kassen, Summers, & Wasser, 1993).

One specific educational approach has been to identify talent and provide "optimal match" experiences to nurture it through multiple means. Early programs focused on the use of special classes to accomplish this end, emphasizing enrichment experiences for core groups of gifted students from second grade on (Barbe, 1955; Hollingworth, 1942). A more recent model has included fast-paced movement through school curriculum, advanced curriculum placement in university-based settings, or mentoring as primary modes of delivery. This approach has been institutionalized nationally through the academic talent search model, developed by Stanley and his colleagues in the middle 1970s (Stanley, Keating, & Fox, 1974).

A more inclusive educational approach to talent development currently being advocated rests on the provision of curriculum for all students at appropriate levels of challenge so that talent may be discerned and encouraged from a broader range of students in the classroom. This idea, initially advocated by Passow (1955), has been recently popularized by Gardner (1983) and others promoting the application of a multiple intelligences theory in regular classrooms. Students are provided opportunities in linguistic, logical, mathematical, musical, artistic, kinesthetic, interpersonal, and intrapersonal modules and allowed maximal development in these various talent areas. Whole schools have adopted this model (Bolanos, 1994).

Another approach has been explored through the development of curriculum that is responsive to students talented in traditional academic areas (VanTassel-Baska, Gallagher, Bailey, & Sher, 1993; VanTassel-Baska, 1994). This approach has relied on the key factors of curriculum reform to guide the development process through an integrated curriculum model that emphasizes talent development.

Historical Development of School-Based Responses to Talent Development

For nearly 20 years, schools have favored a process-product orientation to nurturing talent regardless of the specific area of ability. This approach, popularized by the Enrichment Triad Model (Renzulli, 1977), offered program pioneers in the field a model for initiating pullout resource room programs. This approach gained further support as the cognitive science movement developed, calling for higher-order thinking skills, relevant real-world products, and emphasis on different modes of thinking (Gardner, 1983; Sternberg, 1985). Maker (1982) saw differentiated curriculum for talented learners as a technological issue for teachers by organizing various instructional models to provide for gifted students in any classroom setting. By modifying the strategy model and its components—along content, process, and product dimensions—curriculum for the gifted would result as long as certain differentiating delivery factors were taken into account. Any model of curriculum that followed these early examples of the process-product paradigm tended to gain easy acceptance in schools. The Autonomous Learner Model (Betts, 1991), the Grid System (Kaplan, 1986), the Purdue Three-Stage Model (Feldhusen & Kolloff, 1978), and the Individualized Program Planning Model (IPPM) (Treffinger, 1986) all made the underlying assumption that good curriculum for gifted learners was developed based on individual learner interest and emphasized higher-order skills used in the service of creating meaningful products.

This process-product view of nurturing talent development in schools has limited the development and use of models of curriculum derived from the disciplines of knowledge themselves. Thus, many gifted programs have lacked the rich substance that only the world of content knowledge might bring when linked to important ideas and issues. Some theorists, notably Ward (1981), pressed for a curriculum framework that would honor the traditional disciplines of study at the same time that it extended ideas about differential education of the gifted. Ward sought to provide a meaningful structure to curriculum for the gifted, one that would emphasize systems of thought and great ideas as organizers rather than individual skills or topics. Yet Ward's model was conceptually too abstract for easy translation and use by teachers, although several curriculum efforts were spawned using his approach (Ward, 1979; VanTassel-Baska & Feldhusen, 1981).

Another approach to talent development began to find favor in the late 1970s as a reaction against the trivialization of curriculum brought about by the misapplication of process-product models. Like Ward, Stanley's diagnostic-prescriptive content-based approach to curriculum (Stanley, Keating, & Fox, 1974; Keating, 1976) was concerned about students learning important subject matter. However, Stanley did not advocate radical reorganization of existing school curriculum, but merely its speeding up or acceleration for gifted learners. Based on Scholastic Aptitude Test scores derived from national talent searches that identify over 120,000 middle school-age students each year, the application of this curriculum approach has been widely implemented in university-based summer and academic year offerings. Begun initially as a fast-paced credit-producing series of course options primarily in mathematics, the application of this model has now spread to all content areas, with speed of course completion and mastery of advanced course content the major defining emphases on whether credit is or is not subsequently awarded. However, this approach as an option in schools had limited appeal for many school practitioners since it offered nothing new in curriculum substance, only a prescription for flexible pacing of what already existed. The current practice of curriculum compacting offers a more limited variation of the central ideas of diagnostic-prescriptive intervention at more discrete levels of classroom work (Reis & Purcell, 1993) without addressing issues of advancement in the content area itself.

The Integrated Curriculum Model

A dearth of attention has been given to the relationship of talent development to well-conceived and developed curriculum that is responsive to students talented in specific areas of learning. One such response, however, has been articulated, and it represents the project work on which this book is based. The Integrated Curriculum Model (ICM), first proposed by this author in 1986 (VanTassel-Baska, 1986) and further explicated in subsequent publications (VanTassel-Baska, 1992, 1993a), is comprised of three interrelated curriculum dimensions, responsive to very different aspects of the gifted learner. These curriculum dimensions may be thought of as:

1. *Emphasizing advanced content knowledge that frames disciplines of study.* Honoring the talent search concept, this facet of the model would ensure that careful, diagnostic-prescriptive approaches were employed to ensure new learning as opposed to remedial instruction. Curriculum based on this dimension would represent appropriate advanced learning in all appropriate curriculum areas.

2. *Providing higher-order thinking and processing.* This facet of the model would promote student opportunities for manipulating information at complex levels through employing generic thinking models such as Paul's (1992) and more discipline-specific ones such as Sher's (1993) in the scientific process. This dimension of the model also implies the utilization of information in some generative way, whether it be a project or a fruitful discussion.

3. *Focusing learning experiences around major issues, themes, and ideas that define both real-world applications and theoretical modeling within and across areas of study.* This facet of the model honors the Wardian idea of scaffolding curriculum for talented learners around the important aspects of a discipline and emphasizing these aspects in a systemic way. Thus, themes and ideas are selected based on careful research of the primary area under study to determine the most worthy and important issues and ideas for curriculum development. A theme consistent with new curriculum specifications (Perkins, 1992; Rutherford & Ahlgren, 1989), these ideas become an important framework for curriculum development. The goal of such an approach is to ensure deep rather than superficial understanding of ideas. Figure 1–2 portrays the ICM.

This model synthesizes the three best approaches to curriculum development and implementation documented in the literature for talented learners (Benbow & Stanley, 1983; Maker, 1982; Ward, 1981). The fusion of these approaches is central to the development of coherent curriculum that is responsive to diverse needs of talented students and yet provides rich challenges for optimal learning.

Translation into Curriculum

The ICM model has been successfully translated into two subject-matter areas. Work in other areas of the curriculum is also underway. One of the translations to a curriculum framework and teaching units of ICM was accomplished in the area of science. The second, described in Part III of this book, was executed in the language arts. To date, these two curriculum areas represent the only examples of a deliberate effort to translate the model into written materials. The translation of the ICM was accomplished by developing a curriculum framework addressing each of the dimensions of the model.

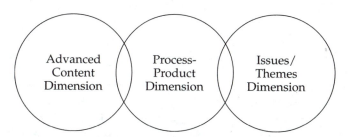

FIGURE 1–2   The Integrated Curriculum Model for Gifted Learners

In order to satisfy the need for advanced content, the language arts curriculum employed the use of advanced literature selections, works where the reading level was two years beyond grade level and sophisticated in respect to meaning. The writing emphasis was placed on persuasive essays, developing argument in written form—a more advanced form of writing than typically taught at elementary levels. Use of advanced vocabulary and the mastery of English syntax at the elementary level were also stressed. The process-product dimension of the curriculum was addressed by use of the embedded model of reasoning developed by Paul (1992) and the use of a research model developed to aid students in generating original work. Products were encouraged through both written and oral work. The issue/theme dimension of the curriculum was explicated by focusing on the theme of *change* as it applied to works of literature selected for the unit, the writing process, language study, and learners reflecting on their own learning throughout the unit. Additionally, selecting an issue of significance to study was emphasized as a part of the research project for each unit. To date, six units have been developed, validated, piloted, and revised using this framework.

The translation of the ICM to the National Science Curriculum Project for High Ability Learners was driven by the overarching theme of *systems*, which became the conceptual organizing influence in each of seven units of study. Students learned the elements, boundaries, inputs, and outputs, as well as interactions of selected systems. Through a problem-based learning approach, they also learned about how science systems interact with real-world social, political, and economic systems. The process-product dimension of the curriculum model was addressed through engaging students in a scientific research process that leads them to create their own experiments and to design their own solutions to each unit's central problem. The content dimension was addressed by selecting advanced science content for inclusion in each unit and encouraging in-depth study of selected content relevant to understanding the central problem of the unit. These units are being used in classrooms across the country to incorporate the new science emphasis and have been found successful in heterogeneous as well as self-contained gifted classrooms.

Curriculum Reform Design Elements

These national curriculum projects for high-ability learners were developed with an understanding of appropriate curriculum dimensions for gifted students, but they also demonstrate the use of key design features of curriculum reform strongly advocated by the national standards projects (O'Day & Smith, 1993) and the middle school movement (Erb, 1994). Thus, the projects employ the following emphases:

- The curriculum is meaning based—it emphasizes depth over breadth, concepts over facts—and is grounded in real-world issues and problems that students care about or need to know. In science, students study the implications of a daily occurrence such as acid spills on interstate highway systems. In language arts, they witness through literature the impact of treatment of minorities in the United States as it has changed over a 60-year period.
- The curriculum incorporates higher-order thinking as integral to all content areas. The units provide students with opportunities to demonstrate their understanding of advanced content and interdisciplinary ideas through strategies such as concept mapping, persuasive writing in language arts, and designing experiments in science.
- The curriculum emphasizes intra- and interdisciplinary connections through using overarching concepts, issues, and themes as major organizers. Thus, in science, students study systems of cities, government, economies, and language, as well as chemistry and biology. The concept of change in language arts is relevant to literature, writing, language, mathematics, art, and music.
- The curriculum provides opportunities for metacognition, student reflection on learning processes. Students are involved in consciously planning, monitoring, and assessing their own learning for efficient and effective use of time and resources.
- The curriculum develops habits of mind through cultivating modes of thinking that resemble professionals in various fields in respect to skills, predispositions, and attitudes. In science, curiosity, objectivity, and skepticism are openly nurtured; in language arts, the mode of reflection and revision is consistently encouraged.
- The curriculum promotes active learning and problem solving through putting students in charge of their own learning. In the problem-based science units, students find out what they know, what they need to know, and how to pursue important knowledge in working on a real-world problem in small investigatory teams. In language arts, students team to discover how language functions and is structured.
- The curriculum is technology relevant in that it uses various new technologies as tools for the learning process, from doing library research via CD-ROM, to composing at the word processor, to communicating with students across the world by e-mail. The units of study in both science and language arts incorporate activities that require these applications.
- The curriculum sets learner outcomes of significance. Expectations for learning are identified at targeted grade levels that reflect the priorities of the new curriculum for being broad based, conceptual, and relevant to real-world applications. In each set of units, learner outcomes reflect content, process, and concept emphases.

- The curriculum employs authentic assessment by tapping into what students know as a result of meaningful instruction. Using approaches such as portfolios and performance-based activities, the units engage learners in assessment as an active part of the learning process.

All of these reform elements formed the basis for initial curriculum development work. Tailoring of the curriculum for gifted learners occurred through ensuring the following kinds of emphasis:

- Provisions for acceleration and compression of content
- Use of higher-order thinking skills (e.g., analysis, synthesis, evaluation)
- Integration of content by key ideas, issues, and themes
- Advanced reading level
- Opportunities for students to develop advanced products
- Opportunities for independent learning based on student capacity and interest
- Use of inquiry-based instructional techniques

Thus, the systematic fusion of integrated curriculum considerations was effected.

Implementation Considerations

The implementation of any curriculum model is based on several considerations in the school setting. Most important among them is the nature of the learner. For students who are talented, regardless of the richness of the core curriculum base, there will be a need to address certain powerful characteristics through flexible implementation of a model.

The Learner: Characteristics, Aptitudes, and Predispositions

There are many characteristics of gifted learners that one might focus on for a discussion of creating an optimal match between learner and curriculum. Several lists have been discussed as a basis for curriculum work (e.g., Maker, 1982; VanTassel-Baska, 1993a). However, it has become apparent that three such characteristics remain pivotal for purposes of curriculum planning and development.

The *precocity* of the learner is a key characteristic to consider in curriculum development. Gifted learners, almost by definition, evidence advanced development in some school-related curriculum area. The most common tested areas for such development are in the verbal and mathematical subject domains. Most students identified for gifted programs are advanced at least two years in one or both areas. Such evidence of advanced development provides a basis for curriculum planning at a more advanced level and the expectation that such students can master new materials in one-third to one-half the time of typical learners. For very gifted learners, there is a powerful motivation to "learn fast and move ahead."

In addition to precocity, another key characteristic that deserves attention for curriculum development is the *intensity* of gifted learners. This intensity may be manifested affectively in the realm of emotional responsiveness when students react strongly to the death of a pet or the classroom injustice committed by a teacher. However, this characteristic also has saliency in the cognitive realm. Students exhibit intensity through the capacity to focus and concentrate for long periods of time on a subject that fascinates them or an idea they find intriguing. Such a characteristic can just as quickly become dissipated in uninteresting busywork or lack of depth in the exploration even of a subject of interest. This characteristic, like precocity, needs curricular attention.

The third learner characteristic of curricular interest is *complexity*, the capacity of gifted learners to engage in higher-level and abstract thinking even at young ages. It also refers to their preference for hard and challenging work, often at levels beyond current functioning. They also enjoy working on multiple levels simultaneously, as when solving complex real-world problems that have many parts and perspectives to study. Just as with precocity and intensity, the characteristic of complexity in learners who are gifted demands a curriculum responsiveness because it is openly desired by the learner as well as indicated by student behavior.

These three characteristics each dictate an approach to curriculum that honors the various facets of the minds and personalities of students who are gifted. Thus, curriculum models for the gifted have responded variously to these characteristics. The Integrated Curriculum Model represents a fusion of these approaches, such that the most powerful characteristics of the gifted are directly reflected in the curriculum intervention. Although this model has salience for all learners, based on a talent development paradigm, the variable of time becomes crucial in implementation. Not all learners will be ready at the same stage of development in each area for advanced, intensive, and complex study.

The Identification of Talent

The identification of talent has been seen as a complex task over the centuries. Plato was known to have remarked on this issue:

Observe them from early on. Note those who stand out from the rest by virtue of their qualities of mind and character of perseverance.

Current approaches to the identification of talent tend to favor a domain-specific orientation, although older models of identification used general ability tests as a primary mode of finding students advanced in verbal, mathematical, and other areas of learning. In fact, one charge leveled against intelligence tests has been their verbal loading, favoring students talented in this area.

There are many specific methods for identifying talent in schools and classrooms (Feldhusen, Asher, & Hoover, 1984; Richert, 1982). Group achievement tests given at various grade levels in school districts provide one way to discern students who are high functioning in areas of school learning. For in-class programming, working with students in high-level curriculum would be warranted if they are functioning above the 80th percentile on the verbal sections of such tests. Vocabulary subscores are particularly useful for detecting verbal talent. For identifying students who are highly talented in the language arts, it may be useful to look at scores in the 95th to 99th percentile range. These students may need more challenging opportunities than even what would be planned for other high-ability learners.

A second way to identify talent in the language arts is to do careful diagnostic testing at the beginning of the year on material in the core textbook used to study this area of the curriculum. For students who test out of substantial portions of the material, anywhere from 30 percent on, advanced work in a given curriculum area should be provided. Diagnostic reading tests and individual reading comprehension tests may also be useful to determine actual prior knowledge in this area. For fourth-graders and beyond, the use of a grammar and usage test would provide insight into grammatical competency.

In the area of writing, a review of writing portfolios is useful to discern writing talent. Another approach would be to give a timed writing assignment that would provide additional diagnostic information at the beginning of the academic year. Autobiographical and product assessment data may be another source of information about verbal precocity. Students who have done independent work in this area—such as additional reading and writing, participation in Junior Great Books or other discussion-oriented programs outside of school, or debate and drama work—may be exhibiting both interest and aptitude in this area.

Another current approach to identifying verbal talent in the classroom is to use behavioral assessment techniques. Through a process observation checklist, a teacher may identify informally students whose behaviors match the following list of characteristics for verbally advanced learners:

- Reads fluently and well
- Interested in words and word relationships
- Uses an advanced vocabulary
- Processes key ideas in what is read
- Enjoys talking about literature
- Writes descriptively and communicates a story
- Reads often inside and outside of class
- Enjoys verbal puzzles and games
- Plays with language in oral and/or written forms
- Exhibits an understanding of the structure of language in speaking and writing

Since the observation of these behaviors is not possible without a rich language arts curriculum base, the teacher must supply a set of activities conducive to eliciting these behaviors in all students. For those learners who are responsive to such activities, more challenging work may be appropriate. Thus, all learners in a context are assessed and given opportunities to demonstrate their linguistic abilities.

One other identification approach needs to be cited—that of off-level testing. If a school is interested in discovering its most verbally able learners, regardless of age or grade, one way to accomplish it is to engage in off-level achievement and aptitude testing. For students in grades 5 through 8, such off-level testing is available on a regional basis from either Johns Hopkins, Duke, Northwestern, or Denver Universities. For younger students in the school, using existing standardized achievement tests at the next higher grade may provide helpful information. Individual assessment instruments, such as the Woodcock-Johnson and the Peabody Individual Achievement Test, may also be useful in discerning advanced verbal learning in younger students. These tests may be administered by teachers or others trained in their use.

The Context Variables

What are the context variables that need consideration in order for a talent development process to work in schools? The need for a match between the learner and the intervention has already been described; it is also important to highlight important contextual considerations that could impact the process in school settings. At least four variables must be considered.

Flexibility in Student Placement and Progress

Even an enriched and accelerated curriculum developed for high-ability learners and addressing all of the educational reform principles cannot be used with such learners without careful consideration of entry skills, rate of learning, and special interests and needs. Thus, ungraded multiage contexts where high-ability learners may access appropriate work groups and curriculum stations is a critical component of the implementation context. Pretesting students on relevant skills is a central part of the new curriculum projects, and diagnosing unusual readiness or developmental spurts that may occur in a curriculum sequence is also important. Schools may notice and use such data as a basis for more in-depth work in an area of a particular teaching unit.

Grouping

As curriculum for high-ability learners is implemented, attention must be paid to the beneficial impact of grouping for instruction. Kulik's (1993) latest reanalysis of the grouping data points out that when curriculum is modified for gifted students, effects of grouping become more prominent. Moreover, recent classroom studies have verified that little differentiation is occurring in heterogeneous classrooms for gifted students (Archambault, Westberg, Brown, Hallmark, Zhang, & Emmons, 1993), and the majority of teachers in U.S. schools are not trained to teach gifted learners (Westberg, Archambault, Dobyns, & Salvin, 1993). Thus, forming instructional groups of gifted students for implementation of differentiated curriculum is clearly the most effective and efficient way to deliver it. Whether such grouping occurs in separate designated classes or in regular classrooms is a local consideration.

Trained Teachers

Recent data confirm the significant role of teacher training in providing differentiated instruction for the gifted (Hansen & Feldhusen, 1994; Tomlinson et al., 1994) and the availability of coursework in the education of the gifted (Parker & Karnes, 1991). Thus, there is every reason to place gifted students with teachers who have received at least 12 hours of professional training. The benefits to the gifted learners become greater when differentiated curriculum is handled by those sensitive to the nature and needs of such students.

A Climate of Excellence

In order for gifted learners to perform at optimal levels, the educational context must offer challenging opportunities that tap deeply into students' psychological states (Csiksenmihalyi, Rathunde, & Whalen, 1993), that provide generative situations (Feldhusen, VanTassel-Baska, & Seeley, 1989), and that also demand high standards of excellence, corresponding to expectations for high-level productivity in any field (Ochse, 1990). More than ever, if curriculum standards are to be raised successfully for any student, the climate of a school must be sensitive to and honor excellence. For gifted students, in particular, such a climate must be in place to ensure optimal development, positive attitudes toward learning, and engagement. Such a climate is also essential for disadvantaged gifted youth, put more at risk by lowered expectations for performance (House & Lapan, 1994).

Conclusion

Talent development offers a viable way to enhance the way schools carry out teaching and learning for all learners, such that the overall level of instruction is raised. At the same time, it is crucial that the "glass ceiling" for gifted students is also removed, encouraging maximal levels of performance. The Integrated Curriculum Model offers one concrete approach for restructuring curriculum for talented learners at the same time that it responds to the curriculum reform agenda for meeting the needs of all learners. It offers practitioners concrete units of study to implement in classrooms nationally by meeting the criteria for exemplary curriculum design, exemplary content considerations, and differentiation for talented learners. For talent development concepts to work effectively for all learners, attention must be paid to student characteristics, aptitudes, predispositions, and the context variables discussed in this chapter. Within a climate of raising standards for all, there must be room for optimizing opportunities for our most talented as well.

Key Points Summary

- Talent development is a complex process involving both internal variables of personality and motivation and external nurturance factors of parenting, schooling, and adult opportunities and experiences.
- Talent development in language arts may be understood from studying the lives of eminent writers.
- Case studies of writers suggest an important path for talent development in the language arts. Key suggestions for nurturance include:
    Encourage early writing behaviors.
    Provide a supportive network of young writers to test out ideas.
    Encourage reflection and writing on student's own life experiences.
    Encourage bookmaking, the phenomenon of product.
    Develop artistic interest as an analogue to literary talent.
    Provide emotional support for the writing process.
- Address the talented students' characteristics of precocity, intensity, and complexity in a verbal arts curriculum.
- Provide flexibility in student placement and progress.

- Group high-ability students for differentiated instruction in the language arts as appropriate, given the nature of the activity.
- Provide training to teachers in the needs of high-ability learners and in techniques to meet those needs.

References

Albert, R. S. (Ed.). (1993). *Genius and eminence: The social psychology of creativity and exceptional achievement.* New York: Pergamon.

Amabile, T. (1983). *The social psychology of creativity.* New York: Springer-Verlag.

Archambault, F. X., Westberg, K. L., Brown, S., Hallmark, B. W., Zhang, W., & Emmons, C. (1993). Regular classroom practices with gifted students: Findings from the classroom practices survey. *Journal for the Education of the Gifted, 16,* 103–119.

Barbe, W. (1955). Evaluation of special classes for gifted children. *Exceptional Children, 22,* 20–22.

Batchelor, J. (1991). *Virginia Woolf, the major novels.* Cambridge, England: Cambridge University Press.

Benbow, C. P., & Stanley, J. C. (Eds.). (1983). *Academic precocity: Aspects of its development.* Baltimore, MD: John Hopkins Press.

Berg, M. (1987). *Jane Eyre, portrait of a life.* Boston: Triangle Publishers.

Betts, G. (1991). The autonomous learner model for the gifted and talented. In N. Colangelo & G. A. Davis (Eds.), *Handbook of gifted education* (pp. 142–153). Boston, MA: Allyn and Bacon.

Bloom, B. (Ed.). (1985). *Developing talent in young people.* New York: Ballantine Books.

Bloom, H. (1987). *The Brontes.* New York: Chelsea House Publishers.

Bolanos, P. (1994, January). From theory to practice, Indianapolis Key School applies Howard Gardner's multiple intelligences theory to the classroom. *The School Administration, 30*–31.

Bronte, C. (1924). *Villette.* Edinburgh: J. Grant.

Csiksenmihalyi, M., Rathunde, K., & Whalen, S. (1993). *Talented teenagers: The roots of success and failure.* New York: Cambridge University Press.

Erb, T. (1994). The middle school: Mimicking the success routes of the information age. *Journal for the Education of the Gifted, 17*(4), 385–408.

Farr, M. (Ed.). (1985). *Advances in writing, research, volume one: Children's early writing development.* Norwood, NJ: Ablex.

Feldhusen, J., Asher, J., & Hoover, S. (1984). Problems in identification of giftedness, talent, or ability. *Gifted Child Quarterly, 28*(4), 149–151.

Feldhusen, J., & Kolloff, M. (1978). A three stage model for gifted education. *Gifted Child Today, 1,* 53–58.

Feldhusen, J., VanTassel-Baska, J., & Seeley, K. (1989). *Excellence in educating the gifted.* Denver, CO: Love.

Feldman, D. (1991). *Nature's gambit.* New York: Teachers College Press.

Gardner, H. (1983). *Frames of mind.* New York: Basic Books.

Getzels, J. W., & Csikszentmihalyi, M. (1976). *The creative vision: A study of problem finding in art.* New York: Wiley.

Goertzel, V., & Goertzel, M. G. (1962). *Cradles of eminence.* Boston, MA: Little, Brown.

Goertzel, V., Goertzel, M. G., & Goertzel, T. (1978). *Three hundred eminent personalities.* San Francisco, CA: Jossey-Bass.

Gordon, L. (1984). *Virginia Woolf: A writer's life.* Oxford, England: Oxford University Press.

Gruber, H. (1976). *Darwin on man*. London: Wildwood House.

Hansen, J., & Feldhusen, J. (1994). Comparison of trained and untrained teachers of gifted students. *Gifted Child Quarterly, 38*(3), 115–123.

Hollingworth, L. (1942). *Children with IQ's above 180*. New York: World Book.

House, E., & Lapan, S. (1994). Evaluation of programs for disadvantaged gifted students. *Journal for the Education of the Gifted, 17*(4), 441–466.

Kaplan, S. M. (1986). The grid: A model to construct differentiated curriculum for the gifted. In J. Renzulli (Ed.), *Systems and models for developing programs for the gifted and talented* (pp. 180–193). Mansfield Center, CT: Creative Learning Press.

Keating, D. (1976). *Intellectual talent*. Baltimore: Johns Hopkins Press.

Kulieke, P., & Olszewski-Kubilius, P. (1989). The influence of family values and climate on the development of talent. In J. VanTassel-Baska & P. Olzewski-Kubilius (Eds.), *Patterns of influence: The home, the self, and the school*. (pp. 40–59). New York: Teachers College Press.

Kulik, J. A. (1993). *An analysis of the research on ability grouping: Historical and contemporary perspectives*. Storrs, CT: National Research Center on the Gifted and Talented.

Maker, C. J. (1982). *Curriculum development for the gifted*. Rockville, MD: Aspen Systems.

McKinnon, D. (1962). The nature and nurture of creative talent. *American Psychologist, 17*, 484–495.

Ochse, R. (1990). *Before the gates of excellence: Determinants of creative genius*. Cambridge, England: Cambridge University Press.

O'Day, J. A., & Smith, M. S. (1993). Systemic reform and educational opportunity. In S. H. Fuhrman (Ed.), *Designing coherent education policy* (pp. 250–311). San Francisco, CA: Jossey-Bass.

Parker, J., & Karnes, F. (1991). Graduate degree programs and resource centers in gifted education: An update and analysis. *Gifted Child Quarterly, 35*, 43–48.

Passow, A. H. (1955). *Planning for talented youth: Considerations for public schools*. New York: Bureau of Publications, Teachers College, Columbia University.

Paul, R. (1992). *Critical thinking: What every person needs to survive in a rapidly changing world*. Rohnert Park, CA: Critical Thinking Foundation.

Perkins, D. (1992). Selecting fertile themes for integrated learning. In H. Hayes Jacobs (Ed.), *Interdisciplinary curriculum: Design and implementation* (pp.67–75). Alexandria, VA: Association for Curriculum and Development.

Perkins, D., & Saloman, G. (1989). Are cognitive skills context bound? *Educational Research, 18*(1), 16–25.

Piirto, J. (1992). *Understanding those who create*. Columbis, OH: Ohio Psychology Press.

Reis, S. M., & Purcell, J. H. (1993). An analysis of content elimination and strategies used by elementary classroom teachers and the curriculum compacting process. *Journal for the Education of the Gifted, 16*, 147–170.

Renzulli, J. (1977). *The enrichment triad*. Wethersfield, CT: Creative Learning Press.

Richert, S. (1982). *National report on identification, assessment, and recommendations for identification of gifted and talented youth*. Sewell, NJ: Educational Improvement Center-South.

Roe, A. (1953). *Making of a scientist*. New York: Dodd, Mead.

Rutherford, F. J., & Ahlgren, A. (1989). *Science for all Americans: Scientific literacy*. New York: American Association for the Advancement of Science.

Sher, B. T. (1993). *Guide to key science concepts*. Williamsburg, VA: College of William and Mary, Center for Gifted Education.

Stanley, J., Keating, D., & Fox, L. (1974). *Mathematical talent.* Baltimore, MD: Johns Hopkins Press.

Sternberg, R. J. (1985). *Beyond IQ.* New York: Basic Books.

Strickland, D. S., & Morrow, L. M. (Eds.). (1989). *Emerging literacy: Young children learn to read and write.* Newark, DE: International Reading Association.

Subotnik, R. F., Kassen, L., Summers, E., & Wasser, A. (1993). *Genius revisited: High IQ children grown up.* Norwood, NJ: Ablex.

Tannenbaum, A. (1983). *Gifted children: Psychological and educational perspectives.* New York: Macmillan.

Tomlinson, C., Tomchin, E., Callahan, C., Adams, C., Pizzat-Timi, P., Cunningham, C., Moore, B., Lutz, L., Roberson, C., Eiss, N., Landrum, M., Hunsaker, S., & Inbeu, M. (1994). Practices of preservice teachers related to gifted and other academically diverse learners. *Gifted Child Quarterly, 38*(3), 106–114.

Treffinger, D. (1986). Fostering effective, independent learning through individualized programming. In J. S. Renzulli (Ed.), *Systems and models for developing programs for the gifted and talented* (pp. 429–468). Mansfield Center, CT: Creative Learning Press.

VanTassel-Baska, J. (1986). Effective curriculum and instructional models for the gifted. *Gifted Child Quarterly, 30*(4), 164–169.

VanTassel-Baska, J. (1989). Case studies of disadvantaged gifted learners. *Journal for the Education of the Gifted, 13*(1), 22–36.

VanTassel-Baska, J. (1992) *Effective curriculum planning for gifted learners.* Denver, CO: Love.

VanTassel-Baska, J. (1993a). *Comprehensive curriculum for gifted learners* (2nd ed.) Boston, MA: Allyn and Bacon.

VanTassel-Baska, J. (1993b). Theory and research on curriculum development for the gifted. In K. Heller, F. Monk, & A. H. Passow (Eds.), *International handbook of research and development of giftedness and talent.* London: Pergamon Press.

VanTassel-Baska, J. (1994). Development and assessment of integrated curriculum: A worthy challenge. *Quest, 5*(2), 1–5.

VanTassel-Baska, J. (1995). The talent development process in women writers: A study of Charlotte Bronte and Virginia Woolf. In R. Subotnik, K. Arnold, & K. Noble (Eds.), *Remarkable women.* New York: Hampton.

VanTassel-Baska, J., & Feldhusen, J. (Eds.). (1981). *Concept curriculum for the gifted K-8.* Matteson, IL: Matteson School District #162.

VanTassel-Baska, J., Gallagher, S. A., Bailey, J. M, & Sher, B. T. (1993). Science experimentation: The importance of strong science education for all students is of concern to schools. *Gifted Child Today, 16*(5), 42–46.

VanTassel-Baska, J., & Olszewski-Kubilius, P. (1989). *Patterns of influence: The home, the self, and the school.* New York: Teachers College Press.

Ward, V. (1979). The governor's school of North Carolina. In A. H. Passow (Ed.), *The gifted and the talented, their education and development: NSSE yearbook committee and associated contributors* (pp. 209–217). Chicago, IL: University of Chicago Press.

Ward, V. (1981). *Differential education for the gifted.* Ventura County, CA: Office of the Superintendent of Schools.

Westberg, K. L., Archambault, F. X., Dobyns, S. M., & Salvin, T. J. (1993). An observational study of classroom practices used with third- and fourth-grade students. *Journal for the Education of the Gifted, 16*, 120–146.

Woolf, V. (1976). *The waves.* Toronto: University of Toronto.

Zuckerman, H. (1977). *The scientific elite: Nobel laureates in the U.S.* New York: Free Press.

2

Talent Identification and Development in the Language Arts

A. HARRY PASSOW
Columbia University

A discussion of talent development in the language arts, as in any general discussion of talent development, must examine three basic questions or issues: (1) What is talent in the language arts area? (2) How is such talent identified? and (3) How is such talent nurtured?

Some three decades ago in the opening chapter of *Talent and Society* titled "Issues in the Identification of Talent," McClelland and colleagues (1958) observed that although we tend to point out "the great advantages that could be provided for promising boys and girls if we were only more certain who they were," what those provisions should be is not all that clear. McClelland asked:

> *Suppose we could locate that sleepy boy in the back row, the potential poet; what would we do for him? Would we offer him a liberal scholarship to one of our better private schools? Would we "enrich" his curriculum with spe- cial readings, or in the Greek classics? Or would we perhaps excuse him from school altogether on the grounds that he would do better as a self-edu- cated man? Or would we supply him with a vocational counselor who*

would help him find his real niche in life? These are not silly questions. The plain fact of the matter is that we do not know what we would do; we do not know enough about what goes into the making of a poet. We may know somewhat more about what goes into the making of a scientist or a professor (based on IQ tests and academic training); but we still know far too little to be confident about how to develop talented performance out of talent potential. (pp. 23–24)

McClelland's query is still quite relevant because it infers that poetic talent potential exists and that it can be identified and nurtured to talented performance standards, even though he is not sure about what we might or what we could do to cultivate such talent. Nor does McClelland suggest how we would know that the third-grader in the back row was indeed a "potential poet." Nevertheless, agreement could probably readily be reached that potential for creating poetry is one kind of talent in the language arts area but not the only kind.

A brief review of the changing concepts of verbal talent over the years will be given here. This will be followed by a discussion of some of the approaches to the identification of verbal talents and an examination of approaches to nurturing such talent development—exploring some of the persistent issues and questions.

Some Conceptions of Verbal Talent

One might ask what concept of talent guides the design of a curriculum framework: Learners who have scored high on tests of verbal intelligence? Learners who have manifested unusual ability by their creative writing or poetry? Learners who exhibit unusual linguistic skills? Learners who are unique in their ability to acquire other languages? Unusually competent dramatists or actors? Persons who do crossword puzzles in ink? All of the above and more?

Consider some of the various conceptions of verbal talent over the years. In their 1956 publication titled *Identifying Students with Special Needs*, drawing on their work with the Quincy, Illinois, Youth Development Commission begun in 1951, DeHaan and Kough (1956) delineated 10 talent or ability areas, including dramatic and creative writing. In a subsequent publication, they discussed ways of nurturing each of these talents. The Portland (Oregon) Gifted Child Project—one of the first programs not limited to general intelligence and one that sought to identify and develop giftedness in areas beyond academic ability—included creative writing ability as manifested in creative thought and expression (Portland Public Schools, 1958).

In the 57th Yearbook of the National Society for the Study of Education titled *Education for the Gifted*, Michael (1958) observed: "Because language is man's chief means for receiving and transmitting knowledge, understanding of language is essential to progress. Gifted persons may be supposed, therefore, to need superior skill in the use of language and superior understanding of, and familiarity with, the media of language expression" (p. 280). Michael discussed the language areas as including the expressive arts of writing and speaking; semantic understanding; the structure of the English language; and reading, listening, and watching the screen.

There is a substantial body of literature dealing with students with high verbal ability, psychometrically assessed. For example, early on, Stanley's Study of Mathematically Precocious Youth (SMPY) added a search for students with exceptional verbal reasoning ability using the SAT-Verbal test score to select youngsters for the language, humanities, and social science courses. Not incidentally, the SAT-Verbal turns out to be a better predictor of success in John Hopkins University for Talented Youths' (CTY) science courses than the SAT-Math.

More recently, Howard Gardner (1983) devoted a chapter in *Frames of Mind* to linguistic intelligence, using poetry and creative writing examples to make his point. Gardner wrote:

> *In the poet, then, one sees at work with special clarity the core operations of language. A sensitivity to the meaning of words, whereby an individual appreciates the subtle shades of difference between spilling ink "intentionally," "deliberately," or "on purpose." A sensitivity to the order among words—the capacity to follow rules of grammar, and, on carefully selected occasions, to violate them. At a somewhat more sensory level—a sensitivity to sounds, rhythms, inflections, and meters of words—that ability which can make even poetry in a foreign tongue beautiful to hear. And a sensitivity to the different functions of language—its potential to excite, convince, stimulate, convey information, or simply to please. (p. 77)*

While focusing on "those domains of expertise in which language itself is at the fore... penning of a poem or the winning of a verbal joust," for example, Gardner noted that in most societies, language is also a tool. Scientists, historians, literary critics, novelists, essayists, and, in fact, all scholars and communicators use language as a tool and some persons use that tool better than others. Those persons are said to have verbal talent.

A writing prodigy is included in David Feldman's study, *Nature's Gambit* (1986), although he observed: "The fact that [Randy's] talents were primarily literary is especially interesting since, for the most part, writing is not a domain where prodigious achievement occurs" (p. 44). Feldman thought this to be the case for two reasons: "The field itself has few organized supports or strategies for instruction in the craft...[and] child writers may be rare because children normally lack the kind of experience, insight, and understanding that writers are expected to convey in their works" (p. 44). Feldman included literary talent as one kind of verbal talent.

Jane Piirto (1992) has reported on a small group of seven students who were identified as having "extraordinary writing talent." Piirto's conception of writing talent focuses on "children who do produce work in writing on the adult level of competence"—that is, young children who use language the way adult creative writers do (p. 387).

A number of researchers have studied the nature and development of precocious readers as still another kind of verbal talent. Precocious readers are relatively easy to identify but, despite a good deal of study, there is no consensus regarding the phenomenon itself—its development, its correlates with other abilities, special strengths as readers, their cognitive and perceptual abilities, and the consequences of reading precocity (Jackson, 1992).

In a *Phi Delta Kappa* publication titled *Educating Verbally Gifted Youth*, Fox and Durden (1982) suggested that a precise definition is difficult due to the difficulty in predicting long-term success in verbal endeavors. Nevertheless, they proposed that verbal talent can be separated into five somewhat overlapping categories: oral expression, reading, foreign language, creative writing, and general verbal reasoning. Perhaps the Fox and Durden categories will suffice to sum up the notion that there are diverse concepts of what constitutes verbal talent, and consequently diverse approaches to identifying and nurturing such talent. The difference between verbal talent conceived as "general verbal reasoning" vis-à-vis verbal talent as more specific aspects of language usage—writing, speaking, acting, and so on—leads to different approaches to identification and development, including curriculum design and instructional strategies.

Identifying Verbal Talent(s)

How do we identify verbal talent? Identification is, of course, linked to the operative conception. Two approaches found in all identification processes apply here: One involves psychometric procedures and the other uses performance and product assessment. The Johns Hopkins CTY program use of the SAT-Verbal test to assess verbal reasoning skills is just one example of the many tests of intelligence and verbal aptitude used to identify high-ability learners. The widespread use of standardized tests to identify children who have high verbal intelligence has been examined relentlessly, with many of the same questions persisting in our quest for identification of verbally talented students.

The *Mental Measurements Yearbook* lists a number of standardized tests designed to identify those youngsters with potential for foreign language acquisition—one of the Fox and Durden (1982) categories. Although such tests predict success, there are those who argue that the actual performance of children using the second (or third) language is a better approach to identify those who might be labeled "language talented." In the United States, foreign language instruction has more often been used as a means for instructional enrichment than as a verbal talent area to be developed.

The Portland Gifted Child Project was one of the first to systematically employ *work samples*. For example, all fifth- and sixth-graders participated in a number of creative writing exercises involving such activities as "developing expressive sentences, developing a paragraph from a sentence, writing a story from descriptive phrases, writing an experience, writing an imaginative composition" (DeHaan & Havighurst, 1957, p. 50). After considerable training, classroom teachers read and rated the children's exercises on a five-point scale using such criteria as: "originality of ideas, depth of understanding of emotion or situation, choice of expressive words, conciseness of expression, developmental logic employed in sentences, good paragraph organization (when appropriate), well-planned plot (when appropriate), maintenance of a point of view" (p. 50).

Although there could be disagreement as to whether this process really identified those with unusual or outstanding creative writing potential, the procedure seems to be one that could facilitate the actual manifestation of potential. Are children unusually creative writers? Do they evidence this ability through their writing?

If we view dramatic ability as a kind of verbal talent, how might it be identified? Performance assessment has been the process most widely used. Knuth (1961) described dramatic talent as follows:

> The gifted child in drama has an aptness to intuit and see relationships of social situations "on the spot." He verbalizes easily, comprehends meanings with insight and definition; he feels human relationships in his peer group with social sensitivity, and he handles his body with ease and poise for his particular stage of physical and emotional maturity. He has an ability to visualize situations, staging, and character roles from the printed page, and he identifies himself as a character. He is attentive, alert, and responsive. He creates a dramatic role through speech and action as he easily tells a story or gives an account of some experience. (p. 352)

The Portland Gifted Child Project had children engage in four exercises: pantomime, word improvisation, reading from a script, and improvisation with hand puppets. The children were judged on their ability to express the situation in a novel way, communicate emotional attitudes convincingly, and command and hold the attention of the group (DeHaan & Havighurst, 1957, p. 51). New York City's former High School of Performing Arts—now a wing of LaGuardia High School for the Art—used a similar approach, assessing students on their actual performance in exercises not unlike those used in the Portland program. Oral expression is also assessed through debate competitions and public speaking contests.

Writing on the identification of children with creative writing ability in a 1951 book titled *The Gifted Child*, Lally and LaBrant (1951) argued that schools have been too eager to exploit the able young writer, even setting up what they referred to as "so-called 'creative' writing" classes. Examining a poem of a 15-year-old boy which they believe teachers would agree clearly evidences unusual writing ability, Lally and LaBrant described the process the child is using as follows:

> *The high quality of the talented child's creative organizational ability brings up the question of aesthetic judgment. The gifted younger child composes in an original fashion but the pattern of his composition as far as we can determine is largely unconscious. No one has told him about emphasis, subordination, balance, rhythm, or any of the other art principles. His work reveals, however, an awareness and a utilization of these elements as a natural expression of his child personality. He composes more or less intuitively. As the child approaches adolescence he becomes more and more aware of himself as a person and begins to examine his creative products with a new and critical sensitivity. ... He looks at his creative products, and if he finds them displeasing he frequently turns away from the work he is doing. (p. 254)*

Lally and LaBrant maintained that every child should have opportunities to explore, work in media of their own choice, and find approval for unusual achievement, but they warn against emphasis in a limited field that, while offering immediate satisfaction, may channel interests prematurely. They underscored the school's responsibility for "providing these children with varied experiences in many areas as well as direction in their special field" (p. 256). This, of course, has meaning for the identification process.

In writing about identifying gifted young scientists—and it could be argued that much the same can be said about verbal talents—Brandwein and Passow (1988) observed that many factors involved do not lend themselves to precise paper-and-pencil tests. Consequently, they proposed an operational approach to identification—"one which created an environment that would facilitate self-identification by offering opportunities for students to demonstrate their abilities, persistence, and questing through their performance and products, and one that would generate activating factors" (Brandwein & Passow, 1988, p. 32). Brandwein's (1955) analogy is as follows:

> *The Operational Approach is more like a training camp for future baseball players. All those who* love *the game and think they can play it are admitted. Then they are given a chance* to learn how to play well *under the best "coaching" or guidance (however inadequate) which is available in the situation operating. No one is rejected who wants to play. There are those who learn to play very well. Whether they can play well (in the big leagues) is then determined after they have been accepted into the big leagues (college and graduate school). (p. 23)*

Piirto (1992) listed some 16 qualities that she found in the writings of the seven children with extraordinary writing talent she studied. These included the use of paradox; the use of parallel structure; the use of rhythm; the use of visual imagery; melodic combinations; unusual figures of speech (e.g., alliteration, personification, and assonance); confidence with reverse structure; unusual adjectives and adverbs; a feeling of movement; uncanny wisdom; sophisticated syntax using punctuation marks, parentheses, and semicolons; prose lyricism; display of a "natural ear" for language; a sense of humor; a philosophical or moral bent; and a willingness to "play" with words (p. 388).

Piirto's list provides the basis for a checklist for identifying young children with extrordinary writing talent and, at the same time, suggests a framework for curriculum and teaching by raising the questions: Do these qualities indeed mark adult creative writers? Can these qualities be taught or enhanced?

Over the years, then, depending on how verbal talent is conceived and defined, tests of intelligence, verbal aptitude, reading, foreign language aptitude, and other standardized assessment instruments have been used to identify those with verbal talent potential. A second, and in this author's view, a much more fruitful approach has been one of creating an environment in which children are provided opportunities to manifest their potential by actually performing and producing. How would we know that the third-grader is a potential poet if he or she had not written poetry of a standard and quality that has been called to our attention? Surely, poetic potential cannot be manifested on a multiple choice test! That is why most programs seeking youngsters who have unusual potential in the areas of writing, drama, and other verbal talent areas use performance and product portfolios in their identification processes.

Nurturing Verbal Talent(s)

Clearly, the operant conception of verbal talent determines how it will be nurtured. There is a difference as to whether one is concerned with *language arts talent, talent in the language arts,* or *verbal talent*—distinctions that are not merely semantic in nature, as has been indicated in this chapter. Moreover, a number of issues are raised regarding the cultivating of verbal talent potential to verbally talented performance.

In considering the nurturing of verbal talents, we need to think in terms of a three-tiered overlapping curriculum—one that provides a basic language arts program for all learners; a second that provides an appropriately enriched and accelerated curriculum for students who have met whatever criteria we have for the general designation as a "high-ability learner"; and a third curriculum that provides for those high-ability learners who have specific "verbal talent" or "linguistic ability"—that is, outstanding potential in some verbal area such as poetry, literary criticism, dramatic arts, creative writing, and so on—and the accompanying characteristics needed to enable them to realize that potential.

The 16 qualities Piirto (1992) identified in her study of children with extraordinary writing talent warrant attention with respect to strategies and experiences that should be provided to those with writing potential. The issue is: If these are indeed the qualities or behaviors of creative writers, can they be nurtured? Can one teach "the use of paradox," "uncanny wisdom," "unusual figures of speech," and other qualities? And, if so, how? How effective can we be in teaching through metaphors?

What are appropriate strategies for developing oral expression? Does one have students listen to great speeches and critique the qualities that make them great? Do we have youngsters analyze the techniques of effective speakers—their figures of speech, grammatical constructions, cadences, and so on? Can we release dramatic talent by disciplined performance?

Obviously, high-ability learners need to go far beyond the acquisition of basic reading skills. Such learners need to acquire the skills of reading different kinds of materials differently. They need to acquire a love of reading for pleasure and for information, as a tool and as an end. Literature is the great depository of life experience, and gifted students must enter that storehouse and mine it for all its riches. Reading is especially important with respect to the affective development of gifted students—their self-identity, self-esteem, social understandings, imagination, visualization, and fantasy.

As noted earlier, there are some youngsters who will have a special interest, motivation, and potential beyond, if you will, the run of the mill high-ability learner. That is, not all high-ability learners have the potential, motivation, commitment, and other qualities for becoming talented writers, actors, orators, or linguists. There are some high-ability learners who need more than we are providing in our enriched and accelerated curricula. These students need opportunities to engage in language experiences at more complex, more abstract, more advanced, and more intense levels. They need opportunities to associate with gifted adults who are *doing* writing, acting, literary criticism, producing, and the like. They need to have opportunities to find out how those who are professionals work, improve their craft, make quality judgments, and relate. They need to move beyond good language usage and begin to examine and critique their own linguistic processes and those of their peers. They need to participate with persons who are high-level producers and performers. They need opportunities to become connoisseurs and evaluators by reflecting on what constitutes excellence in their field and analyzing their own work and that of others. They will need to interact with persons outside the school and the classroom and use resources beyond those found in the school and the library.

Returning to McClelland's challenge regarding the sleepy third-grader who is the potential poet, there is agreement among the experts: what goes into the making of a poet, a scientist, a painter, a musician, an orator, or any other of specialized talent may not be known with certainty, nor is it known if specific learning experiences will result in nurturing particular giftedness. However, it is known that the absence of certain kinds of experiences will either impede or thwart the realization of talent. For example, the potential poet whose mastery of language is not cultivated or enriched, whose understanding of the basic beauty of language is not nurtured, who has had no exposure to various genres of poetry and literature, whose connoiseurship regarding "good and bad" poetry has not been enhanced, who has not experienced opportunities to play around with ideas and words, who has not written poetry that has been subject to criticism, who has not had opportunities to *do* poetry, is not likely to transform his or her potential into performance that will be recognized as talented.

Similar essential basic learning experiences and opportunities can be identified for other verbal talent areas, whether it be creative writing, acting, or foreign language acquisition. Every area of specialized talent has a knowledge, content, and substance of a discipline; special methodologies and processes used by its practitioners; modes of problem definition and problem solving; ways of exercising creativity, innovation, and originality. In nurturing talent potential, then, opportunities must be provided for students to experience these in a climate where they feel comfortable to explore and experiment.

Conclusion

It is now recognized that not all verbally talented learners are going to become creative writers, linguists, translators, actors, dramatists, literary critics, United Nations translators, or even college professors of English or literature. However, all verbally talented learners need to develop their language arts skills of reading, writing, speaking, and listening to the fullest extent possible, since those skills are basic to the development and practice of any talent area. The William and Mary curriculum framework (VanTassel-Baska, Johnson, & Boyce, 1993) is certainly a well-conceptualized, well-designed framework built on sound theory and understanding of this phenomenon.

For those students who have the potential, the motivation, and the commitment needed for outstanding contributions—producers, performers, and creators—we need better ways of identifying that potential and helping to turn talent potential into talented performance. We are not able to give David McClelland (1958) a response to his question of what we would do for the third-grader, the potential poet. However, we do know far more now than we did 35 years ago when McClelland asserted that "we do not know what goes into the making of a poet." In sum, we have a pretty good idea of how to provide a rich and enriching learning experience for verbally talented learners, including the sleepy boy whom we think is a potential poet.

Key Points Summary

- Evidence of effective use of language in a given modality is a key indicator of verbal talent.
- General verbal talent is associated with verbal reasoning, whereas specific verbal talent is seen in areas such as writing, oral communication, reading, and foreign language.
- Both psychometric testing and performance and product assessment may be used to identify verbal talent.
- Performance assessment has been used extensively in the dramatic arts and oral expression.
- Careful assessment of student writing by teachers may reveal specific advanced qualities, including sophisticated structure, unusual word choices, and an ear for language.
- A three-tiered language arts program is recommended that provides a core program that is accelerated and enriched, and one that specifically responds to a key modality of verbal talent.
- Reading is an important avenue for affective development of talented learners.

References

Brandwein, P. F. (1955). *The gifted child as future scientist: The high school student and his commitment to science.* New York: Harcourt, Brace.

Brandwein, P. F., & Passow A. H. (Eds.). (1988). *Gifted young in science: Poten-tial through performance.* Washington, DC: National Science Teachers Association.

DeHaan, R. F., & Havighurst, R. J. (1957). *Educating gifted children.* Chicago: University of Chicago Press.

DeHaan, R. F., & Kough, J. (1956). *Identifying students with special needs.* Chicago: Science Research Associates.

Feldman, D. H. (1986). *Nature's gambit.* New York: Basic Books.

Fox, L. H., & Durden, W. G. (1982). *Educating verbally gifted youth.* Bloomington, IN: Phi Delta Kappa Educational Foundation.

Gardner, H. (1983). *Frames of mind.* New York: Basic Books.

Jackson, N. E. (1992). Understanding giftedness in young children: Lessons from the study of precocious readers. In N. Colangelo, S. G., Assouline, & D. L. Ambroson (Eds.), *Talent development* (pp. 163–179). Unionville, NY: Trillium Press.

Knuth, W. E. (1961). Creative dramatics. In L. Fleigler. (Ed.), *Curriculum planning for the gifted* (pp. 343–370). Englewood Cliffs, NJ: Prentice Hall.

Lally, A., & LaBrant, L. (1951). Experience with children talented in the arts. In P. Witty (Ed.), *The gifted child.* New York: D. C. Heath.

McClelland, D. C., Baldwin, A. L., Bronfenbrenner, U., & Strodtbeck, F. L. (1958). *Talent and society: New perspectives in the identification of talent.* Princeton, NJ: D. Van Nostrand.

Michael, L. S. (1958). Secondary-school programs. In N. B. Henry (Ed.), *Education for the gifted.* 57th Yearbook, Part II of the National Society for the Study of Education (pp. 263–315). Chicago: University of Chicago Press.

Passow, A. H. (1988). The educating and schooling of the community of artisans in science. In P. F. Brandwein & A. H. Passow (Eds.), *Gifted young in science: Potential through performance* (pp. 27–38). Washington, DC: National Science Teachers Association.

Piirto, J. (1992). Does writing prodigy exist? In N. Colangelo, S. G. Assouline & D. L. Ambroson (Eds.), *Talent development* (pp. 387–388). Unionville, NY: Trillium Press.

Portland Public Schools. (1958). *Progress report II, The gifted child project.* Portland, OR: Portland Public Schools.

VanTassel-Baska, J., Johnson, D. T., & Boyce, L. N. (1993). *A curriculum framework in language arts for high ability learners K–8.* Williamsburg, VA: College of William and Mary, Center for Gifted Education.

3

Reading, Writing, and the Construction of Meaning

NANCY NELSON SPIVEY
Louisiana State University

At the beginning of a collection of poems, one author extends this invitation to his readers:

Invitation

If you are a dreamer, come in,
If you are a dreamer, a wisher, a liar,
A hope-er, a pray-er, a magic bean buyer...
If you're a pretender, come sit by my fire
For we have some flax-golden tales to spin.
Come in!
Come in!

This, of course, is Shel Silverstein's (1974) opening poem in *Where the Side-walk Ends*, which includes such other well-loved poems as "Boa Constrictor," "The Crocodile's Toothache," and "Hug o' War." Here we have an author explicitly asking readers to help him make meaning. Although authors are usually less explicit in their invitations, this writer is not unusual in wanting readers to "come in." We can think of different kinds of authors who extend their own invitations to their texts: newspaper reporters and their accounts, biologists and their research articles, business people and their faxes, children and their stories. Authors expect audiences to read (or hear) their texts—to make meaning from them. But what is the nature of this meaning-building process? What are writers inviting readers to do? How do authors' invitations vary, and how do readers' contributions vary?

Writers, drawing from their knowledge and experience, build meanings mentally as they compose texts to accomplish their purposes. They produce texts in order to entertain, to inform, to persuade, to do all these things—or they may have other purposes (Kinneavy, 1971). When their audience is readers other than themselves, they choose textual cues they think will lead their readers to build meanings that are similar to their own. These cues—graphic, lexical, and syntactic—offer different kinds of information. Some signal particular kinds of content, some signal its relative importance, and some signal patterns for organizing and interrelating it. Cues can come not only from the configuration of letters and words and punctuation marks but also from formatting features, such as amount of white space and type of print or manuscript, and from various kinds of illustrations.

Sometimes writers succeed in getting readers to build meanings that are similar to their own and sometimes they do not. Their readers, who have their own purposes, draw from their own knowledge and experience as they use the textual cues to build their own meanings. Not only is there variability between writers' meanings and the meanings of their readers but there is also variability between the meanings different readers create for that same text. The reason for all this variability is that meaning is not *in the text* and it is not carried by the text. Meaning is *in people*, who are in the role of understanders or composers, and people use different knowledge and skills in their literate acts and have different purposes.

This is the constructivist perspective on written discourse that will be developed in this chapter. After a brief discussion of the metaphor underlying constructivism, the focus will be on variability in meaning making as three interrelated aspects of reading and writing are discussed. First will be *reading and writing the text*. This will be a consideration of three operations—organizing, selecting, and connecting—that people perform as they generate meanings in understanding and composing texts. Second will be *reading and writing the intertext*. This will be a discussion of the interrelatedness of texts—how no text is really discrete—and an argument that reading or writing a text also means reading or writing an intertext. Third will be *reading and writing the context*. This will focus on contextual factors that influence the nature of the meanings that people make from and for texts. All three aspects of reading and writing are critical to the development of verbal talent, and the chapter will conclude with some educational implications for that development. The emphasis throughout will be on reading and writing—literacy— but much of what is said is relevant to oral discourse as well.

A Constructivist Perspective on Literacy

The term *constructivism*, as used here, refers to a particular kind of theoretical orientation regarding the nature of communicative processes. A constructivist views understanding texts and composing texts as acts of construction— acts in which language users build meanings on the basis of relevant knowledge brought to the communicative task (Ackerman, 1991; Bransford, Barclay, & Franks, 1972; Frederiksen, 1975; Spiro, 1977, 1980; Spivey, 1987, 1990, 1995; Spivey & King, 1989). There is an architectural metaphor implicit in constructivism: Language users are the *constructors*, mental meanings are their *constructions*, and prior knowledge is the *material* used in the constructive process. Texts themselves are merely sets of cues to meanings. Constructivists would point out that meanings built through reading differ when people bring different knowledge to texts and when they approach texts in different contexts and for different purposes. They would also point out that, because reading involves actively building meaning rather than passively receiving messages, reading and writing have some similarities (they are not simply the inverses of each other). Even though the carpentry imagery suggested by constructivist language may seem to imply the building of some kind of fixed, static structure, a constructivist theory of discourse emphasizes the dynamic nature of meaning and its making.

Constructivism as an epistemological metaphor has roots in the work of such philosophers as Vico (1710/1868) and Kant (1787/1963), but the form of constructivism I discuss here goes back directly to the contributions of Sir Frederic Bartlett (1932). Bartlett was a British psychologist who studied the reading of text early in the century and published his studies in a book titled *Remembering*. In one set of studies, he had his British subjects read a story called "The War of the Ghosts," a Native-American tale. This is the version he used and included in his book:

The War of the Ghosts

One night two young men from Egulac went down to the river to hunt seals, and while they were there it became foggy and calm. Then they heard war-cries, and they thought: "Maybe this is a war party." They escaped to the shore, and hid behind a log. Now canoes came up, and they heard the noise of paddles, and saw one canoe coming up to them. There were five men in the canoe, and they said:

"What do you think? We wish to take you along. We are going up the river to make war on the people."

One of the young men said: "I have no arrows."

"Arrows are in the canoe," they said.

"I will not go along. I might be killed. My relatives do not know where I have gone, but you," he said, turning to the other, "may go with them."

So one of the young men went, but the other returned home.

And the warriors went on up the river to a town on the other side of Kalama. The people came down to the water, and they began to fight, and many were killed. But presently the young man heard one of the warriors say: "Quick, let us go home: that Indian has been hit." Now he thought: "Oh, they are ghosts." He did not feel sick, but they said he had been shot.

So the canoes went back to Egulac, and the young man went ashore to his house, and made a fire. And he told everybody and said: "Behold I accompanied the ghosts, and we went to fight. Many of our fellows were killed, and many of those who attacked us were killed. They said I was hit, and I did not feel sick."

He told it all, and then he became quiet. When the sun rose he fell down. Something black came out of his mouth. His face became contorted. The people jumped up and cried.

He was dead. (p. 65)

Shortly after reading and again after longer periods of time, which might have been a matter of days or years, Bartlett had his subjects write recalls of what they had read. He used these recalls to gain insights into what these readers remembered of the text—what meaning they made of it. He studied his subjects' written recalls for deviations from the original material, and he found various kinds of transformations. Some transformations were not all that interesting: After time had passed, Bartlett's subjects produced shorter recalls with fewer details and proper names. But some transformations *were* interesting: The subjects tended to make elements of the story conform to their own cultural experiences. For example, they recalled the Indians fishing instead of hunting for seals. And some transformations were *very* interesting: The subjects tended to make additions to fill in gaps. For example, they "remembered" reasons for the Indian's realization that the beings he accompanied were ghosts.

Similar methods of studying recall had been used before by other researchers, but it was Bartlett who proposed a constructivist explanation for the transformations that he thought he saw. He suggested that the changes resulted from his subjects' "efforts after meaning" to relate the new information to previously existing knowledge structures. In making sense of the story, they reshaped it with plausible material to make it more consistent with their own cultural knowledge, including how stories "work." Bartlett's research, when it was resurrected in the early 1970s, set the agenda for further studies examining the nature of discourse and the process of meaning making. Researchers today analyze texts for the cues they seem to offer, and they study the transformations that people make as they build their meanings. (For a review of the constructivist tradition in reading, see Spivey, 1987.) For his studies, Bartlett had intentionally chosen material that would be strange to his readers and would be likely to elicit transformations. But reading researchers today tend to study transformations from texts that are more normal reading material for the readers they are studying.

Reading and Writing the Text

Constructivism has been influential in reading theory since the 1970s when it was being articulated by psychologists such as Bransford (Bransford, Barclay, & Franks, 1972) and Frederiksen (1975). Its influence has been felt for years in reading research and instruction (Anderson, Spiro, & Montague, 1977; Spiro, Bruce, & Brewer, 1980; Spivey, 1987; Steffe & Gale, 1995), and it is beginning to be extended to writing research and instruction (Ackerman, 1991; Spivey, 1984, 1990, 1991, 1995). The national report *Becoming a Nation of Readers* (Anderson, Hiebert, Scott, & Wilkinson, 1985) offers a constructivist perspective on the process of reading and on methods of teaching reading.

Reading the Text

Reading, from a constructivist perspective, is a process in which material is generated mentally in response to textual cues. There are three important operations that readers perform on the material they generate. Bartlett (1932) pointed to them when he reported his *Remembering* studies, even though he did not call them operations and did not lay them out explicitly. The terms I use for them are *organizing, selecting,* and *connecting*. Over the past two decades, there have been numerous studies examining one or more of these operations.

Reading is a process that involves organizing—giving structure to meaning. When reading texts, people use their knowledge of how texts are conventionally organized to organize the material they generate. For example, they use knowledge of story patterns (Mandler & Johnson, 1977) for stories and knowledge of expository text patterns (Meyer, 1975) for informational text. The text can help because it offers cues for organizing as well for selecting. Perhaps the text is identifiable as a story with familiar story elements, such as a protagonist's attempt to achieve a goal but experiencing a conflict. The reader following textual cues organizes it as a story. Or perhaps it has elements of an argument in which a problem is posed and a solution is offered. The reader following textual cues organizes the material that way, as a problem-solution from, in memory. Readers can follow organizational cues and let reading be a text-driven process in organizing, but they can supply a different organization for what they read. For instance, someone might be reading the story in order to critique the style. The meaning being built might be organized mainly around points about which to comment. Or someone might be reading a problem-solution argument to compare that author's position on particular points with someone else's. A comparison structure might be the basis for organizing and selecting material.

Reading is the process of *selecting* as well as *organizing*. People cannot usually include everything that texts elicit in the meanings they build for texts; they include what is "important." Constructing meaning requires selecting a subset. Through their texts, writers offer cues of various types as to what might be relatively important. For example, titles and headings can help readers, as can repetition of important themes. Explicit statements of importance, such as saying, "The idea that is most relevant here" and "The third point I want to make," can help. Placement of material, such as putting the most important points at the beginning or end of the text or paragraph, can help. Also, the organizational pattern that is signaled helps indicate to the reader what is important. Through various means such as these, an author presents some material to readers as the figure and lets other material be the ground. The author *stages* what he or she considers most important (Grimes, 1975). Readers, when their reading is a text-driven process, not only follow organizational cues but also staging cues (pick up on the figure). But when they have other purposes or perspectives for their reading, the textual influence can be overridden and the ground can become the figure. Readers might want to acquire some particular information, perhaps about some person or trend. Or they might take a particular kind of perspective on the text, such as a feminist perspective, that would strongly influence what is most important in that reading.

Besides organizing and selecting, a third operation is one referred to as *connecting*. Readers make inferences and elaborations as they attempt to construct meaning that is internally coherent and coherent with what they already know. Texts provide cues for inferencing, but cues vary as to how explicit they are (Clark, 1977). Some additions are anticipated by the author; others are not. People make various kinds of additions in reading as they build meaning, and they do so on the basis of knowledge of various types, such as world knowledge, topic knowledge, and discourse knowledge.

The two texts quoted fully in this text—"Invitation" and "The War of the Ghosts"—provide numerous examples of inferencing required of readers. When reading Silverstein's "Invitation," readers have to infer who the *you* is at the beginning of the poem when Silverstein says, "If *you* are a dreamer, come in." Does that mean anyone who has any kinds of dreams can be a

reader? Do the dreams have to be special kinds? Is the author referring specifically to children? As readers work through the poem, they have to make
inferences about other readers who are mentioned: wisher, liar, hope-er,
pray-er, magic-bean buyer, pretender. Are those who are listed other people
who qualify to be readers (besides dreamers) or are they aspects of the same
reader? Is Silverstein opening up the invitation to anyone or limiting it to
someone with imagination? The figurative language requires inferencing.
Does "come in" mean "read (actively, enthusiastically) the poems in this
book *Where the Sidewalk Ends*"? Does "come sit by my fire" imply "think of
me as a storyteller telling you stories in a comfortable setting like my home"?
Does "flax-golden" suggest value (associated with classical tales), loveliness,
fragility, or something else? Inferences are made unconsciously much of the
time, and they seem often to become an integral part of what someone
remembers of a text—what the text "says."

As mentioned earlier, "The War of the Ghosts" puts a heavy inferencing
burden on the reader. Some places for inferencing are quite obvious. Other
places are not so noticeable because readers can make inferences so unconsciously. Take the first three sentences:

> *One night two young men from Egulac went down to the river to hunt*
> *seals, and while they were there it became foggy and calm. Then they heard*
> *war-cries, and they thought: "Maybe this is a war party." They escaped to*
> *the shore, and hid behind a log.*

For the content to have connectivity, readers must infer that "there" in
the first sentence refers to "at the river" and that "then" at the beginning of
the second sentence means "after the two men had hunted a while." Readers
have to infer that "heard war-cries" suggests some men were nearby making
the kinds of sounds people make when they conduct war and that "this"
refers to the men making the sounds. When reading that the two young men
"escaped to the shore" and "hid behind a log," readers have to add the information that the two men were in a canoe on the river before they went to
shore (readers are not told this) and have to add the information that there
was a log on the ground and that the two men got on the side of the log that
was opposite to the direction from which the war party was coming. Refer-
ential inferences are often easily made because readers have knowledge of
how our language works, and other inferences, such as those that entail adding material, often come readily too because readers draw from other kinds
of knowledge, such as topic knowledge and world knowledge.

As in organizing and selecting, connecting can be something of a text-
driven process—with the reader making only those inferences that seem to
be strongly invited by the text—or it can involve much reading between the
lines. It is interesting that in some settings the people considered good read-

ers make only the inferences that seem to be invited by the text and the people considered poor readers make inferences that seem unconventional and idiosyncratic to others. That is the case in many elementary and secondary school settings, and it is particularly obvious when students are taking standardized reading tests. In some other settings, such as meetings of literary critics and interpreters, the people considered good readers make the unconventional, idiosyncratic inferences—those that are not invited so clearly by the text.

Writing the Text

It seems that constructivists make two major claims that are particularly important for understanding the writing process. One is that meaning and the text are not the same thing. Meaning is in the minds of people, and the text is merely cues to meanings. The cues signal meanings constructed by the writer and meanings to be constructed by readers. The other claim is that meaning is being built mentally *throughout* the process of composing. Composing is a generative process in which the same three constructive operations are performed on material that is generated: organizing content that is generated, making selections of content that is relevant, and making connections among ideas to create coherence (Spivey, 1990, 1995). Writers build meanings over the course of composing: They organize and reorganize. They select some ideas and reject others. They make all sorts of connections between ideas that were unrelated before and thereby create new knowledge. These operations often begin before the writer puts pen to page or touches computer keys, and they continue sometimes even after the writer has stopped producing the written text.

Educators hear a great deal of talk these days about *steps of the writing process*, as if totally different types of cognitive activity are brought to bear in different phases of text production. Some people, harking to Rohman and Wlecke's (1964) three-stage portrayal of composing, think that in prewriting a writer comes up with what he or she would like to say, then in writing he or she puts it down in words, and finally in revising he or she merely tidies up the text. Such a neat, linear process may be true in some unusual cases. But more often, writers generate meaning throughout the process, as they go about selecting, organizing and connecting. Before actually writing down any words, writers come up with possible ways to organize and arrange their material; they do some selecting and rejecting of ideas they generate; and they make connections among related content. They are constructing meaning. During writing, they continue generating material and performing these operations on it. Their meaning develops and changes even as they are producing the text. They are still constructing meaning. And after writing a draft or several drafts, and perhaps still making some changes in the written product, they are using the same operations. At that point, too, they are still constructing meaning. The three-stage view may reflect what the text looks like, but it is not an accurate description of what happens mentally.

In this process of composing, writers produce texts—texts with cues for their readers to build representations of meaning that are somewhat similar to their own. They use the kinds of cues discussed earlier to help their readers in selecting, organizing, and connecting. To guide readers in selecting, they stage certain content. To guide readers in organizing, writers provide organizational cues. To guide readers in connecting the new and the known, writers make various kinds of implications. Writers vary and texts vary in how explicit the cues are. And readers vary in how explicit the cues are to them. This is a balancing act for a writer—determining how explicit to be. Explicitness, as Nystrand and Wiemelt (1991) have pointed out, is a relative notion. What is explicit to one person is not explicit to another. It all depends on the reader—and what the reader knows.

Reading and Writing the Text

Even though we speak of reading and writing as if they are separable processes, it is sometimes difficult—even impossible—to separate them. There are some acts of literacy that involve both processes—comprehending and composing—and they can take place concurrently. People can construct meaning from a text they are reading at the same time that they are constructing meaning for a text they are writing. There are hybrid acts of literacy, as Bracewell, Frederiksen, and Frederiksen (1982) have pointed out. Some of these hybrid acts can be called *writing from sources*. In writing from sources, people build meaning from a text they are reading but they do so for the new text they are going to write. (For more complete discussion of reading-writing acts, see Spivey, 1990, 1995.) It might be that they are writing summaries or critiques of a single text, or it might be they are writing essays (or historical accounts, literature reviews, proposals) based on multiple sources. The fact that they are writing their own text influences how they read other writers' texts.

Verbal Talent in Reading and Writing the Text

The preceding discussion pointed to some important facets of verbal talent—facets that can be seen when one looks at reading and writing processes from a constructivist perspective. In reading, ability involves knowing and using organizational patterns of discourse, being aware of signaling of the relative importance of the content, and supplying inferences for connectedness. It can be using the author's cues when one's purpose is to read the text for the author's meaning. But it can also be overriding those cues to read for another purpose. In writing, ability is generating meaning that has organization, development, and coherence and providing cues in one's text that work well for one's own readers as they build their meanings.

How well someone reads a particular text depends, to a great extent, on the knowledge that the person brings to that text—not only discourse knowledge but content knowledge (topic knowledge, domain knowledge, world knowledge, etc.). A person can build a well-structured, elaborate representation of meaning from the cues of a text if it is a topic for which he or she has relevant knowledge. The same person would not do so well with a text for which he or she has little relevant knowledge. How well someone does in composing a text can also depend, to a great extent, on how much he or she knows about the topic. The point here is that ability is not a totally static phenomenon that can be easily measured. It is relative to the text topic, to the domain, and to the content area or discipline.

Reading and Writing the Intertext

The previous section discussed reading and writing the text. It is relatively easy to talk about texts as units of discourse because those are the units with which we usually deal when we think about reading and writing. But here, we will move to a larger unit, which can be called an *intertext*. The concept of intertextuality has been developed by literary theorists such as Kristeva (1968), Barthes (1971), Riffaterre (1980), Bakhtin (1981), and Miller (1985), who argue that units of discourse are larger than single texts, that a text does not really exist separate from other texts. A text is part of a larger intertext. Leitch (1983) stated the intertextual argument this way: "The text is not an autonomous or unifed object but a set of relations with other texts. Its system of language, its grammar, its lexicon, drag along numerous bits and pieces—traces—of history so that the text resembles a Cultural Salvation Army Outlet with unaccountable collections of incompatible ideas, beliefs, and sources" (p. 59).

Writing the Intertext

Writers, when they compose, draw from the experiences that they have had with other texts. Sometimes they do so consciously and sometimes unconsciously. The writings they produce reflect those experiences, and thus their texts connect with other texts. Some connections with other texts are more explicit than others and are marked by citations or allusions. Some connections are to discourse form, such as conventional openings and closings and text patterns. For example, when children write stories, the form of their stories relates to previous stories they have read, heard, and have composed themselves—in story elements (setting, protagonist, goal, conflict, resolution) and story conventions ("once upon a time," "they all lived happily ever after"). Other connections are to particular content—repeated semantic material. Related content might be particularities of certain characters or settings. Writers have a kind of repertoire of prior texts and knowledge they have abstracted from those texts—not only their own but others' too—that they use when they compose.

Reading the Intertext

Readers come along and they read intertexts as they read the text. A reader has an intertext that is somewhat different from the one the writer used (and different from what other readers create)—because the reader has experienced different prior texts. Intertexts belong to readers as much as they belong to writers. In reading a child's story, a reader might make connections to some stories the writer has read but also some connections to stories that the writer has not experienced. For example, if the child did not say that the princess had blonde hair, but the reader had read plenty of stories in which the princess has blonde hair, that material might be generated by the reader because of intertextuality.

The following excerpt from *Coyote's Canyon* (Telford & Williams, 1989) should help to illustrate intertextuality on the part of the reader. At the very beginning, the creators of that book make a very explicit intertextual connection when quoting words from another author, Judith Fryer (1987). Fryer wrote the words as a sentence in an essay included in an edited collection—just one sentence (p. 44) in a rather lengthy essay. But when borrowing them, John Telford and Terry Tempest Williams presented them in the form of a poem:

> *These things are real:*
>   *desert,*
>   *rocks,*
>   *shelter,*
>   *legend.*

The reader builds meaning for this "poem," which is presented as an epigraph, and that meaning influences—and becomes part of—the meaning that the reader builds for the book *Coyote's Canyon*. This Fryer "poem" might induce some readers to call up texts they have read previously. If they have read Byrd Baylor, for example, the texts in their intertext might include such books as *Everybody Needs a Rock* (1974) and *The Desert Is Theirs* (1975). Then the text of *Coyote's Canyon* has as its first piece an essay that Williams begins this way:

The Coyote Clan

When traveling to southern Utah for the first time, it is fair to ask if the redrocks were cut would they bleed. And when traveling to Utah's desert for the second or third time, it is fair to assume that they do, that the blood of the rocks gives life to the country. And then after having made enough pilgrimages to the slickrock to warrant sufficient separation from society's oughts and shoulds, look again for the novice you once were, who asks if sandstone bleeds.

Pull out your pocketknife, open the blade, and run it across your burnished arm. If you draw blood, you are human. If you draw wet sand that dries quickly, then you will know you have become part of the desert. Not until then can you claim ownership.

This is Coyote's country—a landscape of the imagination, where nothing is as it appears. The buttes, mesas, and redrock spires beckon you to see them as something other: a cathedral, a tabletop, bears' ears, or nuns. Windows and arches ask you to recall what is no longer there, to taste the wind for the sandstone it carries. These astonishing formations invite a new mythology for desert goers, one that acknowledges the power of story and ritual, yet lies within the integrity of our own cultures. The stories rooted in experience become beads to trade. It is the story, always the story, that precedes and follows the journey.

Just when you begin to believe in your own sense of place, plan on getting lost. It's not your fault—blame it on Coyote. The terror of the country you thought you knew bears gifts of humility. The landscape that makes you vulnerable also makes you strong. This is the bedrock of southern Utah's beauty: its chameleon nature according to light and weather and season encourages us to make peace with our own contradictory nature. The trickster quality of the canyon is Coyote's cachet. (Williams, 1989, pp. 16–18)

Readers of this text would vary in the meanings they construct, depending, to some extent, on prior experiences they have had with other texts. The phrases "power of story" and "it is the story, always the story" would elicit different texts for different people. The references to Coyote would have some people remembering trickster stories they have read previously, or at least some aspects of them. Those memories would be embedded in their meanings for the current text and would influence the nature of those meanings. Some people reading the first paragraph would make connections to other texts (perhaps texts they could vaguely remember but could not really recall) simply because of the language patterns, such as the repeated syntactic structure in the first paragraph, or because of the cyclical chronology that seems to be going somewhere but then gets back to the starting point. These are, of course, just a few places in this text where intertextual connections might be made.

Other texts included in this chapter can also illustrate intertextuality on the part of readers. Readers of Silverstein's "Invitation," which began this chapter, would likely experience traces of other texts when they read the words "magic bean buyer" and "flax-golden." Readers of "War of the Ghosts" draw from their own experiences with stories when they make their transformations.

All this discussion about intertext may seem very abstract and intangible. Texts seem more tangible than intertexts do because, with texts, there is the paper and there is the print. Intertexts seem to be someplace else; we cannot see them or touch them. In his book *The Unbroken Web*, Richard Adams (1982/1980) chooses to put them in the space. This is the way he described intertexts of stories:

> *I see in fancy—I have a vision of—the world as the astronauts saw it—a shining globe, poised in space and rotating on its polar axis. Round it, enveloping it entirely, as one chinese carved ivory ball encloses another within it, is a second, incorporeal, gossamer-like sphere—the unbroken web—rotating freely and independently of the rotation of the earth. It is something like a soap-bubble, for although it is in rotation, real things are reflected on its surface, which imparts to them glowing, lambent colours.*
>
> *Within this outer web we live. It soaks up, transmutes and is charged with human experience, exuded from the world within like steam or an aroma from cooking food. The story-teller is he who reaches up, grasps that part of the web which happens to be above his head at the moment and draws it down—it is, of course, elastic and unbreakable—to touch the earth. When he has told his story—its story—he releases it and it springs back and continues in rotation. The web moves continually above us, so that in time every point on its interior surface passes directly above every point on the surface of the world. This is why the same stories are found all over the world, among different people who can have had little or no communication with each other.*
>
> *Both in folk-song and folk-tale there is a paradox. On the one hand they are not attributable to individual authors, but impersonal and universal. On the other, they lose much when they are depersonalized....(pp. 3–4)*

It is fanciful—fun—to think about an intertext up there in space that storytellers can reach. But fancy aside, we have to view intertexts as resulting from knowledge that readers and writers have built over time and that they have available to them in acts of literacy. This knowledge is, of course, socially acquired, so there are going to be commonalities among people who have had similar cultural experiences. Over their lifetimes, people build intertextual knowledge; and something in a text or a situation signals them to use this intertextual knowledge in building their meanings.

Verbal Talent in Reading and Writing the Intertext

The intertextual facets of verbal talent cannot really be separated from the textual facets discussed previously. This is because much of the discourse knowledge and content knowledge people use in comprehending and composing texts is intertextual. Verbal talent is manifested in one's ability to make interesting and appropriate connections to relevant texts. Some of these connections are invited by the author through allusion or reference, and others are not explictly invited. But, whether invited or not, these intertextual links can make for a richer interpretation of (meaning for) the text. Talented writers are able to produce texts that are well connected. In other words, their texts connect to other texts in our culture through form and content. For instance, the texts might have familiar, conventional patterns, when it seems appropriate to be conventional, or might deviate from those patterns, when deviating helps to accomplish the writer's purposes.

Reading and Writing the Context

People read and write texts, they read and write intertexts, and they also read and write contexts. (Perhaps quotation marks should be used here— "read" and "write"—because what is read and written when one interprets and creates context cannot be tied to printed symbols; it is farther from print even than intertext is.) The meanings that people build when reading or writing are influenced greatly by how they construe the context.

Reading the Context

When thinking about context, it is helpful to think of four *wh*- questions: *why, when, where,* and *who.* There is the task—the *why*—why, in the case of reading, readers are performing the task. Sometimes the task (and reader's purpose) might be to see what the author has to say; that would invite a text-driven process. But the purpose might be something else: to find something particular, to find fault, to glean just enough to get the gist, and so on. Purpose in reading can affect how the reader selects, organizes, and connects material. One important study examining task and purpose was conducted by Frederiksen back in 1975. He had one text providing information about "Circle Island." He gave one group of students the task of recounting the material, and he gave another group the task of solving a problem. The representations of meaning constructed by the two groups were dramatically different in terms of selections from what the text offered and what the readers inferred.

Another aspect of context is *when*—when the reading is taking place, how long the reader has to spend or wants to spend. And there is the *where*—the setting. Both can be important in the shaping of meaning: how the reader selects, organizes, and connects. If these are changed, the reading is changed. So is the meaning. It is interesting to think now about all the studies of reading in which researchers attempted to neutralize or eliminate setting as a variable by using a "laboratory" setting—as if the laboratory itself was not a setting that would influence the nature of the reading that the subjects would do.

Yet another element of the context for reading is *who*—who the other participants in the literacy act are. One is the author (who is most likely not physically present but is still "there" through the reader's constructions and can often be very influential). Readers think about the author of the text they read, and the meanings they build are often influenced by how they perceive the author—that writer's persona, that writer's intentions, that writer's credentials, and so on (Haas & Flower, 1988). One recent study (Shanahan, 1993) suggests that young children often create very detailed representations of the authors of the books they read.

Other participants can be people with whom the reader interacts before, during, or after reading. They are part of the social context. The reader "reads" them too, and meanings built for the things they say—the oral or written texts they produce—can certainly influence the meaning that the reader builds for the text and intertext that are read. They are *co-constructors* of meaning (Spivey, 1995). School settings today often involve numerous participants in the meaning-building context. Teachers influence meanings when they give assignments. Other students influence meanings when discussions are held about what is being read.

Writing the Context

Writing is contextualized too. Writers write because they have some exigency—a *why*—for writing; writing is motivated by something they see in that context. They interpret their writing tasks and establish purposes. They continue to develop (and sometimes change) purposes over the course of composing (Flower & Hayes, 1984). As they write their texts, they define and delimit the context; they "write" it as well.

Different tasks, of course, lead to different meanings. The differences may be seen quite clearly when one examines transformations made by writers composing from sources. In a task-comparison study (Spivey & Greene, 1989) reminiscent of Frederiksen's (1975), one group of students in a psychology class had the task of writing a report, and the other had the task of writing a proposal. They all had the same five psychology articles to use as sources. But they made quite different kinds of uses of those sources and different kinds of transformations—constructed different kinds of meaning even though they had the same materials with which to work.

Writers construe and create other contextual factors, including the *when* and the *where*—time and place. The time and place of writing are constraints within which writers work. Time and place can be limiting, as when a writer has only a certain amount of time to produce a text and a limited number of resources where he or she is working. Sometimes writers create their own limitations—impose their own deadlines and confine themselves to one particular place for writing. The time and place of possible readings by the audience are also a very important part of the context writers perceive and imagine. In building meaning for the text, they think about the setting for reading. Is this to be a text read only once next Monday morning—perhaps something on e-mail that will be quickly erased? Is this to be a text to be read by people for years?

And in the case of writing, meaning is greatly influenced by the *who*—how the writer perceives his or her audience. Writers construct meanings with respect to their audience, speculating about the meanings that might be built by that reader or those readers using the textual cues (Kroll, 1985). They make many assumptions about what their readers might know and what might be relevant to their discourse goals. They sometimes add or eliminate audiences or construe the same audiences differently over the course of composing. Roth (1987), who argued that audience "evolves," found writers changing the character of their intended audiences as they wrote their essays for them. Making the audience "easier" seemed to help a writer get through a block, and making the audience "harder" seemed to help a writer develop more complex material.

There are other *whos* in the context. Co-constructors for the writer include responders—people who listen to ideas or react to a draft. In many classrooms today, these social aspects of meaning making are quite visible; teachers build collaborative planning and peer response into their writing curricula (Flower et al., 1989; Nystrand, 1986) as well as their own response through conferences (Freedman & Sperling, 1985). These other people—the responders as well as the audience (whether it is present or not)—influence how the writer selects, organizes, and connects in building a representation of meaning for the text that is being written.

Verbal Talent in Reading and Writing the Context

Verbal talent involves being able to interpret the communicative context and to perform the literacy act in a way that fits that interpretation. A person likely to succeed in verbal interactions is someone who can make smart choices that are appropriate for his or her purpose, audience, and setting. In reading, that can mean knowing when to use a text-driven strategy, following the author's guidance and making organizations, selections, and connections the text seems to invite, and knowing when to use another approach and to restructure. In writing, that can mean knowing about one's options regarding form of discourse and being able to manipulate explicitness to get the desired effect with the intended audience. Talent in communication is, to a great extent, a matter of flexibility. A skilled reader-writer has a repertoire of strategies and approaches from which to draw in performing acts of literacy.

Conclusion

There are important educational implications for the ideas presented in this chapter. Some have to do with the reading and writing of texts, others with the reading and writing of intertexts, and still others with the contexts for reading and writing.

Texts

Students need to learn more about how texts work, about what writers do, and about what readers contribute. Instruction is often too distant from the actual process. Students are assigned readings, and they are judged on their interpretations (or responses to comprehension questions). Students are given writing assignments, and they are given grades on their performance. It is easy to say that teachers need to get into the processes of reading and writing, but it takes work on the part of teachers to actually do it. It requires opening up and taking apart. One way to get into the process—the process of reading or the process of writing—is through think-aloud procedures (letting others "hear" the process one is using [Duffy, Roehler, & Herrmann, 1988]) and discussion of the strategies one actually uses. Another way is on-line commenting or questioning. McKeown, Beck, and Worthy (1993) have developed a method of student commenting called *Questioning the Author*, in which students attempt to figure out why an author has written something in a such a way that it causes problems for them.

By practicing and explicitly noting specific writing techniques, students can benefit in their reading as well as their writing. In their reading, they can begin to be more aware of the signaling of other authors; in their writing, they can begin to use the writing devices themselves when they seem appropriate. It is particularly important for them to become more aware of the room for interpretation that they leave in their own texts—to see the meanings that different people (other students perhaps) make of what they write. The point is not for them to make their texts overly explicit but for them to be able to achieve a level of explicitness to get the desired effect. One way for educators to begin to do all this is to integrate reading and writing instruction: Create a consistent terminology and make connections between the two by having students fill the roles of authors as well as audience.

Intertexts

Intertextual knowledge should be one of the major goals of education. Even though students make their own intertextual connections, their formal education does not do nearly as much as it might to help them build this kind of knowledge so that they can use it in reading or in writing. Texts read as part of the curriculum are often thought of as separate units; they are *compartmentalized*, to use Spiro's (1980) term. They are read, discussed, and tested, and not related to other texts. The process of building intertextual knowledge through reading—making connections—is not fostered to the extent it might be. Sometimes, there are intertextual connections made within a single course but not often enough across courses. This is true in college often for curricular reasons—so that performance in one class is not dependent on performance in another class and so that instructors are not constrained to particular texts. But it tends to be true as well in elementary and secondary years. In writing instruction, students' papers are written, revised, and graded (not related to other texts the student has written, or to texts other students have written, or to texts written by other writers). Students move on to the next text here too.

There are some signs of change in this area. One change can be tied to the computer and hypertext. Hypertext approaches to learning are influencing curricula, even when the computer is not used. Because of hypertext, people are beginning to think in terms of the intertextual connections among readings (e.g., Bolter, 1991; Kearsley, 1988). Another change is tied to use of portfolios, particularly in writing. The student and the teacher can see how the students' writings relate to each other, and a student writer can build on his or her own prior work (Murphy & Smith, 1990).

Contexts

Students need experience in reading for different purposes—seeing how one can modify his or her reading and how different readings can be appropriate for different situations. The same is true in writing. Students need experience in writing for various purposes and for various audiences. Over the course of their lives, people have experiences that help them develop their verbal talent—become better makers of meaning. They bring more and more knowledge to their understanding and interpretation of texts, knowledge that enriches the meanings they build as readers. They bring more and more knowledge to their composing of texts as well—knowledge that enriches the meanings they build as writers and attempt to communicate to other readers through the texts they write. They develop more flexibility.

What makes the school setting so very important in this developmental process is that learning can be accelerated there. This acceleration is possible because the school experiences in literacy can be designed for particular goals and because the environment can be highly supportive (Applebee & Langer, 1983). Teachers can select texts, construct intertexts, and create settings for students to be actively and collaboratively involved in literacy learning. Students can read the same texts and compare meanings that are built, can write texts alone or with others, and can see how others respond to those texts. Students can be led to make connections among the texts with which they work—adding texts that speak to them individually as well as those that are privileged in their culture and selected by their teachers. They can develop a repertoire of approaches to reading and writing tasks so that they have a range of options and can make choices when they accept authors' invitations or extend their own invitations to "come in."

Key Points Summary

- One major claim of constructivism is that the meaning of texts is in the reader, not the text itself.
- The theory of constructivism encompasses cultural group meanings as well as individual meanings in that interpretation of texts may be influenced by cultural norms.
- Organizing, selecting, and connecting are the major strategies readers and writers perform in literate acts.
- Writers build meaning "as they compose"; the text provides only cues to that meaning in the author's mind.
- Writing from sources is a technique of simultaneously reading texts to create meaning and transposing that meaning to one's own writing.
- Intertext involves the world of allusions and references, both explicit and implicit, that can be brought to bear on understanding any text and creating meaning.
- The verbally talented are more expert at manipulating both the reading and writing processes and tend to have larger repertoires of strategies.
- Teachers must be a part of the literacy act through their own experiencing of reading and writing as constructive activities.

References

Ackerman, J. (1991). Reading, writing, and knowing: The role of disciplinary knowledge in comprehension and composing. *Research in the Teaching of English, 25*, 133–178.

Adams, R. (1982). *The unbroken web: Stories and fables.* New York: Ballantine Books. (Originally published in 1980 by Allen Lane as *The Iron Wolf and Other Stories.*)

Anderson, R. C., Hiebert, E. H., Scott, J. A., & Wilkinson, I. A. G. (1985). *Becoming a nation of readers.* Washington, DC: National Institute of Education.

Anderson, R. C., Spiro, R. J., & Montague, W. E. (Eds.). (1977). *Schooling and the acquisition of knowledge.* Hillsdale, NJ: Lawrence Erlbaum.

Applebee, A. N., & Langer, J. A. (1983). Instructional scaffolding: Reading and writing as natural language activities. *Language Arts, 60*, 168–175.

Bakhtin, M. M. (1981). *The dialogic imagination* (ed. by M. Holquist & trans. & ed. by C. Emerson & M. Holquist). Austin: University of Texas Press.

Barthes, R. (1971). De l'oeuvre au texte. *Revue d'Esthetique, 24*, 225–232.

Bartlett, F. (1932). *Remembering: A study in experimental and social psychology.* Cambridge: Cambridge University Press.

Baylor, B. (1974). *Everybody needs a rock.* New York: Macmillan.

Baylor, B. (1975). *The desert is theirs.* New York: Macmillan.

Bolter, J. D. (1991). *Writing space: The computer, hypertext, and the history of writing.* Hillsdale, NJ: Lawrence Erlbaum.

Bracewell, R. J., Frederiksen, C. H., & Frederiksen, J. D. (1982). Cognitive processes in composing and comprehending discourse. *Educational Psychologist, 17*, 146–164.

Bransford, J. D., Barclay, J. R., & Franks, J. J. (1972). Sentence memory: A constructive versus interpretive approach. *Cognitive Psychology, 3*, 193–209.

Clark, H. H. (1977). Inferences in comprehension. In D. LaBerge & S. J. Samuels (Eds.), *Basic processes in reading: Perception and comprehension.* (pp. 243–263). Hillsdale, NJ: Lawrence Erlbaum.

Duffy, G. G., Roehler, L. R., & Herrmann, B. A. (1988). Modeling mental processes helps poor readers become strategic readers. *The Reading Teacher, 41*, 762–767.

Flower, L., Burnett, R., Hajduk, T., Wallace, D., Norris, L., Peck, W., & Spivey, N. N. (1989). *Classroom inquiry in collaborative planning.* Pittsburgh: Center for the Study of Writing at Berkeley and at Carnegie Mellon.

Flower, L., & Hayes, J. R. (1984). Images, plans, and prose: The representation of meaning in writing. *Written Communication, 1*, 120–160.

Frederiksen, C. H. (1975). Effects of context-induced processing operations on semantic information acquired from discourse. *Cognitive Psychology, 7*, 371–458.

Freedman, S. W., & Sperling, M. (1985). Written language acquisition: The role of response and the writing conference. In S. W. Freedman (Ed.), *The acquisition of written language* (pp. 106–130). Norwood, NJ: Ablex.

Fryer, J. (1987). Desert, rock, shelter, legend: Willa Cather's novels of the Southwest. In J. Monk & V. Norwood (Eds.), *The desert is no lady* (pp. 27–46). New Haven: Yale University Press.

Grimes, J. E. (1975). *The thread of discourse.* The Hague: Mouton.

Haas, C., & Flower, L. (1988). Rhetorical reading strategies and the construction of meaning. *College Composition and Communication, 39*, 167–183.

Kant, I. (1963). *Critique of pure reason* (Trans. N. K. Smith). London: Macmillan. (Originally published 1787.)

Kearsley, G. (1988). Authoring considerations for hypertext. *Educational Technology,* November, 21–24.

Kinneavy, J. L. (1971). *A theory of discourse.* Englewood Cliffs, NJ: Prentice Hall.

Kintsch, W., & van Dijk, T. A. (1978). Toward a model of discourse comprehension and production. *Psychological Review, 85,* 363–394.

Kristeva, J. (1968). Problems de la structuration du texte. In *Theorie d'ensemble* (pp. 297–316). Paris: Editions du Seuil.

Kroll, B. M. (1985). Rewriting a story for a young reader: The development of audience-adapted writing skills. *Research in the Teaching of English, 19,* 120–139.

Leitch, V. (1983). *Deconstructive criticism: An advanced introduction.* New York: Columbia University Press.

Mandler, J. M., & Johnson, N. S. (1977). Remembrance of things parsed: Story structure and recall. *Cognitive Psychology, 9,* 111–151.

McKeown, M. B., Beck, I. L., & Worthy, M. J. (1993). Grappling with text ideas: Questioning the author. *The Reading Teacher, 46,* 560–566.

Meyer, B. J. F. (1975). *The organization of prose and its effect on memory.* Amsterdam: North Holland.

Miller, O. (1985). Intertextual identity. In M. J. Valdes & O. Miller (Eds.), *Identity of the literary text* (pp. 19–40). Toronto: University of Toronto Press.

Murphy, S., & Smith, M. A. (1990). *Writing portfolios: A bridge from teaching to assessment.* Markham, Ontario: Pippin Publishing.

Nystrand, M. (1986). *The structure of written communication: Studies of reciprocity between writers and readers.* Orlando: Academic Press.

Nystrand, M., & Wiemelt, J. (1991). When is a text explicit? Formalistic and dialogical conceptions. *Text, 11,* 25–41.

Riffaterre, M. (1980). La trace de l'intertexte. *La Pensee, 215,* 4–18.

Rohman, D. E., & Wlecke, A. O. (1964). *Pre-writing: The construction and application of models for concept formation in writing.* U.S. Office of Education, Cooperative Research Project No. 2174. East Lansing, MI: Michigan State University.

Roth, R. G. (1987). The evolving audience: Alternatives to audience accommodation. *College Compostion and Communication, 38,* 47–55.

Shanahan, T. (1993, April). *Starting a conversation: The development of author awareness during reading.* Paper presented at annual meeting of American Educational Research Association.

Silverstein, S. (1974). *Where the sidewalk ends.* New York: Harper and Row.

Spiro, R. J. (1977). Remembering information from text: The "state of schema" approach. In R. C. Anderson, R. J. Spiro, & W. E. Montague (Eds.), *Schooling and the acquisition of knowledge* (pp. 137–165). Hillsdale, NJ: Lawrence Erlbaum.

Spiro, R. J. (1980). Constructive processes in prose comprehension and recall. In R. J. Spiro, B. C. Bruce, & W. F. Brewer (Eds.), *Theoretical issues in reading comprehension* (pp. 245–278). Hillsdale, NJ: Lawrence Erlbaum.

Spiro, R. J., Bruce, B. C., & Brewer, W. F. (Eds.). (1980). *Theoretical issues in reading comprehension.* Hillsdale, NJ: Lawrence Erlbaum.

Spivey, N. N. (1984). *Discourse synthesis: Constructing texts in reading and writing* (Outstanding Dissertation Monograph Series). Newark, DE: International Reading Association.

Spivey, N. N. (1987). Construing constructivism: Reading research in the United States. *Poetics, 16,* 169–192.

Spivey, N. N. (1990). Transforming texts: Constructive processes in reading and writing. *Written Communication, 7,* 256–287.

Spivey, N. N. (1991). The shaping of meaning: Options in writing the comparison. *Research in the Teaching of English, 25,* 390–418.

Spivey, N. N. (1995). Written discourse: A constructivist perspective. In L. P.Steffe & J. Gale (Eds.), *Constructivism in education* (pp. 313–329). Hillsdale, NJ: Lawrence Erlbaum.

Spivey, N. N., & Greene, S. (1989). *Aufgabe in writing and learning from sources.* Paper presented at annual meeting of American Educational Research Association, San Francisco.

Spivey, N. N., & King, J. R. (1989). Readers as writers composing from sources. *Reading Research Quarterly, 24,* 7–26.

Steffe, L. P., & Gale, J. (Eds.). (1995). *Constructivism in education.* Hillsdale, NJ: Lawrence Erlbaum.

Telford, J., & Williams, T. T. (1989). *Coyote's canyon.* Salt Lake City: Gibbs Smith.

Vico, G. (1868). *De antiquissima Italorum sapientia.* Naples: Stampera de' Classici. (Originally published 1710.)

Williams, T. T. (1989). The coyote clan. In J. Telford & T. T. Williams, *Coyote's canyon* (pp. 16–27). Salt Lake City: Gibbs Smith.

4

Mentors on Paper

How Classics Develop
Verbal Ability

MICHAEL CLAY THOMPSON
University School of Jackson

All questions about what curricular materials are appropriate must rest on a foundation of previously decided questions that collectively comprise a philosophy of education. In essence, you have to know why you are teaching before you can pick your books.

If you are teaching for basic literacy and job skills, then you can be satisfied with ordinary textbooks, basal readers, and high-interest periodicals—maybe. If, however, you are teaching for more, if school is to educate and enlighten students, to teach them to think and to question, to illuminate their place in the world's geography, ecology, and history, then they must be on friendly terms with good books—and with themselves as readers and lovers of good books. Few would dispute this, but there is much debate about what books are good books and about whether classics in particular should be emphasized in the education of verbally talented learners. Despite the debate, there are strong reasons for including the classics as a significant component in the education of these students.

A Consensus against Basals

On one point, authors and researchers in gifted education achieve an unusual consensus: Verbally talented students should not be educated by placement in age-grouped basal reading classes; rather, they should be exposed to good literature (though unsurprisingly there is not consensus about what good literature is). Gallagher (1975) issued a "plea to go beyond the rather sterile presentation of grammar and syntax and to use literature as a means to instill appreciation of past cultures" (p. 198). Parker (1989) stressed that especially for gifted children, the "study of language involves literature—not only reading it, but learning to read it critically and creatively, to interpret an author's meanings and to recognize an author's style" (p. 181). Clark (1988) summarized research by Brown and Rogan:

> *By keeping [gifted] children in the regular basal series, insisting that they adhere to the regular reading program, follow-up, and skill-builder activities, we often frustrate them. This can destroy their belief in school as an interesting, exciting place and in learning and books as the wonderful experiences they thought they were. These researchers point to age-in-grade grouping and the reluctance to provide acceleration or experiences outside of the regular classroom as obstacles to appropriate programming for gifted readers. Allowing young children to read widely, creatively, critically, and with an excellent and motivated teacher is suggested as part of the solution to providing more appropriate language arts instruction. (p. 338)*

Ganopole (1988) called for an emphasis on authentic materials: "Sequenced skills programs and materials which fragment language learning should be shelved along with the controlled-vocabulary basal texts. What should replace these materials? Appropriate replacements include the vast array of real world materials that are whole, meaningful, and related to a context that has a purpose. Such materials include literature—books representing the various genres" (p. 88). Thompson (1990) argued for authentic literature in the teaching of thinking skills: "If we intend to teach our students to think…we must risk giving them something to think about—not the insipid, homogeneous gruel of textbooks, but exposure to the freest minds" (p. 14). Reis and Renzulli (1989) noted the "widespread dissatisfaction expressed by so many school personnel about the use of basal readers for high ability students" (p. 95) and described basal readers for gifted students as "boring and sterile." VanTassel-Baska, Feldhusen, Seeley, Wheatley, Silverman, and Foster (1988) emphasized strong literature:

> *The literature program for the verbally talented child needs to be very rich from the beginning of the language arts experience in school. Children who are reading by kindergarten need a strong literature program at that stage of their development. The use of a basal reading series typically focuses too much time and attention on mastering the reading process, particulary phonics, rather than on allowing gifted students the opportunity for holistic reading of good literature. One way to combat this problem is to build a strong literature program for the gifted K–12, infusing the best and most challenging selections at each stage of development. (p. 156)*

Some light on the failure of basal texts to motivate gifted learners has been shed by Carolyn Fehrenbach (1991), who studied 60 eighth-, tenth-, and twelfth-grade students to compare their reading processing strategies. She found that the "strategies used significantly more by gifted than by average readers were rereading, inferring, analyzing structure, watching or predicting, evaluating, and relating to content area. The strategies used significantly more by average than by gifted readers were word pronouncing concern and summarizing inaccurately" (p. 125). Are basals readers fit material for rereading, inferring, analyzing structure, or predicting? Do they develop strength in critically evaluating literature? If gifted students should not be reading these age-graded, vocabulary-controlled, basal texts, what should they be reading?

The Classics Remain Classic

One part of the answer—if we can agree that education must be more than skill training for jobs and must include a civilizing and ennobling experience in what is and has been human and humane—is that of the numerous ways in which verbal ability can be developed through formal education, a close and constant acquaintance with the classics is one of the most significant. Despite the concern raised by some about the White male bias of the classics—a worthy concern that can (should, yes, but can) be addressed—the classics remain classic; they are at many levels the standards of excellence and the enduring works that must form one strong component in the education of high-ability students. By virtue of their multileveled excellence, and through the influence of these forms of excellence on students' minds, the classics stretch, challenge, and mold students, changing their tastes and giving them a real sense of what the possibilities are for human expression in language. Students, for example, who have become well acquainted with the classics and who have been shown the difference gradually cease to argue for the quality of grocery store–horror novel authors and begin instead to write serious poetry and fiction of their own.

The classics do not mean merely the literature of Greece and Rome, but the rich body of authentic past and contemporary international literature (poetry, fiction, and nonfiction) that is, for various reasons, timeless, and that forms for all of us our sometimes tacit and sometimes explicit sense of good reading. Yes, the classics encompass Homer and Shakespeare, but they also include Harper Lee, Victor Hugo, Chinua Achebe, Cervantes, Pablo Neruda, and Emily Dickinson. No single list of criteria will accurately describe every classic, but as a body, these works possess enduring value, advanced vocabulary and sentence construction, highly developed characters, significant ideas, the potential for open-ended discussions, artistic merit, and significant profiles in intellectual history.

When I reflect on the educational needs of very bright children, it helps me to remember the most intelligent thing I ever heard anyone say. It was said by David, a shy sophomore student of mine in a residential summer program for gifted students. After studying DNA for four weeks, David softly concluded a presentation on his findings by noting that "because of DNA, each of us is the potential ancestor of an infinite number of descendants, and therefore, if anything should happen to us before we reproduce, the consequences to the universe could be catastrophic." In the stunned silence that followed, my 50 students and I looked at each other in a sort of moment of respect. All of us knew that we had just heard a thought of cosmic loveliness and telescopic depth. Now, concerning David—what is the appropriate curriculum for this child? What are the right materials and activities for a child who cares so universally and who comprehends so humanely? What are the books for a child who knows that the abstract is concrete? Well, an education consists of many things, but I certainly want David to read Shakespeare, and Harriet Beecher Stowe, and Richard Wright, and Charles Dickens, and Emily Dickinson, and Dostoevsky, and Emily Brontë, and Victor Hugo, and Walt Whitman, and Tolstoy, and George Eliot, and Homer, and Sophocles, and Chinua Achebe, and...you get the point. I wouldn't want David to miss any of it. I want him to know the lovely and wondrous literature of the world, for through this literature—I want to say *his* literature—he will hear the song of his species, he will encounter his context, he will discover his kin, and he will receive a shimmering mirror of words in which he may learn manifold aspects of himself.

Furthermore, I want David to be given books that will thrill him with quality and respect, and develop the writer in him. I want him not only to reproduce but to *produce*, and to beget new stories, and articles, and essays, and poems. I want children like David to get the literature that will inspire them to the heights of language. To continue David's idea, what are the consequences to the universe that we have neither the descendents nor the precluded literature of Anne Frank?

It is possible, and actually necessary, to discuss the benefits of classics at very great length; it is a subject that cries for clear understanding. But for a chapter-length discussion of the role of classics in developing verbal ability in bright children, a few ideas are especially significant. The classics:

- Are inherently self-differentiating for students of various abilities
- Develop intellectual experience
- Expose students to an educated vocabulary
- Develop critical and creative thinking skills
- Provide a knowledge of intellectual and cultural heritage
- Develop values and humanity
- Demonstrate the universality of genius

Classics Are Inherently Self-Differentiating

I wish I could take credit for this idea. The truth is, I was ambushed into realizing it by the gentleman-scholar, Dr. Harry Passow, who heard me present the value of classics at the symposium that provided the foundation for this book. When my presentation ended, Dr. Passow called me over, a gleam in his eye: "You are advocating classics in the education of *all* children, right?" he asked, and waited, reminding me disturbingly of a lion crouched low in the tawny grass. I suspiciously said yes, I think all students should be given classics. "Well," he pounced, "how would you differentiate the classics for gifted students?" Now, certainly, there are things one can say about differentiating pedagogical processes, but I knew better than to fumble with techniques and small details at this point; I knew something was coming. "Isn't that the beauty of classics," Dr. Passow said, an appreciative kindness in his face. "They are *self*-differentiating. They are so deep that each person is able to read them at his own depth and get something out of them."

Yes. The classics are self-differentiating, and they are also, of course, beautifully appropriate content for the differentiating techniques of teachers who are trained in the education of gifted students. In their very nature, however, classics are inherently a superb curriculum for developing verbal abilities in bright children.

Classics Are Appropriate

Consider that the classics are the products of gifted minds, and more specifically, they are the products of individuals gifted in verbal ability. They are, in essence, mentors on paper. How would you describe the verbal abilities of Melville, Sylvia Plath, Dickens, William Shakespeare, Emily Dickinson,

Dante, or Mary Shelley? Here, for example, are the first words that Herman Melville (1982) wrote in *Moby Dick*. The reader opens the book, finds the first page, and the eyes fall on the first sentence:

> *Call me Ishmael. Some years ago—never mind how long precisely—having little or no money in my purse, and nothing particular to interest me on shore, I thought I would sail about a little and see the watery part of the world. It is a way I have of driving off the spleen and regulating the circulation. Whenever I find myself growing grim about the mouth; whenever it is a damp, drizzly November in my soul; whenever I find myself involuntarily pausing before coffin warehouses, and bringing up the rear of every funeral I meet; and especially whenever my hypos get such an upper hand of me, that it requires a strong moral principle to prevent me from deliberately stepping into the street, and methodically knocking people's hats off— then, I account it high time to get to sea as soon as I can. (p. 1)*

Wham. For the alert mind, Melville's words are the spiritual equivalent of a rocket launch. Other levels aside, the sheer *talent* of the paragraph is dizzying. Growing grim. Damp drizzly. November in my soul. Coffin warehouses. And yet, the most important part of the thrill is not merely through appreciation but through *recognition*; in Melville's words, we see our own brightest potential displayed; in his writing we recognize the best of ourselves. As we read his work, the part of us that loves it finds similarities with the part of him that composed it, and this recognition of similarity kindles a feeling of promise within us, a belief that we, too, might create, might write a world. (The English poet Swinburne compared Victor Hugo writing a novel to God creating spring.) In this moment of recognition, our verbal ability develops. We go from I-like-this-book to this-is-like-me to maybe-I-could-do-this. For children like David, every classic is a self-discovery, a recognition, and a recommendation for being.

Furthermore, the classics are not merely written *by* the verbally gifted, but they are often *about* gifted characters. Gifted children will find classic characters who are like themselves, who think as they do, worry as they do, care as they do. Remember Scout Finch who got into trouble at school for teaching herself to read, Odysseus who solved his way home to his wife, the stubborn Jane Eyre who was a match for Mr. Rochester, Holden Caulfield whose world required no catcher in the rye, the clever Tom Sawyer who got his fence painted white, the Time Traveler whose friends lacked the flexibility to understand his accomplishment, the pretender Becky Sharp whose brilliance illuminated Vanity Fair, the malevolent genius Iago who destroyed a beautiful love, and the introspective Hamlet who was too bright to proceed unthinkingly—even to avenge his father's murder? It would be a simple task to continue this list of gifted characters: Oedipus, Esther Greenwood, Toad (yes, Toad). But better, let's examine the ethical thinking of one gifted character, the little girl Scout Finch, in Harper Lee's *To Kill a Mocking-bird*:

> *Boo and I walked up the steps to the porch. His fingers found the front door-knob. He gently released my hand, opened the door, went inside, and shut the door behind him. I never saw him again.*
>
> *Neighbors bring food with death and flowers with sickness and little things in between. Boo was our neighbor. He gave us two soap dolls, a broken watch and chain, a pair of good-luck pennies, and our lives. But neighbors give in return. We never put back into the tree what we took out of it: we had given him nothing, and it made me sad.*
>
> *I turned to go home. Street lights winked down the street all the way to town. I had never seen our neighborhood from this angle.... Atticus was right. One time he said you never really know a man until you stand in his shoes and walk around in them. Just standing on the Radley porch was enough.*
>
> *The street lights were fuzzy from the fine rain that was falling. As I made my way home, I felt very old, but when I looked at the tip of my nose I could see fine misty beads, but looking cross-eyed made me dizzy so I quit.* (Lee, 1960, pp. 278–279)

Neighbors give in return. Stand in your neighbor's shoes. This thinking, including the principle of reciprocity and the universalizing of consequences, is essential and primary to the great ethical concerns of humankind. We have seen these ideas in the words of Jesus: Love your neighbor as yourself. Do unto others as you would have them do unto you. And we have seen them in the philosophy of Kant's categorical imperative: that action is moral which one can will to be universalized. But there is a special charm in receiving them from a precocious little girl who ponders them spontaneously as she crosses her eyes to see the mist on her nose. And by the way, it *is* a sin to kill a mockingbird; if you have not stopped the world to listen to a mockingbird for a half an hour, lying flat on your back as the spring clouds move through the telescopic blue sky, then you have an insufficient understanding of the word *song*. If you don't believe me, believe Atticus Finch.

Classics Teach Words

One of the obvious developmental benefits of the classics is the vocabulary they contain. Most, though not all, classics are rich in advanced vocabulary that empowers verbal ability. Exceptions—such as the novels of Ernest Hemingway (most of the advanced words are the names of drinks), or Alan Paton's *Cry the Beloved Country* (a gorgeous, biblical simplicity blended with language from South Africa), or Tolkien's *The Hobbit* (intricate grammar, elementary vocabulary)—are rich in other properties and also develop verbal ability. But a great many classics do contain advanced vocabulary, and in ways which may surprise even those who think this point is obvious.

As an example, what one classic do you think the following words come from?

diffidence, placid, adhere, quietus, miscreant, quixotic, reproof, condescend, somber, enigma, phlegmatic, undulate, sublime, resolute, strident, din, amicable, amorous, raconteur, profound, dejection, placid, amiably, tedious, mea culpa, perplex, impede, interpose, incisive, impassive, admonish, aperture, avidly, perfidious, miasma, abject, portal, fain, sanguinary, retort, imperiously, hauteur, patronize, aloof, blithe, boon, cypher, wince, defray, genial, cadaverous, remonstrate, nether, upbraid, solicitous, conveyance, mauve, hitherto, succulent, artifice, proffer, ardent, tremulous, recriminate, assail, virulent, insinuate, intrinsic

Impressive, don't you think? Give up? These are formidable and advanced words—erudite even. One would expect to encounter them not only in SATs but in professional, college, and graduate texts. What book could these come from? I'll reveal the answer below, but first consider a second list. What second classic do you think the following list comes from?

replete, affable, portentous, fractious, despond, subterfuge, dejected, dolorous, countenance, languor, obtuse, vouchsafe, amiable, immure, lurid, sanguine, avidity, paroxysm, allude, wistful, asperity, copse, sinuous, benison, irrevocable, plausible, gesticulate, unction, accouter, placid, revile, stringent, peremptory, artifice, repartee, querulous, retort, assuage, sonorous, plaintive, noisome, athwart, brazen, billow, repast, imperious, listless, privation, voluble, cudgel, comely, victual, contrition, doleful, rancour, habiliment, panoply, tedious, prostrate, turbid, ignominy, fallow, expatiate, sward, errant, sinuous, gesticulate, stipulation, supplicate

Do you think that that average high school senior could comfortably define these words? Or use them in a sentence? Considering what is standard in the age-graded textbooks that most U.S. students receive, what is the probable grade level of the two lists of words? Would the typical student reach these words in elementary school? In middle school? In high school? In college? What book do you think this second list comes from? Let's look at one more list from a third classic:

insidious, remonstrate, pertinacity, paroxysm, innocuous, impending, superfluous, manifest, plethora, weazen, demesne, discomfit, salient, callow, amenities, copious, melancholy, eloquent, dubious, precipitate, placate, diabolical, fastidious, malinger, cadence, ignominy, morose, swarthy, tangible, exquisite, mandate, repose, egotism, progeny, docile, unwonted, pervade, reproof, writhe, eddy, conjure, impel, commingle, latent, palpitant, perplex, repugnance, inexorable, amenities, chronic, importune, wistful, acute, prowess, lacerate, insular, abject, apprehend, vex, bedlam, lugubrious, somber, asunder, effectual, clamor, recur, evince, expedient, wraith, aver

Again, look carefully at this mature vocabulary. What would it contribute to the development of verbal ability for a student to have read the three books which these vocabularies represent? Imagine each of these words used in a clarifying sentence. Well, enough suspense. The three books from which the three vocabulary lists were extracted are, in order, Barrie's *Peter Pan*, Grahame's *The Wind in the Willows*, and Jack London's *The Call of the Wild*.

Children's books! No, children's *classics*. Before you conclude that I tricked you, consider the real trick: Educational practice has tricked us all into thinking that such vocabulary is not for children, that it is developmentally inappropriate, or that it should be postponed until some imaginary later appropriate time. Well, I think that any little child who can handle a big term such as *Sanfranciscofortyniner* or *teenagemutantninjaturtle* can handle *fastidious*, and that we are committing national intellectual suicide with our age-graded pistol. Beyond the earliest elementary grades, I challenge the very idea that there are *children's words*. What should we do? Postpone reading *Peter Pan* until graduate school? If anything, children are *better* able to absorb new words than adults are.

Some may think that the three books I used are extraordinary and that such language is not prevalent even in classics. It is though. This prevalence can be demonstrated through a different way of looking at the vocabulary in the classics: the use of a single word.

If we examine the use of specific words in the classics, we begin to understand even more profoundly why children who read classics are able to amass powerful vocabularies. As I have indicated in *Classics in the Classroom* (Thompson, 1990), good words are ubiquitous in the classics, and the young reader encounters them in myriad contexts. The word *profound*, for example, was used by Melville, Plath, Kipling, Hardy, Stevenson, Barrie, Wells, Conrad, Fitzgerald, Twain, Lee, Hawthorne, Scott, Dickens, and Charlotte Brontë. Atticus Finch has a profound distaste for criminal law. Henry Fleming feels capable of profound sacrifices. Lord Jim finds the sea to be blue and profound. Kipling's Kim salaams profoundly. Sylvia Plath's Esther Greenwood feels the profound void of an empty stomach. Thomas Hardy's Eustacia Vye bends to the hearth in a profound reverie. Peter Pan's eyes show a profound melancholy, though Captain Hook becomes profoundly dejected. Ahab profoundly dines with his officers. Dr. Jekyll experiences the profound duplicity of life. Daisy Buchanan notes that her husband Tom is getting very profound from reading deep books with long words in them. Over and over, the child who reads classics encounters this word—profound ignorance, profound homage, profound silence, profound distress, profound discovery, profound human change, profound intimacy, profound and terrifying logic, profound idea, profound clamor, profound secret, profound affliction, profound grief, profound fatigue, profound blackness of the pupils.

A second example: *Serene* is a lovely word. Judge Taylor's court, in *To Kill a Mockingbird*, is serene. Jane Eyre tells Mr. Rochester that the night is serene. Lord Jim walks under a serene sky. Huck and Tom get out their pipes and go serenely puffing around. (Don't you love that one?) Ahab finds that his pipe is meant for sereneness, and throws it into the profound sea. The Pequod, under indolent sail, glides serenely along. Kipling's Kim is serenely prepared for anything, and a policeman in the same novel is seen to serenely pick his teeth. Hester Prynne has a serene deportment. A woman in *The Bell Jar* has a serene, almost religious, smile. And the Martian invasion in *The War of the Worlds* creates a blank incongruity between the serenity of the sky and the swift death flying yonder. Tom Sawyer hears a stony-hearted liar reel off his serene statement. Henry David Thoreau's serenity is rippled but not ruffled.

This characteristic of the classics—the apt and creative use of words at a level that is brilliantly exciting—is really no surprise. Is it unexpected that humanity's most highly developed verbal talents would use many words and use them well? The best writers *are* the best users of words. If students are to have their vocabularies developed, they should read these writers. These are the writers who define and redefine the limits. These are the writers who show the path.

Consider the language exposure a high school student gets from a single 400-page classic at, say, 20 sentences per page. That is 8,000 sentences, each one a model of a well-constructed thought, absorbed into the student's mind as a subconscious template for his or her own future thoughts and expressions. If, in this single book, there is a higher-level vocabulary word in every third sentence, then the student also receives exposure to over 2,500 uses of advanced words, used in sentence and story context. If the student carefully reads 10 such classics a year, that means exposure to 80,000 well-made sentences and 25,000 good examples of vocabulary usage. For this reason, and others, there is a vast educational difference between reading even 10 good books a year and reading none or few. Through reading, the student acquires a store of language memory that then serves as a foundation for reading, and more speaking, and for writing. (Writing is a skill that follows easily in the wake of large reading experience, but that is almost impossible to teach in the absence of such experience. Reading is the beginning of writing. Anyone who has tried to teach unread students to write knows the frustration of trying to do what you have not begun.) The vocabulary of the classics develops more than vocabulary, though that alone is a shining goal; the vocabulary of the classics, through its context, names the nameless and the subtle, illuminates the mute gaps between things often expressed, and provides moments of creative usage for verbally awakening students.

Classics Develop the Ability to Articulate Ideas

Of course, it is not merely vocabulary that the classics provide for high-ability students. It is ideas, and the way in which the ideas may be articulated. That the classics are insufficiently appreciated as a source of ideas was a sore point for Thoreau. Now that I think of it, a lot of things were sore points for Thoreau, but we should not pause to discuss them here, though when we finish this chapter, we should all go reread his chapter about the loon. Anyway, as Thoreau complained in *Walden*:

> *A man, any man, will go considerably out of his way to pick up a silver dollar; but here are golden words, which the wisest men of antiquity have uttered, and whose worth the wise of every succeeding age have assured us of;—and yet we learn to read only as far as Easy Reading, the primers and class-books, and when we leave school, the "Little Reading," and storybooks, which are for boys and beginners; and our reading, our conversation and thinking, are all on a very low level. (p. 16)*

In fact, the golden words of the classics expose students to a teeming cacophony of contending ideas, as expressed by history's least restrained thinkers. Classics free students from the insipid slumber of textbooks, and shock them awake with the meanings of humanity's dissident heroes: Mohandas Gandhi, Henry David Thoreau, Patrick Henry, Harriet Beecher Stowe, Martin Luther, Martin Luther King, Thomas Jefferson, Mary Wollstonecraft, Voltaire, Emily Dickinson, Frederick Douglass, Jean-Jacques Rousseau, William Blake, and Walt Whitman. Think, these voices say, think. Be free. Be unafraid. Resist tyranny. Protect people's rights. Create. Reject nonsense. Apply your ethics. Pursue happiness. The classics are rife with these ideas, and to read them is to run an intellectual gauntlet, to be struck, and smartly too, by the strongest ideas of the centuries:

> *It is a self-evident truth that all men are created equal—Jefferson. Whenever a government becomes destructive of human ends, it is the right of the peo-*

ple to alter or abolish it—Jefferson. Through nonviolence and passive resistance, even unarmed people can change the world—Gandhi. Impetuous toads in motorcars can get into trouble.—Grahame. The prince must do what is necessary for the benefit of his land, even if it means disregarding conventional moral limitations—Machiavelli. Taking a less-traveled road can make all the difference—Frost. If you fly so high that the sun melts the wax on your wings, you will fall into the sea—Ovid. The love of God must be a leap of faith—Kierkegaard. That action is moral which you can will to be universalized—Kant. As the horses graze, their heads are toward eternity—Dickinson. We should stand at the meeting of two eternities, and improve upon the nick of time—Thoreau. The great expectations you have may be a gift from someone you never realized loves you—Dickens. You must govern the republic of your own mind as a sort of internal philosopher-king—Plato. You must have the mental integrity to change the convictions of a lifetime, if one afternoon's evidence shows you clearly that they are wrong—Malcolm X. Life is a tale told by an idiot, full of sound and fury, signifying nothing—Shakespeare. Everything works out for the best in this best of all possible worlds—Leibnitz. The individual in a modern bureaucratic society can feel as insignificant as an insect—Kafka. The being of Dasein is care—Heidegger. A mouse is miracle enough to stagger sextillions of infidels—Whitman. Some guys become pathologically obsessed with the American Dream, and will do anything to achieve it—Fitzgerald. The masculine and feminine temperaments which we associate with the male and female sex are culturally relative, and are different in other cultures—Mead. A good man may be harder to find than you think—O'Connor. If you want to reach your destination, you must think and be clever in the face of all perils—Homer. The center of Hell is frozen—Dante. (Thompson, 1995, pp. 27–29)

Thousands of pages would not suffice even to allude briefly to the ideas contained in the classics; like stars in the sky, the classics form rich and well-known systems of constellations of ideas. They are the points of reference by which educated people navigate their intellectual courses. They are a cacophonous host of richly conflicting ideas.

Yes, the classics constitute a sort of intellectual hailstorm, but how, exactly, do these ideas influence the development of verbal ability? Once students become accustomed to reading stories that contain ideas, they come, without realizing it, to *expect* ideas. An identification (a truth, I would aver) is established between words and ideas. Words *are* ideas. Ideas *are* words. Words are the liquid medium for the appearance of ideas. To manifest the idea in the wrong words is to have lost it, to have let the idea escape; what results is not the idea. Words are ideas. Language is *real*. "I do not say these things for a dollar," said Whitman in *Leaves of Grass* (1993, p. 70), "or to fill up the time while I wait for a boat; / It is you talking just as much as myself.... I act as the tongue of you, / It was tied in your mouth.... in mine it begins to be loosened." Students who have lived among the words of the classics will not say things for a dollar, either. They will have learned one of the best truths of language: the word and the idea are one. In learning this, students develop; in attempting to apply it, they develop vastly.

Classics Develop Thinking Skills

The encounter with classic ideas cannot be tranquil. The ideas are too gusty and too bracing. It is a tempestuous voyage, in which students simply *must* think. The classics have not been age-graded down or censored through selection to only what can be ignored or to what merely confirms the complacence of the moderate majority—on the contrary. The ill-behaved brilliance of the classics inspires thinking—indeed, *incites* thinking—in everyone who reads them.

For many reasons, the classics are a correct medium for thinking experiences. The classics are complex and profound; they have a bottomless quality that makes rereading an increasingly meaningful and valuable experience. One way to express this is that the classics are what I have termed *Socratic objects* whose answers are not entirely discoverable; they are perfectly appropriate content for open-ended Socratic discussions.

The classics are an excellent content for the excellent processes that have been developed to teach thinking. They are appropriate for Socratic inquiry, but they are also suitable for the application of Bloom's taxonomy and other taxonomy-based activities. In my own classes, I like to assign students to read two classics as homework for each academic term and then to assess the reading through a taxonomy-based individual discussion with each student. I never know in advance what the questions will be; they are spontaneously suggested by the discussion as it grows. The terms I use to create questions are *memory, cognition, synthesis, divergence, convergence, analysis, application, emotion, aesthetics,* and *ethics*—in other words, an amalgam of Bloom's taxonomy and others that I have encountered in education, together with some special focus terms such as *ethics)* that I wish to emphasize.

Note that in offering excellent content for the application of thinking processes, classics rid us of the dread vacuity that sometimes attends the teaching of thinking. Being able to brainstorm how else *A Tale of Two Cities* might have ended, we need not brainstorm how we might survive on the moon with a paper clip and a frisbee.

Literature is often cited as an excellent content for the development of rigorous critical thinking. In both the *Junior Great Books* and *Paideia* programs, not to mention the Advanced Placement program, rigorous analytical

and comparative methods are brought to bear in the interpretation of literature. Students are taught to avoid projecting their own ideas obliviously into
the text, to reread, to make accurate inferences, to cite the text itself as evidence of meaning, to assess character change and philosophical value, and to
respect and hear the views of their peers in the course of a Socratic discussion. The Junior Great Books emphasis on using authentic Socratic questions
that have no foregone conclusion is important since this open-endedness is
essential to successful open-mindedness.

Critical thinking about literature is a process that has wide support. The
programs mentioned, and others, even offer workshops that teachers can
attend in order to receive training in critical thinking about literature. Creative thinking about literature is not as widely studied. Two models of creative thinking that have depth and resonance in using the classics to teach
thinking are by Wallas (1926) and Torrance and Myers (1970). They are
worth mentioning here because they are usually thought of as models of creative behavior, but they yield surprising benefits when applied to the discussion of classics. Torrance's model includes four terms: *fluency, flexibility, originality*, and *elaboration*. In discussing the interpretation of literature, we
should think that way. Fluency: Do we have a number of possible interpretations? Flexibility: Do we have different kinds of interpretations? Originality:
Have we thought of some interpretations that are new? Elaboration: Can we
develop our interpretation in detail, and does it still work with the many
details of the text when we do so? Notice that this model goes against the
grain of the more convergent critical thinking process.

Wallas's 1926 model also has four terms: *preparation, incubation, illumination*, and *verification*. I like to use the Wallas model to help students analyze
literature, both because it helps them do good analysis and because they can
then understand the importance of these steps in other creative experiences.
Recently, for example, my sophomore class and I were reading Shakespeare's *The Tempest*, and I explained to them that one of the primary techniques great writers use to emphasize their themes is repetition. In *The Tempest*, there are a dozen or so words that recur, and a handful of behaviors that
the characters repeat. Without telling the students what any of these things
were, I said, *"Just look for yourself. Study the text. Find out what is repeated. Then
take the time to absorb it. Then develop an interpretation of the play, based on what
you find repeated."* In other words, Preparation: Study and reread the text
carefully collecting the data you will need. Incubation: Allow your study of
the text to sink in, and allow interpretations to bubble in the back of your
mind. (This incubation time is often *very* important in the creation of new
ideas.) Illumination: When you have incubated long enough, your *aha* experience will come and you will suddenly get a good idea for interpreting the
text. Verification: Once you have an idea, patiently work it out, showing how
it helps to explain the many separate details of the story. Students who have

been taught Wallas's model will always remember and appreciate that it takes time to incubate, and will remember that it is possible to force oneself into writing too soon.

Applying Torrance and Wallas's models of creative behavior to the interpretation of literature helps to emphasize the fact that *interpretation is a creative act*, and not simply an act of discovery. Despite the serious reader's high reverence for the text, interpretation is different from pulling sand away from a buried sphinx; it is more like the careful construction of a model that you hypothesize is similar to a hidden meaning you can never directly discern. (As you see elsewhere in this book, *construction of meaning* is, in fact, the term that seems most appropriate to many who study the interpretation of literature.) On the other hand, interpretation as creation does not mean that no interpretation is nonsense, or that interpretation is thrown into the dark realm of relativistic chaos; we cannot say everything, but we can say much. Students who somehow interpret through the obscure glass of callow projection to say that the meaning of *Animal Farm* is that "everyone should just be free to do what he wants" *can* be refuted; the book doesn't mean that.

Clearly, imaginative literature also offers rich opportunities for imagination itself. In fact, rich imagination is the *sine qua non* of one of literature's prime theories—Coleridge's *suspension of disbelief.* Though Coleridge did not put it this way, the point is to separate critical thinking from creative and imaginative thinking and to read literature as a human being rather than as a student. You can always go back and think critically or analytically later, but while you are reading *Frankenstein*, there is a guy made of pieces of corpses, and while you are reading *Dracula*, there are vampires. While you read Oedipus, the blind prophet sees the future and knows your secrets. Suspend your disbelief. Succumb to a literary belief. Fall into what Wallace Stevens called the "mundo of the imagination." (And read Stevens's classic poem/lament for the unimaginative life, "Disillusionment of Ten Oclock.")

Through creative imagination, we can vividly enhance the experience of literature. When we read the first act of *The Tempest* in my class, I like to have one row of students be the wind, another the thunder, another the lightening crack, one student to flash the lights on and off, all of us leaning left and right in unison, while selected students holler out their lines of the text above the howling of the classroom tempest. We don't throw water around. It is uncanny how real the storm can seem; at the end of the first scene, we all feel lucky to have survived. (*Drown* is a word that appears on nearly every page of *The Tempest*.) From that point forward, students can hardly wait to continue the play. Good literature is rich with such imaginative opportunities. Imagine for yourself how you could enhance the reading of the scene in which Hamlet's father's ghost appears on the battlement—the wind, the moonlight, the sea below.

Classics Develop Human Values

We all love Odysseus. Odysseus rejected immortality on a lovely island with the beautiful Calypso to go home to Ithaca and die with the person he wanted to be with: his wife, Penelope. It was a decision the world has never forgotten, and it demonstrates part of what makes classics endure. A few years ago, on reading Castiglione's *The Courtier*, completed in 1518, I was struck by Castiglione's references to authors whose works were classics to him: Homer, Xenophon, Virgil, Caesar, Cicero, Boccaccio, Petrarch, Dante. Like Thoreau 350 years after him, which is now 140 ago, Castiglione discussed Homer and Achilles. This year, my sophomores and I read *The Iliad* and were transfixed by the vivid descriptions of war, by the epic similes, by Achilles and his wrath. This *Iliad* was the same book taught to Alexander by Aristotle and taken on campaign against the Persians. Then we read Dante's *Inferno*—and were amazed by the rain of fire, and prisons of slime, the burning coffins, and the frozen lake, just as Castiglione had been amazed five centuries before.

Why do classics endure? In part, classics endure because of the civilizing effect they have on our spirits. We do not become civilized persons automatically or necessarily. If we become civilized, it is through the benediction of individual civilizing experiences, Odysseus moments, each of which gives us a fragment of the memory and insight we need in order to care about civilized things. One of the most civilizing passages in literature comes in the final words of Stephen Crane's *Red Badge of Courage*. Henry Fleming, the boy who had gone to war despite his mother's entreaties, is coming home from the war:

> *He had been to touch the great death, and found that after all, it was but the great death. He was a man.*
>
> *So it came to pass that as he trudged from the place of blood and wrath his soul changed. He came from hot plowshares to prospects of clover tranquilly, and it was as if hot plowshares were not. Scars faded as flowers.*
>
> *It rained. The procession of weary soldiers became a bedraggled train, despondent and muttering, marching with churning effort in a trough of liquid brown mud under a low, wretched sky. Yet the youth smiled, for he saw that the world was a world for him, though many declared it to be made of oaths and walking sticks. He had rid himself of the red sickness of battle. The sultry nightmare was in the past. He had been an animal blistered and sweating in the heat and pain of war. He turned now with a lover's thirst to images of tranquil skies, fresh meadows, cool brooks—an existence of soft and eternal peace.*

Over the river a golden ray of sun came through the hosts of leaden rain clouds. (p. 134)

He saw that the world was a world for him. He turned now to an existence of soft and eternal peace. In this youth's war-born love of peace, we find the mature knowledge not only of a man but of woman also. Henry has reached the knowledge that wise men and women share in human unity. Does this experience of *civilizing meaning* develop verbal ability for students who read this book? Yes, it is meaning that provides the energy necessary for intellectual growth.

But perhaps the most civilizing truth of the classics is not a passage in any one book but in the passage of all books, for the indisputable evidence of the classics is that literary genius is universal; it is found in all human groups. The classics of the world come to us from men and women, from Americans and Europeans, from Africa and Asia, in Spanish and Greek and Italian, from Argentina and Russia, from young girls and old men. It is possible, through ignorance or intent, to select from the classics in such a way that only one group is represented (and certainly some cultures have a longer heritage of written literature than others), but to do this is to miss the meaning of the classics. They are the best proof of the beauty and promise of our species. Genius is universal, and as new classics are written, the truth of this meaning will become ever more evident. For the moment, consider just a short list of writers whose work has been the implicit subject of this chapter:

William Shakespeare, Dante, Herman Melville, Plato, Charles Dickens, Virginia Woolf, Charlotte Brontë, Malcolm X, Sylvia Plath, Booker T. Washington, Emily Dickinson, Margaret Mitchell, Homer, Maya Angelou, Lorraine Hansberry, Pearl Buck, Geronimo, Garcia Marquez, Anne Frank, James Baldwin, Louisa May Alcott, Mohandas Gandhi, Isak Denisen, Annie Dillard, Confucius, Jomo Kenyatta, Garcia Lorca, Kate Chopin, Victor Hugo, Carlos Fuentes, Phillis Wheatley, Rachel Carson, Goethe, Jorge Luis Borges, Ayn Rand, Chinua Achebe, Ruth Benedict, Claude Brown, Margaret Mead, Emily Brontë, Edith Wharton, W. E. B. DuBois, Mary Wollstonecraft, Mary Shelley, Walt Whitman, Pablo Neruda, Barbara Tuchman, Tu Fu, Harriet Beecher Stowe, Wole Soyinka, Miguel Angel Asturias, Marjorie Kinnan Rawlings, Cervantes, Beatrix Potter, Baroness Emmuska Orczy, Marianne Moore, Dostoevsky, Lady Murasaki, Marco Polo, Chairman Mao, Lao Tzu, Guy de Maupassant, Harper Lee, Mikhail Lermontov, George Eliot, Euclid, Alexander Dumas, Alexander Pushkin, Frederick Douglas, Richard Wright, Ralph Ellison, Castiglione, Chekhov, Frances Hodgson Burnett, Machiavelli,

Henrik Ibsen, Gustave Flaubert, Euripides, Sappho, Wilma Dyke-man, Robert Burns, Calderon de la Barca, Benvenuto Cellini, Con-stantine Cavafy, Elizabeth Browning, Elizabeth Bishop, Rabin-dranath Tagore, Jane Austen

The classics of the world are an accomplishment of humanity, of 10,000 (to use the perfect number from Chinese poetry) brilliant men and women of all ages from all over. Through a familiarity with the true classics of the world, students can be educated above nationalism, ethnocentrism, and elit-ism, and can witness the wisdom and accomplishment of their species. The classics contribute to a global and interdisciplinary perspective that is enlightened and tolerant. This is by no means the least of the benefits to be gained from the classics.

Conclusion

It is impossible in the space of a chapter to address all of the issues pertaining to the use of the classics in the classroom. Thoreau once said that he felt unable to exaggerate enough to express the truth. The classics are like that. To accurately express their importance and the effect they have on the mind is to court disaster by seeming hyperbolic and irrational. But consider the arguments given here, and consider which classic you have read that you would agree to utterly forget, as though you had never read it. Would you forget *The Great Gatsby*, or *Treasure Island*, or *Crime and Punishment*, or *To Kill a Mockingbird*, or *The Odyssey*? Would you part with your memory of any of these books?
Why not?

Key Points Summary

- Basal texts should be replaced with authentic literature that is diverse, advanced, and subject to open-ended exploration.
- The classics are classic for a reason. They endure because of a complex of qualities, such as their language, their artistic merit, their humanity, their intellectual substance, and their originality, and these qualities appeal to and inspire verbally talented learners
- The classics are inherently self-differentiating. The very depth and com-plexity of the classics allow them to be read at different levels by differ-ent students. Outstanding teachers can take advantage of this depth by individualizing and creatively teaching so that each student is able to read and learn in a manner that is most appropriate.

- Classics are an unsurpassed repository of advanced words used in creative, exciting, and talented ways. Even so-called children's classics such as *Wind in the Willows* and *Peter Pan* contain vocabulary that the typical high school student may never encounter in textbooks, let alone master.
- Classics develop the ability to articulate ideas. Each classic is a classic, in part, because it—more than the books that got forgotten—articulates ideas. In the classics, students encounter thousands of examples of things put well.
- Classics develop thinking skills because they give students thoughts to think about; because they contradict each other; because they are ill behaved, tumultuous, and rowdy. The classics are a kind of international published argument over what life means.
- Classics develop human values. If anything really explains why books become classics, it is simply because they are books that matter. There is always something in the story, some loyalty or bravery or curiosity, that matters. The humanity of the classics, including the inherent global perspective of world literature, is a beautiful and critically necessary counterpoint to the culture of violence and brutality that plagues our streets and our entertainment media.

References

Clark, B. (1988). *Growing up gifted*. Columbus, OH: Merrill.

Crane, S. (1961). *The red badge of courage* (pp. 143–144). New York: Macmillan.

Fehrenbach, C. R. (1991). Gifted/average readers: Do they use the same reading strategies? *Gifted Child Quarterly, 35*(3), 125–127.

Gallagher, J. (1975). *Teaching the gifted child* (2nd ed.). Boston, MA: Allyn and Bacon.

Ganopole, S. J. (1988). Reading and writing for the gifted: a whole language approach. *Roeper Review, 11*(2), 88–94.

Lee, H. (1960). *To kill a mockingbird*. New York: Warner.

Melville, H. (1982). *Moby Dick*. New York. Modern Library.

Parker, J. (1989). *Instructional strategies for teaching the gifted*. Boston, MA: Allyn and Bacon.

Reis, S., & Renzulli, J. (1989). Providing challenging programs for gifted readers. *Roeper Review, 12*(2), 92–97.

Thompson, M. (1995). *Classics in the classroom*. (2nd ed.). Unionville, NY: Royal Fireworks.

Thoreau, H. D. (1960). *Walden and civil disobedience*. New York: Signet.

Torrance, P., & Myers, R. M. (1970). *Creative teaching and learning*. New York: Harper.

VanTassel-Baska, J., Feldhusen, J., Seeley, K., Wheatley, G., Silverman, L., & Foster, W. (1988). *Comprehensive curriculum for gifted learners*. Boston, MA: Allyn and Bacon.

Wallas, G. (1926). *The art of thought*. New York: Harcourt, Brace.

Whitman, W. (1993). *Leaves of grass*. New York: Modern Library.

5

The Study of Literature
Insights into Human Understanding

BARBARA ALLEN TAYLOR
Northbrook High School, Northbrook, Illinois

We look to literature as a source of collective wisdom, for insights into our muddled human condition, to be reassured by the record of human heroism or restrained by the corrective drama of human folly. We look to literature for experience that enlarges understanding—understanding accessible only through experience. Indeed, understanding is supposed to be the desired end of all teaching, the goal of all learning. In this chapter, I will discuss what constitutes literary understanding, identify the barriers to the understanding we desire to foster, and suggest a strategy for penetrating those barriers.

Education and Understanding

In spite of much earnest rhetoric to the contrary, guiding students to experience genuine understanding is not an educational priority. The vocabulary of education suggests instead a preoccupation with measurement—an urgency to demonstrate mastery of basic skills, performance of outcomes, the achievement of cultural literacy. This preoccupation is apparently undiminished by the well-documented criticism that the commitment to provide measures of learning tends to trivialize learning endeavors. Measuring the

simplistic and trivial is easy; complex, long-term growth is far harder to document.

However, testing, not understanding, appears to be a high priority on
the agenda of education. Gardner (1991) has documented this sorry fact in
some detail in his recent work, *The Unschooled Mind*. His discussion of understanding provides some insight into how the First National Assessment of
History and Literature came to be a test wholly irrelevant to genuine literary
understanding.

Gardner (1991) has stated that education is the process of constructing
mental models that provide us mechanisms for organizing and integrating
our observations and reflections. Glaser (1984), summarizing the work of
other cognitive psychologists, found that prototypical knowledge structures
play a central role in thinking and ultimately understanding. Each thinker
needs more than one or a multileveled system that will allow for the alternative perspectives of various domains of knowledge and experience. However, building vital and dynamic mental models is complicated by "the persistence of the young child's conceptions of the world" (Gardner, 1991, p. 5).

Gardner identified the ground zero of "prototypical knowledge structures" as the "unschooled" mind: "We have failed to appreciate that *in nearly
every student there is a five-year-old 'unschooled' mind struggling to get out and
express itself.* Nor have we realized how challenging it is to convey novel
materials so that their implications will be appreciated by children who have
long conceptualized materials of this sort in a fundamentally different and
deeply entrenched way" (1991, p. 5). And we have distracted ourselves from
the difficult work of challenging these entrenched structures by settling
instead for what Gardner calls "correct-answer compromises."

That literature is not about answers is decidedly inconvenient. Answers
"that have been sanctioned as correct" are irrelevant. The narrator of Kafka's
(1966) "A Country Doctor" introduces himself to us by stating, "I was in great
perplexity" (p. 21), and to the end of his story, the perplexity persists. Claudia,
the narrator of Toni Morrison's *The Bluest Eye* (1970), summarizes the story
that will follow and concludes as she begins, "There is really nothing more to
say—except why. But since why is difficult to handle, one must take refuge in
how" (p. 9). And when the novel ends, we have no answers—merely confir-
mation: "We are wrong, of course, but it doesn't matter. It's too late. At least on
the edge of my town, among the garbage and the sunflowers of my town, it's
much, much, much too late" (p. 160). Students are perplexed by the story of
Job. What can such a story mean? What can I tell them? Of one thing I am certain: If the story, so dominated by questions, has a meaning, that meaning is in
no sense an answer. To ask my students for answers "sanctioned as correct"
about stories that call what we think and understand, what we feel and
depend upon, into question is silly; worse, it is a violation of literature. And in

practical terms, as a measure of student understanding or knowledge or learning, such questions and answers tell us absolutely nothing.

Literature exists, if we may trust the words of one of its creators, to aid "anyone who aspires to the construction of a mental order solid and complex enough to contain the disorder of the world within itself; for anyone aiming to establish a method subtle and flexible enough to be the same thing as an absence of any method whatever" (Calvino, 1986, p. 99). It introduces us to our "hidden motives" and demonstrates for us that "what matters is the way in which we accept our motives and live through the ensuing crisis. This is the only chance we have of becoming different from the way we are—that is, the only way of starting to invent a new way of being" (p. 100), or to explore "alternate ways of being human, and hence to [find] our undiscovered selves" (Arrowsmith, 1971, p. 7).

Literary Understanding

An understanding of a work of literature requires participation in the world that work creates. Literature renders experience (remembered or imagined), and in an artificial act, holds the flux of experience in place for a moment of illumination. Magically, this moment, frozen but nonetheless vital, may be endlessly relived. So Keats can speak to a "Fair youth, beneath the trees," a living youth, not subject to decay, and comment on the sleight by which time has been eluded: "Bold Lover, never, never canst thou kiss,/Though winning near the goal—yet, do not grieve;/She cannot fade, though thou hast not thy bliss,/Forever wilt thou love, and she be fair!" (Keats, 1974, p. 663).

The dialogue Keats conjures is a highly complex language process. In a powerfully condensed definition, Italo Calvino highlights this complex language process, both invoked by and embodied in literature: "A work of literature might be defined as an operation carried out in the written language and involving several levels of reality at the same time" (Calvino, 1986, p. 101). This operation is urgent and arduous because written language is both miraculous and frustrating.

The opening of *Adam Bede* aptly illustrates the power potential of written language: "With a single drop of ink for a mirror, the Egyptian sorcerer undertook to reveal to any chance comer far-reaching visions of the past. This is what I undertake to do for you, reader. With this drop of ink at the end of my pen, I will show you the roomy workshop of Jonathan Burge" (Eliot, 1987, p. 49).

Commenting on this passage, novelist and critic Lodge (1990) pointed to the miraculous promise offered by "the figure of the drop of ink." Information becomes drama and the reader is invited out of her world into another, a promised escape which Lodge identified as "the fundamental appeal of all narrative" (p. 98).

In a passage with strikingly similar concerns, 15-year-old Genevieve, struggling to write her *Hamlet* essay, describes the other side of the language coin:

> *I have been staring at this screen for hours on end. This is the fourth time that I have clacked away at these keys, created dark squiggles across the screen, then erased, erased, erased, til nothing remained....I have something to say—but how? ...I am limited by the boundaries of my self, and by these two dimensional words, really only squiggles on white paper, not nearly strong enough to carry the souls and lives and realities that they are forced to support.*

She has found her difficulties mirrored in the play she is attempting to discuss:

> *It is ironic that this play, an example of the English language at its finest and most expressive, centers on a character who is ultimately betrayed by his words, and his illusions, and his isolation. Trapped within the web he weaves, Hamlet can never communicate with others, can never explain, or be understood by those who listen to his words for hints of madness, and for nothing more.*

Nonetheless, this student is unable to avoid the critical role of language in her own experience, that in spite of the inadequacy of words, she is compelled to "create with them and explain with them and live and breathe and think in them." She is tormented by language limits and agitated by the desire to narrate her essence: "I know that—for all my words—I can never make you be me. I know this moment, once over, will be gone forever. I know that I shall die one day, and all these words will be only empty husks for others' imaginations."

Genevieve's dismayed outpouring is consistent with the language theories of Mikhail Bakhtin, as summarized by Lodge (1990):

> *Language, according to Bakhtin, is essentially dialogic. Everything we say or write is connected both with things which have been said or written in the past, and with things which may be said or written in response to it in the future. The words we use come to us already imprinted with the meanings, intentions, and accents of others, our speech is a tissue of citations and echoes and allusions; and every utterance we make is directed towards some real or hypothetical other who will receive it. (p. 110)*

Nadine Gordimer's novel *Burger's Daughter* (1970) perfectly illustrates this point. The novel opens with four distinct narrative voices describing and reacting to the same event: the arrest and imprisonment of Rosa Burger's mother. Lionel Burger and his wife are anti-apartheid political activists. We know what they do and have done. The novel's subject, however, is not their actions, but Rosa's character—her identity. The final opening voice is her own, asking a single question: "When they saw me outside the prison, what did they see?" (p. 13).

Rosa then begins to narrate her story. Although Rosa is not the novel's single narrator, what *is* critical to the novel's development is the identity of Rosa's chosen audience, the individual with whom she initiates a self-defining dialogue. She comments on the four opening voices: "My version and theirs." Like Genevieve, Rosa is frustrated with the inadequacy and the vulnerability to misinterpretation of the written word: "And if this were being written down, both would seem equally concocted when read over" (p. 16). Rosa describes instead a "dialogic" process: "talking to you in my mind the way I find I do" (p. 16). The dialogic process is automatic: "One is never talking to oneself, always one is addressed to someone. Suddenly, without knowing the reason, at different stages in one's life, one is addressing this person or that all the time, even dreams are performed before an audience. I see that" (p. 16). To address "this person or that," however, is unsatisfying. Rosa has begun her story by speaking her meaning to "someone who had no importance in their life, someone who stood quite outside it, peripheral, one of the hangers-on drawn by curiosity who had once or twice looked in on it," (p. 17) an unworthy confidant. The novel moves away from this distraction and toward the conversations essential to her being, her confrontation with grief, betrayal, and loss; late in the novel, she addresses her dead father: "I'm told even people who have no religious beliefs sometimes have the experience of being strongly aware of the dead person. An absence fills again—that sums up how they describe it. It has never happened to me with you" (p. 328). But the critical dialogue of Rosa's life has begun, a life in her native country, where, strangely, "there are still heroes," where Rosa will do what she can and learn with the patients she treats to "put one foot before the other" (p. 332).

The critical operation of written language is what Emerson (1957a) named "expression." Our existence is only half of our being, "the other half is...expression." The artist or the poet then creates the medium through which we complete our experience:

> *Every man should be so much an artist that he could report in conversation what had befallen him. Yet, in our experience, the rays or appulses have sufficient force to arrive at the senses, but not enough to reach the quick and*

compel the reproduction of themselves in speech. The poet is the person in whom these powers are in balance, the man without impediment, who sees and handles that which others dream of, traverses the whole scale of experience, and is representative of man, in virtue of being the largest power to receive and to impart. (pp. 223–224)

Wordsworth (1974) made a similar claim. The poet differs from the rest of us in the ability to see deeply what we view only superficially. The poet will consider "man and the objects that surround him as acting and re-acting upon each other, so as to produce an infinite complexity of pain and pleasure" (p. 135); the poet will articulate "the general passions and thoughts and feelings of men" (p. 137).

Literature tells us nothing new; it merely repeats, preparing a familiar situation within a novel script—a script the reader enters to rehearse the dialogue that allows us to define what is of human significance. Flannery O'Connor (1957) has confirmed that "there may never be anything new to say" (p. 76); James Baldwin's story "Sonny's Blues" (1978) also concurs: "For, while the tale of how we suffer, and how we are delighted, and how we may triumph is never new, it always must be heard. There isn't any other tale to tell, it's the only light we've got in all this darkness" (p. 41).

The repetition avoids what Wordsworth described as "savage torpor" (p. 130), the deadening that sets in when we stop looking because we think we have seen it all, or when we thoughtlessly narrate our stories to an unworthy audience. Our poets tell us again and again that appearances are incomplete, that we do not know what we think we know, that a different kind of vision is required, what Flannery O'Connor (1957) described as "anagogical vision... the kind of vision that is able to see different levels of reality in one image or one situation" (p. 72). She explained that she has drawn this term from biblical exegesis, but that the method of which it is a part also expresses "an attitude toward all of creation, and a way of reading nature which included most possibilities" (pp. 72–73). She cited Conrad as an artist whose work embodies this kind of vision, explaining that "he was interested in rendering justice to the visible universe because it suggested an invisible one." (p. 80). Conrad understood with Emerson that "the highest minds of the world have never ceased to explore the double meaning, or shall I say the quadruple or the centuple or much more manifold meaning, of every sensuous fact" (p. 223).

Literature models for us and invites us into the dialogic process—the process that allows us to narrate meaning and the life made coherent by story. In a dialogue, voices speak. Literature's act of giving voice is critical because this operation allows for the possibility of a constant creative imagining of a world beyond the limits we currently accept.

In an essay entitled "Right and Wrong Political Uses of Literature," Calvino (1986) described the vision and voice literature expresses, and he explained the ways in which these qualities are essential to politics:

> *Literature is necessary to politics above all when it gives a voice to whatever is without a voice, when it gives a name to what as yet has no name, especially to what the language of politics excludes or attempts to exclude. I mean aspects, situations, and languages both of the outer and inner world, the tendencies repressed both in individuals and in society. Literature is like an ear that can hear things beyond the understanding of the language of politics; it is like an eye that can see beyond the color spectrum perceived by politics. (p. 98)*

Literature imagines and articulates new possibilities. Newly imagined questions challenge established orders. Old questions return; voices speak across time. The dialogue comforts and challenges us, but only if we actively participate in the conversation. Keats (1974) demonstrated: His narrator addresses the urn; the urn answers and will continue the dialogue eternally, even "when old age shall this generation waste" (p. 664) speaking to the narrator well beyond the wasted generations of its own anciently imagined origins.

Literature dramatizes active dialogue, and our instruction must invite students to participate in that dialogue. Stories and poems ask their readers to indulge in what Coleridge (1971) called "that willing suspension of disbelief" (p. 269) to enter the limited dramatic world the work enacts, to be a part of that experience. Teachers must not interrupt this invitation; we must instead aid the student in entering the awaiting process. Readers learn by experiencing, encountering the text. I learn with Rosa Burger that, like her, I must address the ghosts that haunt my life; avoiding my grief will be disastrous, a spiritually self-destructive act. No one can tell me; to be told about this experience is no substitute for the experience itself. Literature allows me imaginatively to make my own discoveries. Our teaching of literature must nurture this interactive, participatory process, and avoid engendering "savage torpor," the numbed and empty response resulting when we ask for superficial and literal answers—answers that evidence only "familiarity" devoid of understanding.

Barriers to Understanding

To involve students in an authentic experience of literature is a noble aim. But such an ascent must begin in a realistic appraisal of the ragged, scrubby foothills. Any teacher who has introduced students to Shakespeare knows that the initial reality of this endeavor is frustration. The inexperienced reader faces, for the first time, a perplexing and alien text. Literal comprehension requires a narrow and tedious attention to unfamiliar syntax, punctuation, and vocabulary. The reader must divert attention from the text itself to footnotes that explain topical references woven into the play's thematic and figurative patterns. The wailing and gnashing of teeth tends to drown out the music of Shakespeare's language. How little comfort impatient youngsters feel when we explain that this first reading is merely preliminary.

In addition, our guidance and instruction often directly conflict with "the prototypical knowledge structures" of students, those deeply entrenched scripts, stereotypes, and misconceptualizations that characterize the unschooled mind that Gardner (1991) described. Students are sometimes unable to connect a text to their own experience. However, at other times, they cannot separate their understanding of it from their own ideas about human nature and the world around them.

For example, once the literal level of the text is decoded, we confront students with the ambiguity of the text, with the possibility of multiple interpretations, frustrating their belief in straightforward answers and predictable consequences. Thus, we undermine the role of authority, running directly counter to the socialization that has shaped our students to respect and trust authority. In teaching literature, we consistently work against the common sense, the habitual responses, and the long-term socialization of our students.

I was recently reminded of just how formidable their habitual responses are when I observed a group of high school juniors during a final discussion of Kate Chopin's *The Awakening*. They had been working with this text for two weeks, and the discussion I observed was meant to be the conclusion of their study. Prior to this final discussion, students had been engaged in small group projects, each small group responsible for presenting some aspect of this short novel to the whole class. The text itself, though somewhat remote (late nineteenth century), is not taxing in the way of Shakespeare or even Dickens. Nonetheless, students were unable to enter the world Chopin had constructed. The novel's central character, Edna, like Ibsen's Nora, is unwittingly trapped within her role as wife and mother. The social structures that imprison her have choked and thwarted her nature, and she belatedly awakens to a realization of sensuality and individualism—a realization she cannot fulfill. At the end of the novel, Edna, embracing annihilation, walks into the sea.

The students I observed were angry with Edna; the underlying question that controlled their response to the story was, "How could she do this to her husband and children?" Locked in that question, they were unable to ask about the meaning of her action, about the nature of her awakening, about the power of sensuality. Mothers are supposed to love their children, to sustain and protect their children. Family takes precedence over a mother's need for individual fulfillment. This conventional script dominated and blurred the script Chopin had created.

At one point, a young woman offered an insight: "I was just thinking," she said. "You know we really aren't supposed to take characters in stories as positive role models." She paused. "Really, they're negative role models." Such deeply entrenched, unschooled notions play havoc with instruction: Real artists must draw like Norman Rockwell. Poetry must rhyme and be uplifting. Stories teach morals and their characters are role models. And the reality represented in art and literature supports received wisdom, cultural conventions, accepted codes, and social organizations.

Calvino (1986) described another condition that complicates our efforts to elicit understanding: We find ourselves in the middle of a not yet completed intellectual revolution. The condition Calvino described did not come up suddenly; it still has not been resolved today. But as Calvino noted, the muddle reached a noteworthy intensity in the 1960s, when, he said, we faced the fact of "a revolution of the mind, an intellectual turning point" (p. 90).

Our capacity for objectivity is no longer assumed. Evelyn Fox Keller introduced her study, *Reflections on Gender and Science* (1985), with a quotation from Simone de Beauvoir: "Representation of the world, like the world itself, is the work of men; they describe it from their own point of view, which they confuse with the absolute truth" (p. 3). Recognizing this confusion of "point of view" and "absolute truth" is at the heart of the revolution Calvino described. What we have been taught to view as "absolute truth" is instead merely one "point of view." To call one's point of view absolute truth is remarkably self-serving, providing the privilege and power necessary to articulate the "parameters, categories, and antitheses...used to define, plan, and classify the world" (Calvino, 1986, p. 91) and, in so doing, to exclude others from the same privilege and power.

However, the confusion has been duly noted. In a 1977 address to the young women of Douglass College, Adrienne Rich (1979) exposed the fraud:

> *What you can learn here...is how men have perceived and organized their experience, their history, their ideas of social relationships, good and evil, sickness and health, etc. When you read or hear about "great issues," "major texts," "the mainstream of Western thought," you are hearing about what men, above all, white men, in their male subjectivity, have decided is important.*
>
> *Black and other minority peoples have for some time recognized that their racial and ethnic experience was not accounted for in the studies broadly labeled human; and that even the sciences can be racist. For many reasons, it has been more difficult for women to comprehend our exclusion, and to realize that even the sciences can be sexist. (p. 232)*

This final assertion is confirmed by Keller; in the introduction to her feminist critique of science, she argued that both gender and science are socially constructed categories. Our sexual identity and the identity of our natural world are both socially articulated. The purity of our understanding is illusory; what we know is inevitably tainted by our culture, history, and individual psychology.

Nonetheless, objectivist structures of education persist, as do objectivist contentions concerning perception, knowledge, and natural order. Popular culture continues to idealize the authority of science, and educational institutions continue to establish teachers as authorities in an objectivist mode. The student's need to grow into self-understanding and the understanding that the self has both the power and right to construct knowledge is systematically eliminated. The underlying epistemology establishes the primacy of objective and valid knowledge outside the student. Without this knowledge, the student is incomplete, inadequate. And any evidence of inability to take in the knowledge is interpreted as intellectual inadequacy or behavioral perversity.

In discussing the limits of a "strict regime" of basic skills, Gardner (1991) made a crucial point: "What is missing...are contexts in which the deployment of these skills makes sense" (p. 187). Students do not fail to read primarily because they lack decoding skills; rather, they lack "the capacity to read for understanding and the desire to read at all" (p. 186). The critical factor is not absence of skills but "rather the knowledge about when to invoke these skills and the inclination to do so productively in one's own daily life" (p. 187). Such knowledge is self-knowledge and both popular culture and educational institutions automatically dismiss the self as an unworthy focus of educational attention.

For genuine understanding to grow, our students must possess the combination of "knowledge" and "inclination" Gardner described. The inclination arises from the individual's sense that what she is about to do has significance. Genuine inclination cannot be required; it must arise naturally. And when we observe this self-motivated inclination, we have evidence of personal engagement, a willing choice, an autonomous decision.

The authors of *Women's Ways of Knowing* (Belenky, Clinchy, Goldberger, & Tarule, 1986) have described women who grow to this condition, a condition in which they demonstrate an integration of knowledge and inclination. Essential to this stage of development is the capacity for "voice." As Emerson has noted, experience is only half of existence; the other half is expression. In *Women's Ways of Knowing*, the struggle for expression is documented. A way of thinking and knowing comes out of the attainment of "voice": "It is in the process of sorting out the pieces of the self and of searching for a unique and authentic voice that women come to the basic insights of constructivist thought: *All knowledge is constructed, and the knower is an intimate part of the known"* (p. 137).

However, formal education has not capitalized on the connection of self-understanding and intellectual understanding. Belenky and her colleagues explained that women shifting into the position of constructed knowledge have an emergent inner-voice and self, but these emergent capacities have received little encouragement or nurturing, "particularly if the women have learned the lesson of 'weeding out the self,' which our academic institutions so often teach" (p. 136).

When we objectify knowledge by the "weeding out of the self," we invite students to treat learning as meaningless performance. We invite them to discover what we want, rather than to use their own minds to arrive at their own conclusions.

At the end of the academic year, I asked students enrolled in my junior English classes to write an essay in which they described a path of understanding that had opened for them over the course of the year. The course was entitled Habits of Mind. Students had read standard literary works, but had, at the same time, examined epistemology. In reading any given work, we discussed how the individual work itself represented understanding, how language shaped understanding, how particular characters in particular works came to their understandings or failed to do so, how the work dramatized the concerns of a given age, how the work shaped our own minds as we experienced it, and how we inevitably shaped the work to our own ends. I suggested that students could focus on a selection of works read during the year, or they could document the growth of a particular insight, or they could do something as simple as explain the value of a particular assignment. I also left them the option of explaining why they had been unable to learn anything at all in this course and to provide me with guidance for avoiding such a future occurrence.

One student's paper was a particularly telling example of the critical role of self or voice in a student's ability to replace mechanical performance with authentic understanding. Ed began his paper with a paragraph definition of what a real education involves. He explained that individuals must engage themselves "with the uncertain." They must use reason to attempt to answer the "questions of life." And in seeking those answers, the meaning they discover "must be personal." Ed's phrasing was halting, not entirely eloquent; nonetheless, he identified a critical distinction. He realized that what he learned could not remain separate from and unconnected to who he was, and that this was true for all of us. And he credited this insight to his efforts in writing an essay on Hamlet.

Having announced his main conclusion, Ed began to map his progress to insight:

For the majority of my life, and most certainly this year, I regarded educa-
tion as a duty that one must spend time on from kindergarten to college. I
treated the search for learning rather impersonally and I naturally suffered
the consequences. Bad grades, upset and disappointed parents, and low self
esteem to mention a few. When I was faced with the task of reading and
writing essays, I treated this period of time spent on my work just as a slave
fulfilling his duties. I did this almost mechanically, without any thought or
care whatsoever. After fulfilling my obligation, I would go on with my daily
duties with enjoyment. I was so relieved that my work/duty was finished. I
viewed learning as such a hindrance. I would write essays just to get them
finished.

Ed went on to explain that these essays were without any personal signature. His only concern was that they would contain no "wrong ideas." He
specifically described an essay assignment completed early in the year. "The
other day I read my Bede paper and nearly threw up. The paper disgusted
me. My ideas were vague and my assertions were not defended. My paper
was filled with so much ambiguity that paragraphs didn't make any sense."
This paper shamed Ed. He had written the paper early in the year, and in
responding to his paper, I was gentle, but I had communicated that it made
little sense and did not say very much. I had reassured him that as it was
early in the year, he had time and many remaining opportunities to write
something that did make sense. The revulsion he records occurs at the end of
the year, months after having written the paper and as he compares that initial essay to his essay on *Hamlet.*

Ed described his work in reading Shakespeare and writing this later
essay in very different terms:

I promised myself that I would spend the time and dedicate myself to com-
prehend the play completely. As I set forth in this process, something sur-
prising occurred to me. The notion that reading was a duty no longer influ-
enced me. I wanted to read for the sake of my own learning! I spent my free
time actually thinking about the play for myself. The characters became a
part of my life. When I was depressed and suffering, my thoughts went to
Hamlet's suffering.

The student compared the circumstances of his suffering to the specifics
of Hamlet's situation, and concluded in amazement: "See! The characters
would pop into my thoughts in very normal, everyday matters." Ed
explained that because he did understand the play for himself, he did not
dread writing an essay about the play. He did not worry about being wrong,
but felt confident that he could interpret the play. And indeed, his *Hamlet*
essay was a credible piece of work.

His understanding of *Hamlet* and his ability to complete an academic task—that is, to write a coherent essay about the play—are inextricably linked to self-understanding and to "voice." These tasks are critical to finding a place in the world—a place we make with ideas. Ed attends, as do all the students whose work I have cited here, a state-supported boarding school for students who have been identified as gifted and talented, yet the alienation from the world of ideas he described as his initial state sounds very similar to the mindsets of many of the underprivileged women whose experiences are documented in *Women's Ways of Knowing*. To be in this school means that Ed is able to score well on standardized tests, has generally made high marks, has been well behaved, and has provided the requisite "correct-answer compromises." But all along, he has felt the inadequacy of these responses. What had not happened for him was the experience of "expression" that Emerson defines; he had not found himself connected to the ideas and processes his teachers were asking him to master.

Pathways to Understanding

By what means do we avoid "correct-answer compromises" and release our students into language? Delay and repetition do not sound like exciting pedagogical breakthroughs. Yet these are what I recommend: delay and repetition, for these strategies release us into language, into participation and expression.

O'Connor (1957) identified a concern shared by teachers and writers: "a love of the language and what can be done with it in the interests of dramatic truth." She explained that teachers could not serve students nor could writers serve readers "unless our aim is first to be true to the subject and its necessities" (p. 124). For her, this meant teaching literature by thinking about it as writers think about it: "In the act of writing, one sees that the way a thing is made controls and is inseparable from the whole meaning of it. The form of a story gives it meaning which any other form would change" (p. 129). To see the way a thing is made requires of both reader and writer the same methods:

> There's a certain grain of stupidity that the writer of fiction can hardly do without, and this is the quality of having to stare, of not getting the point at once. The longer you look at one object, the more of the world you see in it; and it's well to remember that the serious fiction writer always writes about the whole world, no matter how limited his particular scene. For him the bomb that was dropped on Hiroshima affects life on the Oconee River, and there's not anything he can do about it. (p. 77)

The critical point here is that both writers and readers *must stare;* they *must not get the point at once:* repetition and delay.

Coles (1989) introduced the same theme in *The Call of Stories: Teaching and the Moral Imagination.* He explained that the title of his book is autobiographical: "one keeps learning by teaching fiction or poetry because every reader's response to a writer's call can have its own startling suggestive power" (p. xix)—a fact his parents had conveyed in their habit of reading aloud to him and to one another from works they treasured.

In this book, Coles memorialized his fortunate relationship with William Carlos Williams, poet and medical doctor. Coles spent time with Williams, read his stories and poetry, discussed with him patients and their difficulties, and, in the process, had made clear to him the significance of "expression." Williams told his protege of the importance of "doctor stories"—that is, "short fiction meant to evoke the various events, moods, impasses a doctor experiences" (p. 29). The young Coles at first saw these as not professional: "As a house officer I had to report in detail a given medical or psychiatric reality, and do so in a manner my colleagues could accept and comprehend" (p. 29). He viewed the theoretical language of his medical specialty as "a means of getting to the core of things, focusing precisely on what connects this patient, right here, sitting before me, with others all over the world who belong to a category" (p. 29). But Williams would not allow Coles to be satisfied with this inadequate and truncated "expression." He kept pointing him to the fuller "expression" embodied in story. Willams advised Coles:

> *We have to pay the closest attention to what we say. What patients say tells us what to think about what hurts them; and what we say tells us what is happening to us—what we are thinking, and what may be wrong with us. ... Their story, yours, mine—it's what we all carry with us on this trip we take, and we owe it to each other to respect our stories and learn from them. (p. 30)*

Coles pondered what he had heard and incorporated this insight into his work as a psychiatrist. He also had the opportunity to observe the work of his wife, a secondary English teacher. "Expression" and its "dialogic" process are the central work for teachers of literature and language. Her initial task, indeed the initial task of all of us who teach literature to young people, was to engage a student's growing intelligence and emotions with the line of a story so that the student becomes absorbed with it. This real-world application also points to delay, repetition, and participation.

In another of the end-of-year essays for Habits of Mind, one student described the effects of delay, repetition, and participation. Her essay was written in the form of a letter. Tia opened her remarks by recounting her guarded entry into the class. We had begun the year by reading the episode from Bede's (1968) *The Ecclesiastical History of the English People,* which describes the conversion of King Edwin. In the story, human life is represented in a metaphor of a bird flying from the darkness into the warmth and light of the mead hall and then back out again into the darkness. This metaphor is alluded to in several later poems. We had read two, "Persuasion by Wordsworth" (1976) and "Dark Age Glasses on the Venerable Bede" by Mac-Neice (1976). These two poems deal with the nature of the soul, faith, and religious doubt.

Tia expected merely to read the books, remain silent during discussions, and write an essay, even though she didn't understand the book. However, she surprised herself with her desire to add to the discussion. She described how her participation in class discussion helped her to discipline her critical thinking abilities, to support opinions with assertions, or when evidence was lacking, to discard the assertion. Tia's experience exemplifies the necessity of voice in the growth of intellectual powers. And this strategy enlarged her perspective. As she became more confident, she began to listen to other members of the class and found their comments insightful and eloquent.

Although she had learned to work with her peers, to participate in a community of interpretation, every work was not immediately accessible to her. When it came time to write her essay on *Hamlet,* Tia did not know where to begin. She did not know the characters and found them flat. Her first paper needed to be rewritten.

Repetition seemed in order. Tia needed to revisit this work. She was an intelligent and sensitive reader and a strong writer, but her essay was empty and mechanical. Had she been a student who was still struggling with comprehending the language, I might have made a different decision. But I have challenged enough students over the years to know that if I have made my decision carefully, the repeat performance will pay off.

Tia's academic load was demanding; she reacted with despair at the idea of repeating a task she had checked off her list of things to do. I had not marked the original essay. I simply wrote a note, saying that I knew she could produce a more meaningful essay and that she could talk to me about a new deadline. I handed her the paper; she read the note and burst into tears. I reassured her that I would be flexible, that if other responsibilities were overwhelming, I could accommodate, and that I would adjust her current workload in my class. She dried her tears. Two weeks later, she handed in an excellent essay, and in her year-end essay, she described the process of rereading the entire work, reviewing her notes, and looking deeper into the play. By the time Tia finished the revision of the paper, she not only had a better overall comprehension of the play but she grew to like it. This experience coalesced her understanding of how literature works, of what it asks of a reader, as well as what it can give back to a reader.

In her year-end essay, Tia wrote about her growth as a thinker. She told how she learned to overcome impulsiveness in favor of reflection and how comprehension of any literary work is effected only through close examination of the text, thinking, and questioning. She experienced the results of successful delay, repetition, and participation.

Siebers (1992) argued that ethics is based in experience first and language second. Literature also is more than merely linguistic. Siebers has contended that the grammar of literature does not exist in a hermetically sealed dimension but is itself permeated by the experience which surrounds it. Thus, when we read, we do not rely solely on the grammar of the text to ascertain its meaning.

Readers bring mental structures to the task of deriving meaning from a text: scripts, plans, goals, and life themes. These interpretive devices lie outside the linguistic level of a text and ensure the recognizability of narrative. They are aspects of the prototypical knowledge structures that Glaser and Gardner discuss, and as such, they can also impede understanding of texts, particularly when the text in question challenges the conventions of the context out of which the prototypes have arisen.

In instruction, then, we both depend on and must argue with these structures. Literary interpretation must include more than linguistic analysis; it must recognize "that place where language is used." In our literature classrooms, we must be concerned with the practical domain of literature, and not simply a theory of literature.

Repetition, delay, and participation are the methods we use to immerse our students in the works of literature we wish them to experience. Like life, this experience has the potential to expand and reorient the scripts and preconceptions that both limit and sustain our students' abilities to imagine.

A Strategy for Literary Understanding

I began this chapter by asserting that to evoke literary understanding would require that we make both the mechanisms of literature and the mechanisms of the mind our explicit subjects. I have already noted the affective dimension of intellectual effort. If the self is not engaged in thought, mechanical performance is the best that can be elicited. A thinker's personal alienation from the topic of inquiry precludes the possibility of intellectual integration. Another mental dimension is equally relevant. Literature is written language, and our cognitive response to the written word is directly relevant to literary effect.

Collins (1991) pointed out that we must directly examine reading as a cognitive process in order to further successful poetic interpretation. Students often react to literary texts with the defensiveness of the threatened alien. The text strikes them as incomprehensible. I have too often been guilty of immediately undercutting the reality of that reaction, choosing instead to ignore the uninitiated reader's response, dismissing (rather than exploring) her unsatisfying encounter as the result of inexperience. Collins, instead, credits this experience, identifying this alienation as central to the poetic process.

The experience of mystery begins in the acknowledgment of confusion but is completed in poetic interpretation. The reader's initial alienation partly results from inexperience but, more profoundly, the dissonance is elicited by the text. And to experience the mystery embodied in the text requires access to the reading process: "Reading is rule-governed behavior. It draws upon a culturally determined repertoire of readerly responses, but it also obeys procedural constraints that we might well regard as hard-wired and common to social discourse of all natural languages" (Collins, 1991, p. 151).

The "hard-wired" procedures of reading make possible poetic interpretation. The rule-governed behavior of reading allows us to posit a poetics that can accept the individual reader but also generalize based on our recognition of "hard-wiring." Collins described this poetics:

A poetics must be willing to hypothesize that human subjectivity is not wholly anarchic and, moreover, that a reader engaged in construing a text—in poetic interpretation—is constrained to an appreciable degree by internal, cognitive mechanisms that are in turn prompted by cues established by the text. In short, it must assume in the reader a complex dynamis that is reciprocally activated by his or her engagement with the text. (p. xxii)

The *dynamis* with which Collins is concerned is "the dynamis of texts, a potency that only readers have the causative power to convert into *energia*, or act" (p. xxi). This description of poetics is a powerful example of the release into language cited by Rich (1979). He further described poetic interpretation as "the direct receptive synthesis and interior performance of the text...interpretation in the same sense we speak of a pianist's interpretation of a Mozart concerto or an actor's interpretation of Lear—a performed realization, not a translation" (p. xii).

The operation of written language that is literature, so succinctly defined by Calvino, is elaborated in detail by Collins. Collins defined the literary text as a "stored cultural artifact" that "exists to be reused" (1991, p. xii). That these texts are intended to be reread determines how we proceed and results in the mysterious qualities of cyclic reading. Each reading of a work represents a performance loop. This cycle of rereadings adds depth to the individual loops. Each reading has its own "space," its own "character," but precisely because each reading of a familiar work is variant, we are struck with the dialogic reality of literature in which even very familiar works may take on a feeling of strangeness.

Rereading a text involves us simultaneously with the unfolding "linear artifact" and "information unconstrained by the ordinary rules of linear time" (Collins, 1991, p. xiv). The work has a carefully constructed beginning, middle, and end, but as a rereader, I read the beginning already aware of, not constrained to wait for, the end.

Repetition, delay, and participation are critical elements of ritual. We complete the ritual again and again. We move deliberately through its steps, without haste, pausing at critical moments to heighten our awareness of what is occurring. We participate; we perform. The performance is of the moment and holy in its own right; it is also a reenactment in which participants bring into dramatic reality past events, completing, as in the original moment, actions of the same significance. Ritual has ongoing life; the repeated dramatic moment is both new and ancient, the past carried into and thus informing the present. The ritual participant and poetic interpreter both experience anew and meditate on the already experienced—a meditation that in fact alters the shape of the immediately experienced moment—as though present is not separate from past.

Language has this kind of power—a power students must be released into. They are most effectively released into it when allowed to think about and work with language itself, when, like writers, they work through language to understanding. Challenging students to find their own voice and to render their own visions in language that can cue the "mind's eye" of a reader is a means of releasing students into language.

Conclusion

The understanding that literature has to offer is that born of expression or release into language. We make it accessible to our students by showing them the processes of language, by allowing them to use those processes in the struggle for voice and expression. Instead of requiring them to be familiar with many books, we must delay their encounter with one book until the encounter results in genuine understanding, we must make rereading our real business, and we must make certain that interpretation is the result of "interior performance." By these means, we allow the experience of literature to form and inform their structures of mind. Indeed, we embrace instead the subtlety and complexity of human growth, facing that mystery with the awe it deserves.

Key Points Summary

- Literary understanding is frequently treated as less important than low-level testing on literary conventions.
- Literature invites us to make meaning of the world and of ourselves.
- Literary understanding promotes a deeper appreciation of the complexities of the world.
- Barriers to literary understanding include naive readers inexperienced with complex texts, a desire to simplify life and see it in positive terms, the hero as a role model, and problems with objectification or removal of the self from the enterprise of understanding.
- All students, including the most talented, struggle to find voice in their written work on literary texts.
- Struggling with the meaning of literature in written and oral forms enhances considerably the ability to think critically and well.
- Literary understanding can be enhanced by treating texts from the perspective of the authors who wrote them.
- Texts must be read and reread, discussed, and then rethought in order to be understood. Repetition, delay, and participation are crucial elements in experiencing literature.
- Releasing students into language should be the goal of literature-based experiences.

References

Arrowsmith, W. (1971). Teaching and the liberal arts: Notes toward an old frontier. In D. N. Bigelow (Ed.), *Liberal arts and teacher education*. Lincoln: University of Nebraska Press.

Baldwin, J. (1978). Sonny's blues. *The Norton anthology of short fiction* (3rd ed., pp. 16–42). New York: W. W. Norton.

Bede, the Venerable. (1968). *The ecclesiastical history of the English people, and other selections from the writings of the Venerable Bede*. New York: Washington Square Press.

Belenky, M. F., Clinchy, B. M., Goldberger, N. R., & Tarule, J. M. (1986). *Women's ways of knowing*. New York: Basic Books.

Calvino, I. (1986). *The uses of literature*. San Diego, CA: Harcourt.

Chopin, K. (1964). *The awakening*. New York: Capricorn Books.

Coleridge, S. T. (1971). Biographia literaria. In E. Schneider (Ed.), *Samuel Taylor Coleridge poetry and prose* (pp. 190–400). San Francisco, CA: Rinehart & Company.

Coles, R. (1989). *The call of stories: Teaching and the moral imagination*. Boston: Houghton Mifflin.

Collins, C. (1991). *The Poetics of the mind's eye: Literature and the psychology of imagination*. Philadelphia: University of Pennsylvania.

Eliot, G. (1987). *Adam Bede*. England: Penguin Books, Ltd.

Emerson, R. W. (1957a). The poet. In S. E. Whicher (Ed.), *Selections from Ralph Waldo Emerson* (pp. 222–241). Boston: Houghton Mifflin.

Emerson, R. W. (1957b). Self reliance. In S. E. Whicher (Ed.), *Selections from Ralph Waldo Emerson* (pp. 147–168). Boston: Houghton Mifflin.

Gardner, H. (1991). *The unschooled mind: How children think and how schools should teach*. New York: Basic Books.

Glaser, R. (1984). Education and thinking: The role of knowledge. *American Psychologist, 39*(2), 93–104.

Gordimer, N. (1970). *Burger's daughter*. London: Penguin Books.

Kafka, F. (1966). A country doctor. In W. V. Sparos (Ed.), *A casebook on existentialism* (pp. 21–26*)*. New York: Thomas Y. Crowell.

Keats, J. (1974). Ode on a Grecian urn. In M. H. Abrams (Ed.), *The Norton anthology of English literature* (3rd ed., pp. 662–664). New York: W. W. Norton.

Keller, E. F. (1985). *Reflections on gender and science*. New Haven, CT: Yale University Press.

Lodge, D. (1990). The novel as communication. In D. H. Mellor (Ed.), *Ways of communicating* (pp. 96–112). The Darwin College Lectures. Cambridge: Cambridge University Press.

MacNeice, L. (1976). Dark age glasses on the Venerable Bede. In J. E. Miller, Jr., M. J. Jones, & H. McDaniel (Eds.), *England and literature*. Glenview, IL: Scott, Foresman.

Morrison, T. (1970). *The bluest eye*. New York: Simon and Schuster.

O'Connor, F. (1957). *Mystery and manners*. New York: Farrar, Straus & Giroux.

Ravitch, D., & Finn, C. E. Jr. (1987). *What do our 17-Year-olds know?* New York: Harper & Row.

Rich, A. (1979). *On lies, secrets, and silence: Selected prose 1966–1978*. New York: W. W. Norton.

Siebers, T. (1992). *Morals and stories*. New York: Columbia University Press.

Wordsworth, W. (1974). Preface to the lyrical ballads. In M. H. Abrams (Ed.), *The Norton anthology of English Literature* (3rd ed., pp. 125–140). New York: W. W. Norton.

Wordsworth, W. (1976). Persuasion. In J. E. Miller, Jr., M. J. Jones, & H. McDaniel (Eds.), *England and literature*. Glenview, IL: Scott, Foresman.

Part II

Meaning through
Inquiry in
Language Arts

Part II illustrates the various modes by which students may create meaning from their experiences in the language arts. As such, it operationalizes the constructivist orientation shared by Spivey and Taylor Part I. The chapters in this section also provide a perspective on the content aspects of the language arts, examining in turn the major strands of the discipline: early literacy development, writing, oral communication, grammar and linguistic development, and foreign language. In these chapters, the authors explore ways to scaffold the language arts for purposes of teaching and learning.

Chapter 6 tackles key issues in promoting literacy development in young students and uses case examples of talented learners at various stages of development to illustrate the process. Jane M. Bailey explores the overlapping considerations in developing literacy in all learners. The role of oral communication, clarifying the reciprocal relationship between evaluative listening and oral argument, is explored in Chapter 7, written by Ann L. Chaney. A view of teaching students to engage in higher-level thought through exploration with oral language is stressed. In Chapter 8, Colleen Kennedy's ideas are presented for ensuring student engagement in the writing process. Kennedy also provides important insights on the kinds of writing assignments that enhance the potential for such engagement to occur. Chapter 9, on the teaching of grammar, highlights the interplay between the structure of language and its meaning. Citing a myriad of examples from great literature, Michael Clay Thompson weaves a picture of words and syntax carefully planned for impact on the reader's capacity to recognize and search for understanding. In Chapter 10, Michael Clay Thompson and Myriam Borges Thompson present a case for teaching foreign language as a mechanism for enhancing verbal talent in the areas of communication, culture, and linguistic sensitivity.

Thus, various aspects of the language arts are examined in this section in light of their ability to support the development of verbal talent. It is through these various experiences that students gain understanding of the reciprocal relationships in language arts instruction, of reading and writing, of listening and speaking, and of processing language such that they create meaning.

6

Literacy Development in Verbally Talented Children

JANE M. BAILEY
Christopher Newport University

We are fortunate to live during a time of burgeoning information about literacy development in children. Studies about how children learn language and how their language naturally emerges and evolves in complexity give us important insights about how to shape appropriate learning environments to support their emerging literacy. Lacking in the literature is an exploration of how verbal talent—a particular natural ability to manipulate language—comes into play as students engage in literate acts. What is it that makes some students better readers than others or better writers than others? The more carefully we can pinpoint high verbal potential, the better able we will be to nurture it appropriately. A corollary of defining verbal talent is creating a social network (parents, teachers, facilitators, guides) to act as talent developers.

Who are the verbally talented children? How can they be recognized at an early age and most appropriately nurtured? On the surface, these questions seem simple. Of course, verbally talented children are those who demonstrate at an early age complex listening, speaking, reading, and writing behaviors. Using constructivist theory, all language users are seen as constructors of meaning; those with exceptional native talent as language users ought to be exceptional constructors of meaning. The notion of high verbal intelligence implies a large reservoir of knowledge upon which to draw. It is logical to assume that students who are verbally gifted bring a wealth of material to the meaning-construction process. It seems self-evident that given the right environment, the linguistic constructions created by verbally talented students will be elaborate and versatile, enabling dynamic communicative interchange. The trouble with that view of natural ability is that it assumes the stance of inevitability: Children who have verbal talents will *inevitably* flourish and produce literately productive meaning if placed in an appropriate environment.

Social learning theory reminds us that it is *not* inevitable that children— even children with high verbal ability—will become literate. As parents, teachers, and facilitators, we have a critical role to play in modeling and scaffolding literate behavior at a particularly appropriate level. Theorists such as Lev Vygotsky and Jerome Bruner point to the critical importance of the social (vis-á-vis interhuman) context to literacy development. The beauty of the constructivist approach is that it allows for ever-increasing webs of complexity in literary creation and interpretation, but only through the dynamic social interchange of humanity. This implies that ability alone cannot inevitably make meaning happen. The social interchange—even social history interwoven in intertextual spaces—becomes a key factor in the literate acts of reading and writing. It also implies that even high-ability students have the need for a social guide to help them put together the blueprints of text (or composition or conversation). Whether we act as parent, guide, facilitator, teacher, or curriculum writer, there is a need and place for us to help further literacy talent. In order to do that, we need to understand the full nature of literacy development—what it most often looks like in terms of developmental milestones and how those markers can be moved to different points in a child's landscape.

What Is Literacy Development?

Literacy is the integration of all four of the language arts—listening, speaking, reading and writing—within a framework of *meaning*. In other words, the act of *thinking* and being able to express and understand thought through the use of language is the very essence of literacy. Literacy development can be charted through predictable milestones that mark how this integration comes to fruition. There is a comforting, logical sequence of growth. In each of the language arts, the continuum of development is from awareness to intent: passive awareness of language existence (both sound and print) to the active intentionality of creating or interpreting meaning through the use of language. We know the continuums for each of the language arts intersect and overlap, contributing to the fits and spurts of each other's development. But it is oral listening and speaking development that provides the patterning for all other uses of language.

Generally, oral language begins to emerge in infancy when undifferentiated crying patterns give way to cooing and babbling. By age 6 months, these sounds begin to take on meaning (Glazer, 1989), until single words appear between 9 and 12 months of age. Between the ages of 1 and 2 years, children begin to use telegraphic language, combining two words in meaningful ways, such as "me up" expressing a child's desire to be picked up. Between ages 2 and 3, a child's language evolves into more conventional sentence structure and gets more descriptive. The next year is an important one; most children begin to generalize their knowledge about language. This is when they make up their own grammar rules: "I goed to the store." Between 4 and 5 years of age, children use sentences that are more grammatically correct. They also spend much time describing their actions. This general developmental sequence means that most children are pretty adept at using oral language by the time they get to kindergarten.

Although oral language progress is easily charted, the reasons for its development are hotly debated. Human talk emerges without direct instruction in virtually all cultures. Noam Chomsky's seminal work on a language acquisition device (LAD) provided evidence that the human capacity for oral language is somehow directly wired into our brains, coded genetically into our species. Work on artificial intelligence at MIT (Horning, 1991) is putting Chomsky's structural notions of language to the test of coding language structure into the computer. If a cultureless computer can indeed be programmed to manage language, there may be harder questions for the environmental-nurture side of the language debate to address. At this point, the environmentalists are still safe. Even though there has been exciting progress with computers being able to translate the structure of the world's many languages, the ability of the computer to get at the nuances (p. 54) of language meaning is still a mystery. In contrast, there is clear evidence that a child's facility with oral language is directly related to the environment in which he or she is immersed. We do know that verbal, literate environments generally foster verbal, literate people.

No one pretends that sequences or patterns in language development happen in perfect order or on an exact timetable, even in verbal, literate environments. Linearity of milestones has given way to interrelated stepping stones toward the expression and understanding of meaning in the spoken and written word.

What is discomforting in these logical sequences is the variegated pattern of language learning in children. Quantity and quality of language usage, as well as rate of speed in the acquisition of language skills, are dis-

cerning differences in literacy development. Some children have larger stepping stones than others; some children are able to leap into meaning, over-
stepping marker boundaries. How to account for these developmental
differences and how best to deal with them are issues important to both parents and teachers, for it is we, as both parents and teachers, who are responsible for nurturing literacy growth.

The emergence of writing and reading behaviors is much more slippery
to chart than oral language development. Writing development has its roots
in drawing. Toddler scribbling gives way to representational drawings during the preschool ages. But it is the child's realization that pictures and ideas
can be represented by coded, representational symbols ("writing") that leads
to written expression. During the preschool years, children gradually demonstrate an understanding that writing is different from drawing (Temple,
Nathan, & Burris, 1982); they learn the features of our written code. The
scribbling of early toddlers becomes recursive, with the children repeating
particular patterns (Clay, 1975). They learn that there are certain signs we use
for writing that are put across a page in a straight line, and the particular
symbols used for writing are the letters of the alphabet. The big leap into
actual writing occurs between the ages of 5 and 6 when children generally
make the connection that particular written symbols stand for particular concepts. They need to be able to make those symbols and match them to the
concept or idea they are relating. At this kindergarten age, the symbols are
not usually conventional. That is, most children have their own invented
way of expressing a concept in writing that will get coded more and more
conventionally as particular symbols get connected to particular sounds.

Reading grows out of this sound-symbol correspondence and the attach-
ment of meaning to particular orthographic symbols. Chall (1983) presented
reading development in terms of particular stages. She noted that there are
various ways to chart scope and sequence of skills but reminded us that cognitive, emotional, and linguistic development also relate to changes in reading ability. A general scope and sequence moves from prereading skills
(including basic awareness of print) in preschool to a stage of initial reading
or decoding in the earliest grades. This includes basic alphabet knowledge
usually gleaned in kindergarten. By first grade, children gain a basic sight
vocabulary, enabling them to know a basic group of words by their whole
configuration that makes them single symbols. They are also putting
together phonetic rules enabling them to sound out other words for their
reading vocabularies. Children's decoding skills get heavily taxed in second
grade when they face many more words than are in their sight vocabularies.
This becomes what Chall has cited as Stage 2, where children learn to use
their decoding knowledge. It is between third and fourth grade that the transition takes place between learning to read and reading to learn (Stage 3
readers). Word meaning and context clues lead children to become more able

to read larger amounts of reading material. It is not until the teenage years that students reach Stages 4 and 5. This is when most readers face multiple viewpoints and become discerning, critical readers.

By the time children are in kindergarten, they are able to verbally express themselves quite clearly but are rarely fluent in either writing or reading skills. Average kindergartners can print their first names, but it will be a full year before they can encode or decode a full conventionally written sentence. The complexity of reading and writing behavior may be because we reach a second tier of abstraction. With oral language, we can say that which we think. In comparison to oral language, writing and reading are second-level abstractions based on an additional symbol system: a written code. Somehow, the child not only needs to crack the code of what symbols mean inherently but also has to translate that into its conceptual representation.Thus *a-p-p-l-e* needs to be decoded (or encoded if a child is writing) from its orthographic symbol into its conceptual symbol as a red fruit.

The progess from print to meaning is much more complex than a simple march from letters to words to paragraphs. Rather, it begins from picture-as-symbol-for-thought to picture-as-thought where pictures represent conceptual understanding. Pictures progress into words: written-word-as-symbol-for-thought to written-word-as-thought. It is the progressive facility manipulating the symbol system that moves the learner toward literacy. A verbally competent learner has a certain amount of facility with linguistic symbolism, but a verbally *talented* learner has true agility manipulating linguistic symbols and the language code(s) involved in transmitting thought into expression (or in the case of reading, expression into thought).

One theoretical perspective on language manipulation holds that children create hypotheses; in a search for meaning (or "coherence"), they build an actual interpretation system (Ferreiro, 1990). Children create a world of order and predictability demonstrated by the rules they construct to control their language. It appears that stages of conceptual development are related to the sophistication of the learner's rule system. Langer (1984) has credited Bruner and Piaget for understanding children as active problem solvers whose "conceptual development is characterized by gradually more sophisticated, rule-governed systems of hypotheses or representations of the world" (p. 109).

Advanced Development

Exactly what constitutes advanced language development? Not all early talkers, early readers, or early writers become linguistic geniuses. However, there is a predictive relationship between early reading (those who can read before entering kindergarten) and later verbal ability (Henderson, Jackson, &

Mukamal, 1993; Jackson, 1988; Durkin, 1966). The reason may be that humans learn by doing: Reading begets better reading; writing begets better writing. Vygotsky (1978) perceptively noted that the very act of *doing* an act actually impacts the thought process itself. If the actual literacy event shapes thinking itself, then it makes sense that the longer a child does literate acts, the better he or she will become. Additionally, if a child does not need to spend time learning to read, he or she will be able to use reading to learn. Learning begets learning.

Loban's (1976) longitudinal study of language development clearly demonstrated the adage "Once in front, always in front." The language high-ability group in kindergarten was still the language high-ability in twelfth grade. The group had not only maintained its lead but it also increased in distance from the low-ability group. Early linguistic gains bode well for future success.

Recent work at the Institute of the Study of Child Development (Louis, Feiring, & Lewis, 1992) on the identification of gifted preschoolers has given comparative insight into early verbal development. By comparing the verbal abilities of normal and advanced children at ages 3 and 5, the researchers are able to plot some specific characteristics of advanced verbal development. Using a picture as a stimulus, children are asked to tell a story. The researchers discovered that typical 3-year-olds have a difficult time with this task. Their stories are not particularly logical and they make use of simple vocabulary. The "story" is more of a description of what the children actually see in the picture.

In contrast, a verbally gifted 3-year-old is indeed able to tell a logical story. More interesting, the story is often creatively imaginative. The vocabulary used includes adjectives and descriptive phrases. The sequence of beginning, middle, and end gives structure to the story, which often has a consistent theme.

By age 5, the typical child can tell a logical and creative story. Adjectives are now being used and are beginning to join two thoughts together to form simple compound sentences. However, there is still a problem with beginning, middle, and end sequencing. In contrast, the verbally talented child is now using expressively vivid adverbs, verbs, and compound sentences. Dialogue is used creatively and the story itself can be highly imaginative.

How much the adult can contribute to that development is open to theoretical debate. The Piagetian camp holds that children will construct their own meanings given a requisite literate environment. The Vygotskian camp notes the importance of an adult to bridge the gap between a learner's actual grasp of a concept and his potential conceptual understanding. The adult can provide just the right stimulus or ask just the right question to transcend the gap between what the learner knows and what the learner *can* know. It is the adult (or cognitively more aware peer) who is the converter, acting as catalyst to *help the child* convert potential knowledge to kinetic knowledge.

Studies of individual children can offer specific insight into the nature of verbal talent development. Two children who typify early verbal talent can be met in the following case examples. Both children are typical in their demonstrations of advanced verbal abilities; they also exemplify the variance in how those abilities are manifested. David's reading abilities and Cara's writing talents provide interesting insight into the world of verbally gifted learners.

Case Examples of Verbal Talent

Early Reading Talent

Five-year-old David has the impish grin and human dynamo energy of many kindergartners. David's energy is more than kinesthetic; his mental capabilities are far beyond his chronological years. He can quickly and shrewdly size up an adult to find out if he has an ally or an adversary. David intuitively knows many adults don't understand his needs. He is a special child—one who needs intellectual challenges beyond those presented in most kindergarten classes.

On a recently administered battery of Woodcock-Johnson-R Tests of Academic Achievement (W-J-R), David scored in the 99.9 percentile rank for children of his age (5 years, 6 months) on all seven subtests. For letter-word identification, that places kindergartner David at a grade equivalent of 6.7. For passage comprehension, David scored the equivalent of grade 6.2. Grade equivalencies may mean something in terms of achievement comparison, but they mean more in terms of bottom-line accomplishment. It certainly means David should not be spending time on the usual kindergarten visual discrimination tasks.

To that end, now that David has outgrown the local Montesorri preschool that successfully nurtured his early needs, David's parents will be driving him to another Montesorri school one hour from his home. There is no bus service available and the trip will be grueling for a family juggling two other children, ages 3 and 1. But a careful search of schools has convinced the family that the trip will be worthwhile. The school will provide an environment in which David is used to thriving—one with many materials and the freedom for David to read what he cares to read. He will not be performing any rote exercises for reading readiness that he is already far beyond.

Like his father had done a generation earlier, David had cracked the phonetic code before he was 2 years old. His parents started to read to him when he was 6 months old. By the age of 1, David could listen to stories for 45 minutes to an hour. The family noticed that David was particularly drawn to both letters and numbers before he was even 1 year old. On outings, David would stop and trace the letters on fire hydrants and stop signs. By 18 months of age, he was saying the alphabet, but he always wanted to see the letters he was saying. Mom and Dad bought David six sets of big magnetized letters. David would spend hours playing with his magnet letters. At 20 months, he figured out that letters make sounds.

Although the family did not watch television, David was given the "Sesame Street" video "Getting Ready to Read." That video somehow unlocked the phonetic code for David. He would stare transfixed at that video and then piece together his magnet letters into words that he could say—some were nonsense words, but he was putting letters together in patterns and then sounding out the patterns he created.

By age 2½, David was reading books such as *Ten Apples Up on Top*. His mother says that there was never any formal reading instruction. However, they have a large library of books and had many books available for David that were easy readers. He would pick up books and read them comfortably, progressing in the difficulty of book he was able to handle. By age 5, he was reading *Little House on the Prairie* and the *Chronicles of Narnia*. When banished to his room as punishment for some crime typical of 5-year-olds, David often emerged later than necessary because he got caught up in his world of books. He reads faster than he talks (and David talks fast!) and has a voracious appetite for information. David is a sponge, soaking in knowledge from every available sense. As he begins school this year, we can only hope his teachers will be able to keep ahead of David's cheetah-like pace.

Although David's reading precocity is obvious, his writing abilities mask his full verbal aptitude. David's love for reading tasks was apparent in infancy, but he hated writing tasks. He would color letters and could print letters by the age of 3, but he took no delight in these tasks. His mother feels this may be related to the level of his motor skills, which is below the level of his verbal skills. At this time, David can, but doesn't like or choose to, spend time on writing tasks. The mechanical process of writing is too slow for David's quick mind. He is already looking forward to expressing his thoughts on paper through a word processor, which will match his thinking speed much better. David's lowest Woodcock-Johnson subtest score was in dictation. He indeed was in the 99.9 percentile for his age and scored at a grade equivalent of 3.7, well above his kindergarten placement. However, this was two years below all other Woodcock-Johnson subscores. David does not spend his time putting thoughts to paper; he'd rather be reading. Writing is not (yet?) David's venue for his verbal talents.

The family has no desire to push David into writing, nor any other academic task for which he does not seem ready. They believe in providing

David with the materials to put his own world together. That is why they are willing to drive him an hour away to a Montessori school that provides an individualized approach to learning. For now, the parents are content to answer David's never-ending questions and provide him with the books so he can learn to find his own answers to his many questions. They do know they have a very precocious child—one who is very verbally talented.

Early Writing Talent

Cara is a petite, 9-year old, fourth-grader. Her penetrating twinkling eyes combine seriousness of purpose with humorous insight, exuding a maturity that belies Cara's tender age. I first met Cara when she was a 6-year-old first-grader taking my Young Readers and Writers Saturday class at the College of William and Mary's Enrichment Program for Gifted Learners. Early in the course, each student had to develop a list of potential writing topics.

Emy, a typical child in the class, came up with the following list:

bikes	water
mommy	mouse
rabbit	bananas
dinosaur	clocks
gerbil	earth
cats	brother
dogs	leaves
tree	carrots

Cara's less typical list read:

my two dogs	my food
my two sisters	my clothes
my family	my house
dinosaurs	my birthday
myself	my neighbor
animals	my body
the ornament I made	my teeth (the ones I have)
the book I wrote	my hair
my friends	my bird (Snowey)
my mom	my video camera

It was obvious that Cara had a lot to write about. Compared with the more typical list of Emy's, Cara had more ideas both in number and complexity. Her list demonstrates grammatical development as well—Cara used standard spelling and adjective descriptors. Creatively speaking, Cara demonstrates fluency of ideas as well as the ability to elaborate (e.g., "my teeth [the ones I have"]). Original thinking is perhaps most evident in her video camera topic. Just a simple list comparison enables a teacher to see the different ability levels of Emy and Cara. Emy's list is exclusively nouns—and almost all animals or people. Cara's list is far more expressive than Emy's list.

Whereas many of the students would spend much time "spinning wheels" during writing time, Cara would spend each of the 10 course sessions writing with targeted purpose. Words just seemed to flow from Cara and she was able to get thought to paper without the usual hesitation of 6-year-olds new to the process of writing. However, Cara *was* new to the process of writing. Cara had only recently come to put thought onto paper. It was as if this new venue provided Cara with a spigot for her verbal talent. As I posed questions to Cara about her writing, she metacognitively analyzed her thought processes. I asked, "What are you writing about today, Cara? Why did you choose a home setting for your adventure story? How is your character going to resolve his problem?" Cara bubbled with enthusiastic response. She worked to revise her written stories as she orally explained the rationale behind her writing decisions. Simple description gave way to vivid imagery and metaphorical expression.

By second grade, Cara was prolific with her writing. The ease of getting from thought to paper freed Cara to learn to manipulate written conventions. Now that Cara is in the fourth grade, she has a full portfolio of writing products. She writes in different genres for different audiences—poems, essays, articles; narrative voice, expressive voice, transactional voice. At the age of 9, Cara has control of her written thought processes. Her prize-winning fourth-grade story "Leena and the Magic Shoes" demonstrates Cara's ability to use literary devices such as simile and onomatopoeia: "Leena felt all her blood rushing through her body like a stream in a storm. She could hear her heart beating louder, and louder. Bump, bump, bump. Louder, faster, bump, bump, bump, bump." The mechanics of spelling and grammar are flawless, enabling the meaning of Cara's words to tumble effortlessly across the reams of pages she writes.

Cara's writing talent had shown itself much earlier in other forms of verbal literacy. She is the youngest of four children and her mother says it was obvious from birth that Cara had some special abilities. Whereas most babies enter the world with undifferentiated crying patterns, Cara's mother is convinced that Cara was born making sounds. By 3 months, she was imitating vowel sounds. Mrs. White says that Cara could mimic pitch and intonation at this time as well, which most babies don't do until 8 months of age. Cara was singing "Twinkle, Twinkle Little Star" and the alphabet by 18 months of age.

Mrs. White first took Cara to the library for a toddler reading group at age 2. They always called it Library School and counted Cara's first library story hour as Cara's first day of school. Cara loved her trips to the library and even saved her nametag from Library School.

At age 3, her pediatrician was taken aback by Cara's ability to verbally spar with him. The doctor was verbally quick-witted, and Cara, even though only 3 years old, could one-up him point for point.

By the time Cara began kindergarten, she was reading and so was sent to the first grade for reading lessons. She was also incredibly expressive and garnered the starring role in the entire school production of "Bunny Sue." Cara performed the lead role with such expression that she is still remembered for the production. At age 5, she was able to memorize the entire production easily.

Although she was reading and a capable oral dramatist, Cara was not doing any real writing in kindergarten. Neither Mrs. White nor Cara remembers much at all about drawing, scribbling, or writing until the first grade. Mrs. White feels it might be because Cara's fine-motor skills weren't quite ready for writing yet. But in the first grade (age 6), Cara wrote the following poem:

The Sky

Oh way up high, Where the birds only fly,
A road or a path,
With a really big bird bath,
Somewhere that is very far away—
That you can't see every day.

If you have to see it now,
I really don't know how,
For only in your dreams,
Can you see this magical place
That is covered in pink and lace.
If you have a long sleep.
Your dream, you will keep.

The only thing I'm trying to say
Is that you can't see where the
Sky ends every day.

Signs of writing talent abound. Her poetic ability to rhyme with flow is far beyond her chronological age of 6; but it is the inclusion of symbolism that sets this poem apart. Cara is able to transcend the here-and-now for a glimpse into a world beyond the concrete reality of words. There is a level of abstraction embedded in Cara's poem that raises it to a height of what can be termed "manifestation of talent." Shortly after this poem was written, Cara took the special writing class allowing her to concentrate on writing. She has since taken off with her writing independence. She now does a series of magazines for her mother: "Magazine for Mom." Issue after issue is churned out during Cara's free time—issues wherein the Writer is C. Brianna White; the Editor is C. B. White; the Entire Crew is Cara B. White; and the Publisher is C. B. W. She demonstrates a playful exuberance with words that conveys joy in her artistry. Cara writes in ways that are beyond her years. She is able to descriptively evoke abstract images with the fluid grace of the dancer she also is.

Yes, Cara also reads beyond her years and speaks with an adult vocabulary. Her verbal talents are many. It would be difficult for a parent or teacher *not* to recognize such talent. However, that doesn't make it any easier to deal with such talent. What is it that we as teachers and parents can do to ensure that such talent will be used to its fullest potential? Certainly these case examples of David and Cara offer us some clues.

Patterns of Verbal Talent

Even with their different manifestations, both of these examples of verbal talent demonstrate striking similarities. David and Cara demonstrate the following:

- *Fluid, descriptive oral language:* Both children learned to talk early and by 18 months of age were expressing full conceptual thought processes. As early elementary students, they are able to converse with adults easily, using advanced vocabulary, grammar, and syntax. Their oral language is descriptive and filled with exuberant expression.
- *Early mastery of the phonetic code:* Each child deciphered a sound-symbol correspondence early in the preschool years, well before the usual kindergarten curriculum matching letters to sounds. Interestingly, *Sesame Street* was mentioned by both sets of parents as being influential in helping those children crack the phonetic code of symbol and sound.
- *An advanced ability to use a linguistic symbol system:* Cara and David each translated written words several years beyond their chronological ages. When their peers were reading sight vocabulary readers, Cara and David were able to explore the world of meaningful literature. They were facing the heady realms of imagination through books such as *The Chronicles of Narnia*, giving them networks of meaning upon which to connect literary sequels.
- *Active engagement in reading or writing tasks for extended periods of time:* Whether it is David reading a new book or Cara editing her latest maga-

zine, time gets lost for these children. The interpretation might better be that time is gained as their literary interests clearly enable them to transcend present reality into a world blissfully ignorant of time and its constraints.

- *Playful doing of a skill coupled with seriousness of purpose:* The play of David and Cara is purposeful. Play is a time for the imagination to be fused with their verbal abilities. Cara's writing portfolio brims with the evidence of creative production. Spiral-bound stories, illustrated adventures, and collections of poetry all demonstrate fruition of verbal talent.
- *Ability to express complex thoughts:* Both the complex sentence structure and the high-powered vocabulary of each of these two children enable their verbal expression of complex cognitive thought patterns. It is as if each of them has the ability to link his or her knowledge base (which is significant) to the whole new knowledge base of the future they haven't even gleaned yet.
- *Craving of challenge:* Both children always want to try something new. Whether it's a new writing genre for Cara or a new reading genre for David, they both want to try what they haven't tried before. What for most young children is a safety net—repetition—is the signal of alarm for Cara and David: boredom!

There is no one magical list that can precisely define *verbal talent*. A list such as this is only generally indicative of special talent. If we hold with social learning theory, the list provides us with important cues as to the depth and breadth of the zone of proximal development that these children might have. Their potential is clearly visible. What can we do to nurture the talents of Cara and David, to lead them through their zones of proximal development? How can we as parents and teachers help these children use their gifts to the fullest? Both Cara and David's parents are exemplars of the talent development model. Each of the parents did the following:

- *Noted talent early:* They were well aware that their children were ahead of the usual developmental schedule. The parents noted and charted their child's progress from infancy and kept careful track of development.
- *Bought or made materials that targeted learner strengths:* The parents responded to their children's readiness for particular materials as soon as the skill and interest was noticed. As David was discovering signs, he was given sets of magnet letters to manipulate. The materials matched his interest.
- *Went to great lengths to support talent:* Whether it was a willingness to drive a child to a special school or sacrifice to make tuition payments for special classes, these parents go to great lengths to find special resources to support the talents of their children.

- *Took lead from child:* The parents responded to the children *after* they expressed skill and interest. They didn't coerce their children into tasks for which they didn't express interest.
- *Read, read, read:* It seems that reading to and with the children was important to these families from the start. Reading time was a common denominator for these verbally talented children.
- *Made books and materials available:* In conjunction with time to read is the availability of books and materials at home. These parents value their collections of children's books. They mention sacrificing other purchases in order to buy books for their children.
- *Used the library:* The library for these families is seen as more than just a place to find books. It is a source of special classes and a major resource to support their children's verbal interests. Trips to the library are made regularly and they take advantage of library course offerings.
- *Used video recordings to monitor progress:* Both sets of parents use a video camera to record the special milestones of their children. The children have the opportunity to see themselves succeed in their unique ways. In addition to the presumed enhancement of self-esteem, the video diaries may provide the children with opportunities to metacognitively reflect on their abilities.
- *Took pride in achievements:* Perhaps most important, these parents took great pride in their children. Without bragging, the parents could proudly acknowledge their child's accomplishments. It was obvious that they see their children as individuals and stress the *strength* of that individuality.

Strategies to Foster Verbal Talent Development

If we synthesize the implications from these case studies with the research literature, several specific strategies for furthering verbal talent surface. Students need to be engaged for extended periods of time in complex reading and writing tasks. For Marzano (1991, pp. 5–7), those complex tasks ought to include a variety of response modes that force students to operate at the edge rather than at the center of their abilities. We need to decide what *variety* of tasks can be set up for children that will provide them with a challenge.

A second strategy is the use of targeted questions that get students to examine their own contradictions. Going along with that strategy is the idea of producing a conflict for the learners, forcing the reader or writer to manipulate his meaning-product. The questioning techniques used by the Junior Great Books Foundation often pose conflict for the readers that move them toward arguing a point. Children not only have to answer questions such as "Was it luck or skill that enabled Jack to outwit the giant in *Jack and the Beanstalk?*" but they also have to defend their answer with evidence from the text. This defense and use of evidence forces children to address the *meaning* they get from text.

These strategies are predicated on the use of meaningful text and materials so that students are able to manipulate increasingly advanced and sophisticated content, materials, and delivery systems. This is what engages the student in language manipulation, the ultimate source of mind engagement. Meaningful text and materials must go beyond basal readers. It is *literature* that provides great instrinsic questions buried between its covers. These questions are waiting to be discovered by discerning readers.

Although each of the several individual strategies mentioned for nurturing verbal talent is appropriate in its own right, it isn't nearly as powerful as it can be when used in a coherent and codified manner. That is, a deliberate and conscious choice of objectives, activities, and resources for a young verbally gifted learner can form coherent teaching units that can more powerfully nurture the special needs of early verbal talent. A formalized curriculum can be the difference between total immersion into literacy and just a haphazard sampling of the language arts. Theory points to the necessity of a curriculum that matches the ability level of the students not head-to-head but in an interlocking one step-ahead fashion that builds onto a student's existing schema so as to extend the structure further.

Thus, it is not enough simply to provide reading materials or writing time. Theory points to the need for appropriately challenging content—specific reading materials that engage the proficient reader on multilevels of thought; writing exercises that differentiate audiences and allow written language to be manipulated in complex, meaningful ways; oral discourse opportunities that allow the development of argument and a line of reasoning.

Key to helping a child deal with a core content base of knowledge is the support and guidance of a teacher. The very nature of the questions asked can provide just the help for the student to extend his or her inner scaffold. It is by this extension that the student is able to get to higher mental ground.

One way to trigger this is suggested in the work of Jerome Bruner (1986), who argues for presenting the "hypothetical nature of knowledge, its uncertainty, its invitation to further thought" (p. 126). It is by the nature of this presentation that students are invited to use thought, reflection, elaboration, and fantasy. In other words, we take high-level, captivating material and present it in a way that encourages students to explore its ambiguities. We question and allow children themselves to question to discover patterns or breaks in patterns.

As demonstrated by selected lesson plans found in Part IV of this book, literature can provide a firm foundation for a coherent curriculum that addresses the needs of verbally talented learners. It is great literature that provides sustenance to great minds. Extending the sophistication of student response to literature becomes the purview of curriculum and instruction. Bruner (1986) spoke to a "growing edge" of competence to which we bring learners. Vygotsky accounts for a "zone of proximal development" (ZPD), which is a range of tasks too hard for children to master alone but doable with an instructor (Bruner, 1986). This zone of prixomal development becomes a measure of learning potential that emphasizes the social aspect of learning. From a theoretical perspective, it offers a reason why the instructional process is so important to literacy development.

Conclusion

There is no one way to organize effective instruction for verbally talented students. What is important is that the talent be recognized and nurtured. In all cases, there should be opportunities for challenged thinking since thought is the essence of literacy. This challenge can be presented with stimulating materials and thought-provoking questions. The best support structure for language development that provides both stimulating materials and provokes intriguing questions is quality literature. From the oral traditions of great folktales to the yarns of the modern writer, literature provides a feast of content—through asking the great questions of humanity.

Whether by parent, teacher, or friend (but preferably by all), the talented learner needs a social support network to provide the context that gives literacy its meaning. This social network becomes the audience to showcase the verbal talent as well as discussants to extend and refine the meaning instrinsic to the literature read (or written) by the student. It is this social network that can provide the bridge across the learner's zone of proximal development. It is our job as parents and teachers to lead students across that bridge; to provide the questions and materials that will engage them and convert their potential for independent, autonomous thought into the products of a civilized and cultured society.

In his book on child prodigies entitled *Nature's Gambit*, David Feldman (1986) noted that "proclivities are realized as talent only through the arrangement of conditions that identify, engage, sustain, and fuel its development" (p. xi). Our challenge is to arrange those conditions so that we can indeed identify, engage, sustain, and fuel talent. That is the essence of intellectual engagement. If we succeed, we will have advanced our collective societal intellect—a worthy challenge to us all.

Key Points Summary

- Talented learners may experience developmental spurts or leaps in learning various literacy development skills; teachers and parents need to be attuned to these nonlinear growth patterns and respond with appropriately challenging stimuli.
- The mere practice of literate acts enhances literacy development. Thus, more practice in reading and writing improves learning skills. Daily reading and writing habits are powerful ways to enhance linguistic talent.
- Adult teachers and parents serve the function of helping sudents convert potential understanding to usable knowledge. Implications for adult facilitation, then, are (1) to provide a context for deepening understanding of a skill or concept, (2) to diagnose the appropriate stimulus needed to spark the acquisition of usable knowledge, and (3) to provide support as the learner tries out his or her potential understanding.
- Early readers frequently are not equally precocious at writing, having chosen to spend their time in one language arts area. Practitioners may wish to encourage modes of verbal expression that externalize thoughts and ideas stimulated by reading. Discussion of books read and writing about books read are excellent venues for this broadening of the verbal spectrum.
- Precocious writing talent may also be found in students and should be encouraged through challenging them to write often and in different modes.
- Indicators of early verbal talent include fluid descriptive oral language, mastery of phonetics, advanced ability to use a linguistic symbol system, active extended engagement in verbal tasks, playful use of verbal skills for a specific purpose, complexity of thought, and craving for challenge. Practitioners need to consider these generic behaviors when planning language arts experiences.
- Parents are in an excellent position to encourage early literacy development by recognizing precocious behaviors, using the library, procuring appropriate materials, documenting development, and encouraging individual progress.
- Use of complex tasks, targeted questions, and literature-based reading are strategies for nurturing verbal talent at home and at school.

References

Bruner, J. S. (1986). *Actual minds, possible worlds*. Cambridge, MA: Harvard University Press.

Chall, J. S. (1983). *Stages of reading development*. New York: McGraw-Hill.

Clay, M. (1975). *What did I write?* Auckland, New Zealand: Heinemann.

Durkin, D. (1966). *Children who read early*. New York: Teachers College Press.

Feldman, D. H. (1986). *Nature's gambit: Child prodigies and the development of human potential*. New York: Basic Books.

Ferreiro, E. (1990). Literacy development: Psychogenesis. *How children construct literacy: Piagetian perspectives* (pp. 12–25). Newark, DE: International Reading Association.

Glazer, S. M. (1989). Oral language and literacy development. In *Emerging literacy: Young children learn to read and write*. Newark, DE: International Reading Association.

Henderson, S. J., Jackson, N. E., & Mukamal, R. A. (1993). Early development of language and literacy skills of an extremely precocious reader. *Gifted Child Quarterly, 37*(2), 78–83.

Horning, B. (1991, October). Language busters. *Technology Review*, 51–57.

Jackson, N. E. (1988). Precocious reading ability: What does it mean? *Gifted Child Quarterly, 32*(1), 200–204.

Langer, J. A. (1984, November). Literacy instruction in American schools: Problems and perspectives. *American Journal of Education*, 107–132.

Loban, W. (1976). *Language development: Kindergarten through grade twelve*. Urbana, IL: National Council of Teachers of English.

Louis, B., Feiring, C., & Lewis, M. (1992). *Identifying gifted preschoolers*. Rutgers, NJ: Institute for the Study of Child Development.

Marzano, R. (1991). *Cultivating thinking in English and the language arts*. Urbana, IL: National Council of Teachers of English.

Piaget, J., & Inhelder, B. (1969). *The psychology of the child*. New York: Basic Books.

Temple, C. A., Nathan, R. G., & Burris, N. A. (1982). *The beginnings of writing*. Boston: Allyn and Bacon.

Vygotsky, L. S. (1978). *Mind in society*. Cambridge, MA: Harvard University Press.

7

Oral Communication

Thinking in Action

ANN L. CHANEY
Law Practice, Chicago

"Why should I *take* an oral communication course?" the freshman student groaned in my office, "If I can write an essay for my English class, I can surely write a speech!"

"Why should I *fund* an oral communication course?" the administrator groaned in a budget meeting, "Don't our students score high enough on verbal aptitude tests?"

"Why should I *teach* an oral communication course," the instructor groaned in a curriculum meeting, "when there's nothing to it? 'Tell the audience what they're going to hear, tell them, and then tell them what they've just heard.' That works for me!"

Without passing judgment on what works for some people, at the very least there is an underlying assumption in all three of the above cases—the belief that oral communication is little more than the ability to present a written text to an audience without visibly demonstrating the symptoms of cardiac arrest or hypothermia. This view is a widespread misconception that often prevents students and teachers from realizing the true range and depth of the skills involved in achieving oral communication proficiency.

For talented learners, the need for emphasis in this area cannot be overstated. Speaking and listening activities of a higher order are frequently missing from school curricula (Cramond, 1993; Wolvin & Coakley, 1985) or

115

given very little instructional time. Instructional suggestions have ranged from foreign language to forensics to debate to rhetoric in an expanded view of what high-powered language arts programs need to be (Hansen, 1994; VanTassel-Baska, 1993). These activities may be employed with more talented learners at earlier stages of development, typically by fourth grade (Clark, Willihnganz, & O'Dell, 1985). Moreover, many language arts advocates feel that teaching oral communication directly enhances student performance in other areas of the language arts, such as reading comprehension (Hoyt, 1992) and writing (Sorenson, 1993). Therefore, the need to emphasize a broadened conception of oral communication and its relationship to teaching thinking should be explored.

Striking right at the heart of the "I talk, therefore I communicate" myth, this chapter will explain how oral communication is more properly characterized as "thinking in action." Specifically, it will present a working definition of oral communication, suggest some practical ways to teach oral communication as "thinking in action," and, finally, make some suggestions as to appropriate grading and evaluation methods.

Toward a Working Definition of Oral Communication

Oral communication is a grand and delightful exercise of "thinking in action." As a two-way process involving both the senders and receivers of messages, oral communication necessitates many of the same fundamental skills that are taught in writing. In particular, it requires the organizational and cognitive critical thinking skills that are involved in the sharing of meaning (Barnes, 1992, pp. 108–115).

Although the descriptive term *oral* would seem to exclude such skills as listening and nonverbal communication (commonly known as *body language*), oral communication actually includes these skills and many others. Contemporary theories within the academic discipline of speech communication, most notably *symbolic interactionism*, hold that human communication can be understood as the sharing of meaning through the use of symbols such as language and pictures, or forms of nonverbal expression such as gestures, facial expressions, and manner of dress.

For the oral communicator, messages composed of both verbal and nonverbal symbols are constructed and evaluated with the use of critical thinking skills. This task—uncovering shared meaning—is sometimes complicated further by the myriad of contexts in which oral communication events take place. Contrast a formal public speech delivered before a large audience with the informality of a child watching a 30-second commercial on Saturday morning television. The differences are pronounced and profound. Oral communication contexts may be direct or indirect, formal or informal, instantaneous or delayed, between two people or between millions (or, some would argue, between machines and people).

Recognition of the unique skill demands imposed by each communication context has encouraged a trend toward competency-based communication instruction. Although there remains some disagreement over the inclusion or exclusion of skills such as gender and intercultural sensitivity in language usage, there does exist a set of skills, or *core competencies,* that are widely agreed upon as central to a working definition of oral communication. In an attempt to encapsulate these core competencies into the most efficient format for instruction, the National Speech Communication Association asked 1,200 community and junior college deans and faculty to identify core communication competencies that should be demonstrated by college sophomores (Speech Communication Association [SCA], 1985). See Table 7–1 for a specific listing of these competencies.

At the university level, entire courses are often structured around the skill groupings suggested in Table 7–1. The two communication roles of speaker and listener, combined with the variety of contexts in which these roles are played, clearly indicate that *the ability to read and write at the highest levels of proficiency does not guarantee similar levels of proficiency in oral communication without additional skill development.* Verbal achievement test scores do not adequately measure factors such as nonverbal and interpersonal skills (Goulden, 1992, p. 259).

The key to understanding the interpretation of oral communication as "thinking in action" is to recognize that in either the speaking or listening role, the oral communicator must engage in a multitude of tasks, including information gathering and comprehension, synthesis and analysis of arguments, comparison of alternative choices, identification of values, and giving or responding to feedback. At the same time, the success of oral communication is subject to factors such as the effect of voice and nonverbal characteristics on speaker credibility, the need to give or adapt to audience feedback, time constraints, lack of opportunity for revision, and stage fright.

So now the question becomes, How can a language arts teacher accommodate such an expanded concept of oral communication without subordinating other important aspects of an already full curriculum?

Teaching "Thinking in Action"

From the outset, not all oral communication work needs to be formal, lengthy, or even graded to provide valuable skill development. It is more important that each activity be carefully planned and preceded by clear

TABLE 7–1   Oral Communication Competencies

Speaking Competencies	Listening Competencies
Determining the purpose of the oral discourse.	Listening with *literal* comprehension: • recognizing main ideas • identifying supporting materials
Choosing a topic and restricting it according to the purpose and the audience.	• recognizing explicit relationships among ideas • recalling basic ideas
Fulfilling the purpose by: • formulating a thesis statement • providing adequate supporting material • selecting a suitable organizational pattern • demonstrating careful choice of words • providing effective transitions • demonstrating suitable interpersonal skills	Listening with *critical* comprehension: • attending with an open mind • perceiving the speaker's purpose and organization of ideas and information • discriminating between statements of fact and statements of opinion • distinguishing between emotional and logical arguments • detecting bias and prejudice • recognizing the speaker's attitude • synthesizing and evaluating by drawing logical inferences and conclusions
Employing vocal variety in rate, pitch, and intensity.	
Articulating clearly.	• recalling the implications of arguments
Employing the level of American English appropriate to the designated audience.	• recognizing discrepancies between speakers' verbal and nonverbal messages
Demonstrating nonverbal behavior that supports the verbal message.	• employing active-listening techniques when appropriate

Source: Copyright by the Speech Communication Association, 1985. Reproduced by permission of the publisher.

instructions, and that students have several opportunities to practice new skills in front of an audience, both formally and informally (O'Keefe, 1986, pp. 17–18).

Every teacher is pressed for time and space in the classroom. The following suggested activities are presented by topic and skill grouping and may be easily adapted at the instructor's discretion to the age group, skill, and maturity level of his or her students. The activities were selected on the basis of interest-keeping ability, practicality, and efficiency in developing various oral communication contexts. Most are also characterized by their emphasis on critical thinking skills, and some are also helpful in integrating speaking and writing.

Teaching Response to Persuasion through Evaluative Listening

It has been noted that approximately 75 percent of our daily communication is oral. Much of that is persuasive in nature, designed to influence the attitudes, beliefs, values, or actions of others. We are asked to make decisions continually throughout the day—to buy environmentally safe products, to follow a doctor's prescription, or to let our child stay up an hour later than usual to watch the holiday television specials. Likewise, we act as persuaders when we ask others to vote for our preferred candidate, to turn down the volume on the stereo, or to invest in a particular mutual fund.

Persuasion, of course, does not occur in a vacuum. Speakers may initiate persuasion but listeners participate by evaluating the message and responding. Going back to the set of core competencies presented earlier in the chapter, it is easy to see that the skills of analysis and synthesis are just as important to the listener in receiving and evaluating persuasive messages as they would be to the speaker in developing a thesis and choosing appropriate supporting materials. Both speaker and listener benefit from the ability to differentiate strong from weak evidence: learning to recognize and use, as appropriate, emotional appeals, and value appeals, and learning to recognize strong or fallacious patterns in reasoning.

Listening should be taught as an active, rather than a passive, process so that the listener physically and mentally strives to comprehend spoken messages. An active evaluative listener will use the cognitive skills listed below in combination with verbal and nonverbal skills (asking questions, giving appropriate nonverbal feedback to the speaker such as nodding one's head and smiling or raising eyebrows in disbelief) in responding to persuasion (SCA, 1985).

The Toulmin Analytic Model of argument can be adapted to help young students understand the basic components of an argument. Like diagramming a sentence, the model allows a student to identify and label the parts of an argument. Like all models, the Toulmin model does have its limitations, one of which is that it is more helpful for analyzing arguments than for building them. However, in combination with introductory lessons on building units of proof through inductive, deductive, causal, or analogical reasoning, students will have mastered a number of logical reasoning tools that should aid them in constructing persuasive messages.

The components of the Toulmin analytic model are the *data* (grounds or evidence used in the argument), *warrant* (reasoning pattern or inferences), *backing* (underlying assumptions that tend to support the warrant, usually revealed if the warrant is challenged), *qualifier* (a term used by the arguer to indicate the degree of certainty of the claim), *claim* (the conclusion or proposition the arguer is defending), and *rebuttal* (any exceptions to the claim enumerated by the arguer) (Toulmin, Janik, & Rieke, 1984).

An argument containing all of these elements might look something like this when diagrammed according to the Toulmin model:

DATA

```
There is a police car with flashing:
lights up ahead on the side of the road :        QUALIFIER      CLAIM
stopped behind two cars.               :              :             :
                                       : ---------Most likely/ There has been
It is raining heavily and the roads    :    :                      an accident
are slick.                             :    :                            :
                                       :    :            Unless there is
                                       :    :            construction or the
Traffic is moving slower than usual.   :    :            drivers were
                                       :                 speeding
                            Accidents frequently occur
                            during perilous driving conditions, so
                                       :
                            Police officers patrol the highway
                            to aid motorists and are always
                            present at the scene of an accident
```

Not every argument that students will hear and be expected to respond to as listeners will contain all of these elements. For purposes of building analytical skills, it is sometimes just as productive to limit the model to the three major elements of data, claim, and warrant. Challenging students to pick out the claim made by a speaker (or contained in the text of an argument), then to identify the evidence use by the speaker to support the claim, and then to identify the reasoning or logical assumptions made by the speaker is a very effective exercise in teaching evaluative listening. Students can also learn from this to recognize fallacies in reasoning and to identify alternative ideas that were not considered by the speaker.

Examples:

(D):   It has been raining a lot lately.

I saw some crocus stems poking up through the ground in the garden this morning.

The birds have started to sing very loudly.

(W):   Since these things don't happen when the weather is going to be cold for a long time

(C):   The season must have changed from winter to spring.

(D):   Amy is opening a gift box.

She is sitting behind a table with a big cake that has candles all over it.

Many of her friends are standing around her.

They are all laughing and smiling.

(W):   Since presents are usually given to people for special reasons, and a cake with candles is customarily given for birthdays in this country,

(C):   Amy must be celebrating her birthday.

An evaluative listener can learn to recognize the data, claim, and warrant of a persuasive message and to actively respond to the message by asking questions for clarification, probing the strength of the data, challenging the warrant by proposing alternate inferences, and suggesting ways in which the conclusion might be modified if it seems to be unfounded after closer inspection. Two sample activities that explore evaluative listening in greater depth follow.

Listening Essay

1. Students attend an oral presentation with the teacher or watch one selected by the teacher on videotape.

2. Students write an essay about their reaction to the speaker, focusing on issues selected by the teacher, such as:

What were some of the main points mentioned by the speaker? What sources of information did the speaker draw upon during the speech? What were some of the arguments made by the speaker? Did you find the arguments strong or weak? Why? How do you think other people in the audience reacted to the speaker? What kind of audience feedback led you to draw this conclusion?

Analyze Media Messages

1. Select a series of three or four magazine advertisements, or videotape television commercials that demonstrate strong reliance on visual imagery and "slick" marketing techniques.

2. Instruct students to read/watch/listen to the ad very carefully.

3. Discuss as a class the basic elements of the persuasive message presented in the ad: What is the claim? What is the warrant? What is the evidence? What are some of the reasons that a consumer might have for not trusting the advertiser's message? Ask the class to name as many reasons as they can about why the ad or commercial might be misleading. Are there reasons to be persuaded by the advertiser's message? What are they?

Teaching Persuasive Speaking

No matter how advanced the level of instruction concerning the oral presentation of ideas, the skills of choosing a topic and purpose, outlining, and organizing the presentation should be emphasized. Unlike the writer, the oral communicator is facing an audience that does not have the luxury of following along with a printed text in front of them as the presentation continues. There is also no opportunity for the speaker to revise or rework awkward, confusing passages. Rambling on in a disorganized fashion, circling back to pick up a missed point, and then continuing on in an entirely new direction may have an obvious impact on a speaker's delivery (and perhaps even credibility).

Consequently, persuasive speaking may be more challenging in some respects than other types (such as informative speaking) because it requires mastery of these fundamental organization and content-building skills as well as synthesis, logic, and awareness of the audience's response to the persuasive message. Swicord (1984) found gifted students to be highly challenged by the process of organizing a debate, for example.

Determining the Topic and Purpose

The topic/purpose model is an excellent organizational tool for teaching persuasive speaking. It is comprised of four steps: selection of an appropriate topic, determination of the general purpose of the speech, determination of the specific purpose of the speech, and development of a thesis statement.

Selection of Appropriate Topic.   The student selects an appropriate topic and then narrows or broadens it if necessary, according to time constraints or audience expectations. Students will tend to perform better when they pick a topic area that is interesting to them personally, but assigned topics can work just as well and have the added advantage of giving the teacher more control over the exercise. (Incidentally, there is something to be said for exerting some control over topic selection. One public speaking instructor, who is deathly afraid of snakes, forgot to approve topics one semester and was greeted early one morning by a seven-foot python in the classroom!)

Determination of General Purpose.   General purpose refers to the act of informing, persuading, entertaining, or inspiring, and is always expressed as an infinitive. Students are asked to decide whether their general purpose is "to persuade" or "to inform," for example, after instruction on the implications of each type of purpose. Students learn, for instance, that the goal of a persuasive speech is to change or reinforce the audience's attitudes, beliefs, or actions with respect to the topic; whereas the goal of an informative speech is to increase the audience's understanding of a topic without necessarily attempting to change the audience in any other respect.

Determination of Specific Purpose.   Specific purpose refers to the individual goals the student hopes to achieve through the presentation. The specific purpose can always be articulated in a complete sentence, such as "My specific purpose is to inform the audience about basic first-aid techniques" or "My specific purpose is to persuade the audience to consume less fat and cholesterol in their daily diets."

Development of Thesis Statement.   Once the specific purpose has been determined, the student constructs a simple thesis statement. It should be concise yet include the main points of the message, such as "Three basic first-aid techniques to learn are direct pressure to stop blood flow from an open wound, elevation of bleeding extremities to slow blood loss, and how to stop bleeding through use of a tourniquet" or "We should significantly reduce the amount of fat and cholesterol in our daily diets to reduce and maintain a healthy body weight, to reduce our risk of high blood pressure and cardiovascular disease, and to improve overall nutrition."

The topic/purpose model is especially helpful to students when they are first learning to structure and organize speeches. A good beginning activity that helps students learn how to use the model, and also gets them on their feet early in an informal speaking situation, is the impromptu speech. In this activity, students have five minutes to prepare a speech about a topic drawn from a hat, using the topic/purpose model for development and an outline on note cards.

Building the Speech Outline

The preparation of a speech text begins with a very detailed, complete sentence outline, which is then condensed into what is known as a *speaker's outline*: less detailed; containing cues for effective delivery, such as "Slow down," "Watch eye contact!" or "Emphasize"; and usually written on notecards to allow for a more conversational and dynamic delivery.

Students need to demonstrate a firm grasp of the following critical skills:

1. Formulating significant, mutually exclusive and logically related main points

2. Ordering the main points in an effective, appropriate sequence for facilitating audience understanding and retention (examples include chronological, spatial, topical sequence, problem solution, cause and effect)
3. Correctly identifying differences between main points, subpoints, and sub-subpoints
4. Recognizing and utilizing adequate supporting material
5. Structuring arguments clearly and concisely within the body of a persuasive speech

The activity that follows (see box) may be useful in classroom application of these ideas.

Developing Clear Transitions

Oral communicators should strive for clear transitions in each movement from main point to main point. This practice is necessary to aid the audience in keeping mental track of the flow of the speech. Some examples of transitions that are highly useful for oral presentations follow.

Internal Preview. An internal preview is used in the body of the speech when the speaker's focus is about to shift from one distinct theme to another. For example, "Now that we have seen how serious America's garbage problem is, let's look at some solutions. I will focus on three solutions in particular—reducing our wasteful use of resources, instituting mandatory recycling programs, and developing alternative methods of disposing of our garbage. Let's look at each in turn."

Internal Summary. Similar to the internal preview, an internal summary reinforces the pattern of main points and helps the audience retain the previous information. For example, "Let's pause for a moment to recapitulate what we have found so far. First, we have seen that America's criminal justice system does not effectively deter crime. Second, we have seen that prison programs to rehabilitate criminals have failed miserably. We are now ready to explore solutions to these problems."

Extemporaneous Speaking

1. Instruct students to read newspapers or magazines and to select a current event issue that interests them. Students need to concentrate on an issue that has pro and con aspects.

2. Ask students to prepare a three- to seven- minute speech expressing their point of view on the issue, using the information they have collected from the articles, from personal experience, or interviews with other people.

Signposts. Signposts are key words and phrases that the oral communicator uses to locate a particular point within the overall organizational framework of the speech. A signpost emphasizes the order of a point and the idea to which the next point will be related. Examples include the following:

> Be sure to keep this in mind…
> The most important point to remember is…
> Let me repeat that last statement.
> How can we solve this problem?
> The first cause of the social security crisis is…
> The second cause is…
> The third cause is…
> Finally…

Adapting to the Audience

Audience adaptation involves learning to respect and develop a rapport with an audience while recognizing the impact that its particular characteristics may have on reception of the speaker's message. It may also involve adjusting the message and manner of delivery to audience feedback, verbal or nonverbal.

Students can learn to conduct simple demographic audience analysis by interviewing representatives of the audience or distributing questionnaires. Demographic analysis offers insight into the values, beliefs, attitudes, and general level of understanding presently attained by the audience with respect to a given topic. Good demographic analysis is important not only to avoid offending audience members with stereotypical assertions but it is also helpful in maximizing efforts to build rapport with the audience or to enhance persuasion.

Situational audience analysis is the consideration by the speaker of physical or temporal elements that may affect the presentation, such as the temperature of the speech area, the time of day, the occasion of the speech, or the number of people present in the audience. These types of considerations generally have more of an effect on the length of the presentation and the style (formal vs. informal, manuscript vs. extemporaneous) of delivery more than the content of the speech itself (Lucas, 1992).

Developing Credibility and Nonverbal Effectiveness

Oral presentations may be delivered in several different modes of preparation: manuscript (best for highly formal occasions); extemporaneously (from outline with some preparation and practice, best for situations in which the speaker wants to feel at ease with the audience and wants to maximize eye contact); and impromptu (virtually no preparation). Regardless of the choice of delivery style, good physical delivery includes direct, sustained, and varied eye contact (as opposed to looking over the heads of audience members, around the room, or reading from notes); meaningful, varied hand and arm gestures; appropriate facial expressions; good posture; and absence of distracting nervous mannerisms, such as playing with hair and clothing, shifting weight from leg to leg, or leaning over or gripping a podium.

Good vocal delivery includes the ability to project to the back of the audience; vocal variety in pitch, volume, and tone; absence of vocal pauses such as "uh," "um," "like," "okay," and "y'know;" skillful use of dramatic pauses; an appropriate rate of speed in speaking; and clear articulation.

The single-best tool for building delivery skills is actual speaking practice. Impromptu, extemporaneous, and prepared speeches all build these skills, but frequent attempts to speak before an audience, combined with thorough and sensitive feedback from the instructor, are most important to the beginning speaker.

Constructing Ethical Arguments

The issue of ethics is often neglected, but when one considers the vast number of people who fall prey to unethical persuaders every day, it is certainly worth addressing in class. Just as plagiarism rules are strictly enforced in writing, similar rules should be taught and enforced in speaking. Students should learn to cite their sources in the speech; to use information in its proper context; never to create facts or statistics in an effort to persuade (no matter how "good" intentions may be); and to avoid other types of ethical violations such as omission of potentially significant contrary information, overgeneralizations or overclaiming of evidence, and exaggeration of a source's credentials. The pressures on a speaker to be credible and to achieve personal goals of persuasion, especially when strongly held beliefs are involved, should not be underestimated.

Students can satisfy their desire to be effective persuaders and debaters by mastering the development of "proof" and by learning how to identify the best evidence and reasoning. Instruction in oral communication should include exploration of basic reasoning patterns such as deductive, inductive, causal, and analogical.

Sample Activity

Distribute examples of highly charged political tracts, campaign literature, sales propaganda (such as direct mail), or other intensive persuasive material, and ask students to identify and analyze arguments using the Toulmin Model. Ask them to identify sources of bias in testimony, statistics, or use of examples.

Speech Competitions

The National Forensic League has chapters in many high schools that sponsor weekend interschool speech and debate tournaments throughout the semester. Some junior high schools also have speech and debate teams, as do some 4-H chapters. These activities are a tremendous opportunity for young people to sharpen their oral communication skills in a number of different contexts. The frequent practice of speaking and arguing in front of diverse audiences, when combined with the challenge of competition, can produce unparalleled growth and skill development.

The individual events that make up high school speech competitions are really very interesting, and all of them challenge students to develop key clusters of oral communication skills. Events include the oral interpretation of literature; rhetorical criticism; the production of radio and television programs; the development of humorous or primarily entertaining speech forms (such as the after-dinner speech); and variations of debate events such as parliamentary debate, Lincoln-Douglas debate (one on one) and cross-examination policy or value debate (two-person teams).

Speech competitions are especially useful for observation of traditional public speaking forms such as informative and persuasive original oratories (usually an 8- to 10-minute memorized speech, delivered without a podium); extemporaneous speeches (3 to 5 minutes with limited preparation on a current event topic, without a podium); and impromptu speeches (3 to 5 minutes with 1 minute preparation, usually on a popular quotation or a thought-provoking question). Figure 7–1 contains a criterial checklist to use in ascertaining that all important elements in oral communications have been addressed by students.

Assessment

One question frequently asked by language arts teachers who have not had much experience teaching oral communication is, How do I grade a speech fairly? This section will explore popular approaches to grading oral communication assignments and discuss some alternative means of providing meaningful feedback to students.

Grading Fairly

There is no sure-fire way to avoid subjectivity in the grading process of a performance-oriented or creative arts project; oral communication assignments are no different in this regard. However, teachers should adhere to several

Speaker: _____

Grade: _____   Topic: _____

Comments:

Introduction
____ Gained the interest of the audience
____ Established credibility
____ Previewed main points
____ Clearly introduced topic

Body
____ Main points were clear, mutually
        exclusive, and logically related
____ Main points were well organized
____ Effective transitions
____ Analysis
____ Main points were fully supported
____ Language choice was appropriate
____ Treated audience with respect
____ Recognized and attempted to adapt to or
        establish a rapport with audience

Conclusion
____ Left a strong impact on the audience
____ Clearly brought speech to an end
____ Summarized main points effectively

Delivery
____ Used voice effectively: volume, pitch, tone,
        rate
____ Articulated words clearly
____ Did not use many distracting vocalized
        pauses ("um," "er," "uh")
____ Eye contact was direct, sustained, and
        consistent
____ Good posture
____ Gestures were appropriate and useful in
        contributing to the audience's
        understanding
____ Facial expressions were appropriate

FIGURE 7–1   Criteria Checklist for Oral Presentations

general guidelines in grading an oral communication assignment: establishing clear criteria, applying these criteria consistently to each student, and recording impressions of the presentation while listening to it, either by taking notes or by videotaping the performance.

Establishing Clear Criteria

Where teachers tend to differ the most in grading is in the selection of issues or skills that each sees as most important in effective oral communication. Once the instructor selects the skills to be graded during the exercise, careful thought should be given to the range of performance the instructor expects to see and to the amount of weight to be given to each skill category. Teachers should also consider whether to assign points for each individual skill category or to grade on overall impression of the speech. One sample form using several clusters of criteria is shown in Figure 7–1.

Whenever possible, teachers should give positive, constructive feedback to supplement checkmarks on categories since students need to have substantive feedback in order to improve. Praising students for what they do well is also extremely important in teaching public speaking (or any other kind of oral communication skill) because students tend to approach speaking in front of an audience with much trepidation and because younger students may be more sensitive to criticism about their performance in front of their peers.

An alternative method of grading speeches is the use of a rating scale. The advantages of this method are that it is somewhat less time consuming, provides some degree of assurance of consistency in grading, and allows the students to get a feel of where they are in skill development. The following example below illustrates this approach.

In using the rating scale method, the teacher should determine a range of skill level and apply that criteria consistently to every student. Following is an example of a range in skill that might be developed by a teacher for the skill "clarity of ideas":

Grading Using a Rating Scale (Excerpts of a Form)

Speaker: _____

Grade: _____   Topic: _____

	Excellent	*Good*	*Average*	*Fair*	*Poor*
Vocal delivery	5	4	3	2	1
Physical delivery	5	4	3	2	1
Clarity of ideas	5	4	3	2	1
Analysis	5	4	3	2	1
Support	5	4	3	2	1
Audience adaptation	5	4	3	2	1

Clarity of Ideas

Note: Includes organization, development of concepts, definition of important words where necessary, and absence of phrases or speech patterns that detract from the listener's ability to follow the speech.

5   Ideas are very well organized, transitions clearly mark movement from one idea to another, supporting materials are clearly distinguished from other elements in the speech. Speech flows smoothly from point to point.

4   Some slight misordering of points, some transitions (or lack of transitions), slightly confusing in use of terminology, logic, or use of supporting materials. Speech flows smoothly from point to point for the most part.

3   Organization of main points is basically sound, but other ideas or concepts may be explained in an unorganized or unclear fashion. Speech may ramble at points, may be choppy, or backtrack occasionally.

2   Speech is not well organized; listener may need to rely on context clues within the speech to discern main points. May be extremely choppy or too brief to communicate ideas in much depth.

1   Main points are almost indiscernable without context clues; development of ideas is extremely difficult to follow; points may not be developed at all.

Some teachers prefer a third method of grading—the generic written critique, on which they write comments about their overall impressions of the speech and then proceed to assign a letter grade or points. This method may also be combined with the checklist scale approach in order to provide two types of feedback to students on performance.

All three of these approaches work well as long as they provide adequate support for the grade. Students need to see substantive feedback and need to be able to track improvement. Without constructive, fairly given criticism, students are apt to feel frustrated and have their fears of speaking in front of an audience validated.

Conclusion

Oral communication is best conceptualized as a two-way process involving both the senders and receivers of messages. In this respect, oral communication necessitates many of the same fundamental communication skills that are taught in writing, such as the organizational and cognitive "critical thinking" skills that are involved in the sharing of meaning.

Oral communication instruction can be challenging and rewarding for both students and instructors. In attempts to provide the frequent practice that students need to fully develop a variety of oral communication skills, a series of short classroom activities can be designed or adapted that are fun, interesting, and stimulate critical thinking.

Teachers have a number of options in grading oral communication activities, although many activities can foster skill growth without needing the added weight of a grade. Teachers who wish to grade the more challenging assignments should supplement all grades with clear explanations and positive, constructive feedback.

Key Points Summary

- Oral communication is thinking in action and involves both listening and speaking modalities.
- Core competencies need to be addressed with talented learners in oral communication.
- Listening involves a set of active thinking skills, including detecting bias and drawing logical inferences and conclusions.
- Daily communication is 75 percent oral and much of it is persuasion.
- Teaching students a basic model of "proof" can enhance their understanding of the role of persuasion.
- Determining topic and purpose, building a speech outline, developing clear transitions, adapting to an audience, developing credibility, and constructing ethical arguments are fundamental to teaching persuasive speaking.
- Assessment of oral communication demands the application of clearly stated criteria and qualitative commentary.

References

Barnes, D. (1992). *From communication to curriculum* (2nd ed.). Portsmouth, NH: Heinemann.

Clark, R. A., Willihnganz, S. C., & O'Dell, L. L. (1985). Training fourth graders in compromising and persuasive strategies. *Communication Education, 34*, 331–342.

Cramond, B. (1993). Speaking and listening: Key components of a complete language arts program for the gifted. *Roeper Review, 16*(1), 44–48.

Goulden, N. P. (1992). Theory and vocabulary for communication assess-ments. *Communication Education, 41,* 258–269.

Hansen, J. (1994). Language arts for verbally precocious elementary students. In J. Hansen & S. Howis (Eds.), *Talent development theory into practice* (pp. 105–129). Dubuque, IA: Kendall-Hunt.

Hoyt, L. (1992). Many ways of knowing: Using drama, oral interactions, and the visual arts to enhance reading comprehension. *The Reading Teacher, 45*(5), 580–584.

Janik, A. (1979). *Introduction to reasoning.* New York: Macmillan.

Lucas, S. (1992). *The art of public speaking* (4th ed.). New York: McGraw-Hill.

O'Keefe, V. P. (1986). *Affecting critical thinking through speech.* Annandale, VA: Speech Communication Association.

Sorenson, M. (1993). Teach each other: Connecting talking and writing. *English Journal,* 42–46.

Speech Communication Association. (1985). *Can your students communicate successfully? Speaking and listening compentencies for sophomores in college.* Annandale, VA: Author.

Sprague, J., & Stuart, D. (1982). *The speakers handbook* (3rd ed.). New York: Harcourt, Brace, Jovanovich.

Swicord, B. (1984). Debating with gifted fifth and sixth graders—telling it like it was, is, and could be *Gifted Child Quarterly, 28*(3), 127–129.

Toulmin, S., Janik, A., & Rieke, R. (1984). *An introduction to reasoning* (2nd. ed.). New York: Macmillan.

VanTassel-Baska, J. (1993). *Comprehensive curriculum for gifted learners* (2nd ed.). Boston, MA: Allyn and Bacon.

Wolvin, A., & Coakley, C. (1985). *Listening.* Dubuque, IA: William C. Brown.

8

Teaching Discourse through Writing

COLLEEN KENNEDY

College of William and Mary

As debates about political correctness have dominated recent mainstream media coverage of teaching in college-level humanities courses, so debates about the propriety of cultural criticism in the freshman writing class have dominated the major journals in college composition studies. Although my concern in this chapter will not be on this debate per se, it is crucial to studies of writing pedagogy in classes for college-bound students for two reasons. First, cultural criticism—an interdisciplinary phenomenon rather than one restricted to the Humanities—is not, as some would have it, a passing fad. Today's elementary and high school students will face university curricula that place problems of cultural diversity and of differing constructions of knowledge at the center of many courses; and they will quite probably encounter these concerns in their first college-level writing course. St. Martin's Press alone publishes no less than seven readers in cross-culturalism or cultural critique aimed at an audience of first-year composition students.

More fundamentally, debates about cultural criticism in the writing classroom do not rest solely on issues of politics. Many writing specialists are suspicious of critics' motives on strictly political grounds. Behrens, for example, implies that cultural critics use the writing classroom to prosletyze when he represents their position as being that "the only responsible way to teach writing is to focus on the injustices of the social order" (Trimbur et al., 1993,

p. 257). However, one theme that recurs in these debates—one more ger-
mane to my interests here—is the presumption that the student's voice ought
to be central to the writing classroom. (Indeed, one reason so many journal
articles and conference papers focus on how to respond to racist, sexist, and
homophobic papers is that instructors still assign papers that ask for students' opinions in such matters.) Opponents of cultural criticism, like Hairston, view it as a form of "intellectual intimidation" because it centers the
writing course on something other than students' own "values, preferences,
or interests" (Hairston, 1992, pp. 181, 188). Many of the arguments over pedagogies centered on cultural criticism turn, then, not on issues of "political
correctness" but on whether the writing classroom should be directed
toward students' self-expression or toward the development of strategies for
reading, understanding, and analyzing the discourses of *others* (especially
others with whom the students might disagree).

Lindeman (1993) and Tate (1993) took up a slightly different version of
the debate in paired articles in a recent issue of *College English* (1993). Lindeman argued vehemently against writing courses oriented toward a single
discipline (specifically literature, but the arguments she mustered would
hold for any discipline); Tate, on the other hand, defended such courses.
Their arguments go a long way toward explaining the misgivings many
composition specialists have about integrating cultural criticism into writing
classes: to do so requires that writing courses turn back toward a content-
based pedagogy in which students' writing centers not on their own "values,
preferences, or interests" but on key texts of the discipline and/or the culture.

This chapter will focus not on the issue of politics in the classroom but on
the issue that undergirds it—the need to reintegrate content and analysis into
writing classrooms at all levels of language arts education. This is not to dismiss the invaluable achievements of the "writing-as-process" model. Rather,
it is to use what we have learned about teaching the writing process to help
students understand the complex discourses that, unexamined, can too
strongly determine their "self-expression." The pages that follow describe
the history leading up to the current debates about the best approach to
teaching writing, explain arguments in favor of text-based writing pedagogies (including but not limited to those based in cultural critique), and offer
some exemplary suggestions for implementing the writing process in the
teaching of literary texts. Only writing is emphasized in this chapter, in order
to address contemporary issues emerging from a specific history and to suggest a few practical solutions. However, real pedagogical change will realize
the potential of comprehensive language activities to increase learning at all
levels and in all subject areas, and, more profoundly, to *create* knowledge by
developing sophisticated understanding of disciplinary discourses.

History of Movements in Writing

The widespread preference for writing courses that focus on self-expression emerges from older debates over process versus product. Until the late 1960s, writing was taught predominantly as a series of rules for students to master and by which teachers might measure their proficiency. However, as Richard Larson reminded us, writing is *purposeful*; it is "an act of communication undertaken by one human being for one or more others"—that is, for an *audience* (1986, p. 111). Over the past 20 years, two movements in writing pedagogy—toward teaching writing as a process and toward teaching writing across the curriculum—have shifted the emphasis from rules to communication. Still, much remains to be done toward developing students' and teachers' understanding of purpose and audience.

On one hand, the practical audience for every student's writing is the teacher; the practical purpose is to communicate what the student has learned (about subject matter, method, etc.). However, the implied audience for the most successful academic writing is much larger: a group of hypothetical readers possessing specific knowledge. The implied purpose is much broader as well: to inform, enlighten, and persuade that audience. The implied audience and purpose form the *context* in which sophisticated writers write; the discourse of the discipline provides the rules for and the parameters within which they write.

The most effective writing pedagogy will help students to understand and manipulate context and discourse by encouraging them to write early and often. Paradoxically, all writing is at one point for an audience of one— the writer. Writing is a unique form of learning (Berthoff, 1978; Emig, 1977) because it allows us to see our thoughts and so develop them (Fulwiler, 1987). However, while education in the United States assigns reading as the key learning activity in every subject from kindergarten through college, it often relegates writing to language studies and/or uses it predominantly as a means to evaluate (Fulwiler, 1987). State-of-the-art pedagogy would redefine reading, writing, speaking, listening, and thinking as complex, interrelated comprehensive language activities (Fulwiler, 1987, p. 11). It would integrate all of these activities both horizontally (across subject areas) and vertically (from kindergarten through college).

New developments in pedagogy often occur in response to perennial problems. Larson's definition emphasizes two: (1) students frequently feel they have little to communicate to an audience, or, when they do have something to communicate, they have little conception of what a given audience expects or needs to know; and (2) teachers frequently do not regard their students' writing as the communication of ideas, and therefore do little to help the student determine the appropriate context for that communication. However, Patrick Hartwell's provocative studies of writers at elementary, secondary, and college levels (Hartwell, 1984, 1985) indicate the difference between "good" and "bad" writing reflects not the mastery of rules but the writers' degree of awareness that they have something to say to someone.

In one study, Hartwell (1984) asked teachers to identify the strong and weak writers in their classes. He then asked all students to define "good" writing. At all grade levels, the students identified as "strong" writers defined good writing as communicating interesting ideas in an interesting way ("They share their thoughts with someone," "They are expressing themselves in a way unlike no other"). Again at all grade levels, students identified as "weak" writers defined good writing as mechanical correctness ("Move their fingers. And write neat," "They put the point of the pencil to the paper and start making words," "Using correct usuage and grammer [sic]") (pp. 56–57). Hartwell's findings suggest that the traditional emphasis on "correctness" and "proficiency" actually reinforces less successful writers' misconceptions about the purpose of writing and undermines writing's potential to develop thought.

The movement to teach writing as *process* developed against this rule-bound, *product*-oriented pedagogy. In product-oriented classes, teachers assign papers and evaluate the finished product (especially for mechanical proficiency), but they never actually discuss how to write beyond generalized discussions of the subject area and/or rules for "good" writing. Such "writing" courses are distinguished from other courses in the subject area by their attention to style, usage, punctuation, and so on. By contrast, in process-oriented classes, teachers demonstrate the actual process of writing, taking students through the successive stages of invention/discovery, organization, composition, revision, and editing. Although these stages are conceived as successive, they are also recursive; writers will usually cycle back through stages, learning as they revise, for example, that they need to reorganize the essay or even to rethink the thesis. Process-oriented classes do not dismiss the importance of mechanics; however, they do place them in perspective and treat them late in the process (during revision and editing). The greatest contribution of the movement toward writing as process is its intense attention to the invention/discovery stage and the writer's ideas. At its best, process-oriented pedagogy subordinates mechanical concerns to the writer's purpose; mechanics become a means to help the writer reach an audience rather than an end by which the writer will be judged.

Because of its valuable attention to ideas, process-oriented pedagogy—informed by two different theories of composition—focuses heavily on the individual writer (Berlin, 1988; Faigley, 1986). The first of these theories, the *expressivist*, identifies good writing with the writer's self-knowledge. Its most well-known proponent, Peter Elbow, has defined writing as a process of self-definition and expression; therefore, he argued, the most important audience is the writer. The title of Elbow's most famous book, *Writing Without Teachers*

(1973), suggests his own attitude toward teaching subject areas in the writing classroom. He believes one has to understand oneself before a subject area will have any relevance.

The other theory of composition, the *cognitivist*, is the slightly older one, and concerns itself less with writing as personal expression and more with identifying the psychological processes of writing. Emig (1971, 1977) and Flower and Hayes (1981) defined and refined the successive stages of the writing process as cognitive "steps" every writer must complete. However, Emig's (1971) observations of twelfth-graders led her to conclusions very compatible with Elbow's. She discovered that students spent more time and care on reflexive writing (writing from their personal experience) than they did on extensive writing (writing based on an imposed content); consequently, she urged greater emphasis on personal writing. Emig's and Elbow's theoretical conclusions have been reinforced by more practical matters. Guiding students through the writing process requires class time. As process-oriented pedagogies have developed, teachers have moved away from subject areas (usually literature) in order to free class time for discussion of writing.

Consequently, the other influential movement in writing pedagogy, toward *writing across the curriculum (WAC)*, has come into an unnecessary and unproductive opposition with process models. The best WAC models implement writing into the teaching of the subject areas and approach writing as a process. However, by definition, WAC is content based, and so less conducive to personal writing. Composition theorists have evaded this contradiction through the largely unfounded assumption that personal writing (including narrative and description) is a necessary first step toward analytical writing. Thus, at the university level, the process model frequently dominates freshman composition courses, with the WAC model reserved for advanced courses. At the elementary and secondary levels, if writing is taught as a process at all, it is taught, again, as personal or creative writing.

Text-Based Writing Pedagogies

With the separation of the teaching of writing from the teaching of subject areas, writing has become increasingly isolated rather than increasingly integrated. (Of course, courses throughout the curriculum use writing to measure achievement—for example, in research papers or essay exams—however, these courses do not *teach* writing but use writing only as a *product*.) Expressive and, to a lesser degree, cognitive theories have, in the very process of emphasizing the writer's ideas, neglected the larger and complex issue of *context*, of the hypothetical audience extending beyond the student/teacher. As a result, the last five years have seen an increasing but controversial demand for the reintegration of writing with the subject areas throughout students' education. The introduction of cultural criticism into freshman composition has been the most prominent example; however, even Lindeman (1993), arguing against writing courses based in only one discipline, acknowledged the need for students to develop "a more self-conscious awareness of their behavior as readers, engaged in significant acts of language in every class they take" (p. 314).

Some 25 years ago, Friere (1970) articulated the necessity of critical thinking skills to free and informed choices. Yet college teachers lament their students' inability to think critically, thus indicating where the prevailing process models have failed. The five problem areas cited most often by faculty at the College of William and Mary are representative: (1) students cannot analyze texts; (2) students are unable to draw their own conclusions from secondary research or to discriminate between useful and nonuseful sources; (3) students cannot recognize assumptions or produce appropriate evidence; (4) students are unable to write fluently, to work through a writer's block or a conceptual problem; and (5) students do not write correctly. Although this last point usually means that students make mechanical errors, the specific problems cited—undeveloped paragraphs, turgid writing styles, even punctuation errors—are problems of content and analysis, broadly conceived. Students are unfamiliar with logical patterns of academic thought, which operate at the level of the sentence as strongly as they do at the level of the thesis.

The inability to analyze, to interpret research, and to identify assumptions result from lack of practice: personal writing does not require the student to grapple with someone else's ideas, to test assumptions (their own or the writer's), to take apart an argument and put it back together again. The lack of fluency, too, suggests their unfamiliarity with the elaborate notetaking and revision that sophisticated writers use when struggling with another's ideas. The failure to produce appropriate evidence, to cite useful sources, or to write "correctly" are problems of reaching out to unknown readers (i.e., of context): of knowing what readers will need explained, what they will accept as proof, what they will assume about the writer based on the form of the writing. These problems can best be solved by students' sustained exposure to subject areas as written discourse.

Indeed, the major flaw in arguments directed against text-based writing courses is that it puts off the student's struggle with others' written discourse indefinitely (or, practically speaking, until the student enters a subject-area course where the written analysis of difficult texts is required but not taught). In her argument against teaching "ideology," Hairston (1992) claimed that students are likely to be intimidated by both the difficulty of the assignments and by their instructors' perspectives on the material. Trimbur, responding to Hairston, noted that delaying difficult encounters "can only have the effect of reproducing students as spectators, perpetually on the verge of being overwhelmed by the experts who have the credentials to speak" (Trimbur et. al., 1993, p. 249). Similarly, Thelin (Trimbur et al., 1993) remarked that "Hairston's patronizing predisposition toward students will forever keep them in the role of timid student, and the self-fulfilling prophecy of students freezing in high-risk situations will be complete" (p. 252). The difficulty of the jump to analytical thinking and writing has for several years been held out as the rationale for personal writing in freshman composition: Students can learn to like writing in a nonthreatening atmosphere. However, it is precisely because of the difficulty of this jump that students need to be prepared for it as early as possible. And in fact, because academic discourses vary, sustained examination of a single-subject area (or of related interdisciplinary areas) over the course of a semester is more likely to give students confidence in that discourse, as well as the tools to encounter a new one, than a 10- or 15-week patchwork introduction to writing in several different fields.

The Integration of Writing into the Curriculum

Integrating writing horizontally and vertically in the curriculum raises potential problems the process model hoped to solve: providing adequate class time for both writing *and* content without increasing the workload of already overburdened teachers. However, this false dilemma assumes that what students learn is equivalent to what teachers say. The notion that more writing means more work is to some degree a holdover from the product model. There, the teacher's task was to evaluate the students' mastery of both form and content, under the mistaken assumption that the more the teacher wrote on the essay, the more students would learn from the experience (Hairston, 1986). True pedagogical change thus demands a rethinking of the implied dichotomy of writing versus subject area, a consequent revision of traditional classroom activities, and a reevaluation of the way instructors comment on and evaluate student writing.

Ideally, the horizontal and vertical integration of writing in the teaching of subject areas would raise students' awareness of the subject area as an evolving discourse—that is, a given method of thinking, speaking, and writing about its subject matter. That discourse is dynamic. It has rules, but those are open to change; it has a given subject matter, but that is continually expanding or contracting. And all changes in the discourse are effected through comprehensive language activities—through analysis, debate, definition, discovery, and so on (Berthoff, 1990; Cooper, 1986; LeFevre, 1987). Only through an intimate familiarity with the important writings of a subject area can students come to understand how a discipline takes form and how it can be changed. Such an understanding is crucial to a truly multicultural education because what counts as "knowledge" changes from culture to culture.

Combining the writing across the curriculum and process models—and, further, integrating all of the "comprehensive language activities" into the teaching of content—can actually decrease time instructors spend on certain activities. Many fewer lectures will need to be prepared and, because students' writing tends to improve overall (they are not beginning assignments at the last minute), there will tend to be fewer mechanical problems. Even more importantly, teaching with writing increases students' competence in subject matter, their long-term retention, and their ability to manipulate the knowledge-base of the discipline (Fulwiler, 1987).

The successive stages of the process—invention/discovery, organization, composition, revision, editing—are easily applied to teaching with writing in the subject areas. Described here are general techniques that instructors might employ at each stage, and included in the appendix at the end of the chapter are a few exercises specifically designed for Ernest Hemingway's short story "Hills Like White Elephants."

Invention/Discovery

Instructors can use writing at this stage in two related ways. First, daily writing assignments increase learning (Fulwiler, 1987), even if those assignments are never graded, commented on, or even collected. For example, each day, the instructor might assign a different student to record the crucial points of a day's discussion; students might keep double-entry learning logs in which they take discussion notes in one column and summarize or raise questions about those notes in a second column (legal-rule paper is particularly useful here); they might work in problem-solving groups or read-arounds in which they develop group responses (Schenk, 1986; Nystrand, 1987). Such assignments are most successful when instructors treat them as informal writing— that is, when instructors do not evaluate papers based on concerns of form— although students can profit from constructive comments about repeated difficulties. If instructors wish to introduce *formal* in-class writing, they might ask students to write *microthemes* (short essays written on 5 x 8 index cards that help students to articulate important concepts [e.g., definitions] in a concise and exact form) or *response papers* (one- or two-page explorations of a particular question or further developing a point that came up in class).

Instructors can use these invention/discovery exercises to generate ideas for papers; in addition, they can teach freewriting (Elbow, 1973) and brainstorming as ways of developing theses. Equally important, instructors can build from or adapt informal exercises to help students learn strategies for taking notes on the texts they will write about and research methods appropriate to the discipline. The double-entry learning log, for example, can be used to teach notetaking. Instructors might ask students to write down quotations in one column (from either primary or secondary sources, depending on the assignment) and then to write their own questions or analyses in the margins. Or instructors might require a summary of either primary or secondary texts. They might then ask students to develop questions about the summary that would lead to analysis. (This exercise not only improves students' grasp of the content but it also teaches the crucial distinction between summary and analysis.)

Organization

One of the best ways to teach organization is to ask students to outline a text they will write about, then to answer questions about the organization (e.g., What did the writer have to explain in the second paragraph before we could understand the third?). Students might work in groups to outline the primary text, then discuss how a different organization would change the text; they might also work in writing groups to develop and revise their own outlines based on feedback from their peers.

Composition

This stage is the most individualized—the stage in which the student actually fleshes out the planned paper. Even at this stage, however, group work can prove useful. Students might compose one essay together, keeping track of when and why they have to return to an earlier stage of the writing process. Students should be made especially aware during the composition and revision stages that they will need to return repeatedly to their primary and/ or secondary sources in order to qualify interpretations or supply more evidence.

Revision

Students, even at the college level, can seldom articulate the difference between revising and editing (Sommers, 1980). Instructors need to explain and, where possible, demonstrate that difference, as well as the importance of moving from large-scale to small-scale concerns (Sommers, 1982). Writing groups are particularly useful at this stage (see Lunsford, 1986) because they provide individual writers with an audience that will have questions, need clarifications, and raise arguments. Group tasks should be clearly defined, such as helping the writer develop and qualify arguments or working specifically on revising for emphasis at the sentence level. This stage is the most logical for discussions of paragraphing and style. Instructors can show how the topic sentence of a paragraph, or the main idea of a sentence, is analogous to the thesis in an essay (Lanham, 1987; Crews, 1987). In order to address students' particular needs, instructors might also organize individual conferences during class time, while other students compose or work in groups (Beach, 1986; Harris, 1986).

Editing

Students should learn that although this is the last stage of their writing process, it is frequently the first thing a reader will notice—editing is like dressing for dinner. Instructors should realize that students may find the task of editing overwhelming, given the handbooks full of arbitrary rules about modifiers, commas, and so on. (Indeed, instructors should admit that many rules are simply conventional and that professional writers use handbooks and style sheets rather than memorizing these rules.) Editing groups might read for specific problems, and, where possible, articulate the logic behind certain rules. Instructors should be careful to approach usage and punctuation as logically as possible. For example, commas make sense once the student understands the relationship between the main idea (often the independent clause) and subordinate elements—until the student understands that relationship, teaching comma placement will be frustrating and largely futile. Also, instructors should focus on patterns of error and causes of error rather than on rules or simple correction (Shaughnessy, 1977; Hartwell, 1985; Harris & Rowan, 1989). In all cases, instructors should subordinate mechanical concerns to those of *content*.

Assessment of Student Writing

As teachers rethink what students do in class, they should also rethink the ways they assign, comment on, and assess their students' writing. They should clearly articulate the tasks students must complete, the purpose of the assignment, the relationship of the assignment to the content and/or method under discussion, and their criteria for assessment (Larson, 1986). Each student should submit at least one draft for the instructor to comment on and return for revision; instructors' comments should focus the student's idea: Where does the student need to expand, qualify, return to sources? As much as possible, comments on mechanics should relate to the formal problem, to the logic of the essay. For example, the sentence "It is clear that if you read carefully words are used by Hemingway in an interesting way" seems to indicate a stylistic problem. Actually, this student has nothing yet to say— when he or she finds an idea, the stylistic problems should clear up. Studies on effective comments and evaluation (Sommers, 1982; Hairston, 1986; Anson, 1989) suggest that fewer, carefully selected comments, coupled with increased attention to the student's specific location in the writing process (North, 1982), are much more effective than the massive, time-consuming corrections that characterize essays graded under the product model.

Finally, portfolio analysis (Belanoff & Elbow, 1986; Faigley, Sherry, Jolliffe, & Skinner, 1985) can reinforce the importance of revision and lend instructors' comments more relevance. Portfolios may be submitted at specified points during the semester and always at the end. If an instructor assigns 20 informal exercises and five formal papers during a semester, for example, he or she might require that the final portfolio contain three of the formal papers, revised once more, and five of the student's best informal writings, also revised to formal. None of the student's writing would have been graded to this point; however, the instructor would have commented on all of the formal assignments, assuming they would be revised for the portfolio. Thus, students would receive grades only on the work submitted in the portfolio or on the portfolio plus objective tests. The portfolio thus teaches students that writing is an ongoing process; it prevents students from submitting papers written at the last minute and it gradually increases the student's while decreasing the teacher's participation in the revision process.

Writing pedagogy should help students to understand and manipulate the context in which they write—that is, their extended audience and larger purpose—by integrating writing with the teaching of content areas throughout the curriculum, and from kindergarten through college. Such integration will increase learning in the classroom as it helps students develop critical thinking skills. Practically, implementing a curriculum that teaches with writing will require rethinking the best uses of both classroom and instructor time. Real change will occur only when writing is regarded as but one of the integrally related comprehensive language activities crucial to education in all subject areas.

Key Points Summary

- The emphasis of classroom writing needs to become more integrated with content analysis and less with student self-expression.
- Writing process emphases and writing across the curriculum have underemphasized the importance of contextual analysis in communicating ideas.
- Writing is frequently used as a product of evaluation apart from the teaching of it.

- Writing problems in students cited frequently by college instructors include faulty use of critical thinking and analysis skills, lack of fluency, and mechanical problems in organization and style.
- Students need extensive practice with the critical analysis of texts as preparation for advanced work in any discipline. Not teaching it early merely delays the start of a necessary process for substantive learning.
- Writing defines subject areas. For students to master any content area, they must actively grapple with the writings that continue to define an area.
- Teaching with writing deepens content understanding and long-term retention; in such a model, writing is a part of an integrated comprehensive set of activities used to enhance student learning.
- Daily writing activities enhance learning. The use of microthemes, read-arounds, and double-entry logs provide needed practice without the perceived censure of assessment.
- Developing an outline of how texts are organized is an important tool for teaching good written organization.
- Composition work may be best accomplished in small problem-solving groups.
- Revision needs to be viewed as large scale and small scale, attending to broad organizational considerations as well as sentence-specific concerns.
- Editing should focus students on mechanical problems of their work.
- Assessment of student writing should set criteria, focus the writer for further work (given the stage of the writing process), and employ portfolio analysis techniques.

Appendix

The following sample exercises are based on Ernest Hemingway's short story, "Hills Like White Elephants":

Invention/Discovery

The Read-Around

1. Divide students into groups of five. Ask each student to write, at the top of a sheet of notebook paper, a question he or she has about the story. (These should be legitimate questions, not ones the students know the answer to or ones that cannot be answered based on the story.)
2. After they have written their questions, each student should pass his or her question to the left. Each student attempts to answer the question he or she received in three to five sentences, writing immediately beneath the question.

3. When the students are finished answering, each passes the question once more to the left. The next student reads the question and the answer, then, in three to five sentences, offers a different answer or explains why he or she agrees with the first student's answer.

4. The questions are then returned to the students who initially wrote them. Each student reads aloud the question and the two answers. When all the questions have been read, the group picks what it feels to be the two most important questions and writes a group response to each, developing or qualifying the two answers already written.

The Microtheme

1. Ask students to reply on a 5 × 8 index card: "What is the 'awfully simple operation' the man wants Jig to undergo? Since the operation is never named, explain what in the story leads you to your conclusion."

2. Students may revise once. Answers will be evaluated for ideas, conciseness, and correctness.

The Research Exercise

1. Give students *citations only* to three accessible articles in your school or public library about Hemingway's misogynistic portrayal of women.

2. Ask them to (a) read and summarize one of those articles; (b) look up one other article that the first cites, excluding the three you provided initially; and (c) write a response paper using Hemingway's portrayal of Jig to support or refute the two articles.

3. This paper might be developed into a formal one (e.g., a character analysis or a research paper on Hemingway) or it might be one that a student could choose to revise for his or her portfolio.

The Focused Freewriting

1. Write for five minutes, *without stopping,* on the significance of Hemingway's title.

Organization

1. Divide students into groups of five. Ask them to list events they hear about in the story but that occurred *before* the conversation in the railway station. "What is the real chronology of those events? In what order does Hemingway present them to the reader? Why does he present them in this way—how does the order of presentation determine what the reader focuses on?" Ask students to rearrange the events in some way (e.g., in strict chronology). "How would that rearrangement alter the reader's focus? With what effect?" Each group should prepare a two-page response to present to the rest of the class.

2. Give students 10 minutes in class to draw a rough outline from their focused freewriting toward a short essay explaining the significance of

the title. Then have them present their outlines to each other in groups of three, focusing on whether each step presents the readers with sufficient information to allow them to move to the next one. Students might begin to flesh out the outline as they discuss the problem in groups.

Composition

1. Ask students to prepare their first drafts as homework. Alternatively, students might return to their groups of three, select the best outline, and develop the paper as a group. One student in the group should record how often and why the group has to return to the story to develop the paper.

Revision

1. Ask students, in groups of five, to analyze the style of the first paragraph. Ask them to arrange the sentences in more complex patterns, reducing the six sentences to three or four by subordinating clauses and eliminating repetition. Then ask them how a change in style would change the tone or effect of the description.
2. Have students discuss their papers in groups of three (or, if they have written a group paper, ask groups to exchange papers). Students should comment, the first time, on *content only*, noting where they disagree with an interpretation and why, where they need more evidence to believe an interpretation, and where they don't understand a point. After writers or groups revise once, they should again present their papers the following day. Groups should now work on small-scale revisions: undeveloped paragraphs, sentences lacking emphasis, and so on. If this is a formal assignment, students should then present their drafts to the instructor for comment and further revision.

Editing

1. Use the first paragraph of the story to teach comma punctuation. Ask students to identify where Hemingway left commas out; repunctuate the sentence "correctly" and discuss the effect on the description (or add the commas to "Would you please please please please please please please stop talking?").
2. After you have returned their drafts and students have revised again, have them work on a specific problem (e.g., comma punctuation) in groups of three. For example, if a writer leaves out commas for stylistic effect, ask the others in the group to evaluate the effectiveness. *Note*: This problem, and others you have specifically addressed on previous assignments, should be the only mechanical concerns these groups address.

References

Anson, C. M. (1989). *Writing and response: Theory, practice, and research*. Urbana, IL: NCTE.

Beach, R. (1986). Demonstrating techniques of assessing writing in the writing conference. *College Composition and Communication, 37,* 56–65.

Belanoff, P., & Elbow, P. (1986). Using portfolios to increase collaborative learning and community in a writing program. *WPA, 9,* 27–40.

Berlin, J. (1988). Rhetoric and ideology in the writing class. *College English, 50,* 477–494.

Berthoff, A. E. (1978). *Thinking/forming/writing: The composing imagination*. Rochelle Park, NJ: Hayden.

Berthoff, A. E. (1990). *A sense of learning*. Portsmouth, NH: Heineman.

Bridges, C. (Ed.). (1986). *Training the new teacher of college composition*. Urbana, IL: NCTE.

Cooper, M. M. (1986). The ecology of writing. *College English, 48,* 367–375.

Crews, F. (1987). Sentences. *The Random House handbook* (5th ed., pp. 163–177). New York: Random House.

Elbow, P. (1973). *Writing without teachers*. New York: Oxford University Press.

Emig, J. (1971). *The composing process of twelfth graders*. Urbana, IL: NCTE.

Emig, J. (1977). Writing as a mode of learning. *College Composition and Communication, 28,* 122–128.

Faigley, L. (1986). Competing theories of process: A critique and a proposal. *College English, 48,* 527–542.

Faigley, L., Sherry, R. D., Jolliffe, D. A., & Skinner, A. M. (1985). *Assessing writer's knowledge and processes of composing*. Norwood, NJ: Ablex.

Flower, L., & Hayes, J. (1981). A cognitive process theory of writing. *College Composition and Communication, 32,* 365–387.

Friere, P. (1970). *Pedagogy of the oppressed*. New York: Herder and Herder.

Fulwiler, T. (1987). *Teaching with writing*. Portsmouth, NH: Heineman.

Hairston, M. (1986). On not being a composition slave. In C. Bridges (Ed.), *Training the new teacher of college composition* (pp. 117–124). Urbana, IL: NCTE.

Hairston, M. (1992). Diversity, ideology, and teaching writing. *College Composition and Communication, 43,* 179–193.

Harris, M. (1986). *Teaching one to one: The writing conference*. Urbana, IL: NCTE.

Harris, M., & Rowan, K. E. (1989). Explaining grammatical concepts. *Journal of Basic Writing, 6,* 21–41.

Hartwell, P. (1984). The writing center and paradoxes of written-down speech. In Gary Olson (Ed.), *Writing centers, theory and administration*. Urbana, IL: NCTE.

Hartwell, P. (1985). Grammar, grammars, and the teaching of grammar. *College English, 47,* 105-127.

Hemingway, E. (1927). *Men without women*. New York: Charles Scribner's Sons.

Lanham, R. (1987). *Revising prose* (2nd ed.). New York: Macmillan.

Larson, R. (1986). Making assignments, judging writing, and annotating papers: Some suggestions. In C. Bridges (Ed.), *Training the new teacher of college composition* (pp. 109–116). Urbana, IL: NCTE.

LeFevre, K. B. (1987). *Invention as a social act*. Carbondale: Southern Illinois University Press.

Lindeman, E. (1993). Freshman composition: No place for literature. *College English, 55,* 311–316.

Lunsford, R. (1986). Planning for spontaneity in the writing classroom and a passel of other paradoxes. In C. Bridges (Ed.), *Training the new teacher of college composition* (pp. 95–107). Urbana, IL: NCTE.

North, S. (1982). Training tutors to talk about writing. *College Composition and Communication, 33,* 434–439.

Nystrand, M. (1987). *Using informal writing to teach critical thinking.* Unpublished paper.

Schenk, M. J. (1986). Writing right off: Strategies for invention. In C. Bridges (Ed.), *Training the new teacher of college composition* (pp. 84–94). Urbanam, IL: NCTE.

Shaughnessy, M. P. (1977). *Errors and expectations.* New York: Oxford University Press.

Sommers, N. (1980). Revision strategies of student writers and experienced adult writers. *College Composition and Communication, 31,* 378–388.

Sommers, N. (1982). Responding to student writing. *College Composition and Communication, 33,* 148–156.

Tate, G. (1993). A place for literature in freshman composition. *College English, 55,* 317–321.

Trimbur, J., Wood, R. G., Strickland, R., Thelin, W. H., Rouster, W. J., Mester, T., Hairston, M., Voss, R. E., & Behrens, L. (1993). Counterstatement: Responses to Maxine Hairston, diversity, ideology, and teaching writing. *College Composition and Communication, 44,* 248–257.

9

Formal Language Study for Gifted Students

MICHAEL CLAY THOMPSON
University School of Jackson

In *Growing Up Gifted*, Barbara Clark (1988) reported a typical-sounding conversation between a grandmother and her granddaughter:

"I'm playing with my chalkboard."
"You are?"
"Yes. I played with it yesterday, too."
"Really?"
"Don't you remember? You gave it to me for my happy birthday last Wednesday."

What makes the conversation *atypical*, and significant, is that at the time of the conversation, the granddaughter was less than 2 years old—22 months to be precise. This loquacious toddler's verbal precocity illustrates, as would a thousand other similar stories, the need for what has been called a *differentiated curriculum*. Unfortunately, there has been little agreement about what a differentiated curriculum should contain. Amid increasing calls for rigor and substance, there is widespread agreement that a differentiated curriculum should contain advanced and enhanced reading and writing opportunities, but there is less consensus about what should be read or what should be written.

On the subject of formal language study—including grammar, vocabulary, and other elements to be discussed here—little has been written. In fact, formal language study sometimes receives no mention at all, even in discussions of language arts for the gifted. Gallagher (1975), for example, emphasized reading and the incorporation of values education into language arts. Clark (1988) focused on bibliotherapy and the use of mind maps, developed by Buzan, to assist individualization and improve reading skills. A review of *Gifted Child Quarterly* and *Roeper Review* from 1987 to the present reveals no article in either publication specifically addressing the role of formal language study in the education of gifted students, except for one article on orthography (Olson, Logan, & Lindsey, 1988). It should not be inferred that these and other leading scholars in the field of gifted education do not support formal language study in gifted education; rather, this seems to be an area that remains to be addressed through research. Thus far, research as it refers to language arts in gifted education has concentrated on other important issues: the identification of students who are gifted in language arts, on language arts as one of a multitude of possible forms of giftedness, and on the difficulties associated with identifying some minority and disadvantaged gifted children who might not exhibit superior abilities in language arts. The *Journal for the Education of the Gifted* devoted a Spring 1991 special edition to the "underserved gifted" who might not qualify for gifted programs based on traditional, highly verbal identification instruments (Coleman, 1991).

In recent years, however, strong support for language study in gifted education has come from VanTassel-Baska and colleagues (1988), Parker (1989), and Thompson (1991b). Parker has stressed the importance of morphology, orthography, syntax, and vocabulary development. In addition to stressing the importance of foreign language, VanTassel-Baska noted that a "sound verbal arts program for the gifted needs to include a strong language study element that allows students to understand the English language from a variety of perspectives." (p. 167) Recommended perspectives include syntax, usage, vocabulary development, analogies, etymology, semantics, linguistics, and the history of language.

The fundamental question, then, becomes, Is language study an essential component of the education of the verbally talented, and if so, why?

The unambiguous and resounding answer to this question is that language study is absolutely essential for cogent reasons that can be articulated to anyone's satisfaction. In examining these reasons, I will consider two areas that are traditionally included in discussions of language study: grammar (syntax) and vocabulary (diction, etymology, analogy), and a third area that is not usually, but must be, included in the discussion: poetics, by which I mean, not the study of poetry but the study of aesthetic language structures that interact with and have an impact on syntax. Meaning is accomplished through systematic constructions of grammar, diction, and poetics.

Must we study language? Yes. We are all familiar with numerous, important, practical reasons, frequently cited, for studying language: It prepares the student for advanced intellectual work of all forms, it is necessary to the art of good writing, it is necessary for the advanced levels of communication required in many exciting professions. These reasons are as valid and significant as their advocates believe.

But there are other, even more profound reasons why language must be studied, and it is these reasons that will mean most to gifted children, to whom every living moment seems to be a quest for understanding. *Language is a medium for the mind.* As water to fish, or air to birds, words and sentences are the substance through which our ideas glide. Language is the ecosphere of the mind. Our thoughts pass from sentence to sentence, our thoughts stream forth in sequences of sentences, we receive the thoughts of others in streams of sentences, and we exist continually in a personal, social, and technological environment of sentences. Not to know about language is to be ignorant of the very medium we inhabit. In addition, *language is a manifestation of the mind.* Through spoken and printed language, we may know ourselves, and we may know the selves of others, both living and dead. The complexity, order, and clarity of our syntax; the subtlety, originality, and variety of our diction; the sensitivity, gentility, and aesthetics of our expression—these things reveal, even to ourselves, who we are, what we think about, what we care about, and what the contents of our inmost personalities are. The Oracle of Delphi's dictum, *know thyself,* would be difficult to implement in the absence of language. And for thousands of years, it is this dictum that has, above the myriad mundane concerns of economy and practicality, motivated the still-fundamental concerns of human imagination, which we know by the names of science, philosophy, mathematics, poetry, history, art, music, and literature.

Language study, in other words, is no less a fundamental probing of being than astronomy or microbiology. Therefore, if we ask what is the state of the art in language study, the answer, in part, is that the state of the art is humility in the face of the mysterious. What has been profound remains profound. We are still exploring, still sailing forth into phenomena of language that are yet unnamed, unmapped, or unsuspected. It is wonderful that this is so, that language continues to be a great subject, exciting and fresh. We must remind ourselves that in exploring a thing so wondrous, a state of wonder is highly appropriate: In all language study, a mental state akin to play, to happy exploration, is important. Torrance and Myers (1970) have emphasized the importance of making the familiar strange, and of playing with words and playing with metaphor, and of overcoming the "work-play dichotomy" that makes it sinful to have fun working. Students who study language through poetics, grammar, or etymology should be led to the edge of the deep, probing into the internal organs of sentences as into the protoplasm of protozoans.

In considering the role of formal language study for verbally talented learners, note the following:

- Such students frequently have abilities in language that language study will enhance.
- Language study is a complex, abstract, subtle, and aesthetically resonant content appropriate for them.
- Language study is an inherently interdisciplinary curriculum that will give students insights into virtually all other curricula.
- Language study is an enabling curriculum that will strengthen students' abilities in all other curricula and invigorate their powers of articulation for all purposes.
- Language study is both a method for and an example of higher-order thinking.
- Language study is a form of self-exploration.

Grammar

What is grammar? It is a curious fact that, if asked this question, many veteran students of grammar would be unable to answer. Others would answer by example, saying that it was the study of nouns, verbs, and so on. But why do we study parts of speech, and phrases, and clauses? Because *grammar is a way of thinking about language*. It is an untouted, but superb, form of higher-order thinking. Using grammar, we can think about our ideas, because our ideas are captured in the amber of sentences, where grammar allows us to name their parts, consider their rearrangement, examine the way they are made, and discover their secrets of originality and creativity.

An explanation of the elements of grammar is, of course, beyond the scope of this chapter, but there are a number of points that should be made about the place of grammar in education.

Critical and Creative Thinking

Like logic, mathematics, and creative problem solving, grammar is a rigorous method of higher-order thinking. It is an exceptional tool for making logical, structural, and aesthetic decisions in writing and speaking one's own ideas. Grammar is also an exceptional tool for investigating the differences in style between authors or for peering into the loveliness of a line of poetry.

How does grammar accomplish these things? By bringing the phenomena of thought out of the shadowy realm of spontaneous and intuitive utterance, and into the light of consciousness. With grammar, we learn to identify the parts of ideas, to give them names, to analyze their various functions, and to reflect on their characteristics and benefits. Once these things—such as subjects, direct objects, adverbs, infinitive phrases, and subordinate clauses—have become visible, friendly phenomena, we are suddenly in a position to make critical and aesthetic decisions about them. We know what we are doing. Of course, there are risks: Shakespeare's slobbery monster Caliban rebukes Prospero by saying, "You taught me language, and my profit on't is I know how to curse!"

Interpretation

Because grammar is so often studied as a thing-in-itself—an intellectual amputation severed from its context of living ideas in literature, poetry, and other forms of language—it is easy for us to forget what a decisive analytical thinking technique grammar can be in the interpretation of literature and poetry. Because sentences are ideas, to disclose the sentence's grammar is to disclose the idea's architecture. This disclosing of the underlying construction of the sentence can provide the conclusive insight into the meaning of a poem. Consider, for example, Carl Sandburg's (1956) micromasterpiece, "Splinter":

Splinter

The voice of the last cricket
Across the first frost
Is one kind of goodbye.
It is so thin a splinter of singing.

As we read Sandburg's tiny poem for the first time, we inevitably underestimate it. Why, we even wonder, is this considered to be a poem? If we read it aloud, it sounds like prose, like two simple declarative sentences any middle school student might write. Gradually, however, we begin to notice things. The internal rhyme of *across* and *frost* appears first, followed by the assonance of *kind* and *goodbye* in line three. We notice the short *ih* sound in the words of line four: *it, is, thin, splin, sing.* Well, we think, at least it is a poem. But further examination begins to reveal more wonderful wonders. We hear the music of the frost in the *st* crackles of line two: fir*st*, fro*st*.. And then we notice the beautiful secret of the poem: the singing voice of the cricket: s, s, s, s. The cricket's small chirps rise to our attention: The voi**C**e of the la**St** cricket/Acro**SS** the fir**St** fro**St**/**IS**.... Then, sadly, the cricket's song is gone: *one kind of goodbye.* Having noticed the lovely, small chirp in lines one and two, we miss it in line three. Sandburg's poem now seems rich in music, filled with little-suspected, beautifully concealed touches of genius. Our minds are filled with the scene and the song; we can feel the crunch of the frosty ground beneath our feet, and we poignantly miss the small cricket whose voice was there before but now is gone.

And yet, all of this thinking is not deep enough. Without realizing it, we are still thinking in predictable ways, using our glossary of poetic terms to help us investigate a poem. We are imagining that poetry is self-contained— just as when we study grammar, we imagine that grammar is self-contained. We "disremember" literature and poetry when we study grammar, and we disremember grammar when we study poetry.

Only when we bring the analytic power of grammar into the interpretation of Sandburg's poem do we achieve the decisive insight that transforms the small vignette into a big wisdom. We begin by viewing the poem not as four lines but as two sentences. In the first sentence, we find nothing remarkable at the parts of speech level. It is at the parts of sentence level that the meaning emerges. The subject of the sentence is *voice*, the verb/simple predicate is the linking verb *is*, and having found a linking verb, we look for a subject complement and find one: *kind.* Voice is kind:

subj   pred   subj comp

The **voice** of the last cricket across the first frost **is** one **kind** of goodbye.

Now, under the clear, magic lens of grammar, we see the poem's real idea emerge, and we are not distracted by the beauty of the poetic art or by the imaginative projections of our own minds. This poem, the parts of the sentence reveal, is not about crickets, or frost, or quaint American landscapes. The word *cricket* is nothing but the object of a prepositional phrase. The cricket's song is only one small illustration of a much larger phenomenon—it is only a *kind*, one kind mind you, of *goodbye*. This is a poem about the goodbyes of life, about *all* of the songs, the friends, the moments that are gone and that will not come again. For each of us, as human beings, time moves in one direction, and everything we cherish is deceptively fragile, just a thin splinter of singing. Loved ones, periods in our lives, aspects of ourselves, a thousand things that are important to us—all of these will vanish and cease, like the *s, s, s, s* of the cricket's thin song. Under the magic lens, the small poem's big meaning is laid bare. Far from being a local, rural, insignificant poem about the poignant charms of the fall, it is a deceptively deep poem, forcing our minds to the universal limits and losses of life. The natural comparison for Sandburg's poem is not in some anthology of poems of the American landscape but in Shakespeare's *The Tempest,* in which an Elizabethan genius saw in the evanescence of theater a metaphor for the fragility of life. In the character Prospero's words:

Our revels now are ended. These our actors,
As I foretold you, were all spirits, and
Are melted into air, into thin air.
And, like the baseless fabric of this vision,
The cloud-capped towers, the gorgeous palaces,
The solemn temples, the great globe itself—
Yea, all which it inherit—shall dissolve
And, like this insubstantial pageant faded,
Leave not a rack behind. We are such stuff
As dreams are made on, and our little life
Is rounded with a sleep.

Clarity Clarified

In contrast to its reputation as an arid, definitional subject, grammar is actually a source of profound insight into the meaning of clarity. Like ancient cosmic rays that give contemporary astronomers a ghostly after-image of the big bang (George Gamow's alliterative term), the ordinary sentence—the simple device in which we place our every thought—contains a ghostly image of the hidden binary nature of intellectual being. At the center of the seemingly infinite variations of form that sentences take, there is an astounding consistency: the subject/predicate binary structure. This most common and therefore least appreciated subject/predicate structure, so pure in its simplicity and so well known that its meaning is unsuspected, suggests the two simple things the mind always needs for clarity: *what you are talking about* and *what you are saying about it.* At the sentence level, what is your subject and what are you predicating? At the paragraph level, what is your subject and what are you predicating? At the topic level, what is your subject and what are you predicating? The sentence is a model of the mind; its two parts are the mind's two needs.

This beautiful simplicity at the core of every thought is the very sort of idea that has magnetic appeal for verbally talented learners. When Crick and Watson were searching for the secret of life in the structure of the DNA molecule, they let their search be guided by the strong conviction that the guiding molecule of life would not be an ugly, amorphous molecule, a misshapen tangle, but would be something beautiful—and so it was. The double helix with its twin spirals is both a biological and an aesthetic miracle, a gorgeous secret to the vast biological complexity of our planet. In a precisely similar way, the vast complexities of human thought structures have in common the beautiful subject/predicate nucleus which, if it is understood and appreciated, yields understanding of the very essence of clarity.

Grammar Is Not Self-Contained

Grammar serves meaning, and not conversely. You cannot seek within grammar for the all causes of grammatical structure; these causes are often external. A sentence will not be simple, complex, or compound because of the rules of grammar; it will have clause structure suitable to the needs of the ideas to be communicated. The reason for the structure does not lie within the structure. Rather, the rules of grammar are such that they bend themselves to the needs of meaning and poetics—and these determine the success of the communication. There may be a series of short, simple sentences because the essential nature of the moment to be communicated—say, Cornwall's dying gasps in Shakespeare's *King Lear*—requires a series of terrible silences that position themselves tragically *between* the sentences: "I have received a hurt. Follow me, lady. Turn out that eyeless villain; throw this slave upon the dunghill. Regan, I bleed apace. Untimely comes this hurt; give me your arm." There is nothing, internal to grammar, that dictates the use of these staccato, clipped sentences; rather, it is Cornwall's pain, his inability to utter more than a few words at a breath, that explains the syntax. Cornwall has been stabbed, and in his only 31 wounded words, there are seven clauses, five periods, two commas, and two semicolons. The passage has an average of only four words per clause. It is not Cornwall's words that communicate his agony, but rather the *interwords* that dictate his constricted grammar, forcing itself into the gaps between his death spasms: "I have received a hurt / / / / / / / / / / / / Follow me / / / / / / / / / / / / / / / lady / / / / / / / / / / / / / / / / Turn out that eyeless villain / / / / / / / / / / / throw this slave upon the dunghill / / / / / / / / / / / / / / Regan / / / / / / / / / / / I bleed apace / Untimely comes this hurt / / / / / / / / / / / / / / / / / / / give me your arm." Clearly, the secret of Cornwall's grammar cannot be internally analyzed within the system of grammar itself; rather, the grammar is not a function of itself but of the character's experience: His small gasps of sentence are all he can manage between his large gasps of death.

The example of Cornwall vividly illustrates another insufficiently contemplated aspect of language study—the extraordinary meaning and power of punctuation. Somehow, we give the impression that, say, a comma is a minor technical element that is the object of a small group of rules, and that the whole comma business is wrapped up quickly, like a vo-tech wiring diagram. But in every period and comma of Cornwall's death there is an abyss. One is tempted to suggest that there are as many kinds of commas as there are words, and that a vast and subtle masterpiece could be written on the taxonomy of commas and the profound psychological and spiritual states that they are forced to represent. "Regan," Cornwall whispers, looking to his wife for concern only to see that is not in her countenance, "I bleed apace." What a comma is there.

The Impossible Simplicity Paradox

The paradox of teaching basic, traditional grammar is that it is a small and simple subject that is impossible for students to master. In fact, teachers have had such difficulty teaching basic grammar that many have abandoned the effort, and it is not uncommon to read articles in professional publications advocating the abandonment of grammar instruction. This paradox can be overcome by realizing that grammar is a subject that is not safely sampled. Like a light, it does not come on until all of the wires are connected. Once students have understood all four levels of traditional grammar—parts of speech and parts of the sentence, phrases, and clauses—and have repeatedly used all four levels to examine various sentences, the apparent difficulty of grammar dissolves into a clarity and enthusiasm for looking again at more sentences. Four-level grammar analysis should be applied regularly to sentences from poems and novels, as well as to sentences written by students themselves.

In this connection, note that sentence diagraming, although it has (often beautiful) merits, also has its limitations. It does not graphically analyze the four levels (parts of speech, parts of sentence, phrases, and clauses) that we use in traditional grammar to analyze a sentence. For example, a sentence diagram of Shakespeare's (1967) famous sentence from *Romeo and Juliet*—"A pair of star-crossed lovers take their life"—would look like this:

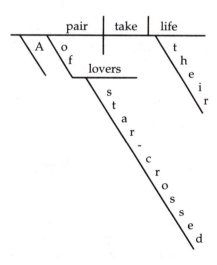

Certainly, the diagram illustrates features of the architecture of Shakespeare's idea. We clearly see the main terms of the sentence, and we see the modifying elements vividly depending from the modified. There is benefit.

On the other hand, the four levels of grammar are visually grouped together into a single form and, more serious, the diagram seems to obscure the essential subject/predicate basis of the idea. The long horizontal line assumes a primary visual importance, allowing the all-important vertical line separating subject from predicate to recede into visual insignificance. In the interest of revealing the binary nature of ideas, we might wish that diagraming called for something more like this:

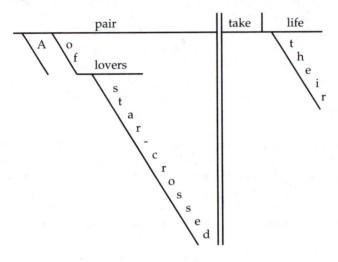

In any case, it is possible for students to diagram a sentence while still failing to understand a great deal about the words and groups of words that they are considering. A different method is to do a four-level analysis:

	A	pair	of	star-crossed	lovers	take	their	life.
Parts of Speech:	adj.	n.	prep	adj.	n.	v.	pron.	n.
Parts of Sentence:		subj.				pred.		direct object
Phrases:				---prepositional phrase---				
Clauses:		Simple, declarative sentence						

Both the diagram and the four-level analysis have their advantages. But notice that much still remains to be said about this sentence. We have not yet noted that *pair* is a common noun or that *their* is a possessive pronoun, which is sometimes called a possessive adjective. We have not indicated whether the nouns in the sentence are plural or singular, concrete or abstract. We have not identified the nature of the preposition (time? space? direction?). We have not indicated the verb tense. But imagine what students would gain from an elaborate Socratic discussion of this sentence, in which the teacher used only questions to have students discover all of the information, beginning with a four-level analysis and ending with a sentence diagram. Imagine that the teacher has just read *Romeo and Juliet* with the students, and they have discussed it to an appropriate depth. The session might begin like this:

Teacher: Now look at this sentence from *Romeo and Juliet* that I have written on the board. Let's examine the grammar of the sentence. What is grammar?

Students: A way of thinking about language.

Teacher: How many levels are there in traditional grammar?

Students: Four.

Teacher: What is the first level?

Students: Parts of speech.

Teacher: What do you mean by parts of speech?

Students: The eight kinds of words in our language.

Teacher: List them for me in a sensible order.

Students: Noun, pronoun, adjective—verb, adverb—preposition, conjunction, interjection.

Teacher: Good. (As students answer, the teacher writes the abbreviations of the parts of speech on the line below the sentence.) What part of speech is *A*?

Students: An adjective.

Teacher: Pair?

Students: Noun.

Teacher: Singular or plural?

Students: Singular.

In this way, the session continues, with the teacher asking detailed questions about the elements as he or she fills in the four-level analysis, followed eventually by the diagram. All of the obvious variations, such as having a student lead the grammar catechism once the class knows the procedure, or having a student come up to do the diagram, work well. This procedure gives students a complete, comprehensive picture, not just of the sentence but of grammar itself. In examining a sentence this way, students finally escape the trees to see the forest, and they realize that traditional grammar is a small, learnable system that yields wonderful insights into the secrets of ideas. Grammar does not have to be an impossible simplicity; it can be simple and possible.

Withholding Grammar

The impossible simplicity of grammar is also a function of the seemingly sensible practice of protracting grammar study throughout the year—studying parts of speech during the first academic quarter, parts of the sentence the second, phrases the third, and clauses the fourth. The effect of this well-intentioned and sincere method is academic catastrophe; it is a method of language study that obstructs the goal of language study: Students cannot use in October what they will not learn until May. Grammar must be studied in its entirety at the beginning of the academic year, and then used throughout the year as a *way of thinking about language* as it occurs in poems, plays, novels, and student writing. Once a four-level review has been completed in September, every sentence examined thereafter serves as a reminder that deepens a student's understanding of grammar's exciting analytical power. Teachers who pride themselves on their year-long thorough and systematic study of grammar should understand that talented students grasp concepts and need applications with astonishing swiftness; these students do not need a protracted trek. An excellent three-week grammar program in September will equip students to study language all year long.

Process and Content

Rote memory is as fatal to the study of grammar as it is to everything else; the study of grammar must be as fully human as possible. The ideas of grammar form an excellent content to which excellent processes must be applied, including such commonly encouraged thinking processes as cognition, synthesis, divergence, analysis, emotion, intuition, imagination, evaluation, aesthetics, and application.

It is important to understand that grammar is beautifully suitable to Socratic teaching, that a sentence is what I refer to as a *Socratic object*, and that an open-ended discussion developing possible alternative descriptions of the grammar of a sentence and their respective merits is one of the most powerful and exciting experiences students can have. Consider, for example, the fun of exploring with students Robert Frost's (1943) wonderful sentence, "Whose woods these are I think I know." This familiar sentence of iambic tetrameter, when examined with grammar, suddenly opens into a chasm of questions and possibilities. The first discovery that students will make is that these eight syllables contain *three clauses*. Gradually, students will realize that the main idea is *I think*, and that *I know whose woods these are* serves as the direct object of the action verb *think*. But within this direct object, the subject/ predicate set *I/know* contains its own direct object: *whose woods these are*, except that this, too, makes a clause, whose subject/predicate set is *these/are*, in which the linking verb takes a subject complement *woods*!

With this surprising examination, we realize that Frost's sentence is enormously compact and elegant, possessing vastly greater energy than its small size would suggest. Like Chinese boxes, it contains objects within objects, but the nested objects are grammatical, which means intellectual. One clause contains a subject complement, and this clause is itself the direct object of a second clause, but these two clauses are themselves the direct object of a primary clause, whose subject and predicate focuses on the idea, *I think*:

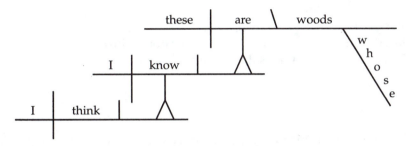

Now consider that a class of verbally talented children has explored this far, discovering, through Socratic questioning methods, the supremely beautiful architecture of this sentence, and then they are suddenly faced with the truly Socratic question: Why? Why did Robert Frost collapse all of these ideas into this form? He could have said, "I think I know whose woods these are," for example. Why didn't he? We have been led, through grammar, to the edge of creative decision, where ideas get moved forward and backward to create differences in emphasis and in sound, where intellectual and artistic awareness form an overlapping zone. Grammar has given us a wonderful problem, and it can be explored in the purest Socratic way, as an open-ended question generating hypotheses and leading to further explorations. In the magic lens of grammar, every sentence becomes a Socratic object.

As explained in *The Magic Lens* (Thompson, 1991b), another exciting way to develop students' ability to think the language of grammar is to use *mystery sentences*, in which the teacher reads a precise description of the grammar of a famous sentence, challenging the students to figure out what the sentence is. The merit of this method is that the students are first given a hollow shell, a transparently empty geometry, and must comprehend it in its abstract architecture before they can make the synthetic connection from the hollow shell to the sentence, whose words alone they thought they knew. Examples of mystery sentences from *The Magic Lens* follow:

Mystery Sentences

1. A children's story contains a famous compound declarative sentence distinguished by three independent clauses. A coordinating conjunction

is used twice to join the three clauses together. Each clause contains a contraction of the first person singular subject pronoun and the helping verb *will*. The third clause contains a direct object and an adverb. The first two clauses contain only subjects and verbs. What is the sentence?

2. A famous sentence from Shakespeare begins with a compound infinitive and ends with a clause that contains a demonstrative pronoun as a subject, a present tense linking verb, a definite article, and a singular common noun as a subject complement. What is the sentence?

Answers:

1. I'll huff, and I'll puff, and I'll blow your house down.
2. To be or not to be, that is the question. (Hamlet)

Vocabulary

Grammar makes visible the abstract architectures of ideas, but it is the words that these structures carry that are the substance of the ideas. Grammar without vocabulary is like a sentence diagram in which no words have been filled in. Students must turn their attention to words themselves, to the fine distinctions between so-called synonyms, to the fact that words empower not just expression but vision itself, and to the interiors of words as a hidden source of knowledge and insight. For the education of high-ability learners, several aspects of word study are important, which are discussed next.

Etymology

For students of English, the great system of Greek and Latin stems upon which thousands of English words are based is an incomparably important—in fact essential—object of study. By using the Greek and Latin etymologies as a foundation for building students' vocabularies,

> *vocabulary is presented not as a set of lists of words but as a* system of thinking, *a way of building, analyzing, spelling, pronouncing, using, and choosing words. Just as a distant galaxy of stars appears in the telescope as a single luminous astronomical object, so in [etymology] it is the vocabulary* system *that appears as a fascinating language object, composed of thousands of sparkling words and word pieces. In this method, the system is not offered as a mere way of learning words, rather the example words serve to illustrate and expand the system in the student's mind. The system is the object of inquiry. The beauty of this approach is that the student finally knows far more than the short list of words encountered in the course; he or she also knows the tens of thousands of words that are not listed but that are*

expressions of the system. *This is an approach that can accomplish much, even in one academic year; it is an approach that can have a significant, visible impact on a student's vocabulary and thought processes. (Thompson, 1990, p. 1)*

Micropoems

A Greek-and-Latin-based vocabulary study accomplishes more than giving students intellectual comprehension of words—it gives students an appreciation of the aesthetic power of words; it reveals the archaeological *micropoems* (Thompson, 1992) of insight and perception captured in the construction of words. Words are made things, and there is reason in their making. Those who made them did so thoughtfully. For this reason, words are often vessels of surprising beauty and insight. They are capsules of philosophy; they are micropoems. Even ordinary words take on a new depth and humanity when viewed in this way. We suddenly realize that to *respect* someone is to see (*spect*) him or her anew (*re*), and we remember the times we ourselves have *looked again* at someone who had been previously insignificant to us. Or in thinking about a *cadaver*, we realize the profound fact that a person has fallen (*cad*) and will never again move about in this green planet's gravitational field, where everything is pulled toward a center with the force, *g*. Or we poignantly realize that a *posthumous* award is granted after (*post*) burial in the earth (*hum*). Or we see the image of the *introvert* turned (*vert*) into (*intro*) himself, back to the threatening world. Though many words, broken down into their Greek or Latin components, are simply logical, many others are micropoems—hidden moments of insight and feeling, testimony to the humanity of our predecessors. Students who know only the dictionary definition surface of words and not the submeanings within the words will scarcely suspect the simplifying logic and poetic power of words, for these qualities are functions of the prefixes, stems, and suffixes that are discovered through etymology.

Perception

Among the great benefits conferred by the possession of a strong vocabulary is the ability to perceive more of the world's phenomena than one would perceive with a small vocabulary. In learning the name of something, we are often apprised of its existence, and having its name, we begin to notice its presence. This enlightenment of vocabulary never occurs to some, who believe that all unknown words are merely unnecessary synonyms of the same words they already know. But once, for example, you learn what an *invidious* compliment is, you begin to alertly perceive the envy-causing compliments that gratify the recipient but leave a companion on the outside, looking (*vid*) in (*in*).

The History of English

Students will love learning about the thrilling history of English, that pile of linguistic rubble: Learish Celts conquered by Romans, Romans withdrawing from the sceptered isle to save the doomed empire from Alaric and his dastardly Visigoths, Germanic Anglo-Saxons crossing the Channel with short words (*cow, pigge, deer*); William's Norman French of Viking descent bringing victorious French words (*beef, pork, venison*); the addition of more Greek and Latin words through scholarship in the Middle Ages; conquerings, battles, soldiers in conflict—grammars and dictions in conflict. English-speaking students should know that they speak a synthesized confusion of tongues and syntaxes left over from 2,000 years of tumultuous history; this too is part of self-knowledge.

Poetics

Though grammar and vocabulary are absorbing and worthy subjects in themselves, it is only when we apply them to wild sentences, encountered unanticipated in novels, poems, and essays, that we discover what breathtaking tools they are. It is then, in the presence of an ill-behaved, stubborn sentence—when we are wrestling with the simplified categories of basic grammar and trying to force the square peg of the sentence into the round hole of the four-level grammar terminology—that our thinking about grammar and diction come alive. And it is then that we often realize that grammar is not enough, that something is still unaccounted for, and that in order to really explain why the sentence used three prepositional phrases, or a series of specific adjectives, of a convoluted Chinese-box clause structure, we must turn to elements of poetics. For upon the poetics, the grammar is based.

I am saying that in studying grammar, one is positively forced—kicking and screaming, if necessary—to study poetics, because the grammar is a function of the poetics. And not conversely.

Just as an explanation of the elements of grammar is beyond the scope of this chapter, so is an explanation of the elements of poetics. But by *poetics*, I mean such typical things as rhyme, meter, and figure of speech. I mean assonance, consonance, and alliteration (Yeats's [1966] "I hear *l*ake water *l*apping with *l*ow sounds by the shore"). I mean end-stopped, enjambed, and endless lines. I mean the interplay of vowels, consonants, and silences; the rhythms (Frost's "Whose woods these are I think I know") and a-rhythms of language. I mean thin, nasal, scratchy sounds (Shakespeare's "Fillet of a fenny sna*k*e, in the *c*auldron boil and ba*k*e") and round, soft sounds (Shakespeare's "Romeo, Romeo, wherefore art thou Romeo?"), bass notes ("Whole lotta…goin' on") and high notes (shakin'); I mean the music of speech. These elements are always present, whether they are deliberately crafted into the sentence or not, and they have much to do with our delight in sentences, our memory of sentences, our admiration of sentences, and our comprehension of sentences. Poetics is typically (and artificially) studied only during the study of poems, but these factors are powerfully present in novels, plays, essays, political speeches, and even in ordinary conversation.

Consider the grammar of Shakespeare's sentences in "Sonnet 29":

When, in disgrace with fortune and men's eyes,
I all alone beweep my outcast state,
And trouble deaf heaven with my bootless cries,
And look upon myself, and curse my fate,
Wishing me like to one more rich in hope,
Featured like him, like him with friends possessed,
Desiring this man's art and that man's scope,
With what I most enjoy contented least;
Yet in these thoughts myself almost despising,
*Haply I think on thee—**and then my state,***
Like to the lark at break of day arising
***From sullen earth**, sings hymns at heaven's gate;*
For thy sweet love remembered such wealth brings
That then I scorn to change my state with kings.

The genius of the poem, though present everywhere, is brightest in the third quatrain, when the narrator turns his eyes away from despair and onto his love: "Haply I think on thee." There follows a soft dash to allow the dear word *thee* some respectful time to realize, and then suddenly, the poem's grammar—which had been occurring in lock-step 10-syllable units, with commas and semicolons at the end of each *end-stopped* line—launches into a 15-syllable *enjambed* burst; *The bird is taking off*, and the iambic pentameter of the sonnet cannot prevent it:

and $_{then}$ ^{my} state, / Like $_{to}$ ^{the} lark ^{at} break ^{of} day ^{a}rising /

from $_{sul}$ ^{len} earth.

Nine wing-flaps. Here, the sensitive reader increasingly learns, as everywhere in language, it is not the grammar which drives the sentence; it is the sense which drives the grammar.

For another, nonpoetry example of why it is necessary to include poetics in a discussion of language study focusing on grammar, let us inspect a well-known political sentence, from Abraham Lincoln's "Gettysburg Address": "Fourscore and seven years ago, our forefathers brought forth upon this continent a new nation, conceived in liberty and dedicated to the proposition that all men are created equal."

We know that the entire speech was so short—in an age when speeches typically lasted one to two hours—that Lincoln was finished with it before the audience had quieted down. A newspaper reporter gasped aloud, "Is that all, Mr. President?" It was. And Lincoln had worked on this tiny speech for weeks; in fact, he had kept it in his hat, taking it out repeatedly during the course of each day to scratch out a word or to insert a phrase. It was a meticulously written speech. And when we look at the words, we begin to wonder about the curiosities and anomalies we see.

Why did Lincoln use the phrase "fourscore and seven" rather than the more direct "eighty-seven"? Why did he choose the words "brought forth"? Why did he disturb the grammar from the expected order? We would have expected something like this: Eighty-seven years ago, our forefathers created a new nation upon this continent.

It is impossible to explain the diction and syntax of Lincoln's brilliant sentence without reference to the poetics, for Lincoln was using the music of the voice to enhance and support his meaning, and only by hearing the music can we understand the grammar. For the first 14 words, Lincoln is playing the bass notes, the *os* and *us* enriched by the *rs*. Hear the sounds: *four score, year, ago, our, forefather, brought, forth, upon, continent.* Lincoln is playing an oboe or a bassoon. And then suddenly, rising above the low tones, we have sounds, alliterated with *ns*, that are higher and lighter—a flute: *new, nation.* And all of this leads to the finale: the most important word, uttered last so that it echoes in the silence at the end of the sentence: *equal.* Equal.

> **Fo**urscore and seven **y**ears a**go, our** **fo**refather**s** **b**rought **f**orth, **up**on this
> **c**ontinent, a *new* *na*tion, conceived in liberty, and dedicated to the prop-
> osition that all men are created EQUAL.

We call these devices *assonance, consonance, alliteration,* and so forth, but language study takes us beyond terminology—whether of grammar, vocabulary, or poetics—to an awareness of the vital interplay and sensitivity revealed by the study of language.

Putting It All Together

We have discussed the importance of formal language study in various aspects: grammar, vocabulary, and poetics. Now let us combine all of these inquiries to explore a single sentence because in real language phenomena, these properties of language *are* always combined; it is only in the arid terrain of textbooks that grammar, diction, or poetics would seem to exist in an unnatural state of isolation. By combining all of the inquiries discussed thus far into a single view of a sentence, we should be able to bring a sentence into extraordinary focus. And so we shall: Just before her suicide, Sylvia Plath, the American poet who married the British poet Ted Hughes and lived in England, wrote a starkly terrible but beautiful poem entitled "The Moon and the Yew Tree." "This," Plath (1963) began, "is the light of the mind, cold and planetary. / The trees of the mind are black.... Fumey, spiritous mists inhabit this place ... I simply cannot see where there is to get to." Plath's "Fumey, spiritous mists inhabit this place" is a sentence of genius, a companion to Shakespeare's similarly evil "Fillet of a fenny snake, in the cauldron boil and bake." If we examine Plath's sentence using grammar, diction, and poetics, we begin to understand why.

A sentence diagram will show us the core of the idea's structure; it is an idea about mists. And these mists, we note, are inhabiting a place, the mind. The diagram shows us the sentence's essential simplicity, and calls our attention to the subject.

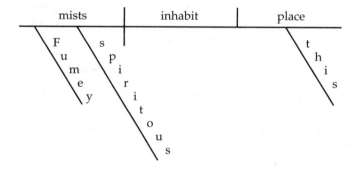

A four-level analysis, however, gives us more detailed information than the diagram does. By analyzing every word and word group in the sentence, one level at a time, we can search every corner of the sentence for signs of life:

Fumey, spiritous mists inhabit this place.

Parts of Speech:	adj	adj	n	v	adj	n
Parts of Sentence:			subj	pred	dir obj	

Phrases:	no prepositional, appositive, or verbal phrases
Clauses:	One independent clause, simple declarative sentence

Parts of Speech: *Fumey* is an adjective modifying the plural common noun *mists; spiritous* is also an adjective modifying *mists; inhabit* is a present tense transitive action verb; *this* is an adjective modifying the singular common noun *place*. There is nothing remarkable about the parts of speech in this sentence; modification is the primary function, since adjectives constitute the most common part of speech. Except for one verb, the entire sentence consists of concrete nouns and their modifiers.

Parts of the Sentence: The subject of the sentence is *mists*, a plural noun that takes a plural simple predicate, *inhabit*; this is a transitive action verb for which the noun *place* serves as a direct object. The parts of Plath's sentence disclose the innermost core of the idea: MISTS INHABIT.

The four-level analysis gives us a clear look at the internal components of the idea, but it shows us that in terms of originality of structure there is nothing anomalous present, nothing that stirs the poetic imagination. The sentence is grammatically ordinary, and depends on something else for its impact.

If we examine the etymology of the words in the sentence, we find that some of the effect of the poem comes from the historical resonances in the words themselves. An analysis of each word shows that most, but importantly not all, of the words have Latin origins:

Fumey, spiritous mists inhabit this place.

fumey: from the Latin *fumus*, smoke, akin to the Greek *thymos*, mind or spirit

spiritous: from the Latin *spiritus*, breath, akin to Latin *spirare*, to blow or breathe

mists: from OE, darkness, mist, dark weather

inhabit: from Latin *in* plus *habitare* to dwell

this: from OE *thes*, this

place: ME, from OF, open space, from Latin *platea* broad street

As we examine this list, we notice that the key word, the subject of the sentence, comes not from Latin or Greek but from Old English (OE). A closer look at the subject word might be in order, and so we consult the supreme source in such matters—*The Oxford English Dictionary*. The *OED*, in its discussion of the word *mist*, provides examples of usage spanning a period of nearly a thousand years. In examples from 10 centuries ago, in fact, only the word *mist* seems recognizable:

1000: ha sunne eode to setle ha sloh haer micel **mist**;

1200: Ne michte ich seon bi-fore me for smike ne for **miste**

1290: A wel deork **mijst** hare com al-so hat swipe longue i-laste

After three more centuries, the sentences begin to sound more like English, but the result is chilling, as it evokes an age of dark forests and iron blades, as mists and clouds gather in the air:

1340: Now gadirs **mystes** and cloudes in he ayre

1398: **Myste** is frende to theues and to euyl doers for he hydyth theyr speyrs and waytynges

Mist is friend to thieves and to evil doers, for it hides their spears and waitings. By the time of Shakespeare, the misty sentences are recognizable as English sentences, but the word *mist* remains virtually unchanged. Milton used it 200 years after Shakespeare, and Scott used it 200 years after Milton.

1450: Han fell sodaynly slike a **myst**

1603: The flagging'st bulrush that ere droopt With each slight **mist** of raine

1667: As Ev'ning **Mist** Ris'n from a River o're the marish glides—Milton

1798: In **mist** or cloud on mast or shroud It perch'd for vespers nine—Coleridge

1831: The **mist** had settled upon the hills, and unrolled itself upon brook, glade, and tarn—Scott

We see from this history that the subject word *mist* has a special role in Plath's sentence. In its present and antecedent forms (*myste, miste, mijst*), it has survived almost unchanged from a dim time before the Norman invasion. Unlike the Latinate words that surround it, it has the monosyllabic, primitive quality that we associate with the dark forests and legends of Roman and post-Roman Britain. It reminds us of Walter Scott's discussion in *Ivanhoe* of how the Norman French words *boef, porque,* and *venison* were the polite courtly words for the crude Germanic *cowe, pigge,* and *deer* of the Anglo-Saxons. It reminds us of *Beowulf* and of the monster Grendel crawling with predatory stealth toward the mead hall. In the line of Sylvia Plath's poetry that we are examining, spiritous mists are inhabiting the blue place of her mind. It is a behavior, we detect, to which mists are not unaccustomed.

And so we have learned that Plath's sentence is a grammatically unremarkable structure based on a subject noun that is rich in suggestive connotation, which possibly operates on our collective unconscious with a context of ancient memories: scents of dark pine forests, silvery moonlight, and the images of the things that mists (as we are reminded by the *OED*) do: gather, hide, fall, glide, perch, settle, unroll. And as Plath would add, *inhabit*.

If we turn from the grammar and etymology to the poetics of the line, we discover a richness that is scarcely detectable in a cursory reading of the poem:

Fumey, spiritous mists inhabit this place.

Meter. The meter of the line is irregular, and at first seems to be without any defining foot, but we notice that it might be regarded as consisting of five feet: a trochee, a dactylic, two trochees, and a spondee: / - / - - / - / - / / . Notice that the dactylic foot, however, is only a trochee with an extra unstressed syllable added, whereas the final spondee is a trochee with the second syllable stressed instead of unstressed. In other words, when we look carefully, we find that the line is *perfectly trochaic except for two syllables* that effectively conceal the soul-beat of the line. Plath, we suspect, wanted to use trochees on our minds, but she didn't want to get caught. Why? The trochee is a foot that is very often used in poetry to suggest *strangeness or evil*, since it is the weird inversion of the normal iambic cadence (e.g., Romeo's "If I profane with my unworthiest hand..."), which is the natural rhythm of English. The double stress of the spondee in the last foot lends weight to the words, *this place*. Plath's line of trochaic pentameter, is a spiritual descendent of Shakespeare's hauntingly evil lines of trochaic tetrameter, spoken by the witches in *Macbeth*: "Fillet of a fenny snake, in the cauldron boil and bake; ... / Double, double toil and trouble; / Fire burn, and cauldron bubble. ... / By the pricking of my thumbs, / Something wicked this way comes."

The concealed trochaic pentameter of the line now casts light on the simple grammar, which had to squeeze itself into the small space afforded by the metrical subtleties. The rhythmic tone is established by the opening trochee followed by a comma, which firmly fixes the trochee, and the two-syllable adjective *fumey* perfectly fills the role.

Figure of Speech. *This place*, remember, is the haunted geography of a mind. In the cold and planetary light of this place, the mind, with black trees silhouetted against the blue light, fumey, spiritous mists are rising. These mists *inhabit*—a word that connotes possession by evil spirits—this place. We have a landscape of isolation and terror, redolent of death, as a metaphor of the mind—one which we now know was one of the final autobiographical moments of a brilliant woman on the tragic edge of suicide.

Sound. There is no pattern of end rhyme in Plath's poem, although subtle resonances of sound exist at the ends of some lines. The real music of the poem is not in end rhyme but in other devices of sound, such as alliteration, assonance, and consonance. "Fumey, spiritous mists inhabit this place" achieves its insidious terror through the insistent hissing of consonants: aspirates (*h*-sounds), fricatives (*f* and *th*-sounds), and sibilants (*s*-sounds), as well as through the thin breathing of the vowels. This can be visually illustrated with a vowel-consonant split, a simple technique I developed to show students the music of a line of poetry:

fumey	**spiritous**	**mists**	**inhabit**	**this**	**place**
f m	sp r t	s m sts	nh b t	th s	pl c
u ey	i i ou	i	i a i	i	a e

A pedagogical note: To really hear the effect of Plath's music with a class of students, create a choral performance to sing the poetry of the line. Assign one row of students to hiss the *s*-sound, another to aspirate the *h*-sound, another to do the *f* and *th* sounds, and have another row sing the thin *ih*-sound. Students should not say the words, only hiss or sing the pure sounds themselves. As teacher, conduct! Bring in the rows one at a time until students can hear all of the dominant sounds combined. The result will sound like this:

Row 1:sssssssssssssssssssssssssssssssssssssssssssssssssssssssssssssssssssssss

Row 2:hhhhhhhhhhhhhhhhhhhhhhhhhhhhhhhhhhhhhhhhhhhhh

Row 3:fffffffffffffthththththfffffffffffthththththtffffffffffffff

Row 4:iiiiiiiiiiiiiiiiiiiiiiiiiiiiiiiiiiiiiiiiiiiiiiiiiiiiiiiiii

This technique will abstract the music from the words, and reveal it in all its insidious evil: Fffumey, ssspiritouss misstss inhhhabit thhhhisss placccce. We can feel the effect of the assonance (repetition of the short *i* vowel sound in *spiritous, mists, inhabit, this*; we feel the consonance in the hissing *s* sounds of *spiritous, mists, this, place*; and we are spooked by the escaping breath in *fff*umy, in*hhh*abit, and *thhh*is.

What has our analysis of the poetics of the sentence shown us? That the genius resides largely in the poetics. That the metaphor of the lost mind as a blue and misty landscape with black trees is emphasized by a disturbing trochaic inversion of the normal iambic rhythm of English thought. That this is supported with a sound track of thin vowels and breathy, hissing consonants. And that all of this provides cramped parameters within which only a very simple grammar can exist, focusing on a single-syllable subject that itself is potent with poetic and historical connotations.

We have examined the grammar, etymology, and poetics of a single sentence, which depicts the inhabiting mists of a mind in the final stages of despair. Which of the three views—grammar, etymology, or poetics—would you choose not to know? Would anyone now prefer not to understand the grammatical simplicity of the sentence, or the evocative associations of the subject word, or the immense music of the line that is paradoxically subtle, or the interplay between these three things? Grammar, etymology, and poetics are essential tools for the appreciation of literature.

Conclusion

For the education of verbally talented learners, formal language study is an essential component, perfectly suited for the differentiated curriculum such students need. When we combine grammar, vocabulary, and poetics, we have a content that is rigorous, abstract, and classic. We have a content that is both practical and intellectual, and that applies with equal import to the words of Kennedy, Camus, Shelley, and Shakespeare.

The 22-month-old granddaughter mentioned at the beginning of this discussion said to her grandmother, "Don't you remember? You gave it to me for my happy birthday last Wednesday." Just 650 days after her birth, she uttered these two sentences. The first is an interrogative sentence consisting of a contraction of the verb *do*, used in its auxiliary function to emphasize the main verb, and the modifying adverb *not*, which derives from the Old English *nought*; a second person singular subject pronoun *you* (traceable back through Middle and Old English *ye* to Sanskrit) used as the subject of the verb *remember*, which comes from the Latin *rememorare*. Her second sentence is a simple declarative sentence consisting of the second person singular subject pronoun *you* used as the subject of the past tense singular action verb *gave* (the verb *give* traces back through Middle English and Old Norse), which acts on the neuter gender third person singular subject pronoun *it* as a direct object. The direct object is followed by an adverbial prepositional phrase *to me*, in which the preposition *to* indicates a relationship of direction between its object of preposition *me* and the verb *gave*, and this prepositional phrase is followed by a second prepositional phrase *for my happy birthday last Wednesday*, which is notable, among other things, for its reference to the chief god of the Germanic tribes, Woden, associated with the Norse god Odin.

Now, this little girl probably never heard of Odin, or even Woden, but on the other hand, her brain whipped these sentences together spontaneously, at the speed of a telephone conversation, and she got it all right: There is no subject/verb disagreement, no pronoun reference error, no misplaced modifier.

Smart girl.

Just imagine what she will know by the age of 2.

Key Points Summary

- Grammar is a way of thinking about language that should be taught early, as completely as possible, and applied as a method of critical thinking to all forms of language.
- Vocabulary study should include the study of Greek and Latin etymology, with special attention given to the aesthetic and intellectual surprises that are not apparent from dictionary definitions but are revealed

References

Clark, B. (1988). *Growing up gifted.* Columbus, OH: Merrill.

Coleman, M. R. (Ed.). (1991). Update: Underserved gifted. *Journal for the Education of the Gifted*, 14(3), 213–350.

Frost, R. (1943). *Come in and other poems by Robert Frost.* New York: Henry Holt.

Gallagher, J. (1975). *Teaching the gifted child* (2nd ed.). Boston, MA: Allyn and Bacon.

Olson, M. W., Logan, J. W., & Lindsey, T. P. (1988). Orthographic awareness and gifted spellers: Early experiences and practices. *Roeper Review*, 10(3) 152–155.

Parker, J. (1989). *Instructional strategies for teaching the gifted.* Boston, MA: Allyn and Bacon.

Plath, S. (1963). *The collected poems of Sylvia Plath* (T. Hughes, Ed.). New York: HarperCollins.

Sandburg, C. (1956). *Good morning, America.* Orlando, FL: Harcourt Brace.

Shakespeare, W. (1967). *Romeo and Juliet.* London: Heinemann.

Thompson, M. (1990). *The word within the word* (Vol. 1). Unionville, NY: Trillium.

Thompson, M. (1991a). *Classics in the classroom.* Unionville, NY: Trillium.

Thompson, M. (1991b). *The magic lens.* Unionville, NY: Trillium.

Thompson, M. (1992). *The word within the word* (Vol. 1). Unionville, NY: Trillium.

Torrance, P., & Myers, R. M. (1970). *Creative teaching and learning.* New York: Harper.

VanTassel-Baska, J., Feldhusen, J., Seeley, K., Wheatley, G., & Foster, W. (1988). *Comprehensive curriculum for gifted learners.* Boston, MA: Allyn and Bacon.

Yeats, W. B. (1966). *Selected poems and two plays of Willian Butler Yeats.* New York: Collier.

10

Reflections on Foreign Language Study for Highly Able Learners

MICHAEL CLAY
THOMPSON
University School of Jackson

MYRIAM BORGES
THOMPSON
University School of Jackson

In any discussion of the development of verbal ability through education, special mention must be made of the importance of foreign language instruction. For reasons that will be discussed here, foreign language study is inherently appropriate and important for high-ability learners. However there are also new realities that affect all U.S. students today. Nearly 20 million Americans speak Spanish as the main language spoken at home, and additional millions speak Spanish as a second language. It has been said that Los Angeles is Mexico's second largest city. American foreign relations with Spanish-speaking nations in our hemisphere continue to increase in importance, as our economies and cultures become more organically connected. International political developments have given historic new importance to the study of foreign language, and have altered the curricular equation, making nontraditional languages such as Russian, Chinese, German, and Japanese more important than ever for U.S. students to study.

All of this is taking place in a technological environment that is making the global electronic village a reality; international live personal video link-ups will soon be as ordinary as neighborhood telephone conversation is today. These changes have relegated the traditional written studies of for-eign language to the scrap heap of anachronisms, and created a bilingual imperative—our abilities in foreign language must be more than silent intel-lectual skills; we must be bilingual. We must be able to speak, understand, and express our ideas in foreign languages. This bilingual imperative calls for classroom experiences involving not only the traditional reading and writing but listening and speaking as well. In fact, the order of importance would emphasize listening first, then speaking, writing, and reading.

Comment on the importance of foreign language to the education of gifted students has been somewhat inconsistent. Some thinkers in gifted education have understood its importance. VanTassel-Baska (1988) has listed foreign language study as one of five key components, (in addition to, literature, writing and composition, language, and oral discourse) in a verbal arts program for the gifted. On the other hand, the words *foreign language, Spanish, Latin,* and *French* do not even appear in the indexes of many core texts in gifted education, although Gallagher (1975) cited the Conant report's recommendation that schools should offer a third and fourth year of foreign language no matter how few students enroll and students who seem able should be urged to complete a four-year sequence of one language. Articles in the *Roeper Review* and the *Gifted Child Quarterly* have focused more on the problems of bilingual education for minority gifted children than on the cur-ricular importance of foreign language study.

Writers who address the question of foreign language study do seem undivided on the need for foreign language study to begin early. Cox, Daniel, and Boston (1985) argued that foreign language study should start early and should continue over a number of years. They have recommended beginning a second language at kindergarten level, and perhaps a third or fourth language for the linguistically able during their elementary years. VanTassel-Baska (1988) has agreed that instruction should begin early: "Whatever the choice of a second language for the verbally gifted, it is important that they have the opportunity to learn one, and preferably much earlier than the typical school curriculum would allow. The primary grades are a good time to start a modern foreign language. Formal study of Latin or Greek can begin by fourth grade. The goal for these students should be pro-ficiency in *two* foreign languages by high-school graduation"(p. 155). Van Doren and Van Doren (Adler, 1984) emphasize the importance of early for-eign language instruction in a Paideia school: "The very early years of a child's life are best for learning to speak and understand a foreign language....At this period of their lives it is not difficult for children to acquire such skills, though they may not yet be able to read and write even their own language" (p. 136).

Foreign Language as Enhancement

For numerous reasons, the study of *foreign* language provides special enhancements to the development of verbal ability that the mere study of one's own native language does not. These new enhancements then turn back and enrich one's sense of the native language, as well as one's understanding of the wonder of language itself. Some of the advantages gained through the study of foreign language include this deeper understanding of language itself, accelerated vocabulary development through cognates, enlightenment through comparative grammar, training of the poetic ear, the ability to read literature in its original language, mental flexibility through acquaintance with language elements that are totally nonexistent in the native language, and an enriched multicultural and global perspective.

Before we embark on a discussion of these points concerning foreign language study, one question deserves preliminary consideration: Should we use the word *foreign*? Are there not some negative connotations associated with the word that requires us to consider alternative terms, such as *modern languages*? The word *foreign* comes from the Latin *foris*, meaning "outside." We use *foreign* to indicate things belonging to other nations or cultures than our own. We also use *foreign* to refer to things that seem strange or alien to us. Certainly, some foreign languages are very distant in time or culture from our own, and will have a quality of strangeness. And some foreign languages, such as Spanish, are spoken as the native language of millions (19 million, in the case of Spanish) of Americans, to whom English is their foreign language. Furthermore, we must remember that *every* language is foreign. We all speak a foreign language, which is our native language; these terms are only matters of perspective. The term *modern languages*, on the other hand, does not encompass the study of ancient tongues, such as Latin or Greek, and it also lacks the exotic excitement of the word *foreign*. This exotic appeal is one of the positive attractions of studying foreign cultures, histories, and languages; as students of the foreign, we are mind-adventurers, seeking with open eyes to learn more about the world beyond our own familiar province. It is this fact—that what we are studying is *not* merely modern but is foreign to our experience and understanding—that gives the study of foreign language the power to illuminate our tolerance and extend our limits. The term *foreign* may thus be seen in its positive light, as an attractive and accurate indication of the value of our study.

On the other hand, the exotic appeal of the foreign language is the beginning, not the end, of a relationship. In teaching a foreign language in the best way, we lead students—as the Latin etymology of *foreign* suggests—*outside* the boundaries of their native experience, helping them to make a foreign language become a second language to them; what had been foreign is foreign no more. It has become internalized. In order for this to happen, English-speaking students and teachers must overcome any Anglocentrism and adopt a seeker's openness and humility that allows them mentally to go from their own language's demands and assumptions to the foreign language. Once they have gone to the other language for what it has to give to them, then they can take it into themselves on its own terms, and what they internalize will be valuable.

To Speak in the Dark

In Alan Paton's classic novel of beauty, fear, and hope in South Africa, *Cry, the Beloved Country* (1987), a small White boy has come to see the local Black minister, Steven Kumalo. The little boy wants to learn Zulu. They address each other with respect, Kumalo calling the small boy *inkosana*, and the boy calling the reverend Kumalo *umfundisi*:

—*Are you ready for the Zulu, umfundisi?*
—*Indeed I am ready.*
—*Tree is umuti, umfundisi.*
—*That is right, inkosana.*
—*But medicine is also umuti, umfundisi.*
And the small boy said this with an air of triumph, and a kind of mock bewilderment, so that they both laughed together.
—*You see, inkosana, said Kumalo seriously, our medicines come mostly from trees. That is why the word is the same.*
—*I see, said the small boy, pleased with this explanation. And box is ibokisi.*
—*That is right, inkosana. You see, we had no boxes, and so our word is from your word.*
—*I see. And motor bike is isitututu.*
—*That is right. That is from the sound that the motorbike makes, so, isi-tu-tu-tu. But inkosana, let us make a sentence. For you are giving me all the words that you know, and so you will not learn anything that is new. Now how do you say, I see a horse?*
So the lesson went on, till Kumalo said to his pupil, It is nearly twelve o'clock, and perhaps it is time you must go.
—*Yes, I must go, but I'll come back for some more Zulu.*

—You must come back, inkosana. Soon you will be speaking better than many Zulus. You will be able to speak in the dark, and people will not know it is not a Zulu.

Reverend Kumalo's words offer insight into the power of foreign language to develop verbal ability, or better, to develop all of the abilities we collectively describe as *verbal*, for who among us could pass the Kumalo Test: to speak in the dark and not be detected? Having studied French, Spanish, German, or even different dialects of our own language, such as Georgia Southern, Australian, or Michigan English, who among us could speak in the dark and be mistaken for a native of France, Spain, Germany, Georgia, Canberra, or Saginaw?

How would native speakers know we were not native? They would know from our diction, from our inability to speak *fluently* enough. But what does *fluency* mean? It means rhythm. It means tone. It means sensitivity to the resonances of meaning we describe as pun, irony, and double entendre. It means using the unconscious contractions common to native speakers of all languages, don'cha think? It means sentences infused with the culture of the place, and not merely the vacuous abstract grammars of the foreign language textbooks. It means singing the music of the language as only a person who *is* the language knows how. It means all of these things and many more.

And so what is required to become speak-in-the-dark fluent in a foreign language? What is required is no less than a profound understanding of levels and nuances of language, *far in excess of what is necessary in studying one's own native language,* for in one's own language, many of these elements are invisible, too natural to be understood. Thus, learning a foreign language forces one to become language conscious.

But this language consciousness does not emerge simply as a way of mastering the elements required for fluency, for in practice the study of foreign language is carried on simultaneously with the study of the native language. The high school sophomore, for example, will be taking English II and, say, Spanish II at the same time. In both classes, the same pertinacious phenomena keep intruding themselves: nouns, verbs, prepositions, contractions, interrogations, compound sentences, past tense, subject/verb disagreements, pronoun case. English is not Spanish, and Spanish is not English, but in each case, language is language. The concept of language itself—what it is, how it works, what its possibilities are—is extracted, or abstracted, in the abstractions to which both languages conform. In fact, Van-Tassel-Baska (1988) has listed "to appreciate and understand language systems" as one of four goals of a foreign language program for gifted students, and Cox, Daniel, and Boston (1985) noted that knowing more than one language opens a student's eyes to the symbolic nature of words, learning that the correspondence between words and ideas in one language may not transfer to another language.

For the alert student, foreign language study will bring the concept of language and grammar—as a tool for communication that satisfies the needs of people to understand each other—into relief as no simple study of one's own native language ever could.

Words That Are Foreign

One of the most obvious benefits of studying the traditional foreign languages (Spanish, French, German, Greek, Latin) is the presence of cognates that strengthen the student's vocabulary in the native language. Families of languages have developed as a function of human history—and these families, such as the Romance languages, the Germanic languages, and the languages of the Muslim world that are related through Arabic—continue to pulse and interpulse within each other. Frequently a word learned in the foreign language, such as the Spanish word for tear, *lágrima*, will have a cognate in English that is erudite or unfamiliar to the student: *lachrymose*. In learning the Spanish *lágrima*, the student is introduced to *lachrymose*. Consider some of the cognates connecting Latin, Spanish, French, and English:

Latin	Spanish	French	English
cantare	cantar	chanson	canticle
speraree	esperar	esperer	esperance
cognoscere	conocer	connoisseur	cognizance
jocare	jugar	joueur	jocular
arbor	arbol	arbre	arboretum

Of course, large numbers of cognates also exist between English and German, between English and Greek, and between English and a host of other languages, including Arabic, American Indian languages, and others. Examples of English words that are of recognizable Arabic origin include *admiral/al-amir-al*, *alchemy/al-kimiya*, *checkmate/shah mat*, and *cipher/sifr*. It is sometimes with a chill that we are caught off guard by the strange familiarity of another language, staring at an unexpected cognate, opening a layer of understanding into ourselves, as when we look at the first words of Greek in the Gospel of John: Εν αρχη ην ο λογοσ, και ο λογοσ ην προσ τον θεον. In the beginning (αρχη, *arche*) was the word, (λογοσ, *logos*), and the word was God, (θεον, *theon*)—as though archeologist Howard Carter had discovered King Tutankhamen's tomb within his own head! (Notice that the word *archaeologist* combines both the Greek αρχη and λογοσ.) These Greek words remind us that in addition to cognates, some language—especially Latin and

Greek—contain word elements that are incorporated into English as pre-fixes, stems, and suffixes, and that aspect of foreign language study holds a special importance for English-speaking students.

Several educators of the gifted have highlighted this issue in their writings. Parker (1989) emphasized the importance of prefixes and stems in learning vocabulary. VanTassel-Baska (1988) noted that "some 60 percent of English words are derived from Latin; thus the study of this language greatly heightens vocabulary power in English" (p. 155) Thompson (1990) advocated the study of Greek and Latin stems in verbal arts programs for the gifted, because in doing so, "vocabulary is presented not as a set of lists of words but as a system of thinking, a way of building, analyzing, spelling, pronouncing, using, and choosing words.... In this method, the system is not offered as a mere way of learning words, rather the example words serve to illustrate and expand the system in the student's mind. The system is the object of inquiry "(p. 1)

Comparative Analysis of Languages

Beginning with the word, we move to other elements of language, including grammar, for it is in the comparative and sensitive study of native and foreign grammar that a student will learn some of the deepest insights into language. The first insight is through similarity; the foreign language will have many of the same parts of speech, parts of sentence, phrases, and clauses as the native language. Using these same concepts in two languages will reinforce them, giving the student a greater command and clarity. But the second insight, and possibly the more important, is through *dissimilarity*; the student will become aware of the untranslatable (more on this later), of the fact that each language can do things that the other cannot do. Each language will have efficiencies, harmonies, rhythms, possibly tenses, and, yes, words and metaphors that the other language simply cannot directly reproduce.

Sometimes, as in the case of poetry, language uniqueness presents fascinating problems for a translator. In the Translator's Note to his translation of Dante's *Inferno*, poet John Ciardi (Alighiere, 1982) calls our attention to a loveliness of Italian which English cannot reproduce:

> *It requires approximately 1500 triple rhymes to render* The Inferno *and even granted that many of these combinations can be used and re-used, English has no such resources of rhyme. Inevitably, the language must be inverted, distorted, padded, and made unspeakable in order to force the line to come out on that third all-consuming rhyme. In Italian, where it is only a slight exaggeration to say that everything rhymes with everything else or a variant form of it, the rhyme is no problem: in English it is a disaster. (p. x)*

If it is only a slight exaggeration to say that in Italian everything rhymes with everything else, it is only a slight exaggeration to say that in English, nothing rhymes with anything else! English is that curious hodgepodge of linguistic rubble, that Latin/Greek/German/ French/Celtic Babylonian babble of languages conquered by other languages. With a grammar descending from the Germanic family, and a vocabulary descending primarily from the Romance family, the wonder is that English works as a language at all, and for this we must thank, for starters, Chaucer and Shakespeare.

Dissimilarities in grammar are interesting. We recently overheard a befuddled student quizzing his fellows to understand why Spanish often uses no subject in a sentence. In English, the subject is often omitted in an imperative sentence, such as "Read further." The subject *you* is understood in such a case. But if we said, "Went to Gibraltar," the thought would be hopelessly incomplete. And yet in Spanish, it would make perfectly good sense to say *"Fuimos a Gibraltar"* or *"Fui a Gibraltar."* Why? Because the English verbs do not inflect through the conjugations as the Spanish verbs do. In English, it is *I went, you went, he went, we went, you went, they went.* And so to say *went* gives us no information about the subject. In Spanish, however, it is *yo fui, tu fuiste, el fue, nosotros fuimos, vosotros fuisteis, ellos fueron.* To say *fueron* is to have specified *ellos.* "Fuimos a Gibraltar" means "We went to Gibraltar," and the subject is one with the conjugated verb in a clean way that English cannot reproduce. In Spanish, *"¡Fuimos!"* could be a sentence, which English would have to translate as "We went!" This nimbleness in the Spanish verbs (Latin works the same way) gives Spanish an efficiency and a clarity that English can only envy, just as English has its own strengths (variety, for heaven's sake) that other languages lack. For the bright student, these fascinating language differences heighten verbal sensitivity and initiate a creative spirit.

From a pedagogical point of view, however, the fascinations of comparative grammar are best realized retrospectively. Students should not go to their foreign languages with English language mindframes, like little Englishmen founding New Londons everywhere and thinking always of *home.* Rather than teach the foreign language with constant reference to English, the teacher should present the foreign language as a thing-in-itself which provides its own frame of reference for vocabulary and grammar. Spanish, for example, should be the vehicle for teaching Spanish; English is not an appropriate vehicle for teaching Spanish because it will inherently Anglicize the concepts and phenomena of Spanish, giving students a misleading and distracting "Spanglish" paradigm for what it is and means to think and speak in Spanish.

It is in this regard that the importance of teaching foreign language orally emerges; native speakers do not study their own languages initially through texts and exercises from books. Rather, they become themselves in a cultural context where they must speak their own French, German, or Spanish, and must understand when it is spoken to them. The oral imperative that emerges gives rise to a different ear for the language and a different thought process entirely than a textbook approach would. A talented teacher can do much to reproduce this oral language environment in the classroom, supplementing it with the written language and formal language study. Van Doren and Van Doren (Adler, 1984) emphasized that "in beginning the study of a foreign language, greater emphasis must be laid on listening and speaking. This is to make up for the head start that the child has with respect to his native language. Of the two methods of teaching foreign language—one in which English is spoken much of the time; the other in which little or no English is spoken—many teachers have found astoundingly better results with the second" (p. 137).

Foreign Sounds

Of course, one of the salient dissimilarities among languages is in sound. Languages just *sound* different. The difference in sound can be a matter of frequency of usage, or it can even indicate sounds which one language entirely lacks. English does not have the *r* sounds of Spanish—either the short *r* as in *gracias* or the rolled *rr* as in *perro*. English also does not have the German *r*, which is not made with the tongue at all but with the uvula. In Africa, there are the click languages of the Bushmen and Hottentots that have a clicking consonant no European language uses. For a Spanish-speaking student learning English, vowels can be a problem. In Spanish the vowels are pronounced in a pure, consistent manner: *o* is pronounced oh, *a* is pronounced ah, *i* is pronounced ee, *e* is pronounced ay, and *u* is pronounced oo. In Spanish, therefore, to pronounce a word is virtually to have spelled it. But in English, it is difficult to determine from spelling alone how to pronounce a word, or conversely. In addition to the basic sounds of each English vowel, we have the pastel vowel sounds as in *it, hat, felt, botch,* and *ugh*. And that is just the beginning; start combining vowels, and all English breaks loose.

And yet these dissimilarities of sound can be one of the greatest delights of language, and can be powerful elements in developing verbal talent. A verbally gifted student once heard a friend read the German poet Rilke's (1955-1966) lovely and poignant poem, "Der Panther." He was captivated by the translation, but was more captivated by the *sound*. Nothing in English, no poem, sounds like Rilke's "Der Panther":

> *Sein Blick ist vom Vorübergehn der Stäbe*
> *so müd geworden, daß er nichts mehr hält.*
> *Ihm ist, als ob es tausend Stäbe gäbe*

und hinter tausend Stäben keine Welt.

Der weiche Gang geschmeidig starker Schritte,
der sich im allerlkeinsten Kreise dreht,
ist wie ein Tanz von Kraft um eine Mitte,
in der betäubt ein großer Wille steht.

Nur manchmall schiebt der Vorhang der pupille
sich lautlos auf—. Dann geht ein Bild hinein,
geht durch der Glieder angespannte Stille—
und hört im Herzen auf zu sein.

Read it again, the student begged. And again. He had his friend write it down, and teach him to pronounce it, and for the next week repeated it to himself nonstop to remember it always. Those sounds: *Vorübergehn, lautlos auf, angespannte, manchmall, durch der Glieder, großer*—English can almost reproduce some of the sounds, but it is not the same. The sounds of the poem, extracted from the context, sounded like moonlight and iron blades, wolves and black forests—like *German*. Eventually, he tried to isolate the sounds of the words and to write pages of English words that had German sounds, such as *mulish* and *fuel*. He wanted to use these words to write a poem in English that would *sound German*. But it didn't work. Regardless of what he wrote, it only sounded English. But what a lesson this student learned from his experiment; these are the lessons students continually learn when they enthusiastically involve themselves in languages that are foreign to them.

Translation as Paraphrase

The more we learn and love a foreign language, the more we understand that all translation is paraphrase. We cannot *translate*; the translated sentence is somehow never quite *translated*. It is not the same. Like the fly sent through the teleportation device, the sentence has come through in mutated form, and is at best a disappointment, at worst a horror. We think, in this context, of Flaubert's laborious effort—satirized by Camus in *The Plague*—to select each word for perfection of sound as well as of meaning, to write a novel possessing the music of a poem. To lose the music of Flaubert's sentences is to lose the sentences. In such cases, translation is especially hopeless; to read Flaubert in translation is to read paraphrase.

Of course, there are brilliant translations and brilliant translators, and some languages are more closely related and seem to survive teleportation better than others. Walter Kaufman's wonderful translations of Goethe and the German philosophers is one example, and sometimes, as in Gretchen's song from Kaufmann's translation of Goethe's *Faust* (1964), the English seems almost to resonate in rhythm with the German: *"Meine Ruh ist hin, / Mein Herz ist schwer, / Ich finde sie nimmer / Und nimmermehr."* Kaufman translates: "My peace is gone, / My heart is sore; / I find it never / And nevermore." It is beautiful.

But the translation is only an illusion after all, *nimmer* is softer and more evanescent than *never*, and Goethe's delicate line has none of the crudeness of the English *gone* and *more.*

Let's explore further. Consider this quatrain from Jorge Luis Borges's (1960) lovely poem "Arte Poética":

> *Mirar el río hecho de tiempo y agua*
> *Y recordar que el tiempo es otro río,*
> *Saber que nos perdemos como el río*
> *Y que los rostros pasan como el agua.*

We could translate the quatrain as:

> *To look at the river made of time and water*
> *And to remember that time is another river,*
> *Is to know that we lose ourselves like the river*
> *And that the faces pass like the water.*

At first, this seems successful enough. Gradually, however, we begin to hear what is lost in the translation/paraphrase/teleportation: the low, water song of the river. Hear it? Here is one river note: *riO, tiempO, OtrO, Río, nOs, perdemOs, cOmO, riO, lOs, rOstrOs, cOmO.* The deep roll of the river, the song of the water moving through its banks, is lost in the English. And anyway, it is not a poem about a *riv-ver*; it is about a *ree-oh. Río. El río* (masculine), mind you. Very different. No self-respecting *río* would make the sounds of the English translation. Those could only be made by a *riv-ver*. (The feminine sound of Spanish is captured by Calderón de la Barca, in speaking of life, *la vida*: "toda *la vida es sueño*, / *y los sueños, sueños son.*" All of life is a dream, and the dreams, they are dreams.

In order to really experience the foreign sounds, values, echoes, and ideas of great foreign literature, we must read it in the original. Unfortunately, few of us are talented or fortunate enough to become fluent in more than a few languages and so must still read translations (paraphrases, that is) in most foreign literature. But the thrill of reading foreign literature in the original, even in one or two languages, is the experience of a mind's time. And this is another reason why verbally talented learners should be continually involved in foreign language study from the beginnings of their educations until the ends of their lives, so that as many as possible can read in the original *Don Quixote, Les Miserables, Plato's Dialogues, War and Peace, The Iliad, Faust, The Divine Comedy, Leaves of Grass, Tao Te Ching,* or *The Tale of Genji.* Such excellent foreign poetry and literature offers a rigorous and meaningful intellectual content for the verbal arts curriculum of talented students, in contrast to the safe, simplified, and selected offerings to be found in most text books.

Furthermore, verbally talented students are quickly attracted to the profound challenges of translation, which offers precisely the sort of open-ended in-what-ways-might-we thinking problems that are so often devised to develop thinking skills. Given, for example, a short poem that they find meaningful, students become deeply involved in capturing the right tone and feel of the poem, in choosing among synonyms, in finding the right words to express what they determine to be the right interpretation of the poem. One of the best assignments a teacher can make is to allow students to work together in small teams to decide on the best interpretation and translated wording of a poem that they care about. In the process, they see first-hand why perfect translation is impossible, and they develop a greater appreciation for language, literature, and the translator's art.

Providing a Multicultural Perspective

Not the least advantage of studying a foreign language is that the endeavor is inherently *multicultural* in its perspective. It is a lesson in the humanities, a lesson in tolerance. To study a foreign language is mental immersion; it is to ride in the thought vehicle of a foreign culture. It is to read and reflect on the writings of people from outside our experience. It contributes to a global awareness, an openness of mind, a geographical alertness, a sense of history, an understanding of unfamiliar norms and mores, a new sensitivity, a new sense of humor, a new interest in current events. In fact, learning a sense of humor in a foreign language is one of the highest forms of intercultural understanding. The Paideia program (Adler, 1984) gives prominence to this aspect of foreign language study: The Paidea foreign language study program has two main purposes. One is to enhance language skills in general and the other is to expand the cultural experience of students and beyond that of their immediate linguistic group. The study of a foreign language with its related culture is one way to avoid cultural provincialism. Cox, Daniel, and Boston (1985) argued that foreign language education provides a valuable "international perspective" both from a pragmatic point of view and also because the cultural receptivity it affords is an end in itself and may be seen as of enormous value in enlightening a global perspective.

An Inherently Interdisciplinary Curriculum

Finally, we note that foreign language study benefits students because it is inherently *interdisciplinary*: Students do not just study foreign vocabulary and grammar; they study literature, history, science, geography, drama, customs, arts, music, and other cultural elements. Students studying Spanish, for example, will typically read dialogues that reflect the social customs of people in Spain and Latin America; they will read passages about the conquistadors, the history of Chile and the life of Simón Bolivar; they will learn songs of Cuba, see travel posters from Puerto Rico, memorize capitals of Central and South America, and practices dances from Spain; they will compare social mores of Latin American countries to those of the United States; they will read about the Spanish American War; they will learn about the philosophy of Seneca; during spring vacation they may take a study trip to Spain where they will tour the museums and galleries; they will discuss the Andes and Machu Picchu; they will compete in the state or regional Spanish fair; they will learn about the Incas, the Mayas, and the Aztecs; they will learn the names of famous composers such as Manuel de Falla, famous poets such as Federico García Lorca, and famous painters such as Velásquez, Picasso, and Goya. And all of this will be naturally, seamlessly, and appropriately integrated into a study of Spanish language, which will serve as the matrix for these interdisciplinary explorations. Very few academic disciplines (unfortunately including history, which is often artificially limited to the study of military and political events) lend themselves as naturally to interdisciplinary thought as foreign language study.

Thus, if our goal as educators is to find concepts and ideas that lend themselves to interdisciplinarity, the study of foreign language and its related culture is an appropriate point of departure. The connections are valid, steeped in a rich history of thought and action, and offer a readily available collage of meaning and experience to learners.

Conclusion

Foreign language is an important and appropriate study for gifted children, one that offers insights into verbal and human phenomena that might go unremarked in a study of a student's own native language and literature. Through foreign language, students acquire a comprehension of variety, both in verbal behavior and in other human behavior, and they also acquire an appreciation of unity. Joseph Campbell once noted that there was really only one mythology in the world, though it manifested itself in many local forms. Language is like that; it is the vehicle through which our common humanity is manifested in English, Spanish, French, German, Russian, Chinese, Japanese, and the other diverse languages of the world. And it is this meaningful quality that appeals to verbally talented students, drawing them deeper into a lifelong appreciation of foreign language.

Key Points Summary

- Foreign language is an important component in verbal arts education for gifted students. It is recommended that foreign language instruction begin *early*, even in kindergarten or elementary school, rather than be deferred to a two- to four-year high school program.
- In contrast to the read-and-translate programs of the 1950s, current foreign language programs should emphasize the *goal of fluency* in listening, speaking, writing, and reading. This goal of communicating in the foreign language, which we have described as the Kumalo Test of speak-in-the-dark fluency, can best be achieved through experiences emphasizing oral language practice, including a wide range of communications, such as humor, cartoons, and word play.
- Fluency can be promoted through the use of native speakers as teachers and classroom guests, through travel experiences that immerse the students in the foreign language environment and supplement the classroom experience, and through video programs and computers that can expose students to a wide range of authentic listening and speaking practice.
- Foreign language is a valuable means of increasing competence in the students' native language, both through comparative insights into grammar and through vocabulary elements such as cognates and word stems. It is recommended that English-speaking students be exposed to a solid foundation of Greek and Latin stems as a key to understanding the foreign background of their own language.
- Foreign language offers verbally talented students an incomparable approach to the rigorous, intellectual content of the great poetry and novels of another culture. Students who read famous foreign works in the original will develop a deeper understanding of both the problems and joys of translation.
- Foreign language study is *multicultural.* In teaching students to appreciate the foreign language, we teach them an anthropological openness and respect for a foreign culture and its norms and mores.
- Foreign language study is *inherently interdisciplinary* since it incorporates into its process and content the history, geography, literature, arts, and social customs of the foreign culture. This interdisciplinary quality of foreign language learning helps students to understand the deeper unities and connections between areas.

References

Adler, M. (1984). *The paideia program.* New York: Collier.

Alighiere, D. (1982). *The inferno* (J. Ciardi, Trans.). New York: Mentor.

Borges, J. L. (1960). "Arte poética" from *El Hacedor,* in *Obras Completas.* Buenos Aires: Emecé Editores

Cox, J., Daniel, N., & Boston, B. (1985). *Educating able learners: programs and promising practices.* Austin, TX: University of Texas Press.

Gallagher, J. (1975). *Teaching the gifted child* (2nd ed.). Boston, MA: Allyn and Bacon.

Goethe, J. W. (1961). *Faust, part one and sections from part two* (W. Kaufman, Trans.) Garden City, NY: Doubleday.

Parker, J. (1989). *Instructional strategies for teaching the gifted.* Boston, MA: Allyn and Bacon.

Paton, A. (1987). *Cry, the beloved country.* New York: Scribner's.

Rilke, R. M. (1955–1966). *Samtliche Werke* (Vols. 1–6) (Complete Works). Frankfurt: Insel Verlag.

Thompson, M. (1990). *The word within the word* (Vol. 1). Unionville, NY: Trillium.

VanTassel-Baska, J , Feldhusen, J., Seeley, K., Weatley, G., & Foster, W., (1988). *Comprehensive curriculum for gifted learners.* Boston, MA: Allyn and Bacon.

Part III

Transforming the Language Arts to Classroom Practice

Part III provides important pathways to classroom practice based on the work presented in the first two parts. More specifically, it serves to provide a coherent translation of ideas about talent development and ideas about teaching the language arts in an integrated approach. As VanTassel-Baska cited in Chapter 1, the use of a model such as the Integrated Curriculum Model (ICM) makes possible a "goodness of fit" between talent development for gifted learners and talent development for all within the language arts curriculum in schools.

The issue of talent development for all and talent development for talented learners needs some clarification. Our work with developing, piloting, and revising the curriculum discussed in the chapters that follow speaks to the areas where the use of the same core curriculum base and the same strategies may be successful for all learners. By the same token, the chapters explore those areas of curriculum implementation that still require modifications for highly talented learners. As has been suggested by the *Prisoners of Time* report (National Commission on Time, 1994), flexibility in the amount of time necessary for talented learners to reach a curriculum standard will typically be shorter and more intensive. Thus, adjustments in expectations for rate of learning have to be made.

A second area of individual differences that needs to be considered is entry-level aptitudes and interests of the learner. Students who are advanced readers at the beginning of fourth grade are ready for more advanced reading material and corresponding vocabulary. Less advanced learners in reading skills require less difficult selections. Thus, variation in the level of the reading stimulus provided is a second area of differentiation.

Last, students talented in the language arts are likely to be ready for in-depth analysis of literature, more complex writing tasks, and more sophisticated project work than other learners. Thus, depth and complexity become issues for curriculum modification in the language arts classroom. The following information may be useful to understand these modifications, even within a rich curriculum framework.

Language Arts Curriculum for All That Stresses Talent Development

- Choice of challenging literature that reflects multicultural selections

- The teaching of reasoning skills applied to literature, language, and writing

- The use of concept mapping to enhance understanding

- Teaching a key concept that encourages intra- and inter-disciplinary exploration

- The use of higher-order questions

- The use of collaborative groups

- The use of authentic assessment approaches

- The use of research projects on significant issues

- The use of homework and unit extensions to enhance learning

Modifications Still Essential for High-Ability Learners

- Advanced reading selections based on reading level and related vocabulary development

- Independent mastery of English grammar and syntax

- Rate and pace of learning attuned to individual readiness

- Early and incremental increase in task complexity

As you proceed through Parts III and IV of this book, it will be useful to keep these distinctions in mind.

In Chapter 11, Joyce VanTassel-Baska introduces the National Language Arts Curriculum Project for High Ability Learners from conception to framework development to teaching unit implementation. The chapter provides the translation of ideas about language arts teaching and learning and converts them to a coherent curriculum system. Chapter 12, written by Phyllis W. Aldrich, reports the results of evaluating existing curriculum materials in the language arts and the paucity of text material suitable for promoting talent development in this area. Dana T. Johnson, in Chapter 13, portrays the landscape of authentic assessment in the language arts, citing viable approaches drawn from the work of the Project. Chapter 14 explores the world of words and its unique effect on high-ability learners. Linda Neal Boyce even uses word play to frame the chapter and illustrates its application to the work of the language arts project. Penny Kolloff carefully weaves the issues of cultural and gender diversity into a discussion of selection of texts and effective utilization of them in Chapter 15. Her commentary on using literature for enhancing student identity and creating empathy for others is an eloquent lesson on the power of literature to impact lives.

Reference

National Education Commission on Time and Learning. (1994). *Prisoners of time.* Washington, DC: Department of Education, OERI.

11

Creating a New Language
Arts Curriculum for
High-Ability Learners

JOYCE VANTASSEL-BASKA
College of William and Mary

How children acquire language is one of the most fascinating areas we can study. Theories of language acquisition abound that view the source of literacy development in various ways—as primarily in the child (Chomsky, 1969, 1986), primarily in the environment (Skinner, 1957), or primarily in the social interactive effect between the two (Cazden, 1983). For talented learners, we know that language development typically occurs early, appears to be spontaneous, and frequently is marked by developmental spurts where students move rapidly toward mastering basic reading processes and developing a large and advanced vocabulary (Durkin, 1966; Jackson, 1988; Roedell, Jackson, & Robinson, 1980). What are the implications of such behaviors for creating an appropriate language arts curriculum at K–8 levels? How might such a curriculum relate to new directions in language arts instruction? These are the central questions that guided the curriculum development work of the National Language Arts Curriculum Project for High Ability Learners.

Although arguments for a high-quality liberal program of study in the language arts have been consistent for more than 10 years (Adler, 1982), the current state of language arts curriculum may be characterized as fragmented by both philosophical orientation and areas of emphasis. The whole language movement has attempted to integrate language arts areas, to provide opportunities for interdisciplinary work, and to encourage "meaning making" on the part of the learner. The cultural literacy movement has attempted to stress the importance of students' developing a rich knowledge base in established works of literature and developing expository writing skills. A third movement has stressed the inclusion of multicultural literature and a global perspective to enhance language development in a culturally pluralistic society. The national standards movement has emphasized the need for world-class standards that set high expectations for learners in the language arts at all levels of instruction. Each of these movements currently has both supporters and detractors in the language arts community.

Recent national reports in the language arts have called for a reconsideration of language arts curricula that use the best of classical and contemporary literature texts to teach language, writing, and literature through an inquiry-based approach (Suhor, 1984). Such reports also stress the importance of using such approaches throughout elementary and junior high school. Close and active reading of various genre is also encouraged, even at the expense of broad coverage (National Assessment Governing Board, 1992). Constructivist theory, as it is applied to the language arts, has focused on the importance of students' creating meaning from using literary sources, particularly in the writing process (Spivey, 1990). Other theorists view the province of teaching language arts as using the classical canon and teaching traditional forms of writing (Hirsch, 1987; Thompson, 1991). Accompanying modes of assessment are being developed that reflect intensive involvement with literary works, focusing more on the processes of reading, the thought patterns of students engaged in it, and the power of thought brought to bear in connecting one work to another (National Assessment Governing Board, 1992). There exists, however, a significant gap between theory and practice. Researchers in literacy development generally have deplored the lack of curriculum research on testing what works in schools (Langer & Allington, 1992). One of the challenges, then, is to find ways to incorporate ideas about literacy development and put them into "testable" practice in the schooling process.

Research on how students learn also is critical to consider in developing new curriculum. Learning is an interactive process that brings together the learner, an activity or task, and the situation that surrounds them (Novak & Gowin, 1984). Thus, there is concern for ensuring a "holistic view" in a language arts curriculum. A literate environment provides rewarding experiences where students construct meaning for themselves in real situations. Students work collaboratively, using the teacher as a model. Learners engage in revising their work as a welcome part of their regular school experience.

An integrated curriculum uses communication skills as interrelated processes that support each other and as enabling skills across all subject areas. Outcome-based curriculum goals focus on whole-thinking processes that are at a sufficiently challenging conceptual level. A "thinking" curriculum requires awareness of one's own thinking, including attitudes, habits, and dispositions, as well as the critical and creative thinking processes about ideas. Such a language arts curriculum encourages and supports student responsibility for learning and encourages and supports student choice, collaboration, and active participation. Such a curriculum also needs to be aligned so that what is written is also taught and tested, allowing instruction and assessment to become interrelated areas.

Tschudi (1991) reviewed the materials on K–12 language arts curriculum and found the following elements a part of successful language arts programs:

- Teaching language in an integrated way rather than as a series of skills
- Teaching language as a tool for learning and encouraging extensive use
- Teaching language to promote community and connectedness, using the social and cultural experiences of students as a base
- Using language study as a social event to encourage risk taking and experimentation
- Teaching to "authentic" assessment measures
- Teaching language through open-ended activities
- Teaching toward learning, with mistakes viewed as fundamental to the process
- Teaching reading and writing as reciprocal acts
- Teaching language as a symbol system that connects to art, music, and other symbol systems
- Teaching language arts through the use of archetypal activities such as inquiry, shared writing and reading, independent writing, independent reading, read aloud and response, and sharing through discussion

Research on the effectiveness of the whole language approach compared to the traditional, skill-based approach to language learning suggests that they are approximately equal in their effects, with some exceptions. Whole language approaches seem to be more effective in kindergarten than first grade, may produce stronger scores on word recognition than reading comprehension, and produce weaker effects with populations labeled specifically as disadvantaged than with those not specifically labeled. More recent studies, however, show a trend toward stronger effects for basal reading programs relative to whole language programs (Stahl & Miller, 1989). The National Assessment of Educational Progress (National Assessment Governing Board, 1992) has depicted reading literacy as a multipurpose, multilevel

set of experiences, moving from initial understanding to developing interpretation, to personal reflection and response, to demonstrating a critical
stance. Through such a model, students contruct, extend, and examine
meaning of texts for the purpose of literary experience, information, or performance.

All of the new directions suggested by the theory and research of those
in the language arts community tend to focus on some common themes for
language arts curriculum reform in schools. These themes include:

- Making the learner the centerpiece for constructing meaning, using
  open-ended inquiry as a primary teaching tool
- Integrating the language arts areas
- Making connections to disciplines outside the language arts
- Setting learner outcomes at high levels
- Using authentic assessment
- Developing in students the skills, attitudes, and dispositions of good
  readers, writers, and communicators
- Using literature that satisfies both classical and multicultural consider-
  ations

The new language arts curriculum must be responsive to these issues in
order to be credible. By the same token, such a curriculum must recognize
the elements of what is uniquely appropriate for high-ability learners in the
language arts. Thus, the following guidelines were important to consider in
framing the work of the National Language Arts Curriculum Project for
High Ability Learners:

- *Select rich and rigorous reading materials.* High-ability students, as all students, need to learn and master the content and the skills deemed by
  society as essential in order to be a good participant in the society. However, as was found in the curriculum assessment process, basal reading
  materials are generally inadequate to guide high-ability students in the
  development of their potential. Language arts programs for high-ability
  students should provide rigorous opportunities for the development of
  their academic and intellectual potential in all major areas of the discipline. Thus, enhancing reading and literature programs through choice
  of substantive texts is a crucial component of appropriate curriculum
  development (Baskin & Harris, 1980; Polette & Hamlin, 1980; Polette,
  1982; Halsted, 1988).
- *Foster the development of reasoning abilities.* Gifted students should have
  opportunities to understand the importance of performing the tasks and
  mastering the structures of traditional K–12 language arts curricula, but
  they should also understand that mastery of a structure frees them to

push beyond the boundaries and constraints of that form, to diverge into more creative patterns of thinking. Gifted students should not see mastery of standardized skills as an end, but as a means to more rigorous thinking. Even the very youngest student should be given repeated opportunities to try out extended modes of inquiry and to ask about the purpose of a piece of literature, its implications for the real world, and its relevance to one's life.

- *Heighten students' awareness and appreciation of cultural diversity.* It is critical that high-ability learners become especially sensitive to differences among and between cultures. Cultural diversity is a valuable resource, and exposure to such diversity can provide genuine opportunities for personal growth. Although not all materials in a language arts program will necessarily or explicitly explore cultural diversity as a central theme, a special effort should be made to incorporate these materials. Given the importance of attitudinal factors in cognitive development, limited English proficiency students and students from minority groups within the dominant culture can be expected to benefit from the inclusion of materials that provide positive depictions of their cultural traditions. Students from the majority culture need an exposure to other cultural patterns as well, to understand in what ways people may be different. Curriculum developers must be careful, however, to ensure that cultural depiction is authentic. For example, are cultural groups represented fairly and accurately in literature, so that stereotyping does not result? Are members of cultural groups portrayed as unique individuals?

- *Use collaborative and inquiry-oriented learning techniques.* Students are a valuable resource to each other, a tenet of learning that can be enhanced through collaborative activities. Some of the most rewarding, unpredictable, and exciting learning occurs when peers collaborate on projects. Students should be given opportunities to work on group projects where one student's ideas supplement, challenge, or redirect a classmate's work. Students also need to understand that knowledge is tentative and our way of knowing is framed in asking the right questions, both of each other and teachers. In particular, students should be given opportunities to ask questions and receive oral and written responses from their intellectual peers. They should come to regard themselves as co-learners in a learning community. Use of discussion groups, work-shopping techniques for the writing process, panels, and debates are all strategies that can enhance collaborative learning and inquiry approaches.

- *Make connections to art, music, and the social sciences.* High-ability students need exposure to material that allows them to explore ideas in a number of areas of study. They should be exposed to the similarities as well as the differences among artistic media. They should also explore the literacies of the written, visual, and performing arts and engage in the excitement of discovering the ways that one artistic medium defines the limits of or merges with another. How does an illustrator portray fantastic characters from a fairy tale? How might one go about setting a poem to music? How does gesture depict a description of an action in a short story? We should encourage gifted students to cross artistic boundaries and to apply the visual, musical, or dramatic to reading and writing. Beyond these applications, high-ability students can make interdisciplinary connections to an understanding of the cultural context within which a work of literature developed and to areas of study that use a common theme such as change.

- *Develop authentic assessment strategies.* If students are to believe that thinking and reflection are valued in the language arts program, then teachers must develop assessment techniques that honor that approach. Use of essays that challenge learners to explore new ideas and connections between ideas, journal assignments that encourage thinking about reading, and other activity-based assessments are critical to the new language arts curriculum. New assessment approaches must become a part of the dynamic teaching-learning process by providing teachers with important diagnostic data as well as documenting student progress. Such assessments must provide a clear sense of where students are in their understanding and skills and how they might improve them. Clearly, portfolios, performance-based activities, and computer simulations all offer promising directions for such augmentation of learning.

Based on these current language arts issues, and an examination of the major areas of the language arts curriculum that are important for high-ability learners, project staff developed the curriculum products described in the next section of this chapter.

The Development of Language Arts Topics Papers

The language arts is not a unified field of study; rather, it has evolved historically from a set of separate traditions and strands of learning. Therefore, it is important to see curriculum development in the language arts that honors the integrity of each strand at the same time that it recognizes commonalities across strands and therefore seeks to unite them.

In the National Language Arts Curriculum Project for High Ability Learners, the topics papers focused on these key strands of learning in the language arts, specifically: (1) language, (2) writing, (3) oral communication, (4) literacy, (5) a general paper on developing curriculum in the language arts, and (6) a paper on the concept of change that was used as a conceptual organizer for individual unit development.

The overall purpose of the topics papers was to aid teachers in understanding the key components of the language arts as related disciplines that could be linked effectively through the concept of change and the process of reasoning. Moreover, providing a rich bibliography of readings on the concept of change and the various areas of the language arts encouraged teachers to engage in the first step of the curricular and instructional process: learning as much as possible about what they are expected to teach.

The topics papers were also guided by current considerations about the content and pedagogy of each language arts strand. Studies of reading that have proliferated in the last 20 years have tended to focus on one of three areas: (1) the social world of reading with particular emphasis on the student as reader and teacher-child interactions (Cazden, 1983, 1988); (2) the basic mental processes of reading and textual features that address them (Palinscar & Brown, 1984); and (3) classroom-based research that advocates more time on task among other recommendations (Cazden, 1988). These three areas have not been addressed in a confluent way at the level of practice, although the studies are not contradictory but rather center on different issues and priorities. However, the world of practice has embraced certain features of these studies. The Reading Commission of the National Council of Teachers of English (1988) recommended a deemphasis on the role of basals and standardized tests and a reconsideration of mandated curriculum. The State of California Framework (California Department of Education, 1987) and the National Assessment of Educational Progress (NAEP) report on reading (National Assessment Governing Board, 1992) both stress the need for student-centered reading curriculum that centers on shared inquiry discussion techniques of authentic and worthy texts. Such recommendations line up well with issues of teaching reading to the gifted learner.

Current NAEP data in writing (National Center for Education Statistics, 1992) demonstrate limited emphasis on expository writing and greater emphasis on more creative forms. Writing samples of students' best work at grades 4 and 8 evidence mediocre control of the writing process and very limited competency in developing argument. Such a result might have been predicted from earlier studies. Applebee (1984) analyzed three popular high school writing texts and found that writing assignments were predominantly evaluative, seeking right answers rather than reflection from students and calling for limited responses. In a comprehensive survey of writing in high school, Applebee (1981) also found only 10 percent of writing time being spent in composing more than a paragraph. More recently, Cooper and Brennenan (1988) recommended more direct instruction in teaching writing and requisite thinking in order to master various forms, wide reading and analysis of texts, and sustained literacy programs for all. Thus, a critical issue to consider in the language arts is how to integrate a comprehensive writing program that provides extensive experiences in expository writing.

Moreover, the language arts program for the gifted should offer opportunities to study language directly. VanTassel-Baska (1993) suggested that the goals for an English language program should be to understand the syntactic structure of English (grammar) and its concomitant uses (usage); to promote vocabulary development; to foster an understanding of word relationships (analogies) and origins (etymology); and to develop an appreciation for semantics, linguistics, and the history of language. Thompson (1992) argued for a strong integration of grammar and vocabulary into the language arts curriculum, as these constitute the structure within which all language functions.

Oral mastery and use of language are also critical parts of the language arts program. The thinking process involved in experiencing literature and writing is linked intimately to and can be enhanced by oral language experience. Through planned experiences in discussion, debate, oral reading and interpretation, oral reports, dramatics, and panel presentations, gifted youth can learn to think effectively in and through the language, and they can learn to write more effectively. Chaney (1992) emphasized the importance of developing critical listening skills as fundamental to teaching students traditional oral forms of presentation.

The Development of the Curriculum Framework

The language arts curriculum framework was developed with a set of generalizations about "change" forming the basis for developing learner outcomes. Also fundamental to the language arts curriculum framework was a set of process outcomes, derived from using a reasoning model to undergird all elements of the project to emphasize higher-order thinking (Paul, 1992). Specific content outcomes derived from the topics papers were developed for each of the four strands of the language arts. Thus, the framework places equal emphasis on concept, process, and content outcomes for high-ability learners at K–8 levels.

The concept of "change" was selected to use for unit development based on its ease of application to various areas of the language arts and other areas of study, as well as its well-documented relevance in the world of scholarship and real life. Integral to understanding this concept were a set of generalizations derived from extensive reading about the concept in the fields of philosophy, the social sciences, and science. The generalizations selected using these criteria were:

- Change is pervasive.
- Change is linked to time.
- Change may be perceived as systematic or random.
- Change may represent growth and development or regression and decay.
- Change may occur according to natural order or be imposed by individuals or groups.

These generalizations were then converted into generic concept outcome statements for use across grade-level clusters. No attempt was made to order these outcomes by grade levels. Rather, the translation of the concept outcomes became more sophisticated through the unit development process as the outcomes were treated from grades 3 through 8. Within the context of each curriculum unit, then, students will be able to:

- Understand that change is pervasive.
- Illustrate the variability of change based on time.
- Categorize types of change, given several examples.
- Interpret change in selected works as progressive or regressive.
- Demonstrate the change process at work in a piece of literature.
- Analyze social and individual change in a given piece of literature.

Just as the project promoted a thematic or conceptual orientation in the teaching of language arts, it also emphasized a strong process orientation toward thinking and reasoning. Based on recent work in teaching critical thinking (Paul, 1992), the project focused on selected elements of reasoning as a generic basis for the teaching of reading, writing, speaking, and listening skills. Virtually all modes of communication are subject to these elements. The elements used extensively in this project follow along with the criteria for assessment of that element.

Although elements of reasoning were not directly assessed in the project, they were translated into generic outcomes that ensured the embedding of critical thinking into the teaching of all the language arts. Within each curriculum unit, students will be able to:

- State a purpose for all modes of communication, their own as well as others.
- Define a problem, given ill-structured, complex, or technical information.
- Formulate multiple perspectives (at least two) on a given issue.
- State assumptions behind a line of reasoning in oral or written form.
- Apply linguistic and literary concepts appropriately.
- Provide evidence and data to support a claim, issue, or thesis statement.

- Make inferences, based on evidence.
- Draw implications for policy development or enactment based on the available data.

Additionally, for each grade-level cluster, content outcomes based on the key strands in language arts were developed. Outcome statements were derived from broad goals for reading/literature, writing, language study, and oral communication. These outcome statements became the basis for teacher development of units and assessment of student learning in each of the units. The content-based goals and learner outcomes developed for this project may be found in Appendix B at the end of this book.

For each grade-level cluster, applications to other areas of study beyond language arts were explored using the generalizations for change as the guiding model. Students were encouraged to apply ideas about change to art and music as well as literature. They also systematically explored ideas of change as they were revealed through social, political, and economic forces of the literary time period studied. These explorations were encouraged as the special project component of the units to be done in class, as homework, or as extensions to the unit.

Figure 11–1 represents the relationship of learner outcomes and teaching strategies employed in the language arts framework and subsequent units. The conceptual structure of learner outcomes on the left provides the basis for the specific teaching strategies to be employed with students on the right. The units are centered on literature selections that provide the source for the conceptual outcomes to be explored and the catalyst for the learning strategies to be employed.

The curriculum framework for developing language arts units for high-ability learners, then, was based on three major types of learner outcomes: concept outcomes organized around the theme of "change," process outcomes organized around the elements of reasoning, and content outcomes organized around the four strands of the language arts—literature, writing, oral communication, and language study. Each set of outcomes drove the development of classroom units such that most lesson plans reflect an emphasis on each type of outcome. Figure 11–2 portrays this idea graphically.

Assessment of Learner Outcomes

Although each set of outcomes was used to guide unit development, only selected content outcomes were used for assessment purposes. The assessment protocols developed were (1) representative of each content strand, (2) incorporated an emphasis on the elements of reasoning, and (3) probed understanding of the concept of change. Thus, the integrated features of the

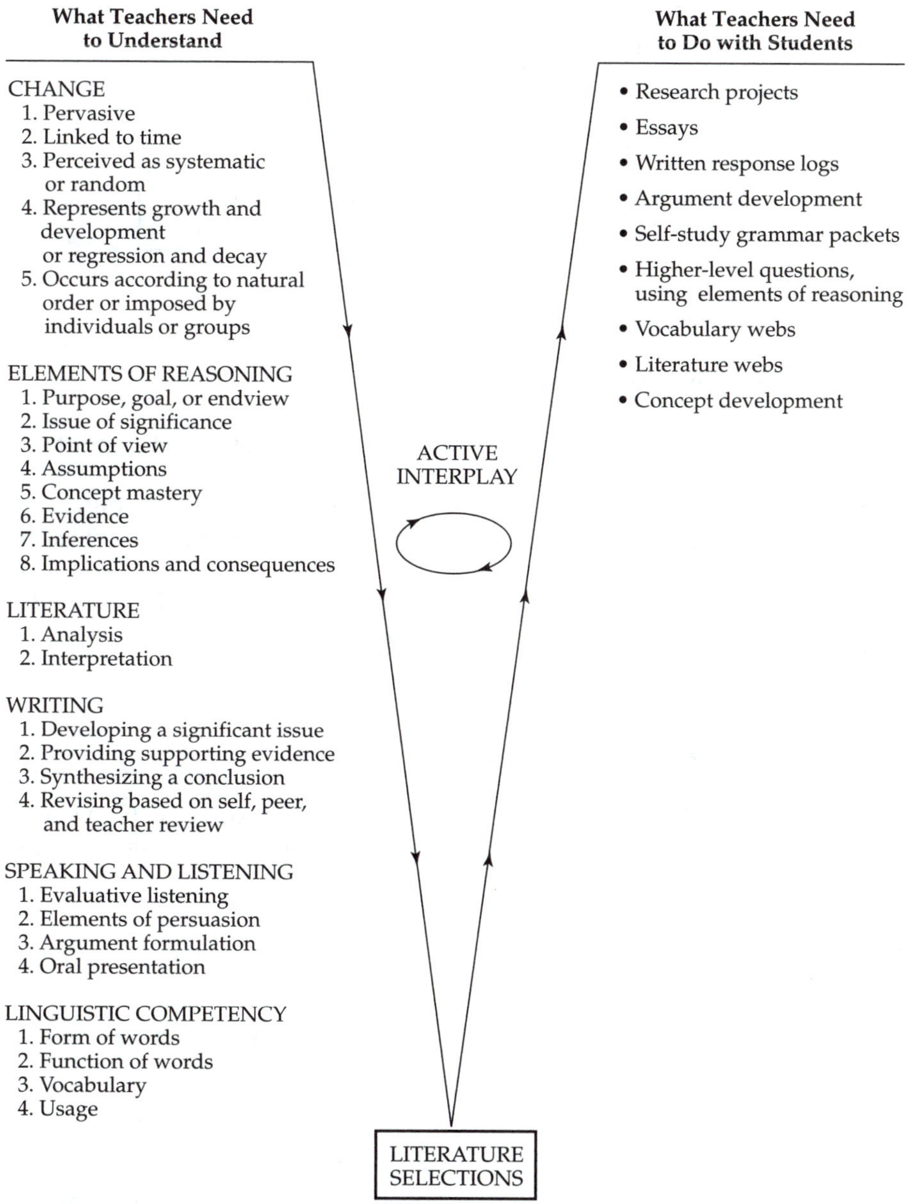

What Teachers Need to Understand	What Teachers Need to Do with Students

CHANGE
1. Pervasive
2. Linked to time
3. Perceived as systematic or random
4. Represents growth and development or regression and decay
5. Occurs according to natural order or imposed by individuals or groups

ELEMENTS OF REASONING
1. Purpose, goal, or endview
2. Issue of significance
3. Point of view
4. Assumptions
5. Concept mastery
6. Evidence
7. Inferences
8. Implications and consequences

LITERATURE
1. Analysis
2. Interpretation

WRITING
1. Developing a significant issue
2. Providing supporting evidence
3. Synthesizing a conclusion
4. Revising based on self, peer, and teacher review

SPEAKING AND LISTENING
1. Evaluative listening
2. Elements of persuasion
3. Argument formulation
4. Oral presentation

LINGUISTIC COMPETENCY
1. Form of words
2. Function of words
3. Vocabulary
4. Usage

ACTIVE INTERPLAY

- Research projects
- Essays
- Written response logs
- Argument development
- Self-study grammar packets
- Higher-level questions, using elements of reasoning
- Vocabulary webs
- Literature webs
- Concept development

LITERATURE SELECTIONS

FIGURE 11–1   Constructing Meaning through Inquiry

Source: From *Learning How to Learn* (p. 3) by J. D. Novak and D. B. Gowin, 1984, Cambridge, England: Cambridge University Press. Copyright 1984 by Cambridge University Press. Adapted with the permission of Cambridge University Press.

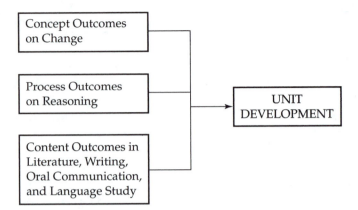

FIGURE 11–2 Emphasis of Learner Outcomes on Unit Development

curriculum were not lost in the assessment process. Moreover, the outcomes measured were also deemed to be the most important for high-ability learners. For example, the emphasis on persuasive writing has been demonstrated to be a weakness among this group of learners at all stages of development. Thus, it is highlighted for special emphasis in the project.

Appropriateness for High-Ability Learners

Each set of outcomes and unit activities were also developed with an eye to characteristics and needs of high-ability learners. The following list illustrates this relationship:

High-Ability Learner Characteristics	*Corresponding Emphases in the Curriculum*
• Advanced reading ability	• Corresponding rich, complex literature selected
• Advanced vocabulary	• Corresponding emphasis on vocabulary development
• Abstract reasoning skills, assignments, and oral presentations	• Emphasis on high-level reasoning in discussion of literature, writing
• Ability to make connections	• Thematic organization of curriculum

High-Ability Learner Characteristics	*Corresponding Emphases in the Curriculum*
• Power of concentration	• Emphasis on analysis and interpretation of literature • Emphasis on long-term projects and meaningful homework
• Concern for moral and ethical issues	• Research on issues of significance
• Emotional sensitivity	• Opportunities for personal response to literature and language
• Ability to generate original ideas	• Emphasis on generative project work

Activities that were used in these units supported advanced levels of complexity that are essential to appropriate curriculum elements for high-ability learners. The following adaptations were made consistently throughout the units:

1. Literature selections used in the units were selected using specific criteria for high-ability learners. In addition, the inclusion of multicultural literature added another dimension of complexity.

2. The inquiry model of discussion moved students from initial reactions to analysis and interpretation of a reading or speech. It invited students to consider multiple perspectives.

3. Vocabulary study in the units went beyond definitions. It modeled study of challenging words, including investigation of etymology, antonyms, synonyms, and related words.

4. Consideration of significant issues was treated on several levels of sophistication. Individual points of view were supported and argued through techniques of persuasion and a claim/data/warrant model. Students were also required to consider and address other points of view.

5. Grammar was treated as a system of thought rather than a set of rules.

6. Interdisciplinary connections were made in the units not only by integrating the language arts themselves but also by linkages with the "sister" arts of music and visual arts and with social, cultural, economic, and political aspects of various societies.

Development of Curriculum Units

A set of six exemplary curriculum units were developed for primary, intermediate, and middle school levels. These units were generated from the selected concept of "change" and flowed from the curriculum framework and related issues already discussed. These units were assessed by eight independent reviewers on the model used to create them. A copy of the development and review critera for the units is contained in the Appendix at the end of this chapter. Each of the six units incorporates four strands of the language arts: literature, persuasive writing, language study, and oral/listening communication. The literature selections in the units were intended to be the springboard for integration of the four strands so that the learner is engaged in a search for meaning through literature. The concept of change served as a central conceptual theme within and across the units. Even though each unit addresses some elements of language study, an additional component was emphasized through the use of student grammar packets that are worked on independently by students. These packets were especially tailored for use by high-ability learners at requisite levels of development (Thompson, 1993). An abstract for each unit is included in Appendix C at the end of the book.

Field testing of newly developed curriculum units was accomplished in the classrooms of the teacher-developers during the fall of 1992. All units were implemented for at least 30 hours of instruction in diverse settings that included: regular classrooms with high-ability learners, pullout programs that met once a week, special classes that met daily, and self-contained programs for high-ability students. The field testing provided valuable data for determining the applicability of the written curriculum to classroom practice. Following the field testing, project staff revised the unit products, based on teacher log data and observational data collected during the field testing. Pre-post data were collected, using authentic assessment protocols developed and validated specifically for the content outcomes of the project. Results of the pilot assessment effort have shown significant growth for students in selected units and areas of the new language arts curriculum.

Implications of the Curriculum Development Project Phase

The first 12 months of curriculum development yielded important data on several issues related to overall curriculum development for high-ability learners. These findings may be characterized as follows:

1. The similarities between curriculum development efforts in general education and the principles of gifted education curriculum development are very complementary. Although the translation of these principles into practice will still require greater flexibility and latitude when dealing with the range of high-ability learners, it is important to note the commonalities of general approaches to curriculum reform with those principles of good gifted education. Because of the complementarity of discipline-specific reform efforts and gifted education tenets, educators of the gifted should align their efforts in curriculum with the work currently going on in all areas of the language arts. As a field, gifted education has much to contribute to the debate on national and international standards in reading, writing, and related areas and much to gain from participating in these conversations. Moreover, the use of the key facets of this curriculum development approach (i.e., learner outcomes of significance, inquiry, authentic assessment) could strengthen existing gifted programs and current school-based efforts.

2. Although there is considerable overlap in the proposed exemplary content-based curriculum for all learners and curriculum differentiation issues for the gifted, there still remain two issues that must be accounted for in working with the gifted. The differentiation for these learners in such a model must still emanate from a clear understanding of the capacity of such learners at a given level to engage in a faster pace of learning at an advanced level. Moreover, high-ability learners require access to more sophisticated curriculum treatment at earlier stages of development. Consequently, curriculum expectations for these students need to reflect such adaptations at advanced levels. Curriculum grounded in intra- and interdisciplinary concepts and higher-order thinking skills such as this project, however, provides much greater opportunities to enhance learning for these students. Curriculum geared to the top 20 percent raises the ceiling and improves overall curriculum, but it still may lack the rigor necessary to challenge our most gifted students, particularly if it is implemented piecemeal or as whole class instruction.

3. The first development phase of the project demonstrated that it is possible to create a set of curriculum materials that are coherent in their treatment of important and desirable features in a curriculum tailored to the needs of high-ability learners. The topics papers, curriculum framework, and the units of study all represent levels of organizing structures that should have facilitated teachers in being able to implement faithfully the progression of the project phases, from the broad framing of a concept to the specific application of classroom activities and/or questions. The curriculum products represent various levels of use from a set of generalizations, to learner outcomes, to classroom units, to lesson plans, to student worksheets. Yet, while written curriculum may be coherent, classroom implementation frequently

is not. Based on the pilot experience, alignment with classroom practice was difficult to effect across all aspects of the framework. Thus, there is a real need to monitor what happens at the classroom level to ensure faithful rendering of ideas into practice.

4. Pilot pre-post results from the language arts effort that used experimental and quasi-experimental conditions showed significant differences favoring the use of the new curriculum with high-ability learners in the areas of literary analysis, vocabulary development, and persuasive writing skills. Results varied, however, from teacher to teacher. Table 11–1 shows the general results by unit. Given that the contact time for the pilot effort was only 30 hours of instruction, these results appear promising for an in-depth future study of curriculum impacts, based on the language arts model used in these units. Also needed are good implementation studies that allow us to understand better the most and least facilitative contexts for classroom and school use.

5. Clearly, one major thrust in curriculum reform in language arts education for high-ability learners must be in the area of teacher training. The need for specific subject-matter training is great if the findings of this project regarding the convergent areas of discipline-specific reform and curriculum efforts for the gifted are to be understood and implemented in all classrooms

TABLE 11–1   Selected Results of Initial Unit Pilots

Unit	Design	Results
Grades 2–3 Journeys and Destinations: The Challenge of Change	Experimental (randomly selected experimental/control group)	A comparison of pre- and post-assessments showed improvement of students in the development of critical reasoning related to comprehension of the main idea of a selection, in understanding the concept of change, and in supporting an answer with valid reasons.
Grades 4–6 Literary Reflections on Personal and Social Change	Quasi-experimental (nonrandom selection of experimental and comparison group)	A comparison of pre- and postassessments indicated significant improvement of students in textual analysis and analytical reading skills as a result of participating in this unit.
Grades 5–6 Changing Ideas and Perspectives through Persuasions	Quasi-experimental (nonrandom selection of experimental and comparison group)	A comparison of pre- and postassessment scorers indicated significant growth in persuasive writing skills for students who participated in the unit.

at the K–8 levels. As found in the review of language arts materials and other studies, teachers are not provided with sufficient grounding in teaching literature, writing, and language through packaged materials in order to teach these subjects effectively. In language arts, all teachers are teachers of the high-ability learner, except in special schools or special classes. Thus, the need to engage with general educators in their staff development efforts to reform education for all learners is a crucial part of our role as educators of the gifted. Major problems that training must address, however, based on data collected during the field testing, include:

- *Lack of content expertise of teachers in the language arts areas.* We tend to think that the serious areas for lack of content knowledge at the elementary level are in math and science; however, there is evidence from our pilot that teachers are not very comfortable with the shared inquiry approach to literature, the reasoning process used to engage in persuasive writing, or techniques for teaching evaluative listening. Moreover, there was limited effort to teach linguistic competency, even though the individual packets were already prepared. Meaningful training must take this lack of discipline-specific knowledge into account and focus on providing for deficits in key areas.
- *Desire to use multiple models rather than teach one well.* Many of the pilot teachers over the years had become hooked on using several ways to teach the fundamental skills of thinking, reasoning, and problem solving. By using multiple models, students were often unable to translate principles in a consistent way, leading to fragmentation and lack of overall understanding of critical aspects of the project. Thus, an individual teacher's desire for creativity and choice interfered with coherence and potentially interfered with enhanced student learning.
- *Ways to integrate and manipulate content, process, and concepts simultaneously.* Teachers need more practice with teaching to multiple outcomes. Although they were comfortable teaching to a single skill, the idea that one activity could be used to address the concept of change, engage students in reasoning, *and* teach content-specific issues was difficult. Teaching more complex materials clearly requires a threshold level of readiness and training on the part of the classroom teacher.
- *Time for teachers to think about what needs changing in a lesson or a unit of study.* Schools are notorious for not providing time for reflection. Our pilot effort demonstrated once again that teachers require more planning time and discussion time at the implementation phase of new curriculum materials than is typically provided in the current school structure. This issue has meaning for teacher trainers as well. The teachers in the pilot effort needed the extended training time provided through this project in order to develop and implement the unit of study. A training model that provides initial input, followed by targeted workshops cou-

pled with on and off site consultation appeared to be essential. A focus group session after the pilot revealed that the teachers needed even more time to reflect on the project than what they had.

6. More than teacher training will be needed, however, to ensure change. Districtwide systems of curriculum management must be developed that encourage teachers to employ new materials and techniques, and that provide adequate planning time for collaboration between and among teachers on how best to deliver instruction. Moreover, new teacher evaluation systems must be constructed that embody the new curriculum emphasis and reward teachers for sharing their expertise with each other and modeling successful practices.

Conclusion

The National Language Arts Curriculum Project for High Ability Learners has demonstrated a key role for educators of high-ability learners in articulating the linkages to national curriculum reform. By helping to determine what high standards might be in language arts, based on our collective knowledge of the brightest learners at each stage of development, we are in a position to enrich curriculum experiences for all learners and focus ever more clearly on the needs of top students who can reach those standards earlier and through differential pathways. Yet upgrading the quality of general curriculum in any area is an enormous task that will require creative strategies for making change and further research and development on what constitutes best practice. Hopefully, this project will have served an important function in providing a blueprint for the general direction to be taken and the potential benefits to be accrued for high-ability learners as a result.

Key Points Summary

- Creation of appropriate language arts curriculum for talented learners requires attention to (1) the needs of high-ability learners, (2) a working knowledge of curriculum reform principles, and (3) an understanding of key issues to incorporate from the language arts communities.
- The National Language Arts Curriculum Project for High Ability Learners provides a model of what curriculum products might be for elementary and middle school students.
- The units employ the concept of change to make connections among selected pieces of literature, other language arts areas, and other disciplines like the social sciences, art, and music.

- The units foster reasoning abilities by employing key questions and activities that require students to infer, to support arguments with data, and to draw implications.
- The units emphasize and integrate all four strands of language arts content.
- Rich, complex literature provides the basis for unit activities and the catalyst for student learning.
- Inquiry-oriented learning experiences are a primary feature of the units.
- Collaborative and interdisciplinary experiences are provided throughout the units.
- Heightening awareness and appreciation of cultural diversity is a major element emphasized in the project.

Appendix: Criteria for Development and Review of Language Arts Units

	Not Observed	Observed	Exemplary Use
I. General Criteria			
Student Outcomes:			
• Are the student outcomes significant or contrived for convenience?	1	2	3
• Do outcomes include both content and process?	1	2	3
Comments:			
Topic/Content:			
• Is the area of study important to the understanding of the language arts?	1	2	3
• Does the area lend itself to inter-disciplinary study?	1	2	3
• Can the selected concept be honestly represented in this area?	1	2	3
Comments:			
Assessments:			
• Are the assessments "authentic"?	1	2	3
• Do the assessments measure the student outcomes?	1	2	3
• Are the assessments varied in type and structure?	1	2	3
Comments:			

	Not Observed	Observed	Exemplary Use
Resources:			
• Are multiple resources being used?	1	2	3
• Are opportunities for learning how to use resources built in?	1	2	3
• Are nonprint resources being utilized?	1	2	3
Comments:			
Technology:			
• Are students required to use technology as a writer and researcher would use it?	1	2	3
• Is the technology relatively current?	1	2	3
• Is the technology appropriate for the age level of the student and the nature of the task?	1	2	3
• Does the technology require learning or simply operational knowledge of a machine?	1	2	3
Comments:			
Extended Learning Opportunities:			
• Are students challenged to engage in learning beyond the school year, on vacations, and weekends?	1	2	3
• Are students provided with high-level homework asssignments?	1	2	3
• Are parents oriented to their potential role in extended learning?	1	2	3
Comments:			

II. Specific Language Arts Emphases

	Not Observed	Observed	Exemplary Use
Whole Language Approach:			
• Does the unit integrate the language arts areas as much as possible?	1	2	3
• Are there interrelated opportunities for reading, speaking, and writing?	1	2	3
• Do students engage with the richest literature possible?	1	2	3
Comments:			

	Not Observed	Observed	Exemplary Use

Multiculturalism/Globalism:

	Not Observed	Observed	Exemplary Use
• Is there evidence of global thinking and interdependence in the perspectives presented?	1	2	3
• Is there an emphasis on futurism as seen in approaches to problem solving, use of scenarios, etc. ?	1	2	3
• Do the units incorporate the best of multicultural literature and culture?	1	2	3
• Is there a balanced perspective on at least three diverse cultures?	1	2	3
• Are the contributions of various cultural groups embedded rather than treated separately?	1	2	3

Comments:

Critical and Creative Thinking:

	Not Observed	Observed	Exemplary Use
• Does the unit incorporate techniques for enhancing thinking skills?	1	2	3
• Does the unit include questions for discussion that emphasize higher-level thinking?	1	2	3
• Do the unit activities engage the learner in reflective thought?	1	2	3

Comments:

Inquiry-Based Instructional Techniques:

	Not Observed	Observed	Exemplary Use
• Are students allowed to discuss new ideas?	1	2	3
• Are students provided an environment where risk taking (and making mistakes) is considered an important part of learning?	1	2	3
• Do students discover ideas and concepts more often than they are told?	1	2	3
• Does the teacher model good thinking practices for students?	1	2	3
• Does the teacher reflect on the students' thinking as well as their knowledge?	1	2	3

Comments:

	Not Observed	Observed	Exemplary Use
Metacognition:			
• Are there opportunities built into the unit to allow students to think about their thinking strategies?	1	2	3
• Are there opportunities for teachers to reveal their thinking to students (model metacognition)?	1	2	3
Comments:			
Research Process:			
• Are students provided the skills and responses necessary to explore a relevant issue?	1	2	3
• Are the students encouraged to engage in research?	1	2	3
• Is there enough latitude for students to develop their own issues?	1	2	3
• Does the issue of significance allow students to act as social scientists?	1	2	3
Comments:			
Interdisciplinary Applications:			
• Does the topic naturally bring language arts and other disciplines together?	1	2	3
• Can the concept being studied also be demonstrated in other disciplines?	1	2	3
Comments:			

III. Specific Language Arts Strand Emphases

	Not Observed	Observed	Exemplary Use
Literature			
• Do the units reflect choice of literature based on intellectual, affective, and multicultural considerations?	1	2	3
• Do the units emphasize expectations for advanced reading behaviors?	1	2	3
• Do the units incorporate textual analysis of conceptually rich material?	1	2	3
• Do the units emphasize inquiry-based discussion?	1	2	3
• Do the units link reading activities to other language arts activities?	1	2	3
Comments:			

	Not Observed	Observed	Exemplary Use
Writing:			
• Do the units use concept mapping to teach outlining?	1	2	3
• Do the units emphasize persuasive writing?	1	2	3
• Do the units focus on strategies for developing a thesis statement, providing supportive evidence, and drafting a conclusion?	1	2	3
• Do the units reflect the use of revision in the writing process?	1	2	3
• Do the units reflect the use of work-shopping techniques (peer review and discussion of each other's writing)?	1	2	3
Comments:			

	Not Observed	Observed	Exemplary Use
Language Study:			
• Do the units emphasize the development of word relationships, such as synonyms, antonyms, and analogies?	1	2	3
• Do the units include opportunities to learn appropriate-level vocabulary?	1	2	3
• Do the units encourage the development of linguistic competence in English, with equal emphasis on grammatical structure?	1	2	3
• Do the units include opportunities to learn about the history of language, etymology, and/or semantics?	1	2	3
Comments:			

	Not Observed	Observed	Exemplary Use
Speaking/Listening Communication:			
• Do the units provide opportunities for students to engage in active speaking and listening activities?	1	2	3
• Do the units promote the use of persuasive speaking?	1	2	3
• Do the units promote involvement of students in responding to each other's presentations through questions, discussion, and critique?	1	2	3
• Do the units address critical thinking skills through listening and speaking?	1	2	3
Comments:			

References

Adler, M. (1982). *The Paedeia proposal: An educational manifesto.* New York: Collier Books.

Applebee, A. N. (1981). *Writing in the secondary schools* (Research Monograph No. 21). Urbana, IL: National Council of Teachers of English.

Applebee, A. N. (1984). *Contexts for learning to write: Studies of secondary school instruction.* Norwood, NJ: Ablex.

Baskin, B., & Harris, K. (1980). *Books for the gifted child.* New York: Bowker.

California Department of Education. (1987). *State of California language arts framework.* Sacramento, CA: Author.

Cazden, C. (1983). Adult assistance to language development: Scaffolds, models, and direct instruction. In R. P. Parker & F. A. Davis (Eds.), *Developing literacy.* Newark, DE: International Reading Association.

Cazden, C. (1988). *Classroom discourse: The language of teaching and learning.* Portsmouth, NH: Heinemann.

Chaney, A. L. (1992). *Issues in contemporary oral communication instruction.* Topics paper developed for National Language Arts project. Washington, DC: U. S. Department of Education.

Chomsky, C. (1969). *The acquisition of syntax in children from 5 to 10.* Cambridge, MA: MIT Press.

Chomsky, C. (1986). *Knowledge of language.* New York: Praeger.

Cooper, C., & Brennenan, B. (1988). *Writing achievement of California eighth graders: A first look.* Sacramento, CA: California State Department of Education.

Durkin, D. (1966). *Children who read early.* New York: Teachers College Press.

Halsted, J. (1988). *Guiding gifted readers from preschool through high school.* Columbus, OH: Ohio Psychology Press.

Hirsch, Jr., E. D. (1987). *Cultural literacy: What every American needs to know.* Boston, MA: Houghton Mifflin.

Jackson, N. E. (1988). Precocious reading ability: What does it mean? *Gifted Child Quarterly, 32*(2), 234–243.

Langer, J., & Allington, R. (1992). Curriculum research in writing and reading. In P. Jackson (Ed.) *Handbook of research on curriculum* (pp. 687–725). New York: Macmillan.

National Assessment Governing Board. (1992). *Reading framework for the 1992 National Assessment of Education Progress.* Washington, DC: United States Department of Education.

National Center for Education Statistics. (1992). *National assessment of educational progress's 1990 portfolio study.* Washington, DC: United States Department of Education.

National Council of Teachers of English. (1988). *Reading commission report.* Urbana, IL: Author.

Novak, J. D., & Gowin, D. B. (1984). *Learning how to learn.* New York: Cambridge University Press.

Palinscar, A. S., & Brown, A. L. (1984). Reciprocal teaching of comprehension-fostering and comprehension-monitoring activities. *Cognition and Instruction, 1*(2), 117–175.

Paul, R. (1992). *Critical thinking: What every person needs to survive in a rapidly changing world.* Santa Rosa, CA: The Foundation for Critical Thinking.

Pollette, N. (1982). *3 R's for the gifted: Reading, writing, and research.* Littleton, CO: Libraries Unlimited.

Polette, N., & Hamlin, M. (1980). *Exploring books with gifted children.* Littleton, CO: Libraries Unlimited.

Roedell, W. C., Jackson, N. E. , & Robinson, H. B. (1980). *Gifted young children.* New York: Teacher's College Press.

Skinner, B. F. (1957). *Verbal behavior.* New York: Appleton, Century, and Crofts.

Spivey, N. (1990). Transforming texts. *Written Communication, 7(2),* 256–287.

Stahl, S., & Miller, P. (1989). Whole language and language experience approaches for beginning reading: A quantitative research synthesis. *Review of Educational Research, 59(1),* 87–116.

Suhor, C. (1984). *1984 Report on trends and issues in English: A summary of reports from the NCTE commissions.* (ERIC Document Reproduction Service N. ED 239290.)

Thompson, M. (1991). *The magic lens.* Unionville, NY: Trillium.

Thompson, M. (1992). *The word within the word.* (Vol 2). Unionville, NY: Trillium.

Thompson, M. (1993). *Inspecting our own ideas.* Saratoga Springs, NY: Board of Cooperative Extension Services.

Tschudi, S. (1991). *Planning and assessing the curriculum in English language arts.* Alexandria, VA: ASCD.

VanTassel-Baska, J. (1993). *Comprehensive curriculum for gifted learners* (2nd ed.). Boston, MA: Allyn and Bacon.

12

*Evaluating Language
Arts Materials*

PHYLLIS W. ALDRICH
Coordinator for Gifted Education, BOCES

This chapter discusses a curriculum review of the leading language arts reading and writing textbooks commonly used in many U.S. schools. From 1989 to 1991, a team of researchers and practitioners convened by the Saratoga-Warren Counties Boards of Cooperative Education (BOCES) developed a Curriculum Assessment Guide (CAG) based on current research in literacy and in the education of gifted children. The CAG was field-tested extensively by two different teams of curriculum raters and revised for clarity. In addition to commercially published basal texts, we (the members of BOCES) reviewed the few supplementary language arts resource materials that we could identify as exemplary for highly able verbal learners. The search for content that was meaningful, based on rich literary texts, and that held out the promise of genuine stimulus for inquiry was illuminating. We found few challenging curriculum avenues for teachers of highly able verbal students to follow. The scanty collection of worthy materials dramatically underscores the need for curriculum development meeting world-class standards.

Our findings corroborated Chall's (1991) study about the diminishing difficulty of most textbooks over the last 50 years. To provide historical perspective, we decided to review the McGuffey readers that had sustained teachers and students in the United States from the 1830s to the 1920s. We

218

found persuasive evidence that, according to measures of rigorous content, vocabulary, syntax, grammar, sophistication, and complexity of thought, the McGuffey series offered far more challenge than the more elaborate modern basal readers.

There are critical implications of this materials deficit. As programs for able children are increasingly eliminated in the name of "detracking," honors programs disbanded in the name of equity, and therefore more classrooms composed of students spanning wide extremes of ability, teachers will face a daunting task. Without a rich array of quality curriculum materials to guide them, teachers will not be able to challenge the most able. Those students' talents will languish and accelerate the disturbing trends labeled by Singal (1991) as "the other crisis in American schools"—namely, the demotivation of talent.

Rationale and History

The recent reform efforts energized by the National Education Goals and tempered by concerns for equity that promise all children the opportunity to "learn to use their minds well" have led to particular quandaries with respect to high-ability students. Specifically, in language arts, U.S. students at all levels have lost ground. Analyses of scores on the SAT-Verbal show that the number of students earning a score of 600 or higher has declined 35 percent since 1972, even though the number of test takers has increased by 1 percent (National Excellence, 1993).

On one hand, the public's tendency to assume that bright students' talents will develop without any special interventions has been fueled by Kozol's (1991) study of "savage inequalities" in classrooms and Oates's (1985) vivid personal observations about the injustices of tracking. Popularization of these accounts has lent momentum to the critics of gifted programs and led to dissolution of many of those programs.

The crusade against the "elitism" perceived in programming for the gifted has led to the reduction of advanced placement and honors classes— and has spurred national leaders such as Al Shanker of the American Federation of Teachers to emphasize that the renewed push for equity does not require that models of excellence and academic rigor be dismantled. Indeed, the Governors at the National Education Summit of 1989 agreed that, in order for U.S. students to compete internationally, all quartiles had to demonstrate improved achievement. The formulation of the national goals refrained from including a national policy against ability grouping.

However, in the past several years, many national reports that have documented alarming facts about the actual achievement of the top-ability students underscore that this desired achievement does not happen without nurturing. Stevenson and Stigler's (1992) 10-year study comparing U.S. students' math performance to those in Japan, Korea, and Taiwan revealed that not only were most of our students behind, but also the most able U.S. students did not score in the top 10 percent. Although the International Education Assessment (IEA) reported that among 10 industrial nations U.S. 9-year-olds ranked near the top, it cautioned that this study measured only the most basic comprehension skills (Institute for Educational Research, 1988). In the arena of advanced inference skills, the 1990 National Assessment of Educational Progress report on reading showed that since 1971 at the upper levels of performance, achievement had increased little and, at the top, is declining. The report concluded that "there has been a substantial decline in the percentage of 17-year-olds who have reached the 'advanced' level signifying ability to synthesize and learn from specialized reading materials" (Mullis, Owen, & Phillips, 1990). When students were asked to construct a written response that involved analyzing, interpreting, or evaluating what was read, very few were able to examine meaning by providing arguments or evidence to support their interpretations.

The 1992 NAEP study on student writing portfolios painted an even bleaker picture of deficiencies in students' skills. Even though most of the data in the study came from more affluent schools and the work was not produced in a test situation, the quality of written samples was poor. In the category of persuasive writing, only a few samples were submitted, and none of them earned scores beyond minimal levels (Gentile, 1992). Thus, it appears that teachers need guidance in knowing how to teach persuasive writing to all their students. Increasingly, evidence seems to suggest that talent does not emerge without deliberate cultivation.

Singal (1991), a history professor at Hobart and William Smith Colleges, concerned about the dismal state of reading and writing skills of college freshmen attending selective colleges, analyzed 20 years of SAT scores, grading practices, and curriculum. He concluded that there had been an alarming decline in rigor—in the quantity and quality of reading in elementary and secondary schools and a 70-point drop in verbal SAT scores between 1966 and 1976 before changes in testing demographics. He maintained that the drop could not be explained by the newer groups taking the SAT, but by a real drop in skills of the most able. The extent of the decline was highlighted more recently in the *Chronicle of Higher Education* (Shea, 1993), which reported that "the number of students who scored above 600 on the verbal section of the Scholastic Aptitude Test has dropped by 35 percent since 1972."

The development of verbal ability, even when conscientiously attempted, is proving to be a complex task. Researchers from The Johns Hopkins University Center for Talented Youth have conducted several studies of disadvantaged fifth-graders who showed intellectual promise but who had been omitted from local programs for the gifted due to lack of skills. Results from five years of an ambitious intervention program for at-risk students of high potential reveal the difficulty of the redressing of verbal weaknesses (Lynch & Mills, 1993). The Skills Reinforcement Program (SRP) found that, while the students were able to show strong growth in the math area, improvement in the verbal area was far more difficult to achieve. After a year of intensive intervention through the Skills Reinforcement Project, students in the treatment group made significantly greater gains than a control group in mathematics but not in reading. The researchers noted that "the students' mathematical skills and reasoning ability proved more amenable to dramatic change than their verbal ability" (Lynch & Mills, 1990, pp. 375–376). They went on to speculate whether "verbal development may simply require more instructional time and 'homework' time to produce greater advances in proficiency "(Lynch & Mills, 1990).

In another study (Lynch & Mills, 1993), the authors again found that increases in language arts achievement "were not as dramatic as the mathematics gains" and suggested that "the language arts program might be improved by increasing the length of the intervention or with curricular modifications." In a third study, the researchers found the same pattern of results: The "gains made by students in the language arts classes on standardized reading tests were less impressive [than in math]." They hypothesized that "it is also possible that growth in language skills is harder to achieve with academic intervention...owing to the nature and content of the two disciplines" (Mills, Stork, & Krug, 1992). Their tentative conclusion vividly underscores the need for new language arts curriculum. The task of building language arts strength in high-potential students has proven to be a serious challenge resistant to quick or superficial solutions.

In Yonkers, New York, special magnet schools for the gifted, "P.E.A.R.L.S.," which enroll 55 percent minority students, have found similar difficulty in improving verbal scores. After an intensive intervention program designed to narrow the apparent achievement gap between minority and majority gifted students in language arts and mathematics, "results indicated significant growth in the area of mathematics, but there was little change in the language arts area" (G. Pack, personal communication, February 1, 1992).

One of the only advanced language arts-based programs for highly able elementary students in rural upstate New York is the Saratoga Warren BOCES Young Scholars program. It was begun in 1987 to offer intellectual challenge in the humanities for students who reason better than four grades above their agemates. In 1992–93, 233 students from 35 different schools attended one of 15 sites for a full day per week to study classics such as *The Odyssey, Medea, Gilgamesh, Beowulf,* and *The Once and Future King* with intellectual peers. Significant growth in inference, reading comprehension, vocabulary, and writing skills has been carefully documented under the guidance of evaluators from The Johns Hopkins University (Aldrich & Mills, 1989). The success of this program seems to suggest that rigorous curriculum based on in-depth study of challenging literature can bring about meaningful growth in language arts among the verbally talented.

Not only on the national level, but also within the field of gifted education, researchers have documented special curriculum needs of gifted learners. Durden and Tangherlini (1993) vividly described the challenge in their recent book: "For talented students, proceeding from kindergarten to the twelfth grade in the nationally prescribed lockstep is often a torturous procedure" (p. 3). Other writers as well have focused strongly on this area (Kaplan, 1986; Maker, 1982; Passow, 1982; VanTassel-Baska, 1992).

The recent study of 7,300 third- and fourth-grade teachers by Archambault and colleagues (1993) concluded that classroom teachers make only minor modifications in the regular curriculum to meet the needs of gifted students. For instance, in 92 days of observing teachers, they noted that less than 22 percent of the questions required the students to think beyond the factual level. The researchers found this disturbing, since many districts have eliminated resource room programs due to economic problems or concerns about equity of grouping students homogeneously. To counteract this situation, they call for more concentrated efforts to help classroom teachers to provide gifted students with an enriched curriculum—efforts that include curriculum materials specifically designed for classroom teacher use.

A recent study analyzed the efficacy of curriculum compacting procedures in which highly able students were allowed to demonstrate beforehand that they had mastered the required skills in a unit. In many cases, they were then freed to engage in more meaningful work (Reis & Purcell, 1992). Although this study offers persuasive evidence that teachers can learn how to compact and that their students benefit, the practice is not common. A serious challenge suggested by the Reis study is that for teachers to learn how to compact, they first need to know where to find rigorous curriculum materials and how to use them.

Even at the level of state language arts frameworks and curriculum guides, the needs of the gifted are almost invisible. Dunkleberger (1992) analyzed documents from 44 of the states and found that "only seven even acknowledged the existence of highly able learners." Such a lack makes this project's goal to offer model curricula that reflect the elements of "new" language arts and standards appropriate for the gifted learner even more compelling.

Langer (1992) identified teachers' needs for knowledge about effective instructional strategies for using literature. She has been able to identify "general principles of instruction that underlie classrooms where literary understandings are supported" (p. 1) and has delineated the kinds of scaffolding teachers need to provide to enable such learnings to take place. She finds that even though the theory may be valid, "teachers need clear guidelines to use on a day to day basis to guide them in creating the classroom contexts where they can move beyond facts, and teach 'thoughtfulness. '" Thus, a first step to ensure classrooms as places where thoughtfulness is prized and practiced is to identify good materials.

Existing Practice

Conflicting opinions about the best ways to teach reading and writing abound. In spite of the current widespread popularity of articles, books, and research that praise literature-based instruction and whole language and that call for the integration of reading and writing, many teachers still rely heavily on commercial reading programs for the majority of their instruction (Mullis, Owen, & Phillips, 1990). Indeed, in the 1990 NAEP Reading Assessment, over 90 percent of fourth- and eighth-grade teachers sampled noted that they used a basal reading program for a major part of their instruction. Consequently, one major task for the National Language Arts Curriculum Project was to analyze several of the leading series for their appropriateness to the needs of highly able learners.

Goodman, in his *Report Card on the Basals* (1989), cited these major problems with basal reading programs: Most student texts prescribe a controlled learning sequence; most selections are excerpts with simplified vocabulary; the ethnic balance is contrived; the teacher must closely follow the prepared script; only 10 to 15 percent of the instructional time is spent in the actual reading experience; emphasis on prereading activities constricts the role of student interpretation; assessments usually consist of narrow, skill-based exercises; and reading is seen only as an act of identifying words. Goodman concluded by endorsing Frank Smith's major objection to basals: They overlook the possibility that the student might have a worthwhile idea to pursue as part of the reading experience (Smith, 1988). Teachers faced with the challenge of teaching highly able learners are particularly mindful of the need to encourage independent thinking and deal with student-generated issues or ideas.

New Understanding of Reading

In response to these limitations of basals, many reading researchers have proposed several antidotes that seem much more compatible with the needs of children. Editors of commercial reading programs also have shown increased sensitivity to these issues (Walmsley & Walp, 1991). The following

1992 guidelines from D. C. Heath, a textbook company, illustrate this trend. The editors state that their goal is to produce thinkers instead of robots or decoders of isolated words; that reading is a conversation with great minds; that reading is a meaning-seeking process; that the language arts should be integrated; that students should have the best language models; that the students' own language is viewed as a major resource; and that language is not assumed to be only a solitary activity.

If effective reading is viewed as a transaction or conversation between the reader and the author from which the reader builds meaning, then the challenge for teachers of verbally talented learners is to put the reader in touch with the broadest range and depth of thinkers. In effect, the teacher's role is to find "idea partners" for the students. The teacher needs to assume that readers bring a variety of thoughts and questions to the "conversation" and must not underestimate either the students' background knowledge or their capacity to generate their own ideas (Wolf, 1988).

Curriculum Assessment Guide: Guidelines to Good Language Arts Materials

The Consumer's Guide to English-Language Arts Curriculum underscores the difficulties teachers face when looking at the major basal reading and writing series (Aldrich & McKim, 1992). From 1989 to 1991, a team of researchers and practitioners convened by the Saratoga-Warren Counties Boards of Cooperative Education (BOCES) developed a Curriculum Assessment Guide (CAG) based on current research in literacy and on the education of gifted children. The CAG was field-tested extensively by two different teams of curriculum raters and revised for clarity.

The teams of reviewers included teachers of the highly able verbal learners from the Saratoga Springs, New York, area, experienced classroom teachers with heterogeneous groups of students, curriculum specialists, professors from the National Research Center on Literature Teaching and Learning, and a member of the National Assessment Governing Board Reading and Writing Committee.

The curriculum review project began with the steering committee's design of a research-based Curriculum Assessment Guide, which grew out of three guiding ideas: rigorous curriculum content, unique needs of the gifted learner, and learning environment. The design of the CAG took far longer than we anticipated and required many different revisions in order to create a document with which researchers would be happy and one which teachers could use comfortably. Our first step was to engage our lead scholar and linguist in a thorough literature review of the research in language acquisition, reading, and writing so that we could be sure that our document would be firmly grounded in current and thoughtful research.

Synthesizing findings proved to be a difficult task. If we included everything from research, we ran the risk of producing a document that was far too unwieldy for daily practitioner use. After three revisions and field tests among our staff and outside teachers, we finally arrived at consensus on the scope and nature of the document

The purpose of the Curriculum Assessment Guide is to assist teachers and curriculum planners in weighing the merits of a particular curriculum in order to determine where it fits into current research on literacy research and the needs of gifted children. We felt strongly that classroom teachers needed to have an authority to guide them through the plethora of alluring but unsubstantive commercially published materials that did not genuinely challenge highly able learners. After developing the CAG in this iterative fashion, we received encouraging feedback from superintendents and language arts specialists around the country.

What Is the Curriculum Assessment Guide (CAG)?

The CAG was designed to be used by administrators, curriculum specialists, and classroom teachers to apply not only to comprehensive language arts series but also to supplementary materials with more specialized focus. The CAG is organized around three interlocking features, all of which are important to consider when making curriculum choices.

The first CAG concern is *literacy content*: What exactly will be taught? Challenging content offers the verbally able student issues, problems, and themes through a variety of texts, formats, and purposes in reading, writing, and oral communication. Strong literacy content that supports multiple pathways for creating meaning invites vigorous exploration and promotes attitudes and habits for lifelong learning.

The second CAG emphasis is *learner needs*: What do the highly able need from their language arts experience? Rich engagement for verbally talented students offers both structured and open-ended opportunities that promote high-level critical thinking and metacognitive skills. Challenging language arts experiences expand students' curiosity and foster interpretive and evaluative judgments. Even among the highly able, learner needs vary. Therefore, a broad range of experiences to meet those needs is desirable.

The third area that the CAG addresses is *literacy community*: How might the teacher in the classroom create a community of inquiry? The teacher's roles are those of facilitator, colearner, and problem solver. The development of literacy community emphasizes language as a common and essential bond of communication. It provides an interactive model of literacy behavior

through multiple literacy events involving both independent and collaborative learning.

How Was the CAG Applied?

Project staff reviewed three categories of language arts materials: comprehensive reading and language textbook series known as *basals*, state language arts curricula, and supplemental texts and literature-based
approaches designed expressly to challenge gifted learners by not-for-profit
publishers such as districts, universities, or foundations.

Two separate groups of reviewers used the CAG to analyze the same
materials. One group was composed of experienced classroom practitioners
and language arts teachers from local schools; the other group was made up
of researchers from the State University of New York at Albany. We found
the perspectives from these two different kinds of reviewers to be very interesting. For the most part, the researchers from the Center on Literature
National Research Center on Literature Teaching and Learning were more
critical of the commercially produced materials than the teachers from regular classrooms. However, teachers from programs devoted solely to highly
able verbal learners concurred with findings from the Center on Literature
National Research Center on Literature Teaching and Learning. In brief, we
found no one set of commercially prepared materials that would challenge
gifted learners.

The reviewers rated the materials described on both holistic and numer-
ical scales. In the summaries of findings that follow, the reviewers' intention
was to assist teachers in practical ways to select suitable challenging language arts materials from an array of published and teacher-made lessons.
The target audience for the *Consumer's Guide* is the teacher who might ask:
What materials might I choose to challenge those students whose verbal abilities seem by far to exceed others in my class? or How can I plan lessons that
will stimulate students' thinking and provide opportunities for fruitful
group interaction and solitary pondering? or If my school requires a basal,
what might I choose and how can I justify this decision to administrators or
parents? or If selection of materials is unlimited, in which ways might I best
move highly able verbal learners toward acquisition of valuable skills and
deeper thoughtfulness?

We were looking for exemplary curriculum material to help verbally
able students develop these habits of mind:

- To look for the pivotal ideas in the text
- To become sensitive to/aware of ambiguity, irony, and nuance in text

- To be able to recognize an author's "voice" and how it is achieved
- To put forward their own ideas about the text supported by textual references
- To appreciate the power of syntax
- To understand how the arts illuminate and add dimensions to meaning
- To approach and engage with text through the sister arts—music, painting, drama, and sculpture
- To become aware of authors' assumptions about cultural background
- To recognize similar themes expressed by writers from different cultures (i.e., through comparative literature)
- To propose connections between texts and different disciplines
- To read widely among the classics in all genres
- To become sophisticated consumers of various genres
- To appreciate the relationship between form and format
- To develop fluency, flexibility, and one's own voice as a writer
- To develop a lifelong love of reading
- To become critical, questioning thinkers
- To appreciate the multiple pathways to pursue meaning and arrive at solutions

Of the more than 300 books and supplementary materials that we initially reviewed, barely a handful matched the criteria that we set forth in the CAG. This meant either that our standards were too high or that we were demanding curricula to be strong in too many different ways. We hypothesized that perhaps there could be no one completely packaged approach to challenging highly able verbal learners.

In addition to commercially published basal texts, the team reviewed the few language arts resource materials that are commonly in use with highly able verbal learners. Those materials that pass through our Stage One Review and merited a fuller analysis did not earn high scores in every category but were deemed highly effective as supplementary approaches. Programs such as Junior Great Books, the McGuffey Readers, and the Center for Talented Youth (CTY) reading and writing course guidelines offered rich examples of materials worth teaching and expanding upon. For instance, we found that the McGuffey Readers earned very high scores in most of our criteria except for varied assessment forms and the multicultural aspects. The Junior Great Books emphasis on shared inquiry discussion techniques and their rich array of literature selections were deemed appropriate for all learners, including highly able learners, even though assessment suggestions were limited. The CTY materials were ambitious in concept and scope but offered limited guidelines for specific lessons.

General Observations about the Reading Series

The reviewers' conclusions corroborated Goodman's (1989) criticism of most commercially produced language arts materials and Chall's (1991) observation about "dumbed down" texts. The reviewers found that the basals' gap between introductory rhetoric and actual lessons offered little to challenge the most verbally able. A set of specific concerns found in the review follows:

1. The philosophy statements that the publishers include in the opening sections of a teacher's manual often reflect current research in reading education. Concepts such as the following are addressed: *multicultural perspectives* (linking themes and thought from many different cultures); *critical thinking* (analysis, synthesis, and evaluation); *fluency* in speaking and writing (generating many ideas); *teaching skills in context* (as opposed to drill-and-practice exercises unrelated to any content); *emergent literacy* (the theory that young children develop reading and writing skills as part of a gradual process that cannot be plotted on a strict time line and that the entire print and spoken environment exerts a powerful influence on this development); *reader response* (an attitude that encourages the child's interpretations of a story that may be displayed in many ways such as art, play writing, or invented spelling); and the treatment of both students and teachers as members of a *literacy community*. (This term recognizes the vigor of a classroom in which the teacher and the students engage in inquiry.)

2. Some of the publishers suggest strategies teachers can use to make the literature/language arts classrooms into environments where literacy is supported in a way that encourages growth. These approaches are sometimes described in an appendix and other times included in the introductory sections of the manuals. At least four of the six publishers we reviewed outlined either a process approach to writing, a reader response to literature, or both.

3. Three of the publishers—Scott Foresman, Houghton Mifflin, and Heath—supplied what we would consider rich literature selections. The others offered very short selections that might be difficult to use to encourage multiple interpretations, a critical stance, or rich responses to the readings. Supplemental reading selections would be necessary for all the programs, but would not be helpful unless the problem of the publishers' viewing literature in a subordinate role is addressed. One publisher, for example, has moved toward featuring literature as a model of writing to be copied, or as a springboard for activities that seem more additive or associative than self-contained. Within these activities, students can explore multiple perspectives. This trend is particularly important because the literary experience is essential to full literacy development.

4. The unit activities, in many instances, do not reflect the stated philosophies. Lessons often are teacher directed to the point of devaluing the students' thinking. As an example, questions are often posed by the teacher and the expected responses are supplied in the manual. There seems to be little room for students to engage in, and be supported in, ever-deepening thinking. There seems to be little attention to increasing sophistication within the material; unit formats remain consistent throughout the year, and even from year to year.

5. Mechanics and discrete skills still seem to be the driving forces behind many aspects of the programs. The concept of teaching skills in context has not been well developed in most of these materials. There seems not to be an understanding that these skills, in order to be relevant to the students, have to grow out of student needs. Students should be invited to hone their skills for the purpose of supporting lively engagement in a true literacy event rather than a routine answer to a teacher's contrived question.

Summary of Findings from the Review of the Basal Writing Series

Overall, the review of basal writing series substantiates concerns about both substance and emphasis likely to be found in programs using these texts.

1. All of the series attempt to reflect current research; some are more successful at the task than others. Their philosophy statements promise integration of the language arts (reading, writing, speaking, listening) with each other and with thinking. All series attempt to achieve integration by having students read a literature selection, analyze it for structure and use of language, and use the selection as a model for their own writing. The series seek to encourage students to become successful lifelong communicators by applying language arts skills to other academic areas and to real-life situations.

2. All of the publishers suggest teaching strategies intended to promote literacy community within the language arts classroom. These approaches occur throughout the annotated teacher's manuals in unit/lesson-specific examples and, sometimes, through generic suggestions in a discrete manual section. All publishers outline a process approach to writing.

3. Despite the literacy model approach supported by the publishers, no series includes a majority of rich or rigorous literature selections. Within a unit, students consider only one or two brief inclusions of no more than three or four pages. Literature in a subordinate role does not offer students occasion to savor the style, tone, or message of writers. It permits brief glimpses instead of providing multicultural perspectives.

4. Unit activities, for the most part, fall short of the philosophy statements' promises. The series lack significant, in-depth writing topics that foster problem solving, innovation, and extended thinking. Reading and writing are emphasized, whereas speaking and listening are secondary and receive scant development. Many activities use a consistent, predictable format and are traditional, teacher-led instruction of predetermined grammar content. There is little attention to increasing sophistication within each series level.

5. Grammar, mechanics, usage, and adherence to the various stages of the writing process are the driving forces behind the programs. Although attempted, contextual skills development is underdeveloped. Much of the material in these series consists of unimaginative formats and sets of rules dispensed through contrived content area exercises.

Implications for the Teacher

If effective reading is viewed as a transaction or conversation between the reader and the author from which the reader builds meaning, then the challenge for teachers of gifted learners is to put the reader in touch with the broadest range and depth of thinkers. In effect, the teacher's role is to find *idea partners* for the students. The teacher needs to assume that readers bring a variety of thoughts and questions to the "conversation" and must not underestimate either the students' background knowledge or their capacity to generate their own ideas (Wolf, 1988).

An interactive model of literacy behavior suggests that it may no longer be appropriate or pedagogically useful to focus on language arts content and/or skills in isolation, as has frequently been the practice. In many instances, content has been relegated to the role of providing materials for skills practice (Babbitt, 1989). For instance, a work of literature might be used as an example of sequencing or student writing could serve as an exercise in paragraphing. When content does occupy center stage in commercial reading programs, classroom activities typically focus on recognizing teacher-based, preordained expectations and demonstrating recognition in teacher-determined formats.

The model of *idea partners* implies that the teacher must make room for and actively seek out the nature of the students' ideas and thoughts. Educators must no longer assume that "one size fits all"—or that the student responses to the same piece should be similar to be correct. In fact, different interpretations should be encouraged.

To the language arts classroom, teachers must bring their own assumptions about students as meaning makers and creators of ideas, their own sensitivity to writing, their own judgments about content, and their own sense that the entire classroom comprises a literacy community. Most importantly, teachers must not underestimate a gifted student's ability to engage with rigorous content.

The two criteria found most wanting in the review of basal materials were rigor and richness, both critical to providing optimal materials for talented learners in the language arts.

What does *rigorous content* mean? How might a teacher know how and where to find rigor for gifted learners? In current discussions about school reform, there is much discussion about world-class standards. These have varied connotations. On one level, *standards* may imply a comparison. For instance, how might one compare essays written by twelfth-graders on an Advanced Placement English test? What makes the difference between those rated as 5 and those rated as 1? How do performance expectations for fourth-graders deemed to be doing advanced work in England or Japan compare to those in the United States?

Rigor is an elusive concept. It may be viewed simply as reading works considered too difficult for most students at a certain age. But it should not be confused with *rigor mortis*—something stiff and lifeless. Instead, it might be seen as a backbone or tree trunk that has the potential to support many branches. Rigor implies something difficult, something requiring a student to stretch to understand, something that eludes instant recognition, something that is subtle, below the surface, perhaps beyond a reader's immediate experience; it is something hinting at many layers or patterns. *Rigorous content* means that the reader needs to work to make sense out of the text, but that the process of wrestling to achieve meaning is worth the effort.

Rigor means that the ideas inhabiting the words are worthy of pondering, that adequate responses cannot be forced to fit the mold of habitual or commonly perceived "relevant" responses or clichés. Rigorous content does not condescend to, or underestimate, the student's ideas. Rigorous content lures, cajoles, and invites students to think and make connections.

Rich content must be viewed in the context of a specific domain or discipline (Ochse, 1990). It contains conceptual depth and often reaches across disciplines. Highly able students, like most students, learn best when the level of difficulty extends just beyond their grasp (Vygotsky, 1978) and when the range of association from the context is highly diverse. Students flourish when challenged by text that is filled with implied meaning, rich vocabulary, irony, and subtle humor. They appreciate varied viewpoints (Ochse, 1990).

The failure of curricula to include the classical foundations of Western literature such as mythology, the Bible, and Shakespeare have left students less able to appreciate the literature that expands on those themes and images. In the admirable current push to seek out rich sources of literature in other cultures, teachers must not overlook some of the major sources of inspiration central to much Western literature.

The emphasis in textbooks on controlled vocabulary and short noncomplex sentences has depleted the richness and range of children's reading experiences. Diane Ravitch's query, "Where Have All the Classics Gone?" (1987), documented the stark contrast between the content of late nineteenth-century readers and reading textbooks published since 1940. Children's stories by Alcott, Defoe, Tennyson, Longfellow, Keats, Audubon, and Thoreau had been expunged due to the length of their sentences and complex vocabulary. She noted another deprivation. Poetry selections have declined from 30 percent of the total content of nineteenth-century readers to less than 30 percent in the 1980s. By 1986, "informational material and realistic stories about boys and girls had replaced most myths, fairy tales, fables, and legends." Since then, it appears that this trend has been partially reversed, but "relevance" and a social reform agenda still seem to guide many text selections (Ravitch, 1987).

Conclusion

The review of published curriculum turned out to be a far more time-intensive and difficult process than we had anticipated. In order to be fair to the publishers, we spoke with them about their goals and then analyzed carefully not only their introductory remarks in the basal readers but also the way actual lessons had been designed. We often found a large gap between what publishers said they were trying to do and what they actually did. From this, we conclude that the new research in reading and writing has just begun to be absorbed into the thinking of the actual basal lesson writers.

We also gained new respect for the decisions required in order to assemble a coherent, challenging curriculum design that would leave enough room for teachers and students to make choices but would also fill in enough of the gaps for the less-informed teachers. The reviewing process made us far more critical and careful about our curriculum development efforts. In effect, we became not only far more careful consumers but also far more discriminating producers of materials

After a 12-month review of all the major series and of other commercially available materials, we concluded that none of them provided enough challenge for the highly able truly different learner. There is little evidence of multistranded, in-depth activities or projects from which a student might be able to gain interdisciplinary perspective. Few of the writing or reading tasks invite thoughtful inquiry. These findings about the "dumbing down" of textbooks corroborate studies from other disciplines. For instance, Chall (1991) has noted that "in spite of recent improvements, texts are much less demanding than 60 years ago." She maintains that basals are not, and never have been, appropriate for the most able.

We believe that curriculum material for the verbally able should have richness, complexity, and literary merit that provides issues, themes, and ideas that are meaningful. With literary habits of mind as guiding beacons, we can help teachers to make curriculum content decisions that are truly world class.

Key Points Summary

- Current national and international data suggest a decline in verbal capacities of our top students and a lack of rigor in examination questions in comparison to other countries.
- Developing verbal skills among talented students must focus on enhancing critical reading and thinking.
- *The Curriculum Assessment Guide* provides criteria for considering the appropriateness of any language arts material.
- *The Consumer's Guide* presents recommendations based on comprehensive reviews of language arts materials; it was found that basal texts were not appropriate for use with verbally talented students.
- Literature-based materials such as Junior Great Books and McGuffey's Readers were found appropriate for developing verbal talents.
- The criteria of rigor and richness of content are crucial to consider in selecting appropriate classroom materials in the language arts.

Appendix A: Rater's Holistic Review of Curricular Features

Note: This chart provides an holistic appraisal of _____
as reviewed through the Curriculum Assessment Guide. The following data reflect reviewers' scores of textbooks averaged according to grade-level cluster.

The overall rating average rating for this series is _____.

Scoring Key: Extensively—6, Adequately—5, Moderately—4, Infrequently—3, Rarely—2, Not at all—1

General Curricular Design Features			
	Grades K–2	*Grades 3–5*	*Grades 6–8*
Curricular Scope	6 5 4 3 2 1	6 5 4 3 2 1	6 5 4 3 2 1
Materials	6 5 4 3 2 1	6 5 4 3 2 1	6 5 4 3 2 1
Learner Considerations	6 5 4 3 2 1	6 5 4 3 2 1	6 5 4 3 2 1
Pedagogical Approaches	6 5 4 3 2 1	6 5 4 3 2 1	6 5 4 3 2 1
Assessment	6 5 4 3 2 1	6 5 4 3 2 1	6 5 4 3 2 1

Language Arts Curricular Features			
	Grades K–2	*Grades 3–5*	*Grades 6–8*
Curriculum Content	6 5 4 3 2 1	6 5 4 3 2 1	6 5 4 3 2 1
Activities	6 5 4 3 2 1	6 5 4 3 2 1	6 5 4 3 2 1
Instructional Practices	6 5 4 3 2 1	6 5 4 3 2 1	6 5 4 3 2 1

Literacy Content			
	Grades K–2	*Grades 3–5*	*Grades 6–8*
Provides appropriately challenging issues, problems, and themes	6 5 4 3 2 1	6 5 4 3 2 1	6 5 4 3 2 1

Provides variety of texts, genres, formats, and purposes for R & W	6 5 4 3 2 1	6 5 4 3 2 1	6 5 4 3 2 1
Supports processes and multiple paths for creating meaning	6 5 4 3 2 1	6 5 4 3 2 1	6 5 4 3 2 1
Adds to student information storehouse	6 5 4 3 2 1	6 5 4 3 2 1	6 5 4 3 2 1
Allows for student definition of significant questions and topics	6 5 4 3 2 1	6 5 4 3 2 1	6 5 4 3 2 1
Integrates skills with content	6 5 4 3 2 1	6 5 4 3 2 1	6 5 4 3 2 1
Heightens awareness and appreciation for cultural diversity	6 5 4 3 2 1	6 5 4 3 2 1	6 5 4 3 2 1
Encourages lifelong habits	6 5 4 3 2 1	6 5 4 3 2 1	6 5 4 3 2 1

Learner's Engagement		
	Grades K–2	*Grades 3–5*	*Grades 6–8*
Challenges high verbal abilities	6 5 4 3 2 1	6 5 4 3 2 1	6 5 4 3 2 1
Provides open-ended experiences	6 5 4 3 2 1	6 5 4 3 2 1	6 5 4 3 2 1
Provides structured experiences that teach logic and syntax and grammar	6 5 4 3 2 1	6 5 4 3 2 1	6 5 4 3 2 1
Promotes high-level critical thinking	6 5 4 3 2 1	6 5 4 3 2 1	6 5 4 3 2 1
Offers opportunity to experiment	6 5 4 3 2 1	6 5 4 3 2 1	6 5 4 3 2 1
Develops students' discourse skills	6 5 4 3 2 1	6 5 4 3 2 1	6 5 4 3 2 1

Expands curiosity that leads to deeper aesthetic appreciation	6 5 4 3 2 1	6 5 4 3 2 1	6 5 4 3 2 1
Fosters evaluative judgment	6 5 4 3 2 1	6 5 4 3 2 1	6 5 4 3 2 1
Promotes metacognitive skills	6 5 4 3 2 1	6 5 4 3 2 1	6 5 4 3 2 1

Literacy Community Development			
	Grades K–2	*Grades 3–5*	*Grades 6–8*
Encourages lifelong engagement with literature	6 5 4 3 2 1	6 5 4 3 2 1	6 5 4 3 2 1
Develops literacy community	6 5 4 3 2 1	6 5 4 3 2 1	6 5 4 3 2 1
Provides multiple literacy events	6 5 4 3 2 1	6 5 4 3 2 1	6 5 4 3 2 1
Fosters collaborative learning	6 5 4 3 2 1	6 5 4 3 2 1	6 5 4 3 2 1
Promotes self-reflection	6 5 4 3 2 1	6 5 4 3 2 1	6 5 4 3 2 1
Provides flexible pacing for meaningful engagement	6 5 4 3 2 1	6 5 4 3 2 1	6 5 4 3 2 1
Encourages teachers as facilitators, colearners, and problem solvers	6 5 4 3 2 1	6 5 4 3 2 1	6 5 4 3 2 1
Suggests engagement with outside resources	6 5 4 3 2 1	6 5 4 3 2 1	6 5 4 3 2 1
Evokes sense that language provides common bonds of human experience	6 5 4 3 2 1	6 5 4 3 2 1	6 5 4 3 2 1

Appendix B: Rater's Holistic Review of Curricular Features Specifically Related to Highly Able Verbal Students

Note: This chart provides an holistic appraisal of _____ as reviewed through the Curriculum Assessment Guide, Part III. The following data reflect reviewers' scores of textbooks averaged according to grade-level cluster.

The average rating for this series' relevance to highly able verbal learners is_____ .

Scoring Key: Extensively—6, Adequately—5, Moderately—4, Infrequently—3, Rarely—2, Not at all—1

Curriculum Correlation with Research about *Content* for Highly Able Verbal Students		
	Grades K–2	*Grades 3–5*	*Grades 6–8*
Uses broad-based issues, problems, themes	6 5 4 3 2 1	6 5 4 3 2 1	6 5 4 3 2 1
Uses range of rich, sophisticated literature	6 5 4 3 2 1	6 5 4 3 2 1	6 5 4 3 2 1
Includes range of genres/ writing formats	6 5 4 3 2 1	6 5 4 3 2 1	6 5 4 3 2 1
Crosses multiple disciplines	6 5 4 3 2 1	6 5 4 3 2 1	6 5 4 3 2 1
Incorporates sister arts	6 5 4 3 2 1	6 5 4 3 2 1	6 5 4 3 2 1

Curriculum Correlation with Research about *Process* for Highly Able Verbal Students		
	Grades K–2	*Grades 3–5*	*Grades 6–8*
Uses rigorous techniques, materials, forms	6 5 4 3 2 1	6 5 4 3 2 1	6 5 4 3 2 1
Extends existing ideas or produces new ideas	6 5 4 3 2 1	6 5 4 3 2 1	6 5 4 3 2 1
Uses research/primary source skills/methods	6 5 4 3 2 1	6 5 4 3 2 1	6 5 4 3 2 1

Encourages open-ended tasks/experiences	6 5 4 3 2 1	6 5 4 3 2 1	6 5 4 3 2 1
Requires in-depth work on significant topics	6 5 4 3 2 1	6 5 4 3 2 1	6 5 4 3 2 1
Uses collaborative engagement	6 5 4 3 2 1	6 5 4 3 2 1	6 5 4 3 2 1
Requires relationships with varied audiences	6 5 4 3 2 1	6 5 4 3 2 1	6 5 4 3 2 1
Allows for student creation of assessment tools	6 5 4 3 2 1	6 5 4 3 2 1	6 5 4 3 2 1
Requires rich opportunities for reflection	6 5 4 3 2 1	6 5 4 3 2 1	6 5 4 3 2 1

References

Aldrich, P., & Mills, C. (1989). A special program for highly able rural youth in grades five and six. *Gifted Child Quarterly, 33*(1), 11–14.

Aldrich, P., & McKim, G. (1992). *The consumer's guide to English–language arts curriculum.* New York: Saratoga–Warren Board of Cooperative Educational Services.

Archambault, F. X., Westberg, K. L., Brown, S. W., Hallmark, B. W., Zhang, W., & Emmons, C. (1993). Regular classroom practices with gifted students: Findings from the classroom practices survey. *Journal for the Education of the Gifted, 16*(2), 103–119.

Babbitt, N. (1989). The rhinoceros and the pony. *Horn Book, 65*(6), 728–731.

Chall, J. (1991). *Are the textbooks too easy?* New York: Teachers College Press.

Dunkleberger, D. (1992). *State language arts guides.* Paper prepared for Saratoga Warren BOCES Javits Project.

Durden, W., & Tangherlini, A. (1993). *Smart kids: How academic talents are developed and nurtured.* Gottingen, Germany: Hogrefe & Huber.

Gentile C. (1992). *Exploring new methods for collecting students' school based writing: NAEP's 1990 portfolio study.* Washington, DC: National Center for Education Statistics.

Goodman, K. (1989). *Report card on the basals.* Portsmouth, NH: Heinemann.

Institute for Educational Research. (1988). *The IEA study of written comprehension.* Jyvaskyla, Finland: Author.

Institute for Educational Research. (1992). *The IEA study of reading.* Jyvaskyla, Finland: Author.

Kaplan, S. (1986). The grid: A model to construct differentiated curriculum for the gifted. In J. S. Renzulli (Ed.), *Systems and models for developing programs for the gifted and talented*(pp. 180–193). Mansfield Center, CT: Creative Learning Press.

Kozol, J. (1991). *Savage inequalities.* New York: Crown.

Langer, J. (1992). Teaching the process of literary understanding. *National re-*

search center on literature teaching & learning update, 2(11), SUNY–Albany.

Lynch, S., & Mills, C. (1990). The skills reinforcement project (SRP): An academic program for high potential minority youth. *Journal for the Education of the Gifted, 13*(4), 364–379.

Lynch, S., & Mills, C. (1993). Identifying and preparing disadvantaged and minority youth for high level academic achievement. *Contemporary Educational Psychology, 12*(1), 66–76.

Maker, J. (1981). *Teaching models in education of the gifted.* Rockville, MD: Aspen.

Maker, J. (1982). *Curriculum development for the gifte*d. Rockville, MD: Aspen.

Mills, C., & Stork, B., & Krug, D. (1992). Recognition and development of academic talent in educationally disadvantaged students. *Exceptionality, 3*, 165–180.

Mullis, I. V. S., Owen, E. H., & Phillips, G. W. (1990). *Accelerating academic achievement: A summary of findings from twenty years of NAEP.* Washington, DC: Government Printing Office.

National excellence: A case for developing America's talent. (1993). Office of Educational Research and Improvement. Washington, DC: United States Department of Education.

Oates, J. (1985). *Keeping track: How schools structure inequality.* New Haven, CT: Yale University Press.

Ochse, R. (1990). *Before the gates of excellence: The determinants of creative genius.* Cambridge, England: Cambridge University Press.

Passow, H. (1982). *Differentiated curricula for the gifted/talented.* Ventura, CA: Leadership Training Institute on Gifted and Talented.

Ravitch, D. (1987, May 17). Where have all the classics gone? *New York Times.*

Reis, S., & Purcell, J. (1992). *An analysis of content elimination and strategies used by elementary classroom teachers in the curriculum compacting process.* Storrs, CT: National Research Center on Gifted Education.

Shea, C. (1993, January 13). Fewer test takers get top scores on the verbal SAT. *Chronicle of Higher Education,* pp. A29, A33.

Singal, D. (1991). The other crisis in American schools. *Atlantic Monthly, 268,* 59–62.

Smith, F. (1988). *Audits of meaning.* Portsmouth, NH: Heinemann.

Stevenson, H. W., & Stigler, J. W. (1992). *The learning gap: Why our schools are failing and what we can learn from Japanese and Chinese education.* New York: Summit Books.

VanTassel-Baska, J. (1992). *Effective curriculum planning for the gifted.* Denver, CO: Love.

Vygotsky, L. (1978). In M. Cole, V. John–Steiner, S. Scribner, & E. Souberman (Eds.), *Mind in society: The development of higher psychological processes.*) Cambridge, MA: Harvard University Press.

Walmsley, S., & Walp, T. (1991). *A study of second graders' home and school literary experiences.* SUNY–Albany, NY: National Research Center on Literature Teaching & Learning.

Wolf, D. (1988). *Reading reconsidered: Literature and literacy in high school.* New York: College Entrance Examination Board.

13

Assessment in the
Language Arts
Classroom

DANA T. JOHNSON
College of William and Mary

Traditional forms of testing have been used to monitor student progress but the content monitored has been primarily skills and facts. However, current trends are moving away from objective paper-and-pencil testing toward approaches that incorporate meaningful tasks into the assessment process (Herman, Aschbacher, & Winters, 1992; Stiggins, 1991; Resnick & Resnick, 1989; Mitchell, 1992).

In the context of this chapter, the terms *authentic assessment* and *performance-based assessment* are used synonymously to mean assessments where students are required to generate a response or product in the context of the learning environment rather than take a standardized paper-and-pencil test of multiple-choice items. Students are required to perform behaviors in which they must demonstrate competency. These are nonintrusive, integrated tasks that combine instruction and assessment into one act. Thus, the assessment experience is also a learning experience for students. The word *assessment* comes from Latin derivatives that mean "to sit down and weigh." In authentic assessment, we are striving for our best approximation of sitting next to each student while judging his or her breadth and depth of understanding and application of what we are teaching. Current trends toward performance-based and authentic assessment are helping to move the evaluation process in that direction.

Authentic assessment has a number of advantages over traditional forms of testing. Among them are direct measurement of what students should know; emphasis on higher-order thinking skills, judgment, and collaboration; encouragement of active participation in the learning process; and allowing teachers to teach to the test without undermining validity (Hacker & Hathaway, 1991). High-level, open-ended outcomes are possible instead of low-level forms of learning that are rewarded by most traditional tests (Resnick & Resnick, 1989). Assessments should teach students that tasks in school are part of the inquiry process and should provide valuable feedback to teachers and students (Wiggins, 1991). A move to more authentic tasks and outcomes will improve teaching and learning (Wiggins, 1990).

Research in authentic assessment approaches has shown that the use of authentic assessment taught students to assume increased responsibility for their own learning (Scott, 1992). Disadvantages have also been cited, however. These include expense, difficulty in making results consistent and usable, and undemonstrated validity, reliability, and comparability (Hacker & Hathaway, 1991). Authentic assessment must include important content (Peters, 1991) while common standards should drive the integrated learning and assessment process; they should be taught and practiced with students in conjunction with authentic tasks (Wiggins, 1991).

The use of authentic assessment not only reveals what students can do but also sets a standard for what is expected of students. It helps build habits of mind rather than recall of facts and allows integration of content, process, and concept outcomes assessment. This is consistent with the idea that reading is not a specific skill but an interaction with the text, intertext, and context as discussed by Spivey in Chapter 3 of this book.

Key Features

Various components of an authentic assessment program in language arts can monitor different emphases while giving students the opportunity to perform tasks and receive feedback. These might include:

- *Open-ended writing assignments*: Students may write on a topic of their choice, use a genre of their choice, or set the parameters of the assignment according to their sense of creativity and what is appropriate. An autobiographical piece might be a poem, a personal narrative, or a short story.

- *Writing portfolios*: These provide opportunities for multiple measures of performance over an extended period of time. A number of examples of student work are assembled in a purposeful way. A portfolio might include work selected by the student, a series of drafts of a particular work, or examples of different types of writing. The portfolio gives patterns of progress an opportunity to surface.
- *Speech making*: Short and long, formal and informal speaking opportunities help students improve speaking skills and sharpen their thinking. Feedback from peers and the teacher on both the content of the speech and its delivery help students improve.
- *Self-evaluation*: Reflection on one's own work is not only an assessment technique but part of the learning experience. The ultimate aim should be to train students to assess their own progress.
- *Peer evaluation*: By looking at the work of their peers, students may gain insights into their own writing and speaking. Peer writing groups encourage collaboration.
- *Observational assessment of discussion, especially of responses to open-ended questions*: Classroom responses can be recorded on a student roster or on stick-on notes to be included in a folder. When observational forms are used by teachers, they are documenting actions and comments of students in a more formal and explicit way than is often done.

The National Language Arts Curriculum Project for High Ability Learners chose to use a number of authentic assessments for multiple purposes in the six language arts units that were developed and piloted in grades K–8. Although authentic assessments are beneficial for all students, they may be especially advantageous in the assessment of the work of high-ability learners since they avoid the ceiling effect of low-level questioning that is often found in traditional forms of testing. First, preassessment and postassessment instruments were designed to address learner outcomes in the language arts emphasis areas of literature interpretation, persuasive writing, and language study. The purposes of this assessment approach were:

- To assess learner outcomes of significance in the classroom
- To derive important data for planning appropriate instruction
- To determine needed emphases in the instructional process

The first and last literature selections of each unit were used as the basis for the literature interpretation and writing assessments. After students had responded to questions in writing, class discussion and other lesson activities followed. In this way, the assessments were integrated into the learning experiences of the unit instead of being administered in an isolated testing setting. The oral communication assessments required students to listen to a persuasive speech, summarize the main ideas of the speech, and use a graphic organizer to organize the ideas of the speech.

Not all pre- and postassessment instruments were authentic in nature. Those used in language study were more traditional; they used objective grammar items and multiple-choice vocabulary lists. The project staff felt that a combination of assessment approaches would address some of the concerns voiced over a single approach. The objective instruments were also used in the interests of shortening the testing and scoring time.

Rubrics for scoring the assessments were adapted from the National Assessment of Educational Progress (NAEP) Portfolio Study (Gentile, 1992) and the 1992 NAEP Reading Framework (National Assessment Governing Board, 1992). Oral communication assessment procedures were treated more informally in later versions of the units. Sample assessment protocols and scoring rubrics used for this project are included at the end of this chapter.

As students engaged in each piece of writing, they used self-evaluation, peer evaluation, and teacher evaluation forms to monitor progress and get feedback. These included opportunities for assessment of language mechanics and vocabulary in context. Sample criterial standards incorporated in each form were:

- Clarity of ideas
- Logical organization of ideas
- Support for arguments
- Correct capitalization
- Use of rich and varied vocabulary
- Correct use of language

Portfolios of student writing were kept by students. This helped assess progress of each student over the course of the unit. At the end of the unit, students were asked to write an evaluation of the changes they saw in themselves as writers; this was intended to help students view themselves as writers as well as to assess their progress, clarity, content, and quality of expression. In addition, since "change" was the conceptual focus of the unit, this activity contributed to the understanding of generalizations about change. Thus, assessment and learning were combined in one task.

Observational checklists were used to assess classroom discussion. This is an area that teachers traditionally fail to document. In addition, speech assessment forms were provided for students and teachers to evaluate student speeches. Key criteria included in these checklists were:

Observation of Discussion

- Listens attentively
- Makes many contributions
- Justifies with evidence
- Contributes original ideas

Speech Evaluation

- Clear purpose of speech
- Clear and logical reasoning
- Audible voice, good eye contact
- Held interest of audience

Assessment of final products was also addressed. Students' persuasive speeches were evaluated by both peers and teachers using the form that is included at the end of this chapter. Each unit features a research strand that required students to produce a paper documenting the process and its results. The form used to evaluate the product may be found at the end of this chapter.

The reasoning and conceptual strands of the units were also assessed by means of assessments that were tailored to reasoning skills and generalizations about the concept of change that were emphasized in the units. The Concept of Change Assessment is a good example of a rich learning activity that also serves as an evaluation tool. The reasoning assessment form is one that can be used with various oral or written communication throughout the unit.

Issues of Implementation

The bridge from theory to practice is not always smooth. Such is the case in implementing new assessment techniques. The scope of this language arts project did not attempt to assess all stated language arts outcomes. Similarly, not all of the outcomes that were highlighted could be assessed through the pre- and postassessment instruments due to time constraints in the 20 to 40 hours allotted to the piloting of individual units. The chosen instruments addressed a representative sampling of outcomes yet were able to be administered in a classroom within a reasonably short period of time.

One clear issue is that authentic assessment is time consuming. A recall test is faster to administer and much faster to score. Grades are easier to assign according to a given percent of correct answers. But does this kind of test really document learning? Parents will need to be educated about advantages of authentic forms of assessment (which may actually give them more information about their child's performance even if there is not a percentage score on every "test").

Another area that may pose difficulties to classroom teachers is the scoring or assigning of ratings to various products and responses of students. A scoring rubric needs to be developed that indicates criteria for each score on the scale. It should be complete without being so narrow that scorers look for a specific response or so that it does not allow room for an unusual response. By making the assessment process a more open-ended one, we are opening up the possibility of getting responses that span a wide range. Since there can be a very fine line between a brilliant answer and a bluff, the authentic assessment procedure should provide the opportunity for the teacher to ask a student a follow-up question if necessary to adequately ascertain the level of competence of the student's response. Higher scores should indicate higher levels of complexity and differentiated demonstration of competence. In situations where the stakes are high, such as graduation or admittance into a class or program, a level of acceptable performance must be specified. In other situations, the information gained may serve as feedback to teachers and students and as such should enlighten the next phase of instruction. Scoring rubrics were developed by project staff for the pre- and postassessments used in the units piloted for this project. Sample scoring rubrics are included later in this chapter.

Observational assessment of discussion is an area that needs some careful attention. Teachers say they think they know what students do, but it is important to document examples and frequencies. If we say that our classroom activities are valuable learning experiences, then we must document the performance of students during those experiences. Class participation cannot be accounted for by a check on a report card without some record about the frequency and quality of student responses or specific notations about the level of contributions to small groups. If a class list is transformed into a comment sheet and a teacher is committed to making at least one notation each week for each student, then all students will be noticed and remembered, not only the most dominant. However, this is not an easy task for teachers to take on. It is time consuming, especially if written comments are recorded rather than check marks entered on a grid. Even though it is a subjective process, it is far easier (and more fair to students) to document several specific performances than to be faced with a report card or a questioning parent and have only general memories.

Authentic forms of assessment are beneficial to all learners in that the open-ended nature of the required tasks allow for differentiated responses. Thus, for high-ability learners ample opportunities are provided for exceptionally insightful, creative or proficient responses, products, or performances. Traditional tests, on the other hand, inhibit anything beyond a convergent response.

Implications

In light of current trends in educational reform, students will no longer be allowed merely to memorize facts and rules to be recalled on tests as evidence of competence. They will be expected to deal with the flow of new information, think critically, communicate effectively, and work cooperatively (Hacker & Hathaway, 1991; National Commission on Testing and Public Policy, 1990; National Council of Teachers of Mathematics, 1989; Sizer, 1992). Demonstration of these outcomes must come about in appropriate ways. The following are implications of the educational reform movement and the trend toward authentic assessment:

1. Assessment needs to be an integral part of curriculum and instruction. A system of authentic or performance-based assessment can accomplish this. When these techniques are used, "teaching to the test" is appropriate. However, the "test" may not be a traditional one. Opportunities for teacher and student feedback must be integrated into the instructional process. Students should not have to ask the question, Will this be on the test? since the focus should not be on a culminating test but should instead incorporate frequent and varied feedback. Standards of performance for final products such as speeches, essays, or presentations should be clear in advance so that students will know what they are working toward.

2. No single assessment instrument will monitor all outcomes; various instruments should be used both during and at the end of a unit of study. Preassessments provide valuable information that aids teachers in planning for instruction; frequent input on student progress helps teachers monitor progress; and final assessments enable students to show what they can do. Multiple data points give a more complete picture of student strengths and weaknesses.

3. Programs for gifted and talented students, especially pullout programs, do not always assign letter grades for student work. However, assessment needs to be a strong component in curriculum used for these students. Feedback for students, teachers, and parents can be substantive and rewarding when authentic means of assessment are used.

4. Setting performance standards and establishing criteria for meeting those standards will improve curriculum and instruction for all students. By choosing appropriate language arts tasks with open-ended possibilities for performance and criteria that recognize exceptional responses, verbally talented students will be given appropriate opportunities to engage in demanding work and to demonstrate their competence.

Authentic Assessment in the National Language Arts Curriculum Project for High Ability Learners

This section describes the pre- and postassessment procedures and results of pilot testing of six language arts units for high-ability learners that were developed as part of the National Language Arts Curriculum Project for High Ability Learners.

Establishing Content Validity of Pre- and Postassessment Protocols

The content validity of the assessment protocols was achieved through three approaches:

1. Each protocol was modeled after an existing protocol found in the literature. For example, the literary analysis assessment was modeled after the items used in the National Assessment of Educational Progress (NAEP) Reading Framework model (1992). The writing assessment was modeled after the NAEP Portfolio Writing Study (Gentile, 1992), and the oral communication protocol was modeled after a piloted assessment used with freshman college students (Chaney, 1992). The grammar assessments were adapted by Thompson from his grammar text, *The Magic Lens*, (1991) and consist of multiple-choice questions. The protocols were similar in structure in all units but were tailored for each of the unit topics.

2. Selected protocols were piloted during the Summer Enrichment Program of the Center for Gifted Education. Teachers in this program volunteered to administer the instruments to their classes of high-ability students. The assessment instruments were scored by project staff and were modified as a result of the feedback obtained from the pilot. The following instruments were piloted:

> Literature Analysis and Interpretation Assessment in Grades 3, 5, and 8
> Persuasive Writing Assessment in Grades 5 and 8

The assessment pilot provided great assistance in determining the appropriateness of protocols for particular developmental levels, the need for more and clearer prompts, and the level of task difficulty within development levels.

3. Additionally, each assessment protocol was reviewed by a panel of six experts, including individuals representing the language arts areas and gifted education. The experts also represented teaching, administrative, and university backgrounds. Overall ratings for the assessment area was 2. 0 (sufficient) on a scale of 1.0 to 3.0 regarding appropriateness for measuring the specified learner outcomes. Assessment ratings procured across the six units averaged 2.5, a score indicating a midpoint between appropriate and exemplary, in respect to the "authenticity," "appropriateness," and "variety of the assessments used." Minor modifications of unit assessments were done at the revision stage of the project, using the comments from experts to guide the process.

Scoring and Interrater Agreement

For the evaluation of student performance in the four language arts strands, scoring protocols were developed. Before actual scoring began, the three raters selected for the task reviewed and discussed the various criteria for scor-

TABLE 13–1   Percent of Interrater Agreement

	Same	1 Apart	2 Apart	3 Apart
Literature Interpretation (0–3 scale)	66. 7	33. 3		
Persuasive Writing (0–5 scale)	75. 8	23. 7	0. 5	
Listening Main Idea (0—5 scale)	81. 6	17. 1	1. 3	
Relationships in Concept Maps (open-ended scale)	66. 7	20. 8	9. 4	3. 1
Levels in Concept (open-ended scale)	90. 5	8. 2	1. 3	

ing the different components of each goal. The raters scored sample student responses and discussed the results in order to clarify their understanding and interpretation of the evaluation criteria. For Goals 1, 2, and 4 (literature, writing, and oral communication), the student products were evaluated in terms of specific criteria by a combination of raters. Each rater reviewed the student product and scored it accordingly. After the data were collected, they were examined for discrepancies. When scores exceeded a one-point difference, the raters reexamined the particular item and rescored it based on interrater discussion. (With regard to the evaluation of Goal 3 [vocabulary], the pre- and posttest items were scored by only one rater since only one answer was acceptable.) Percent of interrater agreement is summarized in Table 13–1. The scores were then averaged across reviewers to obtain a composite score.

Under Goal 1, the project staff assessed students' ability to develop analytical and interpretive skills in literature. Students were asked to read a particular story or passage and then answer four questions. A sample set of questions for a fifth-grade unit is included here. The questions are based on "Poor People," a short story by Leo Tolstoy.

1. **State an important idea from the story in a sentence or two.**

   0 No response

   1 Simplistic statement about the story is made with no elaboration; includes only part of the main idea; vague or confusing response; creates title rather than stating the main idea; shows little grasp of the main idea

   2 Cites simple story line and includes some detail and description of the story line; summary

3 Shows a comprehensive grasp of significance of passage or story; shows some insight to theme

2. **Use your own words to describe the significance of the following sentence:**
   (page 201) "They had been covered carefully with the mother's threadbare shawl and with her dress."

   0 Misses the meaning/No response/Restates the author's words
   1 Incomplete/Response hints at the meaning but expression of it is vague
   2 Accurate but literal/Response shows good grasp of meaning but does not elaborate
   3 Interpretative/Response is on target with some elaboration; shows some insight

3. **What does the author say about change in this story? Support what you say with details from the story.**

   0 Misses the mark/No response
   1 A statement about change is made but it is disjointed, vague or shallow
   2 A valid, understandable statement or generalization about change is made (perhaps a hint of support is included)
   3 A valid statement/generalization is made and supported
   4 A valid statement/generalization is made and supported with some elaboration

4. **Create a title for this story. List two reasons based on the reading.**

   0 No response given or title makes no sense/Is off base
   1 Utilitarian title; no reasons given or they are merely a rewording of the title
   2 Insightful title accompanied by one reason that supports the title
   3 Insightful title that captures meaning and is supported or title accompanied by two reasons that support the title

Under Goal 2, project staff assessed students' ability to write persuasively. Following a prompt provided by the teacher, students were asked to list three reasons for and against a particular statement or decision. This prompt was intended to serve as a prewriting exercise. Part C, however, asked students to write an essay related to the story. A sample assessment for persuasive writing in a fifth grade unit is included here. It is based on a short story, "Poor People," by Leo Tolstoy.

Do you think that the story "Poor People" should be required reading for all students in your grade?

Directions: **Write a paragraph to answer the question. State your opinion. Include three reasons for your opinion, and write a conclusion to your paragraph.**

An *opinion* is stated:

0 No opinion stated or only yes/no answer provided
1 Simplistic statement or partial sentence
2 States opinion well

Reasons are given for the opinion:

0 No reasons provided or illogical statement provided
2 Provides one valid reason to support opinion and other tenuous reasons
4 Provides two to three valid reasons to support opinion with limited or no elaboration
6 Provides at least three substantive, insightful reasons with elaboration and/or evidence from the story or poem

Conclusion

0 No conclusion is stated
1 Limited conclusion or sentence fragment provided
2 Well stated conclusion

Under Goal 3, project staff evaluated student performance on knowledge of grammar and standard written English using a multiple-choice format. The assessment measure was adapted by Thompson (1991). Pre- and posttests were administered, scored, and evaluated.

Under Goal 4, project staff examined students' ability to interpret and analyze oral communication skills. Students were asked to explain each of the main points developed by the speaker, then organize the content of the speech using a graphic organizer. The concepts of relationships, levels of hierarchy, and cross-links (Novak & Gowin, 1984) are used in the criteria for scoring concept maps. The following is the rubric that was developed for evaluating student papers:

1. **Explain each of the main points that were developed by the speaker.**

    5 All main points are clearly identified and explained in great detail
    4 All main points are clearly identified with some elaboration
    3 All main points are identified with minimal or no explanation
    2 Some main points are identified, but description is incomplete
    1 Only random facts from speech cited; listing of phrases rather than summary
    0 No response

2. Organize your information by using a graphic organizer such as a concept map or web.

- *Relationships:* Assign 1 point for each valid relationship (count the number of connectors)
- *Levels of hierarchy:* Assign 2 points for each hierarchical level in the longest path of the map; do not count words that have simply been strung together without clear subordinate relationships
- *Cross-links*: assign 2 points for each cross-link showing a correct relationship between two concepts in different sections of the map

This rubric was not included in most of the pilot classrooms. Thus, limited data have been obtained using it.

Discussion of Pilot Results by Unit

When applicable, comparisons between pre- and posttest measures were conducted using independent t-tests. Significant levels of growth were noted in at least one area of each of the piloted units. See Table 13–2 for an overview of gains observed in the pilot data for the four outcome areas.

In four of the five pilot classes where independent study grammar packets were piloted, students showed significant levels of improvement from pre- to postassessment. The eighth grade pilot class did not register significant growth. However, out of all the pilot classes, this class had the most infrequent contact with the teacher (at best, one full day every other week). The project staff and the teacher concluded that even though the packets were designed to be completed independently, some monitoring and support from the teacher was crucial to ensure maximum benefits to students and in the successful completion of the packets.

When applicable, results from both treatment and control groups were also compared using t-tests. Data were selected for comparison groups for selected outcomes at selected grade levels. The data tended to show treatment groups outperforming comparison groups on postassessment measures. See Table 13–3 for an overview of comparisons of treatment and comparison group data for the four outcome areas.

Conclusion

Modes of assessment are changing as part of current educational reform movements. Authentic assessment techniques that evaluate learning in ways that blur the distinction between instruction and testing are becoming a major part of that movement. Although there are some difficulties associated with authentic assessment techniques, they are advantageous to the learning

TABLE 13–2 Pre- and Postassessment Gains in Treatment Groups by Levels of Significance

	Literature Interpretation	Persuasive Writing	Language Study	Listening/ Concept Maps
Change as a Part of Life Grade 3	$p < 0.001$	NA	NA	NA
Exploring Through Literature Grade 5	Question 3 $p < 0.05$	--	Grammar $p < 0.001$	NA
Language, Literature, and the Future Grade 5	NA	NA	Vocabulary $p < 0.001$ Grammar $p < 0.001$	NA
Changing Ideas, Changing Perspectives Grade 6	--	$p < 0.01$	Grammar $p < 0.05$	NA
The 1940's: A Decade of Change Grade 7	$p < 0.05$	--	Grammar $p < 0.01$	--
Threads of Change Grade 8	--	--	Grammar --	Cross-links in concept mapping $p < 0.05$

process. The National Language Arts Curriculum Project for High Ability Learners has incorporated a number of these elements into its units for high-ability students. The pilot data from pre- and postassessments provide some evidence of growth in student achievement as a result of participating in the units. Moreover, the project staff have found these assessment techniques effective in eliciting open-ended responses from students, thereby providing an appropriate medium for high-ability students to demonstrate the true nature of their understanding and accomplishments. However, a more extensive systematic study of these issues is needed. Teachers who are interested in authentic assessment may find the examples from these units helpful in tailoring the techniques for their own lessons.

TABLE 13–3 Postassessment Performance in Treatment Groups to Comparison Groups by Levels of Significance

	Literature Interpretation	Persuasive Writing	Language Study	Listening/ Concept Maps
Change as a Part of Life Grade 3	$p < 0.001$	NA	NA	NA
Exploring Through Literature Grade 5	Question 3 $p < 0.001$	NA	NA	NA
Language, Literature, and the Future Grade 5	NA	NA	Vocabulary $p < 0.001$	NA
Changing Ideas, Changing Perspectives Grade 6	--	$p < 0.05$	--	NA

Key Points Summary

- Authentic assessment offers teachers the opportunity to ensure that testing of students is directly related to their teaching and becomes a reiterative part of it.
- Authentic assessment tools such as performance-based activities and portfolios enhance the involvement of students in the process, promoting self-responsibility.
- Authentic assessments promote a strong emphasis on higher-order thinking and understanding ideas rather than on low-level skills.
- Use of authentic assessment approaches aids instructional planning.
- The National Language Arts Curriculum Project for High Ability Learners employed prepost literature, writing, and grammar assessments, coupled with teacher-student-peer observational assessment techniques.
- Scoring authentic assessment is a valuable learning experience in itself. Training for small teams of teachers in a particular protocol may be the best approach to using such assessments.
- Pilot data from the project suggest that students show significant growth in key areas of the language arts through using such protocols, and teachers find them useful in deciding on needed lesson emphasis.

Appendix: Sample Assessment Forms

Writing Self-Assessment

Name _____

Exercise _____

Directions: Use the following rating scale to evaluate each quality.

3 = Excellent   2 = Satisfactory   1 = Needs Improvement

	Needs Improvement	Satisfactory	Excellent
Content			
• My main idea is clear.	1	2	3
• My details support the main idea.	1	2	3
• My ideas are organized logically.	1	2	3
• My arguments are strong and well supported.	1	2	3
• My vocabulary is rich and varied.	1	2	3
Mechanics			
• My spelling is accurate.	1	2	3
• My capitalization is correct.	1	2	3
• My punctuation is correct.	1	2	3

My writing sample is strong in these ways:

_____

_____

My writing sample could be improved in these ways:

_____

_____

Teacher Assessment for Writing

Name _____ Date _____

Directions: Use the following rating scale to evaluate each quality.

3 = Excellent   2 = Satisfactory   1 = Needs Improvement

	Needs Improvement	Satisfactory	Excellent
1. Expresses good ideas	1	2	3
2. Shows smooth and orderly flow of ideas	1	2	3
3. Displays appropriate level of detail	1	2	3
4. Demonstrates appropriate elements of structure (introduction, body, conclusion)	1	2	3
5. Uses descriptive language, vocabulary	1	2	3
	1	2	3
6. Uses correct language	1	2	3
7. Demonstrates correct use of language	1	2	3

Particular strengths:

_____

_____

Areas needing improvement:

_____

_____

Teacher Reasoning Assessment

Name _____

Date _____

Directions: Please rate each student on his or her reasoning skills evidenced in oral and written communication.

3 = To a Great Extent   2 = To Some Extent   1 = Not at All

	Not at All	To Some Extent	To a Great Extent
1. To what extent is the reasoning clear?	1	2	3
2. To what extent is the reasoning specific as in citing appropriate examples or illustrations?	1	2	3
3. To what extent is the reasoning logically consistent?	1	2	3
4. To what extent is the reasoning accurate?	1	2	3
5. To what extent is the reasoning complete?	1	2	3

Particular strengths:

_____

_____

Areas needing improvement:

_____

_____

Research Project Assessment

Name _____ Date _____

Directions: Use the following rating scale to evaluate each quality.

3 = Excellent   2 = Satisfactory   1 = Needs Improvement

	Needs Improvement	Satisfactory	Excellent
1. Issue and problem are clearly defined	1	2	3
2. Sources are diverse	1	2	3
3. Literature sources are summarized	1	2	3
4. Interviews and/or survey questions are included	1	2	3
5. Interviews and/or surveys are summarized	1	2	3
6. Results are reported appropriately	1	2	3
7. Interpretation of data was appropriate	1	2	3
8. Implications were made from the data	1	2	3
9. Given the data, reasonable conclusions were stated	1	2	3
10. The project paper was mechanically competent	1	2	3

Strengths of the project:

_____

_____

Areas for improvement:

_____

_____

References

Chaney, A. (1992). *Issues in contemporary oral communication instruction.* Williamsburg, VA: The College of William and Mary, Center for Gifted Education.

Gentile, C. (1992). *Exploring new methods for collecting students' school-based writing: NAEP's 1990 portfolio study.* Washington, DC: U.S. Government Printing Office.

Hacker, J., & Hathaway, W. (1991, April). *Toward extended assessment: The big picture.* Paper presented at the Annual Conferences of the American Educational Research Association, Chicago, IL. (ERIC Document ED 337494).

Herman, J. L., Aschbacher, P. R., & Winters, L. (1992). *A practical guide to alternative assessment.* Alexandria, VA: Association for Supervision and Curriculum Development.

Mitchell, R. (1992). *Testing for learning.* New York: The Free Press.

National Assessment Governing Board. (1992). *Reading framework for the 1992 National Assessment of Educational Progress.* Washington, DC: U.S. Government Printing Office.

National Commission on Testing and Public Policy. (1990). *From gatekeeper to gateway: Transforming testing in America.* Chestnut Hill, MA: Boston College.

National Council of Teachers of Mathematics. (1989). *Curriculum and evaluation standards.* Reston, VA: NCTM.

Novak, J. D., & Gowin, D. B. (1984). *Learning to learn.* New York: Cambridge University Press.

Peters, C. W. (1991). You can't have authentic assessment without authentic content. *Reading Teacher, 44,* 590–591.

Resnick, L., & Resnick, B. (1989). *Tests as standards of achievement in schools.* New York: Center for Technology in Education. (ERIC Document ED 335421).

Scott, L. (1992). *Improving evaluation of third grade literacy using authentic techniques and self assessment.* Ft. Lauderdale, FL: Nova University. (ERIC Document 347510).

Sizer, T. (1992). *Horace's school.* Boston, MA: Houghton Mifflin.

Stiggins, R. J. (1991). Facing the challenges of a new era of educational assessment. *Applied Measurement in Education, 4,* 263–273.

Thompson, M. (1991). *The magic lens: A spiral tour through the human ideas of grammar.* Unionville, NY: Trillium.

Wiggins, G. (1990). *The case for authentic assessment.* Washington, DC: American Institutes for Research. (ERIC Document ED 328611).

Wiggins, G. (1991). *Toward one system of education: Assessing to improve, not merely audit.* Denver, CO: Education Commission of the States. (ERIC Document ED 348400).

14

In the Big Inning
Was the Word

Word Play Resources for
Developing Verbal Talent

LINDA NEAL BOYCE
College of William and Mary

By words the mind is excited and the spirit elated.
—*ARISTOPHANES*

Introduction : Chapter ::
Word Play : Verbal Talent

All language is a game according to Peter Farb (1973/1993), who sees the language game as serious and complex, but never trivial. "True word play," Farb stated, "employs linguistic virtuosity while still operating within the general framework of a language's rules" (p. 113). Farb further stated

> *The adult poet also plays with his language and manipulates it in much the same way that children manipulate nonsense verses. But as a self-conscious craftsman, the poet possesses an intuitive knowledge of the abstract patterns of his language and a feeling for the extent to which he can use them*

creatively. Whether he is discovering new and expressive uses for sound, reviving an archaic word, borrowing words from other languages, or forcing old words into novel grammatical structures, he is always exploiting the linguistic resources already in his spoken language. (p. 120)

Verbally talented children work on developing their linguistic virtuosity from an early age. VanTassel-Baska (1994) cited gifted learners' fascination with words, early reading, large vocabularies, and high-level reading comprehension as a few of their characteristics. Tuttle (1991) has asserted that the characteristic that distinguishes the verbally gifted from the good student is the ability to comprehend and synthesize relationships among a variety of sources. He warned, however, that verbal abilities pose potential problems when gifted students dominate class and informal discussions, use sarcasm, argue for the sake of arguing, and engage in humor that is not always understood or accepted by others.

Verbal humor, in particular, seems to be a double-edged gift. Shade (1991) reported that gifted students respond to and comprehend verbal humor to a greater degree than students from the general population. He noted, however, that teachers often see humor as disruptive in the classroom and that they discourage humor as well as the students who produce it. Likewise, gifted adolescents reported to Ziv and Gadish (1990) that their humor was often neither understood nor appreciated by their classroom peers and that they used it with close friends only. Although teachers and friends frequently discourage humor, it serves important functions for gifted students. It fosters creativity, it provides coping strategies, it allows self-expression, and it facilitates the development of insight and understanding (Shade, 1991; Silverman, 1993; Ziv & Gadish, 1990).

This chapter looks at ways to nurture gifted learners' verbal ability and their penchant for humor through vocabulary study within the arena of word play. Calfee and Drum (1986) reported that serious vocabulary study is a neglected area for all students, consisting of defining words already known and using them in sentences. Baumann and Kameenui (1991) recommended a comprehensive program of vocabulary instruction wherein students read and listen to a wide variety of literature and oral discourse, generate oral and written compositions on a regular basis, use dictionaries and specialized word tools, learn strategies for analyzing and remembering words, learn the words necessary for comprehension in specific situations, and engage in word play. For gifted readers, Catron and Wingenbach (1986) asserted that vocabulary development is crucial to creative and to critical reading. They recommended that gifted learners study figurative language, connotations, and etymology. Within the broad parameters of word play described in this chapter, students have the opportunity to use dictionaries and specialized word tools, learn strategies for analyzing words, study figurative language and discriminate among connotations of words, read a wide variety of literature, and generate compositions that display their unique abilities and insights.

This chapter explores word play as a deliberate strategy to develop verbal talent through two approaches. First, it presents a case study of Nadine, a gifted learner who is described by one of her professors as "representing the extreme high end of verbal talent." The case study chronicles Nadine's experiences with vocabulary study, demonstrates her hunger for exploring language, and reflects her delight as well as mishaps in playing with it. Second, the paper describes resources that support a quest for understanding words and encourage the synthesizing of relationships. By playing with words, able students master the game of language.

Nadine : Words :: Juggler : Balls

Nadine says of herself, "As a child I was excessively verbal to the point of annoyance to my parents and others. My father used to say, 'She started talking at six months and she hasn't stopped since!' I became a pest by going into neighbors' yards and talking to them until they fled into their houses."

Nadine recalls that as a young child, certain words conjured intriguing visual images. The word *purpose*, for instance, she saw in her mind's eye as a blue flame like the pilot light in her family's oven. Although these visual images puzzled and even worried Nadine as a child, they may reflect a heightened sensitivity to language that helps to explain her intense interest in words.

Nadine taught herself to read before the age of 4. She remembers playing with the sounds in *The Ear Book* (Perkins, 1968) and becoming a fluent reader with *The Fire Cat* (Averill, 1960). By age 5, she was investigating the dictionary, fascinated with the idea that it contained "all the words."

In the second grade, Nadine was confused by the partial information about words that she received in the classroom. After hearing about the prefix *trans* in the word *transportation*, Nadine wondered about other words and asked her teacher about them. She remembers the following inauspicious exchange:

Nadine: "Where does the word *tooth* come from?"

Teacher: "What do you mean, 'Where does the word *tooth* come from?'"

Nadine: "Why do we call a tooth a *tooth*; why do we use that word?"

Teacher: "Because that's just the word we use, that's all!"

Nadine concluded that she had misunderstood the lesson about prefixes and that people made up words however they pleased rather than through the use of a logical system.

Nadine has always liked big words, and words that are old or rare. Some of her favorites include *lycanthrope*, a folklore term for the ability to turn into a wolf, and *antejentacular*, meaning before breakfast. As she reads, Nadine often writes down the words she doesn't know.

Not until she took Latin in high school did Nadine find the intellectual substance about words that matched her voracious appetite. Nadine says, "In Latin, I enjoyed memorizing vocabulary; I could memorize it instantly. My favorite Latin root is *sequ*—consequence, sequel, consecutive, sequence— a cool word!" Nadine's only memory of vocabulary study throughout her school career is of her Latin classes. Her own voracious reading and her constant compiling of word lists nurtured the ability that school neglected.

Nadine was able to learn words instantly and to remember interesting literary passages and movie dialogue verbatim. One of her long-time friends confirms Nadine's self-assessment of her rapid learning. The friend says, "She's so quick; she can think so fast; and her vocabulary is so big. I remember when my son was studying fish, Nadine started teasing him about the Humuhumunukunukuapuaa. After peels of laughter from my son, everyone bet that Nadine was making up a fish story. But Nadine won, the Humuhumunukunukuapuaa is a real Hawaiian fish. Nadine always does that; she remembers everything."

Nadine is a master of impromptu parody. She rewrites literary pieces, mimics the speech patterns of others, and authors her own hilarious verses. Over the years, her teachers' reactions to this trait have ranged from amusement to outrage.

In fact, this profile of Nadine neglects a central issue of her precollegiate education—her underachievement. Nadine routinely failed courses at her parochial girls' school and was eventually expelled. She attributes her failure to boredom and refusing to complete work that she considered pointless. In her local public high school, Nadine fared slightly better and managed to graduate second from the bottom of her class. She then enrolled in a small private college known for its flexibility and for giving people a chance. Currently, Nadine is working on a doctoral degree at a major university.

When asked what compels her constant investigation and play with words that continues to underscore her adult life, Nadine responds, "More than anything else, meaning motivates me—I want to know the meaning behind it; it's the fact that words carry meaning." She also admits that she enjoys studying people's reactions and figuring out how to get just the reaction she wants, whether it be entertainment or persuasion. Nadine says that she constantly refines ways to say things that will make people laugh.

Finally, she says, "I like to discuss ideas. If I can persuade somebody, I am motivated to say it the right way and to use certain examples to get a point across. "

Verbal Dexterity : Linguist :: Muscles : Athlete

As seen through the profile of Nadine, verbally talented individuals have a love affair with words—relishing images and sounds, striving to understand a word's origin and history, collecting words, making people laugh with parodies and outrageous use of words, searching for meaning, and honing the ability to make an exquisite word choice. Rather than discourage talents such as Nadine's, educators can nurture them by providing access to appropriate advanced resources. The following sections of this chapter discuss word play resources and their value for developing verbal talent.

Dictionary : Wordsmith ::
Census Data : Demographer

From an early age, children are exhorted to "look it up in the dictionary!" Parents and teachers often fail to realize, however, that all dictionaries are not "created equal." Some dictionaries discourage use with stultifying definitions, whereas others invite reading by including special features and notes. *The American Heritage Dictionary of the English Language* (1992), for instance, includes a word history note for the word *tooth* that would have satisfied Nadine as a second-grader. Here, she would have learned that the words *eat, tooth,* and *dentist* are all related through a Proto-Indo-European form of *dent* with sound changes that resulted in the Germanic word *tanthuz,* which eventually became the English word *tooth.*

Similarly, *The Lincoln Writing Dictionary for Children* (1988) is based on the premise that dictionaries are meant to be *read*, not just to correct spelling or define words. Numerous short essays inform the reader about words and writing. For instance, a highlighted insert accompanying the word *counter* states:

> The word counter *is used as a prefix meaning "in the opposite direction" or "against." Knowing this, you can probably figure out the meaning of words such as* counterattack, counterclockwise, counteract, *and* counteroffer. Counter- *is close in meaning to "anti-," as in "anti-terrorist laws." But it is broader in meaning. Notice you could not make an "anti-offer" when bargaining to buy a car. "Anti-" means one is strongly opposed, as in "anti-communism." (p. 182)*

For authoritative information on words, students should be introduced to the joy and the luxury of delving into the monolithic *Oxford English Dictionary (OED)* (1992), or one of its editions such as the *Shorter Oxford English Dictionary* (1993), or the compact disk version. Here, students will find, for each entry, literary quotations in chronological order that illustrate how a word has been used over time and how that use has changed.

Two other dictionaries of particular interest include the *Webster's Third New International Dictionary of the English Language, Unabridged* (1961), a comprehensive unabridged dictionary, and its abridged counterpart *Merriam-Webster's Collegiate Dictionary* (1993). The definitions in these two resources are listed in chronological order. The abridged version includes the date when each usage first came into the language. *Merriam-Webster's Collegiate Dictionary* (1993) thereby provides a convenient way for students to study change in the English language.

Students deserve to meet and to have ready access to a variety of lively, informative dictionaries that entice reading about words. Dictionaries should be evaluated for features such as etymologies, word usage notes, notes that show the relationship of synonyms, definitions illustrated with quotations from literature and the media, and the inclusion of dates that show when meanings have come into the language. Teachers and students should beware that the name *Webster* is in the public domain and that it can be used by any publisher. Likewise, a dictionary can be *unabridged* but lack important features. Therefore, the name *Webster* or the word *unabridged* in the title of a dictionary does not guarantee quality.

In addition to the well-known thesaurus, various word finding tools such as reverse dictionaries (Bernstein, 1975; *Reader's Digest Illustrated Reverse Dictionary*, 1990) and visual dictionaries (*Facts on File Visual Dictionary*, 1986; *Macmillan Visual Dictionary*, 1992) offer intriguing ways to learn words. A reverse dictionary attempts to help readers find words "on the tip of the tongue" by listing definitions that lead the reader to the half-remembered target word. For instance, when trying to remember the word for sentences that read the same backward as well as forward, it is possible to look up *backward* and to find the word *palindrome*. In visual dictionaries, labeled illustrations and diagrams provide the words for items such as the parts of a sailing ship, the bones in the body, or a knight's suit of armor.

The selection of dictionaries within a classroom or school library may be limited. However, public libraries and academic libraries offer an extensive collection of dictionaries; some are designated as reference books for use within the library while others circulate for home and school use. By inviting students to bring dictionaries from home and by checking others out of libraries, teachers can amass an interesting and diverse array that might include the *Compact Edition of the Oxford English Dictionary* (1971), which comes with a magnifying glass for reading its reduced pages or fascinating old copies of Johnson's (1773) *Dictionary of the English Language,* which set the standard for dictionaries meant to be read. Whenever possible, dictionaries such as the ones mentioned here should be purchased for classrooms, thereby creating readily available resources for students.

Etymology : Word :: Paleontology : Fossil

Although dictionaries provide brief histories of words, books such as Flexner's *I Hear America Talking* (1976) and *Listening to America* (1982) provide both a history of the language used in the United States and a look at United States history as seen through language. Illustrated with reproductions of primary source material such as photographs, prints, and cartoons, Flexner's chapter on World War I, for instance, chronicles the major events of the war by explaining its language and terminology which included *khaki, the duration, red tape,* and *whizzbang.* In his historical discussions, Flexner includes the slang and derogatory terms of the era as well as the cultural, literary, and political words.

Other books such as *101 Words and How They Began* (Steckler, 1979) and *Words: A Book about the Origins of Everyday Words and Phrases* (Sarnoff & Ruffins, 1981) introduce young children to words that entered English from around the world. Steckler links breakfast cereal to mythology with his explanation that Ceres was the Roman goddess of the crops; and Sarnoff explains that *corduroy,* which comes from French words meaning "cloth of the king," was a word invented by English weavers to help them sell fabric.

Studying the history of words introduces not only individual words but the entire system of languages and language history. In *Sumer Is Icumen In,* Greenfeld (1978) focused on the history of the English language by considering its origins, changes, and future. As if to answer Nadine's question, "Where does the word *tooth* come from?" Cooper (1992) investigated ideas about the first spoken words and traced the development of languages throughout the world in her book *Why Do You Speak As You Do?*

Sperling has proven that old words are entertaining and that playing with them is fun. In *Poplollies and Bellibones* (Sperling, 1977), she introduced funny-sounding obsolete words with circular definitions in which one unknown word leads to another. She also created dialogues to translate and annotated stories to read. In *Murfles and Wink-a-Peeps,* her book for young children, Sperling (1985) began with a letter to *boonfellows* (friends, companions) in which she talked to readers about how words change and die. She then entertained them with her circular definitions and her own old-word play.

Lexicographer : Word :: Numismatist : Coin

As Sperling demonstrated with her books and Nadine mirrored with her lists, word collecting can become a passionate hobby. In his classic *An Exaltation of Larks*, which identifies and illustrates collective nouns, Lipton (1991) invited readers, like Tom Sawyer whitewashing his fence, to take a brush from the bucket and help paint the fence. In one school, teachers and students accepted Lipton's invitation, picked up the brushes, and spent the year expanding his list that included a *gaggle of geese*, a *sentence of judges*, and a *clutch of eggs*. Items such as a *brace of reporters* found in the local newspaper that captured the essence of the named group inspired students to keep hunting or to invent their own.

In *Chin Music*, Schwartz (1979) played with his collection of words from folklore and regional speech, which included gems such as *fumadiddle* and *snallygaster*. Following his list of synonyms, anecdotes, and definitions, Schwartz expanded his text with research notes that provided a context for the words. He offered students a glimpse of an intriguing research path that crossed several disciplines as well as a romp with words.

Willard Espy's (1972) homonym lexicon in his *The Game of Words* listed 547 pairs of homonyms that range from *acclamation, acclimation* to *you'll, yule*. Espy demonstrated that collecting words isn't enough; rather, collections must be displayed and used. Following his list, Espy challenged readers to complete couplets to which he provided teasing definitions such as:

> *I found a shaggy mare in ***** (an American state)*
> *With might and **** (reinforces might)*
> *I trimmed her **** (hippy hairdo)*
>
> *(Answer: Maine, main, mane) (p. 125)*

In *Eye Spy: A Mysterious Alphabet*, Bourke (1991) played with homonyms through a visual guessing game. Each double-spread page in the picture book consists of four illustrations of homonyms. The illustrations for the letter *M*, for instance, show a queen, two kings, and a monarch butterfly. Because the last illustration in each set contains a clue to the next set, *Eye Spy* is as much fun to "read" (there are no words) backwards as it is forward. Terban's *Hey, Hay! A Wagonful of Funny Homonym Riddles* (1991) and *The Dove Dove* (1988) challenge readers with riddles such as "What do you call the person who inherits what we breathe?" (an *air heir*) or puzzles such as "When I *see* the right *place*, I will *quote a passage* from Shakespeare" (*sight, site, cite*).

Teachers can encourage students to look for homonym word play that is both intentional and unintentional. Comic strips in the daily paper such as "Calvin and Hobbes," "B.C.," and "Shoe" frequently depend on homonyms and puns. Beauty salons go by monikers that include "The Mane Shop" and

"Shear Madness." A local plumbing contractor advertises, "For Plumb Good Plumbing." Conversely, students may locate unintentional but equally entertaining homonym blunders in the press or in business correspondence. A bulletin board or a center where students can display their discoveries encourages everyone to join the fun.

Flying Chaucer : Ufologists :: Pun : Wise Guise

Numerous resources exist to assist teachers looking for word play ideas and word games for the classroom. In *The Oxford Guide to Word Games*, Augarde (1984) described games such as riddles, crosswords, anagrams, spoonerisms, and concrete poetry. Especially interesting for language study, *The Oxford Guide* provides historical and literary context for the games as well as information for playing them. Augarde traced the game of charades, for instance, from 1711 when it was a written game to its present dramatic form which was played by Lewis Carroll, used by Noel Coward in *Hay Fever*, and disdained by Winston Churchill.

Compendiums that specifically address educational objectives through word play include Kohl's (1981) *A Book of Puzzlements: Play and Invention with Language*, Geller's (1985) *Wordplay and Language Learning for Children*, and Golick's (1987) *Playing with Words*. Kohl addressed classroom needs by arranging his games into categories, such as letter games and games that play with parts of speech. He encouraged adaptations for making the games more complex and offered suggestions for inventing original games. Geller arranged her games by age level and focused on children's developmental language play such as the rhymes of preschool children and the metaphors in older children's riddles. Although Golick's collection also depends on children's traditional language games, she used them as tools to help students with specific language needs or disabilities.

In *Playing the Language Game*, Shepherd (1993) presented original role-play simulations that enable older students to act as field linguisticians so that they can observe and speculate on language. In her game, "Knowing the Rules," for instance, students are asked to listen to two lines of "Jabberwocky" by Lewis Carroll and then to draw whatever they imagined either individually or in small groups. Shepherd has used "Knowing the Rules" to dispel anxiety about grammar study and to convince students that they intuitively understand the rules of grammar.

Rather than describe how the games are played, Richard Lederer and Willard Espy have actively involved readers in playing the games. In *The Play of Words*, Lederer (1990) provided brief information on a group of words such as *clichés* or *metaphors*, or games such as "Inky Pinkys" and then offered lists to complete and puzzles to solve. Willard Espy has proven that word play is appropriate for every day of the year with his *Almanac of Words at Play* (Espy, 1975) and *A Children's Almanac of Words at Play* (Espy, 1982). His games include puns, Tom Swifties, long words, and circular stories accompanied by explanations and ideas for further play.

Formal analogies such as *reading : pleasure :: writing : frustration* (stated "reading is to pleasure as writing is to frustration") demonstrate a particular type of word play that serves as a tool for thinking as well as entertainment. Thompson (1990, 1991) has argued that analogies teach students to gain clarity by identifying a clear relationship between words. He uses analogies not only as a "verbal diversion" but as part of a comprehensive and challenging system of vocabulary study. In *Challenge of the Unknown* (1986), the authors stressed that in order to use analogies as a problem solving tool, students must be able to create the analogy and to define the relationship that is implied. For instance, the analogy, *pit : peach :: sun : solar system* demonstrates the relationship of part to whole. Other examples of relationships cited by the *Challenge of the Unknown* curriculum include:

- action to object   *race : track :: swim : pool*
- synonyms   *blast : gust :: blare : roar*
- degree   *walk : run :: add : multiply*
- part to part   *hand : elbow :: foot : knee*
- place   *England : London :: Canada : Montreal*
- association   *silk : rayon :: butter : margarine*
- antonyms   *birth : death :: introduction : conclusion*
- purpose   *surgeon : scalpel :: butcher : cleaver*
- cause and effect   *rain : flooding :: ice : skidding*
- characteristic   *sinks : rock :: floats : feather*
- sequence   *May : February :: November : August*
- object to action   *dishes : break :: clothing : rip* (p. 116)

Word Play : Literature ::
Drafting Materials : Architecture

Literature serves as the ultimate arena for word play. For young readers, Graeme Base's (1986) *Animalia* provides an alphabet of collectible words such as "diabolical dragons daintily devouring delicious delicacies" or "quivering quails queuing quietly for quills." Base's elaborate illustrations that surround the words entice readers to supply their own words for items and characters, such as a decanter, a dirigible, a quiver, and Don Quixote. In another type of word play, young readers delight in their superior knowledge and laugh at Amelia Bedelia's (Parish, 1963) misinterpretation of homonyms and idioms as she attempts to "dust the furniture," and "draw the drapes."

Although *Animalia* and the *Amelia Bedelia* books are widely read, other classic word play literature often needs to be introduced by an enthusiastic teacher or parent. Milo's journey through Dictionopolis in *The Phantom Tollbooth* (Juster, 1961) doubles in fun when read with a group intent on finding the puns, idioms, and word play embedded in every paragraph. After chuckling through *The Phantom Tollbooth*, students may want to take a serious look at the word play of Lewis Carroll, a master of the art. The Pennyroyal editions of *Alice's Adventures in Wonderland* (Carroll, 1982) and *Through the Looking-Glass and What Alice Found There* (Carroll, 1983) which interpret Lewis's texts with scholarly annotations and woodcuts by Barry Moser are of special interest to bibliophiles.

Louis Untermeyer (1979) has reminded us, "Poetry is essentially a form of play—a play of metaphor, a play of imagery, a play of rhyme" (p. 77). Untermeyer has gone on to say that the pun is a form of verbal dexterity and springs from the same combination of wit and imagination that speeds the poetic process. For students who have learned to play with words, literature and all language become the playground.

Chapter : Book :: Resources : Knowledge

For verbally talented learners, word play harnesses their facile language ability with their keen sense of humor. It builds vocabulary, provides an opportunity to manipulate language structure, nurtures creativity, elicits critical thinking, and honors humorous insight. As with any other sport, word play builds a community of players who enjoy the company of one another and the challenge of the game.

The resources discussed in this chapter demonstrate the power and joy of playing with words. For students, they provide opportunities for independent reading and lifelong learning. For teachers, the resources offer ways to build on the unique abilities of verbally talented learners and to honor their special needs. Word play in the classroom can provide a safe place to experiment with words, to strive to understand a system, to take risks with humor, and to enjoy special abilities and insights.

Key Points Summary

- Words are the tools of verbally talented students and should be emphasized in any language arts experience.
- Exploration into verbal humor provides a way to capitalize on the inherent interests of the verbally talented at the same time such opportunities promote sophisticated understanding of communication in many forms.

- Vocabulary development should be a highlight of language arts experiences for the verbally talented.
- Advanced resources such as quality dictionaries, thesauruses, and other reference materials can provide a strong basis for potential language development.
- Books that focus on word play and word games are wonderful resources to use in classrooms or to pass on to interested students.
- Verbally oriented games promote language development and have high interest appeal for the verbally talented.
- The study of analogies enhances higher-level thinking skills in verbal terms.
- Encouraging word play in the classroom builds communication skills and insights into the world of the language arts.

References

American heritage dictionary of the English language (3rd ed.) (1992). Boston: Houghton Mifflin.

Augarde, T. (1984). *The Oxford guide to word games.* Oxford: Oxford University Press.

Averill, E. (1960). *The fire cat.* New York: Harper & Row.

Base, G. (1986). *Animalia.* New York: Abrams.

Baumann, J. F., & Kameenui, E. J. (1991). Research on vocabulary instruction: Ode to Voltaire. In J. Flood, J. M. Jensen, D. Lapp, & J. R. Squire (Eds.), *Handbook of research on teaching the English language arts* (pp. 604–632). New York: Macmillan.

Bernstein, T. M. (1975). *Bernstein's reverse dictionary.* New York: Quadrangle.

Bourke, L. (1991). *Eye spy: A mysterious alphabet.* San Francisco: Chronicle Books.

Calfee, R., & Drum, P. (1986). Research on teaching reading. In M. C. Wittrock (Ed.), *Handbook of research on teaching* (3rd ed., pp. 804–849). New York: Macmillan.

Carroll, L. (1982). *Alice's adventures in wonderland.* (Selwyn H. Goodacre, Ed.). Berkeley: University of California Press.

Carroll, L. (1983). *Through the looking-glass and what Alice found there.* (Selwyn H. Goodacre, Ed.). Berkeley: University of California Press.

Catron, R. M., & Wingenbach, N. (1986). Developing the potential of the gifted reader. *Theory into Practice, 25,* 134–140.

Challenge of the unknown. (1986). New York: W. W. Norton.

Compact edition of the Oxford English dictionary (Vols. 1–2) (1971). New York: Oxford University Press.

Cooper, K. (1992). *Why do you speak as you do? A guide to world languages.* New York: Walker.

Espy, W. R. (1972). *The game of words.* New York: Bramhall House.

Espy, W. (1975). *An almanac of words at play.* New York: C. N. Potter.

Espy, W. R. (1982). *A children's almanac of words at play.* New York: Clarkson N. Potter.

Facts on File visual dictionary. (1986). New York: Facts on File.

Farb, P. (1993). *Word play: What happens when people talk.* New York: Vintage. (Original work published 1973).

Flexner, S. B. (1976). *I hear America talking: An illustrated treasury of Ameri-*

can words and phrases. New York: Van Nostrand Reinhold.

Flexner, S. B. (1982). *Listening to America: An illustrated history of words and phrases from our lively and splendid past.* New York: Simon and Schuster.

Geller, L. G. (1985). *Wordplay and language learning for children.* Urbana, IL: National Council of Teachers of English.

Golick, M. (1987). *Playing with words.* Markham, Ontario: Pembroke.

Greenfeld, H. (1978). *Sumer is icumen in: Our ever–changing language.* New York: Crown.

Johnson, S. (1773). *A dictionary of the English language: In which the words are deduced from their originals, and illustrated in their different significations by examples from the best writers. To which are prefixed, a history of the language, and an English grammar* (Vols. 1–2) (4th ed.). London: W. Straham.

Johnson, S. (1986). *Dictionary of the English language: Selections.* (Richard L. Harp, Ed.). Lanham, MD: University Press of America.

Juster, N. (1961). *The phantom tollboth.* New York: Epstein & Carroll; Random.

Kohl, H. (1981). *A book of puzzlements: Play and invention with language.* New York: Schocken.

Lederer, R. (1990). *The play of words: Fun & games for language lovers.* New York: Pocket.

Lincoln writing dictionary for children. (1988). San Diego: Harcourt Brace Jovanovich.

Lipton, J. (1991). *An exaltation of larks: The ultimate edition.* New York: Viking.

Macmillan visual dictionary. (1992). New York: Macmillan.

Merriam-Webster's collegiate dictionary (10th ed.) (1993). Springfield, MA: Merriam-Webster.

Oxford English dictionary (Vols. 1–20) (2nd ed.). (1992). New York: Oxford University Press.

Parish, P. (1963). *Amelia Bedelia.* New York: Harper.

Perkins, A. (1968). *The ear book.* New York: Random.

Reader's Digest illustrated reverse dictionary. (1990). Pleasantville, NY: Reader's Digest.

Sarnoff, J., & Ruffins, R. (1981). *Words: A book about the origins of everyday words and phrases.* New York: Charles Scribner.

Schwartz, A. (1979). *Chin music: Tall talk and other talk.* New York: Lippincott.

Shade, R. (1991). Verbal humor in gifted students and students in the general population: A comparison of spontaneous mirth and comprehension. *Journal for the Education of the Gifted, 14*(2), 134–150.

Shepherd, V. (1993). *Playing the language game.* Philadelphia: Open University Press.

Shorter Oxford English dictionary (Vols. 1–2) (2nd ed.). (1993). New York: Oxford University Press.

Silverman, L. K. (1993). A developmental model for counseling the gifted. In L. K. Silverman (Ed.), *Counseling the gifted and talented* (pp. 51–78). Denver: Love Publishing.

Sperling, S. K. (1977). *Poplollies and bellibones: A celebration of lost words.* New York: Clarkson N. Potter.

Sperling, S. K. (1985). *Murfles and wink–a–peeps: Funny old words for kids.* New York: Clarkson N. Potter.

Steckler, A. (1979). *101 words and how they began.* Garden City, NY: Doubleday.

Terban, M. (1988). *The dove dove.* New York: Clarion.

Terban, M. (1991). *Hey, hay! A wagonful of funny homonym riddles.* New York: Clarion.

Thompson, M. C. (1990, 1991). The word within the word (Vols. 1 & 2). Unionville, New York: Trillium.

Tuttle, F. B. (1991). Teaching the gifted. In J. Flood, J. M. Jensen, D. Lapp, & J. R. Squire (Eds.), *Handbook of research on teaching the English language arts* (pp. 372–379). New York: Macmillan.

Untermeyer, L. (1979). The pun. In A. Moger (Ed.), *The complete pun book* (pp. 75–81). Secaucus, NJ: Citadel Press.

VanTassel-Baska, J. (1994). *Comprehensive curriculum for gifted learners* (2nd ed.). Boston: Allyn and Bacon.

Webster's third new international dictionary of the English language, unabridged.

(1961). Springfield, MA: G. & C. Merriam.

Ziv, A., & Gadish, O. (1990). Humor and giftedness. *Journal for Education of the Gifted, 13*(4), 332–345.

15

Windows and Mirrors

Gender and Diversity in the Literate Classroom

PENNY KOLLOFF
Illinois State University

> *All students deserve a curriculum which Mirrors their own*
> *experience back to them—thus validating it in the public*
> *world of the school. But curriculum must also insist upon*
> *the fresh air of Windows into the experience of others—*
> *who also need and deserve the public validation of the school*
> *curriculum.—EMILY STYLE (1988)*

What was it about the Melendy family that enfolded the 10-year-old girl so many summers ago? Was it the easy-going interplay among sisters and brothers? Perhaps it was author Elizabeth Enright's imaginative plot and expressive language. *The Saturdays* invited readers into a family in which both girls and boys have adventures in equal numbers, one in which youngsters know who George Bernard Shaw is and appreciate opera. I took my place in that family, right between Randy and Rush, through this book and its several sequels.

I also had much in common with April Bright, main character of *Bright April*. We were both members of close-knit families and we were both Brownie Scouts. Marguerite de Angeli's April became my first Black friend. The sisters in Sydney Taylor's *All of a Kind Family* reminded me of my own sisters and also introduced me to Jewish traditions and holidays. In keeping with Emily Style's concept of curriculum as window and mirror, each of these books served as both a mirror of elements of my own life and a window into areas of the lives of others about which I knew little.

I led a charmed life. My parents were avid readers, our home was filled with books, and I lived two blocks from the public library to which I could walk alone from the time I was 6 years old. Within those book-lined walls were two librarians who loved children who loved to read. Miss Nada and Miss Lucy bent the rules about how many books could be taken out at a time, understanding a reader who might not be sure which book she wanted to read first, or a reader who feared that she might finish her book after the library closed for the evening or the weekend.

In school, my experiences with literature were mixed. Although I have no clear memory of my reading experiences in the primary grades, other than *Fun with Dick and Jane* and round-robin reading in groups, I did have teachers in fifth and sixth grades who read aloud books, including *Black Beauty, Daniel Boone,* and *My Friend, Flicka.* It did not occur to me to wonder why the main characters (the human ones, anyway) of all of these books were male, but I do remember becoming especially caught up in the events relating to Jemima Boone's kidnapping by Indians, and I can still recall the visual images evoked by that part of the book. Looking back, I wonder if my teachers consciously chose books they knew would appeal to and hold the attention of boisterous boys, believing that girls will listen to anything.

Because I read so much outside of school (and during school, since I was one who finished my work quickly), I had no problem finding captivating books populated with characters with whom I could identify. I did not think about my classmates who lived a greater distance from the library or those who lived in homes where reading was not valued or encouraged. If their exposure to literature consisted of what they encountered in school, their experiences would have been quite limited.

These memories surfaced several years ago when I questioned a teacher about high school required reading lists comprised of a disproportionate number of books by and about males. His straight-faced, serious reply was that until about senior year, male students simply would not read about females and their experiences, therefore the lists were designed to keep the boys interested because "the girls will read whatever is assigned." Perhaps this is one of the reasons that 9 of the 10 authors most frequently read in secondary schools are male (the lone female is Harper Lee).

Recent Trends in Reading

Decades have passed since the "golden days" in the life of a child from a fairly homogeneous population and a school with a rather narrowly prescribed curriculum. In those years, several things have happened that threaten the development of verbal talent in all students. One significant change, education watchers tell us, is evidence of the systematic "dumbing down" of the curriculum (Hirsch, 1987; Ravitch & Finn, 1987; Singal, 1991). Singal, describing the decline of rigorous literature curriculum in the wake of the spontaneous, creative 1960s and 70s, wrote, "Students are all too often given works that…are 'age appropriate' assignments that reflect their interests as adolescents, that they can read without constant recourse to a dictionary and from which they can take whatever they are inspired to take. Feed a student the literary equivalent of junk food and you will get a lackluster command of English" (p. 65).

A second trend is marked by recent evidence that we are becoming a society where reading is not valued. According to a 1991 survey by the National Association of Booksellers, 60 percent of U.S. households did not purchase a single book during the previous year. The 1992 National Association of Educational Progress survey of fourth-, eighth-, and twelfth-graders found that one-third of those surveyed never read in their spare time, while two-thirds of eighth-graders and 40 percent of twelfth-graders report watching more than three hours of television a day.

Not only are the reading habits of children in jeopardy, but there is evidence that another group, upon whom many of our hopes for a literate society are based, is also at risk. Jipson and Paley (1992), writing about literature-based reading programs, studied the reading habits of education students at the graduate and undergraduate levels. Results of their research revealed that undergraduate education majors engaged in very little recreational reading. When these future teachers reported reading for pleasure, the materials were generally magazines and popular fiction. Contrast this with reports from graduate education students, a majority with undergraduate liberal arts degrees who had worked for a period outside of education before beginning their teacher training work. These individuals engaged in reading for pleasure, read diverse materials, and reported that reading was important to them. For literature programs to be enriched and stimulating, there must be teachers who are well read and enthusiastic about reading.

The Emergence of Gender and Diversity Issues in Curriculum

In addition to these trends, any consideration of language and literature must take note of broader changes in society, their impact on schools and effects on curriculum. Two recent issues significantly affecting the larger society, and therefore the schools, are (1) a recognition of the increasing diversity of the population and the concomitant need for the society to become more culturally and ethnically aware, and (2) a growing sensitivity to women's concerns and roles. As these issues have come to the fore in society, schools have acknowledged the need to address them within the structure of educational institutions. The first of these intersections of society and school may have become evident several decades ago when textbooks, particularly basal readers, took note of the fact that vast numbers of children in our nation's schools did not live in the environment portrayed in *Fun with Dick and Jane* or its sequels and counterparts. Basal reading materials changed to reflect the lives of children who were not White and who did not live in suburban, two-parent families.

More recently, the controversy heightened with the conflict surrounding the place of the "canon" in the curriculum for an increasingly diverse population in the schools. Those who supported the traditional approach—consisting of works by male authors representing European cultures, exemplified by the Great Books—battled with advocates for a broader, more representative group of authors in the curricula of high schools, colleges, and universities. It is noteworthy that none of the 10 authors most frequently read by high school students is from another culture.

The second of these issues, attention to the needs and development of women, riveted the public's attention in response to the release of results of studies commissioned by the American Association of University Women (AAUW, 1991, 1992). These studies showed, among other things, that the self-esteem of girls declines precipitously in comparison with boys as they progress through the elementary grades and into junior and senior high school. Also a part of the AAUW reports is a compilation of research evidence that supports the notion that girls and boys are treated quite differently in school. Differences are documented in the nature and amount of teachers' attention they receive, the encouragement of teachers and counselors, the responsiveness of the curriculum and setting to their needs, and the structure of classroom learning experiences as they relate to the particular ways in which girls and boys learn best.

The intersection of societal changes with knowledge about how people learn requires careful evaluation of both the content and the methods of teaching the curriculum. Dynamically interacting with factors relating to gender and diversity is a fundamental change in our understanding of the ways people learn. Current thinking looks to the constructivist philosophy to explain how learning evolves as learners strive to make sense of their worlds, in contrast with the earlier, more traditional view that learning results when content is presented to students who practice in order to demonstrate mastery. Constructivism emphasizes that learning through language is a dynamic and active process requiring that learners make meaning by bringing personal and individual experiences to bear on the literary encounter, by interacting with the material and with others who engage in the process, and by writing about the process in order to clarify and extend their thinking. Given the very personal nature of the learning process, it is obvious that, in order to engage all students, it must be relevant and responsive to each individual.

Goals for the Development of Verbal Talent

In the face of these complex trends and challenges, it is appropriate to formulate larger goals relating to the emergence of verbal talent in all students. First is the goal of building patterns of reading behavior that will lead to life-long habits. Second is the goal of producing individuals who can make meaning of high-level, challenging literature. Additionally, the curriculum must respond to the changing society by ensuring that every segment of the student population has the opportunity to reach these goals. Therefore, a third goal is suggested that centers on this need: to provide both content and metholodogy that will encourage the overlooked groups to develop their voice. For this to take place, the curriculum must become, as Style (1988) so aptly put it, both mirror and window for all students.

For all students to develop their verbal talents to the greatest degree possible, their reading and listening must nurture their understandings of human experience and provide the basis for them to speak and write about literature. Literature that will enhance these talents in all students must be truly representative of the entire human heritage, the heritage of all, not just a segment of this group.

Those who wish to encourage the verbal talents of all must provide the environment and the materials that will allow each individual—regardless of race, regardless of gender, regardless of social or economic background—to have access to the best and broadest selections of literature, the most stimulating and supportive forums for discussion and the most motivating and inspirational inducements to write. In general terms, the curriculum content must be representative and the methods must engage full and enthusiastic participation by all students.

Fulfillment of the goals listed here begins with the earliest encounters between children and literature. In order to achieve the goals, with special emphasis on the third, both content and methods for teaching literature and language in the classroom must change. Traditional content and methods must be revised in order to respond to the needs of students who have previously encountered literature that does not allow them to relate in terms of their own experiences, cultures, psychological makeup or world view.

Content Modification for the Development of Verbal Talent

Content modification must involve the incorporation of stimulating and enriching literary experiences. For fortunate children, these experiences begin virtually at birth and become ingrained in the years before they enter school as parents read to them, talk with them about books, and make books readily available and integral in their lives. Should these children's good fortune continue, they will be in classrooms with teachers who are readers themselves; who read aloud to their classes, regardless of the age of the students; who select thought-provoking, rigorous, important literature for their students to read and write about. These teachers will introduce literature with complex characters and ideas and themes that inspire discussion and ultimately lead to greater understanding of the human experience (the windows to which Style refers). Encounters with this literature will also allow children to relate to their own lives through their reading and listening (Style's mirrors).

To ensure that the curriculum is responsive to all students, special attention must be focused on the inclusion of contributions from groups that are not sufficiently represented in literature. Specifically, these groups include females and members of minority cultures. Obviously, females who are also from minority groups are even less likely to find literature to serve as mirrors to their lives and experiences. Equally important are opportunities and needs for other students to see through windows into lives different from their own. Such curriculum can be created by teachers who are cognizant of characteristics of literature that speaks to females and minorities and adequately and accurately echoes their experiences.

The following suggests some general characteristics with examples to guide the search for materials that more appropriately represent and portray females and minorities in ways that may benefit all students and enrich their learning.

Stories That Counteract Typical Formulas.   Because concepts of self and others begin early, attention to these issues must begin when young children first encounter literature. One approach to balancing literature for all children is to introduce stories that offset conventional fairy tales to which most children are exposed early, and that establish and reinforce numerous views of roles and behaviors. *The Fourth Little Pig* by Teresa Celsi suggests an alternative to the traditional story of the three little pigs. In this book, three little pig brothers are joined by their sister who coaxes them out of the house where they are hiding from the wolf. *She* is the adventurer who goes off to see the world while her brothers stay close to home. Unlike typical fairy tales in which the active, adventurous characters are male while female characters remain in the background and wait to be rescued, stories like this offer parents, teachers, and children a chance to challenge the stereotypes before they are fully embedded in the child's experience.

Another story for young children that reverses typical patterns is *Princess Smartypants* by Babette Cole. A thoroughly modern princess, Ms. Smartypants prefers her pets to her male suitors and devises impossible tasks for those who seek to woo her. Much of the humor derives from the illustrations, names of characters, and contrasts with what children and adults recognize as the formula for a fairy tale in which the princess awaits the arrival of a prince who will meet with the approval of her father, sweep her off her feet, and "rescue" her from perpetual maidenhood.

Characters Who Exhibit a High Degree of Creative Thinking and Creative Risk Taking. Among common depictions of both females and members of minority groups are characters who defer difficult problems and decisions to others, who support rather than lead, whose aspirations for their futures are limited, who denigrate themselves and their abilities, and who do not take intellectual and creative risks. Fortunately for those who want to select materials that show females and characters from different cultures in positive, active roles, there are books—some older, some more recently published—that make this possible.

Elementary classrooms consciously seeking balance in the literature curriculum will introduce positive role models for girls and for those from different racial and ethnic groups. An example of a book that dispels both racial and gender stereotypes is *Amazing Grace* by Mary Hoffman. Grace is an African American girl who loves to imagine and play out her fantasies. She can be Joan of Arc or a pegleg pirate, Hiawatha or Anansi, the Spider. When her class is to present Peter Pan, Grace resists her classmates' protests that *Peter Pan* is not a girl and is not Black, and with encouragement from her sensitive and supportive grandmother, she decides to try out for the title role. Children in early elementary grades should meet Grace and talk about imagination, setting goals, taking risks and overcoming artificial barriers that limit potential.

Characters Who Make Nontraditional Choices. A thoughtful work is *Miss Rumphius,* by Barbara Cooney, about a young girl who grows up to fulfill her goals by visiting interesting places, living by the sea and making the world a more beautiful place. Her choices reflect the philosophy of life that she has created, and although these choices are not traditional ones for a woman, Miss Rumphius lives and travels alone, making things happen, rather than waiting for things to happen to her. She is an independent woman, a role model for her grand-niece, Alice, who also vows to visit exotic places, live by the sea, and make the world more beautiful.

Half a world away in Pakistan lives Shabanu, title character of *Shabanu, Daughter of the Wind,* by Suzanne Fisher Staples. This young Muslim has experienced much more freedom than other girls her age, but when she is faced with an arranged marriage, she must make decisions and take risks. This book reveals cultural differences that determine significantly contrasting lifestyles between young people in the middle east and this country.

Characters Who Are Problem Solvers.   A work of fiction that is based on fact is Deborah Hopkinson's book *Sweet Clara and the Freedom Quilt,* the story of a young field worker who learns to sew and begins to work in the Big House. When she hears of the Underground Railroad and the difficulty slaves have following the trail, she creates a quilt that is a map showing the route to liberation. Clara is a young woman who solves problems and takes risks. She takes the lead and traces her quilted map to freedom, with others following along her route.

Characters Who Exhibit Positive Responses to Insecurities and Fears.
Madeleine L'Engle, an author who spans both fiction and nonfiction, both adult and children's literature, speaks to verbally talented individuals everywhere. Long a favorite of children for her series beginning with *A Wrinkle in Time,* she exhibits a best fit between criteria for excellent literature and works that speak to talented girls. Her stories are populated with bright children who often experience rejection, misunderstanding, and difficulty relating to others because of their extraordinary abilities, advanced vocabularies, and unusual interests. Madeleine L'Engle experienced many of these difficulties herself as a gifted child who was particularly talented in writing. Her books are rich in language and imagery, the plots are complex and unpredictable, and her underlying messages are deeply moral. A creative teacher may intersperse readings from the fiction with selections from L'Engle's published journals (*A Circle of Quiet, The Summer of the Great-Grandmother*) to offer students rare insights into the mind of a creator of uncommon literature, as well as the mind of the brilliant and sensitive woman behind the literature.

In *A Wrinkle in Time,* Meg, her brother Charles Wallace, and their friend Calvin face the scorn and distrust often thrust upon intellectually precocious children by classmates, teachers, neighbors. Meg also suffers the typical frustrations of adolescent females concerned with physical appearance and feelings about being different from others. These insecurities result in negative self-perceptions that cause her to doubt her abilities and her strengths. Madeleine L'Engle's journal, *A Circle of Quiet,* contains the antecedents of this characterization in her reflections from her own childhoood. She writes poignantly of the long-term outcomes of experiences in a private school where she did not fit in and where she was labeled not very bright and accused of plagiarism.

> *How much pain and rejection and failure and humiliation can a child take? The span of endurance varies from child to child; it is never infinite. What would have happened if my parents had not been able to remove me from that particular school where teacher and student alike had me pegged as different and therefore a failure? . . . I still tend to think of myself in the mirror set up for me in that one school. I was given a self-image there and not a self, and a self-image imposed on one in youth is impossible to get rid of entirely, no matter how much love and affirmation one is given later. Even after all these years, my instinctive image of myself is of someone gawky, clumsy, inadequate, stupid, unwanted, unattractive, in the way.* (p. 145)

Works That Complement and Supplement Other Curricular Material. Literature in the classroom can extend other text materials and fill in some obvious gaps. For example, even recently published history and social studies textbooks have paid only perfunctory attention to the involvement of women and members of other cultures in settling, defending, leading, and moving the country forward. The history of the United States, traced in the curriculum of elementary and secondary schools, is largely the history of white males, reported by them. For middle school and high school students, these accounts may be enriched by both diaries and fictionalized accounts based on journals of those whose points of view are not presented in standard texts. For example, to supplement accounts of the Westward movement and the Oregon Trail, there are actual diaries of women who made the trip. *Women's Diaries of the Westward Journey,* by Lillian Schlissel, contains excerpts from the diaries recounting the daily lives of those who made the trip. Women are the ones who recorded births and deaths, illnesses, and daily struggles against land and weather.

Drawing on journals and diaries of her female ancestors who pioneered and settled new territories, Molly Gloss wrote *The Jump-off Creek,* a fictional account of one woman who set off for Oregon to homestead alone. Chapters alternate between Lydia's first-person journal entries and third-person narrative of her experiences and those of other inhabitants of the Blue Mountains. Lydia claims her homestead, clears the land, builds her home, cares for her animals, and endures separation from the friendship of other women, even as she vows not to be lonely. This account of a woman's struggle to shape her life on her own terms brings perspectives of women to the classroom not only for the benefit of girls, who find characters with whom they share values, dreams, strengths and fears, but also for boys who gain knowledge of women's experiences and points of view.

For somewhat younger readers, *The Endless Steppe,* by Esther Hautzig, is a recounting of one Polish family's exile to Siberia following their arrest by the Russians in 1941. Esther, who was 8 years old at the time of the banishment, spent the next five years living a life very different from the life she lived as the daughter of wealthy Jewish "capitalists." She and her family learned to do without those comforts that had been part of their lives and to adapt to life where fulfilling every basic need was a struggle.

The voices of Native Americans, silent in most curricular materials about the history of this country, are readily available for inclusion into classroom study. Books such as *Spider Woman's Granddaughters,* edited by Paula Gunn Allen, brings into one collection both traditional and contemporary story telling by Native Americans. Materials such as these contribute to students' understanding that there are alternatives to such literary constructs as the unities of time, place and action and the concept of hero.

Autobiographies and Journals.   One of the most effective ways to examine the perspectives of others and become more sensitive to their experiences is to read their own accounts of their lives. Writers are, for obvious reasons, especially talented at presenting themselves in ways that help others see through the windows of their life-shaping experiences. Madeleine L'Engle's journals allow readers to learn more about her life, her philosophy, and her values. Several other writers are worth noting for their considerable ability to speak to readers about growing up female and, in one case, Black and female. In each of these examples, the works cited here are selected because of the richness and exceptional quality of the writing as well as the account of the writer's life itself.

Maya Angelou has written several autobiographical accounts of various periods of her life. The first and best known of these is *I Know Why the Caged Bird Sings,* a book that is read in many middle school and high school classes. Angelou creates for the reader a picture of what it was to grow up poor and Black at a time and place in this country where both conditions would seem to be insurmountable. There were, in her life, relationships with understanding adults, concerned mentors like Mrs. Flowers who gave the young Marguerite Johnson a love for books and an appreciation for the sound of the written word read aloud. And so she flourished and advanced, overcoming early obstacles to become a poet, actor, teacher, and articulate spokesperson for women and for African Americans.

One Writer's Beginnings, by Eudora Welty, tells of her early childhood and events that led to her emergence as a writer who uses words and images to create characters and settings that have collected readers throughout the years. Among the reasons this work is compelling is Welty's description of a childhood in which books and language were celebrated.

> *Ever since I was first read to, then started reading to myself, there has never been a line read that I didn't hear. As my eyes followed the sentence, a voice was saying it silently to me. It isn't my mother's voice, or the voice of any person I can identify, certainly not my own. It is human, but inward, and it is inwardly that I listen to it. It is to me the voice of the story or poem itself. The cadence, whatever it is that asks you to believe, the feeling that resides in the printed word, reaches me through the reader-voice. I have supposed, but never found out, that this is the case with all readers—to read as listeners— and with all writers, to write as listeners. It may be part of the desire to write. The sound of what falls on the page begins the process of testing it for truth for me. Whether I am right to trust so far I don't know. By now I don't know whether I could do either one, reading or writing, without the other. (p. 13)*

A particular strength of Welty's work is her ability to recall and convey such vivid recollections of her early life, her writer's acute sensitivity to her external and internal surroundings.

Another autobiographical piece reflecting a different time and place is *An American Childhood* by Annie Dillard. A generation and the distance between Jackson, Mississippi, and Pittsburgh, Pennsylvania, separate Welty and Dillard, but both have a facility with language and a way of capturing and communicating the joys and miseries of growing up that earns them a place in the literature curriculum.

Dillard is unique among those who write of their early lives in her ability to capture the essence of adolescence in vividly striking images.

> *When I was bored I was first hungry, then nauseated, then furious and weak. "Calm yourself," people had been saying to me all my life. Since early childhood I had tried one thing and then another to calm myself, on those few occasions when I really wanted to. Eating helped; singing helped. Now sometimes I truly wanted to calm myself. I couldn't lower my shoulders; they seemed to wrap around my ears. I couldn't lower my voice although I could see the people around me flinch. I waved my arm in class till the very teachers wanted to kill me. When rage or boredom reappeared, each seemed never to have left. Each so filled me with so many years' intolerable accumulation it jammed the space behind my eyes, so I couldn't see. There was no room left even on my surface to live. My rib cage was so taut I couldn't breathe. Every cubic centimeter of atmosphere above my shoulders and head was heaped with last straws. Black hatred clogged my very blood. I couldn't peep, I couldn't wiggle or blink; my blood was too mad to flow. (pp. 223–224)*

Strategies for Developing Verbal Talent through Speaking and Writing

Content is not the only consideration in classrooms where the development of verbal talent takes place in an environment that is responsive to differences. Once content is altered, methods and strategies for teaching must also be modified so that all students have the opportunity to participate comfortably and equally in activities. Research on differences in teacher behaviors toward female and male students (Sadker & Sadker, 1985) suggests some ways in which instructional practices should be modified to include all students equally. Teachers in classrooms where boys are allowed and encouraged to speak more can become more aware of these patterns and carefully structure discussions so that all students are called on and are given the positive feedback that supports their contributions. Since male students are more likely to call out answers and girls tend to be less impulsive, teachers might require students to jot down ideas before making a response. This will help teachers pay closer attention to the flow of the discussion and any under- or overrepresentation of groups in the response patterns and it will also give the more reflective students (sometimes female, sometimes students from minority groups) more time to organize a contribution.

Increasing numbers of classrooms include cooperative learning strategies as an organizational pattern. Although teachers often structure cooperative learning groups to reflect a representative balance of ability, gender, and diverse attributes, it may be helpful to allow some groups to come together on the basis of like characteristics, thus allowing students to interact and benefit from the support of classmates with whom they share common interests, backgrounds, and perspectives. A cooperative learning group of girls might read and discuss a biography of an eminent woman, or relate certain events or elements of a piece of literature from the point of view of a female character. An example of this took place in a class studying *The Odyssey*, where a group of girls focused their attention on perspectives of the women in the book.

A related method capitalizes on teachers' use of students in leadership roles, a common variation on the Junior Great Books process often employed in classes for academically talented students. Students take turns being responsible for developing and conducting class discussions of the literature, using the shared inquiry techniques modeled by the teacher. Having the chance to prepare thoroughly, those students who are more contemplative and therefore may be slower to respond in group discussions will assume leadership roles and be well prepared and secure as they undertake them.

Another aspect of the development of verbal talent is attention to oral communication, an area deserving attention for several reasons. Oral interaction is a means of articulating and clarifying thinking for the speaker. Some students who do not participate in discussions are denied the opportunity to achieve this clarification and articulation. Since there is evidence that male students dominate class discussions because teachers call on them more frequently and because they often command the floor by speaking out without being called on, it is clear that attention needs to be directed to the development of oral communication skills in those who are less likely to be heard in discussion. Certainly one way to encourage discussion is to ensure that the material to be discussed is relevant to most or all of the students. But oral communication cannot be assured by simply modifying the content of the literature curriculum.

Several elements of oral communication skills are especially beneficial to those students, frequently females or minorities in the classroom setting, who are less likely to be effective in situations where discussion and oral presentation are required. Direct instruction should be given in both formal and informal communication so that oral contributions by these students will receive appropriate attention. Characteristics that should be fostered include speaking with confidence and conviction, making oral assertions directly and without hesitancy, matching oral assertiveness with appropriate nonverbal behaviors such as direct eye contact and correct posture, and ensuring that oral messages are free from physical and vocal distractors. There are several ways that this can take place. First, teachers can offer direct instruction when students are in small groups such as the homogeneous cooperative learning groups. Students in these groups will be less sensitive or self-conscious when a teacher points out behaviors or habits that detract from oral communication.

A second technique is to offer specific models of speaking techniques, noting the behaviors that make the communication effective. Videotape can be a useful tool for showing examples of females and minorities exhibiting model oral discussion techniques. Programs such as "Meet the Press," selected portions of "The Oprah Winfrey Show," and other examples of good discussions could be useful for focusing on the target behaviors.

Videotape may also be effective if used carefully to look at the oral skills of students in the class. If class size permits, and particularly in assignments that culminate with formal oral presentations, teachers may employ videotape with follow-up individualized conferences to help students recognize and practice good oral skills. Another beneficial use of videotape is for teachers to tape themselves in order to identify some of their own behaviors such as those cited by researchers of gender differences in classrooms.

Writing must also undergo change if it is to be responsive to all students and instrumental in the development of verbal talent. Since writing serves several purposes (communication of thoughts and ideas to others and a means by which ones own thinking can be clarified), it is important that students be able to write from meaningful experiences and interactions with literature. Successful integration of students' writing experiences with literature requires that they be able to relate on a personal level to their reading and that they be able to bring to their reading and writing a background that allows them to construct meaning and explore and elaborate that meaning for themselves and an audience, whether that audience is the teacher or other readers.

One meaningful writing experience is the use of journals. Frequent journal writing allows students to record their thoughts and perceptions and their reactions to literature and to discussions. Often, students who are not yet comfortable speaking in class will be able to write their ideas and elucidate their thinking processes in a journal that no one other than the teacher will read. Teachers may gain insight into students' responses and feelings by reading their journals and may begin a productive dialogue by making written comments in the journals.

The process approach to writing may also appropriately involve cooperative groups that consist of students who have similar backgrounds and may bring similar perspectives to their reading and writing. This could be an effective strategy early in the year as the class begins to work together. As they study a literary selection, the opportunity to read and discuss the writing of other group members builds a supportive environment among students who are not yet at ease with a larger, more diverse group.

Conclusion

The development of verbal talent among all students is the goal of the literate classroom. Too often in the past, the needs of particular groups of students have been neglected in the teaching of literature and related language skills and processes. More recently, we have come to the point of recognizing the importance of including in the curriculum a rich and diverse body of literature that speaks to all students. This chapter has suggested some characteristics of literature that meets this requirement. A number of specific selections have been listed and described. Methods of modifying the related processes of speaking and writing have also been suggested.

Attention to these issues provides an environment that ensures that all who study literature and who speak and write about literature will be able to bring to their study those characteristics that make them who they are. At the same time, the curriculum will offer the breadth of content and process that will allow all students to learn from the diverse internal and external lives of others.

Key Points Summary

- Reading selections in schools have been simplified and therefore made less challenging for all learners.
- American reading habits have changed; fewer students and adults are choosing to spend leisure time reading.
- Cultural diversity and gender issues have sparked concerns ensuring representations of literature depicting minority groups and girls and women in literature selections used in educational contexts.
- Constructivist thought dominates current learning models for the teaching of literature in schools; the learner, not the text, makes meaning.
- To attain cultural and gender representation in content and active involvement of students in the learning process are the critical variables for developing a rich language arts curriculum.
- Literature that contains the following specific characteristics promotes the possibility of students optimal identification with it and benefit from it:
  Stories that counteract typical formulas
  Characters who exhibit thinking behaviors
  Characters who make nontraditional choices
  Characters who are problem solvers
  Characters who respond proactively to danger and fear
  Multicultural works that complement/supplement other frequently used material
  Autobiographies and journals
- Use of strategies such as cooperative learning, oral communication activities, and writing process workshops all enhance total student engagement and are particularly appealing to minority students and girls.

Young People's Literature Cited

Angelou, M. (1970). *I know why the caged bird sings*. New York: Random House.

Allen, P. G. (Ed.). (1989). *Spider woman's granddaughters*. New York: Ballantine Books.

Celsi, T. (1990). *The fourth little pig*. Austin, TX: Steck-Vaughn Company.

Cole, B. (1986). *Princess smartypants*. New York: G. P. Putnam's Sons.

Cooney, B. (1982). *Miss Rumphius*. New York: Penguin Books, USA.

de Angeli, M. (1946). *Bright April*. Garden City, NY: Doubleday & Company.

Dillard, A. (1987). *An American childhood*. New York: Harper & Row.

Enright, E. (1941). *The Saturdays*. New York: Dell Publishing.

Gloss, M. (1989). *The jump-off creek*. Boston: Houghton Mifflin.

Hautzig, E. (1968). *The endless steppe*. New York: Harper & Row.

Hoffman, M. (1991). *Amazing Grace*. New York: Penguin Books, USA.

Hopkinson, D. (1993). *Sweet Clara and the freedom quilt.* New York: Alfred A. Knopf.

L'Engle, M. (1962). *A wrinkle in time.* New York: Farrar, Straus & Giroux.

L'Engle, M. (1972). *A circle of quiet.* New York: Farrar, Straus & Giroux.

L'Engle, M. (1974). *The summer of the great-grandmother.* New York: Farrar, Straus & Giroux.

Staples, S. (1989). *Shabanu, daughter of the wind.* New York: Alfred A. Knopf.

Schlissel, L. (1982). *Women's diaries of the westward journey.* New York: Schocken Books.

Taylor, S. (1972). *All of a kind family.* Chicago: Follett.

Welty, E. (1983). *One writer's beginnings.* New York: Warner Books.

References

American Association of University Women. (1991). *Shortchanging girls, shortchanging America* (Executive summary). Washington, DC: AAUW Educational Foundation.

American Association of University Women. (1992). *How schools short-change girls* (Executive summary). Washington, DC: AAUW Educational Foundation.

Hirsch, E. D., Jr. (1987). *Cultural literacy: What every American needs to know.* Boston: Houghton Mifflin.

Jipson, J. A., & Paley, N. (1992). Is there a base to today's literature-based reading programs? *English Education, 24*(2), 77–90.

National Center for Educational Statistics. (1992). *Reading in and out of school: Factors influencing the literacy achievement of American students in grades 4, 8, and 12, in 1988 and 1990.* Washington, DC: U.S. Department of Education.

Ravitch D., & Finn, C. E., Jr. (1987). *What do our 17-year-olds know?* New York: Harper & Row.

Sadker, M., & Sadker, D. (1985). Sexism in the schoolroom of the '80s. *Psychology Today, 19*(3), 54–57.

Singal, D. (1991). The other crisis in our schools. *The Atlantic, 268,* 59–62.

Style, E. (1988). Curriculum as window and mirror. In E. Style (Ed.), *Listening for all voices: Gender balancing the school curriculum* (pp. 6–12). Summit, NJ: Oak Knoll School of the Holy Child.

Part IV

Teacher Reflections and
Model Lesson Plans

Part IV, the final section of the book, will share the perspective of the teachers responsible for the initial development of the language arts units described as a part of the National Language Arts Curriculum Project for High Ability Learners. Their observations of various facets of the project, along with illustrative parts of their units, provide an important touchstone of reality testing for this book. Just as Part III examined practical implications of talent development in the language arts, these teachers ground those implications in actual classroom practice. All of these teacher-authors were initial developers and piloters of the curriculum of the project that is currently being disseminated nationally. Their observations emerged from reflecting on their pilot experiences with a particular language arts unit coupled with years of classroom experience working with all students as well as talented learners. Each chapter concludes with relevant sample lessons from their units of study that reflect the ideas expressed in their individual chapters.

Chapter 16, by Becky M. Crossett and Connie W. Moody, links issues of the middle school to aspects of interdisciplinarity developed in their units. Practitioners looking for ways to promote interdisciplinary instruction with language arts as the base will find this chapter informative and useful.

Chapter 17 focuses on the art of teaching persuasion to intermediate students through written and oral modes of communication. Sandra Coleman and Chwee Geok Quek's use of classical literature to evoke argument and debate provides an interesting application for practitioners.

Carol Cawley and Jan Corbett explore in Chapter 18 the development of inquiry skills in young learners at the primary level through the use of literature and its related activities. They place emphasis on question asking as a process but also on the structure of questioning and ensuring use of higher-order (or "fat") questions.

The last elements found in Part IV are the teaching models that are used throughout all of the units to support the delivery of the curriculum structure. These models represent the organizing basis of lesson development and incorporate the major teaching strategies employed in the classroom.

16

Constructing Meaning through Interdisciplinary Instruction in the Middle Schools

A Blueprint

BECKY M. CROSSETT
Middle School Teacher, York County,
Virginia

CONNIE W. MOODY
Summit High School, Frisco,
Colorado

Presently, there are no commonly agreed on best practices in the middle grades. Over the next three years, schools are likely to slowly but steadily adopt various practices to create more responsive programs for early adolescents (Epstein & MacIver, 1990). However, several "signature" practices that reflect the basic middle school values can be identified and labeled as "characteristics of a middle school" (Carnegie Council on Adolescent Development, 1989; Epstein & MacIver, 1990; George, Stevenson, Thomason, & Beane, 1992). These include organizing students into teams, using teacher interdisciplinary teams, focusing curriculum on student needs for connectedness and relevance, and promoting flexibility in learning situations.

Few middle schools have fully integrated all of these recommended educational practices. The transition from the traditional forerunner—the junior high school—is a slow process and much remains to be accomplished. Many research studies focusing on middle schools have found that most remain, programmatically, far from achieving the goals of middle school education

(George, Stevenson, Thomason, & Beane, 1992). However, as educators have long known, while waiting and working for plenary changes from without, many significant changes from within can take place.

Young adolescents, who are experiencing dramatic physical, social, emotional, and intellectual or cognitive changes as a result of maturation, are even more acutely aware of how bewildering and perplexing life really is. Between the ages of 10 and 14, more biological changes take place in the human body than at any other time, with the exception of the changes that take place in the first three years of life (Wiles & Bondi, 1993). Some of the personal and social concerns of young adolescents may be seen in Table 16–1.

Just as one of the characteristics of a middle school is to allow early adolescents to "construct" their own meanings from information and materials with which they are confronted, so too must it be the attitude of practitioners in the middle grades. That is, teachers, administrators, parents, and other adults who work with young adolescents must construct some personal meaning from and commitment to the ideals that constitute an effective middle school program and begin, in their own ways, to institute such a program. As a matter of fact, it is the creation of these fundamental changes within the school by practitioners that may have the most impact on the complete transition to a true middle school as the wheels of the school bureaucracy spin slowly.

TABLE 16–1   Personal and Social Concerns of Adolescents and Corresponding Curricular Themes

Early Adolescent Themes	Curricular Themes	Social Concerns
Understanding personal changes	Transitions	Living in a changing world
Developing a personal identity	Identities	Cultural diversity
Finding a place in the group	Interdependence	Global interdependence
Personal fitness	Wellness	Environmental protection
Social status	Social Structures	Class systems
Dealing with adults	Independence	Human rights
Peer conflict and gangs	Conflict Resolution	Global conflict
Questioning authority	Justice	Laws and social customs
Personal friendships	Caring	Social welfare

Source: From *A Middle School Curriculum: From Rhetoric to Reality* by J. A. Beane, 1990, Columbus OH: National Middle School Association. Copyright 1990 by National Middle School Association. Adapted by permission.

The key characteristics of middle school programs include the following topics of emphases.

- Providing a balanced curriculum based on the needs of early adolescents
  - Using questions and concerns of early adolescents to drive curriculum
  - Helping students construct knowledge and understanding about themselves and the world around them
  - Promoting individuality by allowing students to construct their own meanings and see things through their own lenses
  - Expanding instructional objectives to include the posing and clarifying of self and social questions; identifying overarching themes and concepts; and finding resources
  - Developing metacognition and habits of mind

- Concentrating on interdisciplinary and intradisciplinary curriculum approaches that transcend separate subject areas
- Using a variety of instructional strategies including inquiry
- Fostering health and fitness to improve academic performance
- Integrating fully the cognitive and affective aspects of the curriculum

By working closely with other teachers on a team, educators can design interdisciplinary units of study that reflect the real-life concerns and needs of young adolescents organized around a universal theme or concept. Through such proactive efforts, small groups of practitioners can be instrumental in making middle schools a reality.

A Rationale for Interdisciplinary Curriculum

Examples from two exemplary interdisciplinary units developed as part of the National Language Arts Curriculum for High Ability Learners Project. *Threads of Change in 19th Century American Literature* and *Literature of the 1940's: A Decade of Change* will be cited frequently throughout this chapter as illustrations of key points of interdisciplinary unit construction. Specific lessons from the units may be found at the end of the chapter. These units demonstrate that interdisciplinary curriculum planning is a powerful way to address the needs and characteristics of the middle school learner. Even though an interdisciplinary approach is appropriate for all middle school students, these units have been constructed with the needs of the verbally talented in mind. Why is interdisciplinary curriculum so important?

Interdisciplinary curriculum causes students to become thoughtfully involved with important content. Specific disciplines are critical, yet educators must find or create learning experiences that will allow students to manipulate information/data from within the content areas and to see relationships and connections across the various disciplines. If this is allowed to occur, curriculum relevance will be heightened because students will interact in meaningful real-world activities. Thus, important social and cognitive needs of young adolescent learners will be met. For example, In *Threads of Change in 19th Century American Literature*, the writings of Ralph Waldo Emerson and Henry David Thoreau are examined with an eye to the threads of change that surrounded these writers during the Romantic Period in literature. Students investigate feminism, abolitionism, industrialism, and transcendentalism through the writings of the times in order to explore how these "isms" affected life in the nineteenth century. Students can also consider how these aspects of change affect contemporary society. Such an interdisciplinary emphasis contributes to a cohesive, in-depth study of the literature of nineteenth-century America.

Interdisciplinary curriculum also offers alternatives for students as they are encouraged to become producers and not merely consumers of knowledge; they become productive thinkers, not reproductive thinkers. By focusing on real-life themes and issues, teachers create curriculum that is emerging, changing, and continually adapting to the needs of the middle school learner. Research projects in both units require students to create a comparison model of life in nineteenth-century America and the 1940s, respectively, that examines how life today is similar or different in respect to societal attitudes toward key issues such as racism and sexism.

The multifaceted nature of interdisciplinary curriculum is a way of honoring the social, emotional, cognitive, and physical characteristics of each developing individual learner. For example, *Literature of the 1940's: A Decade of Change* views the changes in U.S. thought and culture in the 1940s through a language arts lens, an art lens, a drama lens, as well as a historical lens. Thus, this interdisciplinary unit provides students with more "hooks" on which to hang their personal meanings.

Moreover, interdisciplinary curriculum is an excellent tool for implementing an integrated program rather than emphasizing isolated parts. Resources are organized in order to help students make connections between what they know and what is to be learned. Emphasis is on the learning process; students construct meaning, discover relationships, solve problems, and develop skills through meaningful experiences. The growth rate of knowledge today challenges educators to reflect on what should be taught and what can be eliminated from a course of study. If the disciplines are integrated, a study can become more in-depth without sacrificing important intradisciplinary issues. Thus, less becomes more!

Finally, the real world is interdisciplinary. Consequently, schools must become a true microcosm of contemporary society by engaging students in interdisciplinary learning.

Employing Interdisciplinarity: A Method of Facilitating Meaning Construction

Interdisciplinarity is a "knowledge view and curriculum approach that consciously applies methodology and language from more than one discipline to examine a central theme, issue, problem, topic, or experience" (Jacobs, 1989). It provides comprehensive and integrated learning opportunities for students and an assurance that students will receive substantive rather than superficial learning experiences. An interdisciplinary curriculum should stress linkages, connections, and relationships among the disciplines in order to help each student construct personal meaning as he or she confronts relevant concepts, problems, or issues; gathers resources and data; and generates conclusions or solutions from among alternatives.

As the instrumental change agents in middle school reform, classroom practitioners must create and deliver interdisciplinary units of study for young adolescents. This may sound like an ominous task, but, while it is not easy, it is very "do-able" and extremely rewarding. There are many models for interdisciplinary curriculum construction available. It is recommended that teachers seek professional development opportunities that provide hands-on training in this type of unit construction. As the developers of the units cited throughout this chapter and as teachers ourselves, we hope that the following outline of our method of unit construction will be helpful to others.

Developing an Interdisciplinary Unit

Although there is a definite process for developing interdisciplinary units, the steps within the process are fluid. Each practitioner who engages in interdisciplinary planning will find the need to adapt the following steps into his or her own personal method for successful curriculum development.

Select the Organizing Center or Concept

The organizing "center" is the concept that is chosen to act as the specific focus for the unit as it becomes the "lens" through which the teacher(s) and students will view the various subjects or disciplines. It provides cohesiveness to the unit as it unifies the learning experiences and points the students in the direction of some common goals, thereby making the learning activities mutually reinforcing.

Some curriculum developers would state that the "lens" might also be a theme or topic. This may simply be a matter of semantics, but using a concept is important because it allows for a broader scope of learning and provides an overarching construct under which multiple disciplines will find vital roles in the interdisciplinary planning and teaching process.

The following questions will be helpful when a teacher attempts to choose a "lens" or concept for developing interdisciplinary units of study:

- Does the concept allow for meaningful contributions to be made from existing core curriculum?
- Have the needs and characteristics of the middle school learner been addressed by the concept?
- Does the concept apply to the "real" world?
- Can generalizations be made about the concept that will promote future learning or transfer of understanding?
- Are resources readily available for curriculum to be developed around the concept?
- Does the concept provide broad options for teaching and learning?

For example, although there are various resources available on the topic of *spiders*, this topic is not a concept because it does not allow for meaningful contributions from the various disciplines nor does it provide broad options for teaching and learning. *Structures*, on the other hand, not only includes the study of spiders and their webs but can also include other topics and themes to be considered, such as community or governmental structures, human-made or natural structures, or even how language is structured for meaning.

The Metaphor of a Lens

When writing interdisciplinary curriculum, an organizing center or unit concept must become the focus for content selection. This center becomes the "lens" through which the curriculum writer views various subjects in order to merge disciplines and to provide cohesiveness to the curriculum. The lens serves a multiple role because it is applied broadly to serve as a "wide-angle" lens that integrates various disciplines, yet it allows students to "zoom-in" as they examine minute details within the unit of study. This center, or lens, discloses patterns, relationships, connections, and contrasts within and across the disciplines. It allows students to delve deeper into a concept for close examination.

In order to decide on an organizing center or lens, the teacher should consider two criteria:

- The center or lens should not be so broad or general that it is beyond the scope of a reasonable investigation.
- It should not be so narrow that it restricts investigation from within multiple disciplines (Jacobs, 1989).

Often, teachers use various "filters" that slightly alter the emphasis of the lens. These special filters provide opportunities to extend and enrich the subjects, topics, or themes explored within the concept lens that directs the entire unit of study.

Use a Graphic Organizer to Create Concept Applications

After choosing an organizing concept, the teacher should brainstorm associations which relate to that concept. This aspect of the interdisciplinary planning process provides a means for the unit developer to view the concept from various perspectives. The units developed under the Javits Curriculum Development Project used "change" as the conceptual focus of the units. The developers of the units referred to in this chapter each constructed webs that attempted to answer each of the following questions:

- How do writers view the concept of change?
- How do scientists view the concept of change?
- How do historians view the concept of change?
- How do mathematicians view the concept of change?
- How do anthropologists view the concept of change?

Determine the Generalizations or Universal Truths about the Concept

When planning interdisciplinary curricula, it is important to state the underlying generalizations about the concept. These will be evidenced by the strong connections, relationships, and patterns that emerge in the graphic organizer. For example, project staff and unit developers derived these generalizations about the concept of change:

- Change is linked to time.
- Change is pervasive.
- Change may occur according to natural order or may be imposed by individuals.
- Change may be systematic or random.
- Change may represent growth and development or regression and decay.

They were then tested for validation against a careful review of the change literature (Boyce, 1993).

Develop Student Outcomes

Outcomes for each of the Javits units were developed for the four strands of the language arts, the process of reasoning, and the concept of change (Van-Tassel-Baska, Johnson, & Boyce, 1992). A complete list of outcomes is included in Appendix B at the end of this book. The outcomes for the concept of change evolved directly from the derived generalizations. Once established, the student outcomes became the ends toward which the units were taught.

Design the Means for Reaching the Unit Outcomes

To design the means by which outcomes may be realized is to map the way. The teacher must choose the most appropriate materials and resources, plan the most meaningful activities, integrate the most applicable strategies, and design the most effective assessments in order to develop a worthwhile interdisciplinary unit that will accomplish its stated outcomes. Some activities and strategies found to work well in these units with young adolescents were problem solving, case studies, debates, simulations, and seminar discussions.

Although deciding on strategies and collecting materials and resources for teaching the unit are important, it is the creation and use of effective guiding questions that will link these strategies, materials, and resources into a cohesive unit of study. For instance, in *Threads of Change in 19th Century American Literature*, student inquiry was fostered by two guiding questions that drove the unit:

- How did the various authors respond to the change agents of their respective time periods?
- How have the threads of change you have discovered throughout the unit shaped U.S. culture today?

Implementing the Unit

This step needs little explanation, but it is important to remember to be flexible during implementation. Due to the many different factors such as administrative requirements, individual student needs, and schedule conflicts that impact all teachers on a daily basis, it is often necessary to amend and adapt one or more components of any given lesson on any given day.

Assessing Student Learning

Another crucial part of interdisciplinary curriculum work is to assess regularly how students are progressing toward the stated outcomes. In the exemplary units described in this chapter, a combination of tools were used to tap into student learning, including observation data, student products, writing portfolio samples, and formal pre- and postassessments in literary understanding and persuasive writing.

Assessing the Effectiveness of the Unit

Throughout the implementation of an interdisciplinary unit, the teacher should document the success of each lesson. Even though a lesson may be successful overall, some component of the lesson may need adjustment—perhaps the video wasn't as useful as was previously thought, for example. The two authors of this chapter kept a log in which student and teacher reactions to all elements of every lesson were noted. The information gleaned from such documentation was used to refine and revise the unit for others to implement. Videotapes were compiled for specific teaching lessons and analyzed for ways to enhance the unit teaching.

Unit Descriptions and Application to Model of Development

Threads of Change in 19th Century American Literature begins with an in-depth study of the change agents that affected the writings of Ralph Waldo Emerson and Henry David Thoreau in nineteenth-century America. Students are given the opportunity to explore the agents of change that were affecting U.S. society: Romanticism, Feminism, Abolitionism, Industrialism, and Transcendentalism. Small groups of students choose to research one of these issues by selecting a literature box that contains articles, books, audio- and videotapes, literary works, and so on, on each of the "isms." The students work in teams and develop a class presentation. After each presentation, students are asked to discuss important issues during the nineteenth century that continue to have an effect on U.S. society today.

A second emphasis of the unit is dedicated to the reading and analysis of *The Adventures of Huckleberry Finn* by Mark Twain. Students are presented with situations that encourage them to reflect on personal change as well as changes in human behavior. They are asked to trace political, social, economic, internal, and external changes that are presented in the novel. Individual student literary packets provide guidelines and guiding questions for study. Essays and persuasive speeches are required throughout the unit. Language study, vocabulary, and grammar activities are also featured.

Assessment throughout the unit includes student conferences, reaction logs, videotaped sessions, and portfolios of individual and group work. Students are asked to produce graphic organizers of arguments, issues, and themes. They are asked to identify bias in various writings and to provide supporting evidence for different points of view. They use established criteria to evaluate arguments and are asked to verbalize opposing viewpoints in spoken argument.

Students produce writing entries in a reaction log and create concept maps, persuasive essays, literary analysis of two novels, an oral presentation of independent investigations, videotapes sessions, and pretests and post-tests. Grouping practices used throughout the unit allow students opportunities to work independently as well as in groups. The unit emphasis on U.S. culture today makes this historical study relevant to students.

Literature of the 1940's: A Decade of Change is an interdisciplinary unit that fully integrates the language arts, the social studies, and the fine and performing arts. Shaken by the events of a world war that included the Holocaust and Hiroshima, America and Americans underwent great change during the 1940s. How do we know things changed? We can read it in the literary works of the day; we can interpret it in the dramas of the day; and we can see it in the artwork of the day.

A study of these social issues and historical events is best done by reading period literature, watching period films, and analyzing primary documents that include letters, diaries, photographs, paintings, and the like. By so doing, the students are able to make their own hypotheses and draw their own conclusions about the concept of change and its application to life, thought, and culture in the United States in the 1940s. They are also encouraged to consider what impact the events and people of World War II and the 1940s continue to have on U.S. culture today. The civil rights movement and the idea of women in the workplace are two examples treated in the unit.

The introductory literary piece is an excerpt from *The Moon Is Down* by John Steinbeck. This propagandistic piece helps the students begin their inquiry into the impact of World War II on America. Subsequent lessons include The Changing Face of War (students contemplate how wars have changed by reading several poems); America Reacts to War (a study of the internment of Japanese-Americans accomplished by reading poetry and magazine articles); and The Holocaust (the book *Maus II* by Art Spiegelman serves as the backdrop to an investigation into the terrible events that haunt us today). Several of the lessons are augmented by audio, video, and laser disc presentations. Guest speakers also provide a vital primary link to the past as students embark on independent investigations.

Seminar discussions that focus on interpretive reading occur regularly. When reading a piece for discussion, students are required to "interact" with the piece by noting key ideas, words, phrases, and so on and by making connections within the test. During the discussion, students are asked interpretive questions and encouraged to support their thinking with text references.

Students create many different types of products, including persuasive essays, critical reviews, graphic organizers, drawings and paintings, oral communication opportunities, technology applications, and more. The creative expression of each individual is honored and shared throughout the course. Students are given an active role in their own assessment. They are asked to give a self-assessment rating on each "graded" assignment.

As the unit draws to a close, the separate strands that have been studied become intertwined as two postwar pieces are read and discussed. *The Mem-*

ber of the Wedding, a play by Carson McCullers, and *The Lottery,* a short story by Shirley Jackson, are both viewed as U.S. responses to the events and attitudes that were indicative of the war years. The students determine in these pieces how America was reshaped by World War II.

Key Features of Interdisciplinary Units

Each of the interdisciplinary units that was developed employed key features that made it distinctive and easy to follow as a model for others. The major features discussed here are graphic organizers, questioning strategies, multiculturalism and globalism, and independent investigations.

Graphic Organizers

Graphic organizers are instruments that can be used to create a visual image of written text or spoken words for the purpose of analysis. Graphic organizers become an image of the relationships or connections between or among the ideas conveyed in speech or in text. They also can be developed by learners as preparation for writing or speaking.

In *Literature of the 1940's: A Decade of Change,* graphic organizers were used extensively to help students analyze pieces of literature, persuasive speeches, documentary videos, and artwork. Students were also required to develop graphic organizers as methods of prewriting for both creative and persuasive essay writing assignments as well as to represent the concept of change. Students were exposed to many different types of graphic organizers through illustration and demonstration.

It is important that the teacher model how graphic organizers can be used. As much as conveying information about graphic organizers, this is an important method of demonstrating their power. The students see the teacher "thinking out loud." For a lesson on persuasive speaking in the 1940s unit, the lecture notes of the teacher on effective persuasive speaking were developed as a graphic organizer that was displayed on the overhead during the lecture. The students were also supplied with copies so that they could visually see what they were hearing.

For middle school learners, the use of graphic organizers is important as young adolescents are striving for a sense of control and identity. By developing such skills, these learners gain control of their own thinking processes and are able to think more deeply about what they read, hear, and see.

Questions as Scaffolds for Higher-Level Thinking

Questions are key elements in thinking. They allow teachers to raise the level of productive thinking from recall and knowledge to one that requires evaluative reasoning. However, encouraging teachers to pose questions that require higher-level responses from students is not sufficient. Students also need to correlate their thinking processes and response modes to the different types of questions being asked. The Richard Paul model of reasoning (1992) was employed in the units and is reflected in the questions developed. This model requires students to engage in actively discussing purpose, evidence, inferences, concepts, and implications of what they read.

One effective way to develop discussion in a classroom is to ask probing questions that require students to give more than superficial answers. Since the probe depends on an individual student's response, teachers must be acutely aware of the discussion process in order to appropriately support student contributions in class.

In interdisciplinary unit work, guiding questions can provide the scaffold for addressing student outcomes. Educators can guard against imposing their own agenda, interpretation, or expected response on students by carefully wording questions and honoring student interpretations. Questions can be used to help *link* literary selections to their personal lives, for example.

Guiding questions may also be used by the curriculum developer in order to link the unit's lessons and activities. For example, in *Threads of Change in 19th Century American Literature*, the questions that networked throughout the entire unit of study included:

- How did Romanticism affect the writing, art, and music of nineteenth-century America?
- How would you evaluate feminist thought in nineteenth-century America compared to today?
- What was the impact of abolitionism on American law from the nineteenth century to now?

Multiculturalism and Globalism

"During the early adolescent years, young students become aware of the many cultural differences among people in both their immediate environment and in the world brought home to them through media. As budding moralists, they naturally make comparisons and wonder why things are" (George, Stephenson, Thomason, & Beane, 1992, p. 75). At this time, when young adolescents are attempting to define their own identities and to find their "niches" in the world, it is imperative that they investigate the world as a global community of diverse cultures that coexist on this planet. It is also important that they begin to see diversity as a strength of the human race rather than as a weakness.

Schools, as institutions and microcosms of the greater U.S. society, must encourage students to explore, and thereby develop respect for, the ethnic diversity of our national heritage. In an effort to overcome a powerful human frailty, we must also deal realistically with the ethnic and racial conflicts that are trademarks of our individual and societal failures (George, Stevenson, Thomason, & Beane, 1992). By helping students to analyze and understand their own cultures as well as the cultures of others, students will develop deeper kinship among their contemporary peers and powerful friendships between the generations. Understanding, tolerance, and respect are important life skills and should be fundamental goals at the middle school level. By inviting students to investigate multiculturalism through various disciplines, we invite them to become part of the human heritage. A contribution to the richness of interdisciplinary curriculum is the consideration of multiculturalism and global perspectives.

In studying the impact of World War II on American thought and culture in the interdisciplinary unit *Literature of the 1940's: A Decade of Change*, students discover some of our American heritage and social history through literature. The pieces of literature are deliberately chosen to allow students to experience various cultural perspectives on and reactions to key events. For instance, the students read "Second Blood," a short story about an American Jew's reactions to the horrors of the Holocaust, written by Jo Sinclair, a female Jewish writer. Four tanka poems by Yukari, an issei Japanese-American woman interned during the war, vividly illustrate the demoralizing blow of racial prejudice. Langston Hughes and other Black writers and poets bring to life the struggle of African Americans fighting for liberty, equality, and democracy not only on the front lines but on the U.S. homefront as well. By reading such pieces by authors of diverse cultural backgrounds about people of diverse cultural backgrounds, young adolescents are given first-hand, authentic, and concrete experiences to help them understand and assimilate their own cultures.

Just as multiculturalism as a concept engages the learner in a search for understanding group identity and heritage, so too middle school students crave a sense of belonging to a group. Thus, teachers can guide students on social inquiries into our pluralistic culture and human heritage. Such experiences allow teachers to be co-learners and to model values and attitudes of multicultural appreciation and understanding.

Multicultural and global understanding is also promoted by ways of organizing students in the middle school. The development of closer ties between teachers and students are encouraged and supported by the practice of teaming, thereby creating in students a sense of security and belonging—a keen need for young adolescents. It is this sense of security and belonging that gives students confidence to look at the issues and problems of the greater world community and contribute ideas and possible solutions. "The first day or so we all pointed to our countries. The third or fourth day we were pointing to our continents. By the fifth day we were aware of only one Earth."—*Sultan Bin Salman al-Saud, Discovery 5, June 1985* (Kelly, 1988).

Independent Investigations

Independent investigations are student centered. Young adolescents become independent, self-directed learners as they study an area of interest. Opportunities also exist for peer interaction as students work together to make choices and decisions about an important issue. Independent investigations are a type of inquiry that encourage students to pursue an in-depth study of an area of interest as they incorporate the research process. Such investigations begin with students selecting a topic for study and continues by allowing them to define a problem, explore alternative solutions, develop a plan of action, implement the plan, and present the results of the investigation.

In both of the teaching units, *Threads of Change in 19th Century American Literature* and *Literature of the 1940's: A Decade of Change,* students were required to engage in a major independent investigation. Other types of inquiries, or mini-investigations, were featured in both units that required that the students incorporate certain research steps and processes. For example, in *Threads of Change in 19th Century American Literature,* the students selected a topic from a list of alternatives, gathered data, synthesized it, and critiqued resources in order to understand the Romantic period in American literature. Focusing on the investigative process is a valuable way of preparing students for more demanding independent investigations.

Issues of Implementation

The teacher's role in interdisciplinary curriculum development and instruction is to collaborate and network with other educators, parents, students, and community resources in order to make relevant curriculum decisions. The teacher should create a "laboratory" environment that encourages students to feel free to investigate, inquire, and to be willing to take necessary risks as they pursue a course of study.

The teacher must also model a spirit of inquiry by examining and questioning students' thinking, encouraging them to consider alternatives when forming opinions, making assumptions, and drawing conclusions based on evidence. Helping students to become willing to admit uncertainty as they question and consider all points of view is another important role of the teacher. Becoming a metacognitive coach by actively demonstrating the use of thinking skills is imperative as the teacher encourages self-monitoring that creates learners who are conscious of how they are manipulating knowledge and thinking processes throughout the unit of study.

Both units cited in this chapter employed grouping strategies that were deliberately varied to place students in many different "learning" communities. In this way, students explored their strengths and made valuable contributions to collaborative efforts. They experienced the give and take of learning that hopefully will transfer to the necessary give and take of peaceful and productive coexistence on this planet.

Conclusion

Contemporary society is characterized by an information explosion, ever-changing technological innovations, and increasingly more diverse popula-tions. Middle schools must break from the traditional educational approaches in order to address more closely these characteristics of modern society while being ever mindful of the needs of young adolescent learners. One powerful means of accomplishing this goal is interdisciplinary planning and instruction that benefits both teachers and students as it allows them to make decisions about relevant content and to establish connections between the disciplines while also allowing the construction of personal meaning.

Key Points Summary

- Interdisciplinary curriculum is appropriate for middle school students since it reflects real-world issues and relevant modes of learning as well as provides a thoughtful approach to learning content.
- The language arts have many rich connections to other disciplines, such as social studies, art, and music.
- Teachers can develop their own interdisciplinary units as shown by the examples in this chapter.
- Independent investigations offer alternatives for students so they are not merely consumers of facts.
- A concept rather than a topic needs to be chosen carefully as the organiz-ing center of the unit.
- Graphic organizers can be used effectively to analyze text, to illustrate connections between ideas, and as a strategy for organization of thoughts.

Sample Lessons

Sample Lesson from Literature of the 1940s: A Decade of Change

Lesson 22

Curriculum Alignment Code					
Goal #1	Goal #2	Goal #3	Goal #4	Goal #5	Goal #6
				✕	✕

Instructional Purpose:
- To trace changes in the social, political, and economic climate from the 1940s to the present and predict changes into the future.

Materials Used:
1. A Changing World: Key Issues and Events (see page 307)
2. Reference materials from the unit

Activities:
Note to Teacher: This in-class activity will take two 90-minute periods to complete.

1. Have students use A Changing World: Key Issues and Events (handout at end of lesson) to organize their thinking about how key social, political, and economic issues have changed since the 1940s and predict how they might change by the year 2050.
2. Students should work in the same small groups used for exploring research issues originally. For this activity, however, they should *explore across issues* rather than just tackle one.
3. Answer the following key questions:

   - How has American foreign policy changed after World War II, particularly in respect to adversaries of that time?
   - How have the global alliances created during World War II affected international events in the last 10 years?
   - How were soldiers returned from wars after WWII treated in comparison to Vietnam soldiers? Trace these changes up through the Gulf War of 1990.
   - How have society's views of minority groups—such as African Americans, Jews, Asian American, and women—changed since WWII?
   - What changes in world view regarding economics has occurred in the last 10 years?
   - How has communication technology affected our perspective on war and its atrocities over these periods?

4. Groups will need to spend the *entire period* exploring these issues.

Homework:

1. Write a persuasive essay in which you argue for one of the following positions:

   a. The 1940s constituted the most significant decade of the twentieth century.

   b. The 1990s will constitute the most significant decade of the twentieth century.

A Changing World: Key Issues and Events

Past (1940s)	Social	Political	Economic
Present (1990s)	Social	Political	Economic
Future (2050s)	Social	Political	Economic

Sample Lesson from Threads of Change in 19th Century American Literature

Lesson 4

Curriculum Alignment Code					
Goal #1	Goal #2	Goal #3	Goal #4	Goal #5	Goal #6
×				×	×

Instructional Purpose:
- To review the characteristics of Romanticism and discuss the various categories from the timeline.
- To understand how the *Threads of Change* influenced the literary works of Henry David Thoreau and Ralph Waldo Emerson.
- To introduce literature boxes and related assignments.

Materials Used:
1. Biographical sketch of Henry David Thoreau
2. Biographical sketch of Ralph Waldo Emerson
3. Literature Box Data (see page 310)
4. Guidelines for Literature Boxes (see page 313)
5. The Research Model (see page 367)

Activities:
1. Write on the board: *What was life like before the telephone?* Students can brainstorm ideas. They should be encouraged, through discussion, to trace changes and their connections throughout history. They should consider how communication changes people's lives, society, and culture.

   - How have these changes affected people's work? Their leisure? The sense of time and place? Relationships?

   - How have these "change agents" affected the American culture as we know it today?

2. While Henry David Thoreau and Ralph Waldo Emerson lived and wrote in Concord, Massachusetts, in the 1800s, an irreversible process of change and exchange began, producing the foundation for a new world—the world we live in today. The unit we are studying, *Threads of Change*, examines the encounter through the primary agent of change, which was Romanticism. However, each of the following forces of social change also affected this period in our history: Feminism, Abolitionism, Transcendentalism, and Industrialism.

   From these five threads grew a series of events that reordered the thinking of the new nation. The consequences of this nineteenth-century exchange continue to influence our lives and events today. We will examine how connections within cultures are most often revealed through change. Throughout our study of *Threads of Change,* we will examine how events and processes of change make the past understandable, help explain the present, and help us plan more wisely for the future. This unit is about cultural themes and how the United States changed as a result of their dominance.

3. Explain that the five *Threads of Change* have been developed into five *Literature Boxes* that contain data about a particular "change agent" that affected nineteenth-century American society.

4. In the examination of the Literature Box on Romanticism, students will explore the literature and biographies of Thoreau and Emerson. Divide the class into Groups A and B. Ask each group to write in their Response Journals on the meaning of the following quotes:

   Group A: If a man does not keep pace with his companions, perhaps it is because he hears a different drummer. Let him step to the music which he hears, however measured, or far away.—Henry David Thoreau

   Group B: In the woods, too, a man casts off his years, as the snake his slough, and at what period soever of life is always a child. In the woods is perpetual youth.—Ralph Waldo Emerson

5. Share the reactions and ask the following questions:

   • What inferences can you draw about the philosophy of these two writers from the quotations?
   • How do they illustrate the tenets of Romanticism?

6. Ask Group A to read the biographical sketch of Henry David Thoreau; Group B is to read the biographical sketch of Ralph Waldo Emerson.

7. Each group will share the data with each other concerning these two giants in nineteenth-century American thought.

8. Discuss Thoreau's and Emerson's influence on eminent people in various fields.
   Example: The people listed below expressed a debt to Thoreau's concept of civil disobedience:

   • Leo Tolstoy, in his opposition to Czarist Russia
   • Gandhi, in his resistance to British rule in India
   • Martin Luther King Jr. in his struggle for civil rights of Black Americans

   Emerson's influence through his concepts of self-reliance and nature is current when we consider environmental issues in contemporary society.

9. Pass out the Literature Box Data/Artifacts handout (next page) to students. To embark on a group investigation, have students choose one of the four *Literature Boxes* #2–#5 to study. Each box contains data concern-

ing each of the *Threads of Change* that helped shape the U.S. culture as we know it today:

#2 Feminism

#3 Industrialism

#4 Transcendentalism

#5 Abolitionism

Have them review Handout 4B, Guidelines for Literature Boxes, as they begin to explore the boxes. (Allow group time of 30 minutes for this activity.) Share the results of the initial exploration activity. Who will do what? How will the central question be systematically explored? Hand out the Research Model (see page 367).

10. To check on the progress of the Grammar Self-Study packets, ask students to discuss the form and function of the underlined words in this sentence from *Walden:*

I went to the <u>woods</u> <u>because</u> I wished to live <u>deliberately,</u> to confront only the <u>essential</u> facts of life, and see if I could not learn what it had to teach, and not, when I came to die, <u>discover</u> that I had not lived.

Homework:

1. Continue research on the *Literature Box.*

Note to Teacher: A good source for artifacts from this period is The National Center for History in the Schools Project at the University of California in Los Angeles. The address is 231 Moore Hall, 405 Hillgard Avenue, Los Angeles, California 90024-1521. The phone number is 310-825-8388.

Literature Box Data/Artifacts

All boxes include short biographies of Louisa May Alcott, Herman Melville, Edgar Allen Poe, Mark Twain, Walt Whitman, Nathaniel Hawthorne, Rebecca Harding Davis, Emily Dickinson, Ralph Waldo Emerson, and Henry David Thoreau. Suggested data/artifacts for each of the individual *Literature Boxes* include:

Box #1: Romanticism

A list of environmental quotations from the writings of Henry David Thoreau

A Yearning Toward Wildness by T. Homan

Excerpts from the following:

Self-Reliance: The Wisdom of Ralph Waldo Emerson by R. Whelan

Walden by H. D. Thoreau

Civil Disobedience by H. D. Thoreau

Where I Lived and What I Lived For by H. D. Thoreau

A Week On the Concord and Merimack Rivers by H. D. Thoreau

Biographies, letters, newspaper articles, diaries from the period

The Civil War Video Series by Ken Burns

"Earth's Holocaust" by Hawthorne

Emerson's poetry

Paintings by Thomas Cole

Wordsworth's poetry

Romantic music by Chopin, Schubert, and late Beethoven, Tchaikovsky, Schumann, and Stravinsky

Box #2: Feminism
Debate at Seneca Falls

Characteristics of feminism

Art prints by Mary Cassatt

Sojourner Truth's speech found in *The American Reader* edited by Diane Ravitch

Susan B. Anthony: Pioneer Suffragist

"This Is My Letter to the World" found in *Selected Poems, Emily Dickinson* by S. Applebaum

"Declaration of Sentiments" by Elizabeth Cady Stanton

"A Pair of Silk Stockings" by Kate Chopin

Biographies, letters, newspaper articles, diaries from the period

"Plans for Improving Female Education" by Emma Willard

Woman in the 19th Century by Margaret Fuller

Massachusetts legislature address by the Grimke sisters (1830)

"Sweethearts and Wives" by T. S. Arthur

Box #3: Industrialism

Photographs of the Industrial revolution (taken from various history texts)

"Child Labor: Working Conditions"

"The Factory Girls of Lowell"

"United States Geography: Industrial America"

"A Woman's Place Is in the Factory"

"Big Business and Industry"

Characteristics of industrialism

Packets of information on the Industrial Revolution

Biographies, letters, newspaper articles, diaries from the period

20th Century: Dos Passos's *USA*

Sturbridge Village in Massachusetts

"Paradise for Bachelors" by Herman Melville

Autobiography of Lucy Larkham (1840s)

Photographs by Louis Hines

Art depicting the Industrial Revolution

Box #4: Transcendentalism

The Dial (a collection of writings by Emerson, Thoreau, Bronson, Alcott)

Characteristics of transcendentalism

Unitarianism data

Data on Brook Farm and Communitarian Experiments

"Brahma" by R. W. Emerson

Concord, Massachusetts (history, prominent citizens, key activities, etc.)

Biographies, letters, newspaper articles, diaries from the period

Works by Margaret Fuller

"Transcendental Wild Oats" by Louisa May Alcott

"Brook Farm" by Hawthorne

Works by Orestes Brownson

Works by Bronson Alcott

Box #5: Abolitionism

Harriet Tubman: The Moses of Her People by Langston Hughes

"The Underground Railroad" by American History Illustrated

Excerpts from history books

Sojourner Truth's speech found in *The American Reader* edited by Diane Ravitch

My Folks Don't Want Me to Talk about Slavery edited by Belinda Hurmence

Abolitionist poetry

William Lloyd Garrison speeches

Uncle Tom's Cabin by Harriet Beecher Stowe

"On the Slave Trade" by Benjamin Fanklin

The writings of Lowell, Whittier, Horace Mann, and Frederick Douglass

Liberator by William Lloyd Garrison

"Appeal to Blacks" by David Walker

Works by Nat Turner

Works by Sarah and Angela Grimke

Works by John Brown and Marcus Garvey

Guidelines for Literature Boxes

1. Read and study the information/artifacts in each box.
2. Research the topic in depth, using a variety of resources. Consult resources; these might include library resources and experts in history or literature.
3. Prepare a group presentation to share your findings. You may create symbols to represent significant events during the period of the individual *Thread of Change*; summarize the research. Create artwork to tell the stories of the changes throughout this historical period; create maps, charts, and other illustrations of the various "threads" represented. Incorporate the information/artifacts in the *Literature Box* in your presentation as appropriate.
4. Help your audience examine how events and processes of change make the past understandable, explain the present, and help us plan more wisely for the future. Recall the guiding question: How is this area a change agent that helped shape U.S. culture as we know it today?

5. Use the Research Model (see page 367) to structure your overall project. Use the "Need to Know" Board (see page 332) in Lesson 3 to aid in guiding the research process.
6. You will make an oral presentation about your research in Lesson 20. The written product is due in Lesson 22

Note to Teacher: You will need to work with your librarian to gather the necessary materials for each box. Be as creative as possible in displaying the boxes for students. You are encouraged to add to the list of artifacts suggested for each box as well.

References

Beane, J. A. (1990). *A middle school curriculum: From rhetoric to reality.* Columbus, OH: National Middle School Association.

Boyce, L. N. (1993). The concept of change: Interdisciplinary inquiry and meaning. *Topics papers.* Williamsburg, VA: College of William and Mary, Center for Gifted Education.

Carnegie Council on Adolescent Development. (1989). *Turning points: Preparing youth for the 21st century.* New York: Carnegie Corporation.

Epstein, J. L. & MacIver, D. J. (1990). *Education in the middle grades: National practices and trends.* Columbus, OH: National Middle School Association.

George, P. S., Stevenson, C., Thomason, J., & Beane, J. (1992). *The middle school—and beyond.* Alexandria, VA: Association for Supervision and Curriculum Development.

Irvin, J. L. (Ed.). (1992). *Transforming middle level education: Perspectives and possibilities.* Boston: Allyn and Bacon.

Jacobs, H. (Ed.). (1989). *Interdisciplinary curriculum: Design and implementation.* Alexandria, VA: Association for Supervision and Curriculum Development.

Kelley, K. (Ed.). (1988). *The home planet.* New York: Addison-Wesley Publishing Company.

Paul, R. (1992). *Critical thinking: What every person needs to know in a rapidly changing world.* Rohnert Park, CA: Critical Thinking Foundation.

VanTassel-Baska, J., Johnson, D., & Boyce, L. N. (1992). *A curriculum framework for language arts.* Williamsburg, VA: College of William and Mary, Center for Gifted Education.

Wiles, J. & Bondi, J. (1993). *The essential middle school.* New York: Macmillan Publishing Company.

17

Enhancing Oral Communication for Intermediate Students

SANDRA COLEMAN
Teacher of Gifted,
Colonial Heights, Virginia

CHWEE GEOK QUEK
Ministry of Education in Singapore

Systematic oral communication instruction is necessary to foster effective communication, and research shows that special instruction can increase students' level of sophistication in oral communication (Chaney, 1992). A sixth-grade unit, *Changing Ideas and Perspectives through Persuasion,* was developed as part of the National Language Arts Curriculum Project for High Ability Learners at the College of William and Mary to give high-ability students instruction in oral communication and persuasion. Why such a strong emphasis on oral communication?

Oral communication is a vital skill for all students because throughout life they will have many opportunities to share information with others (Frith & Mims, 1984). In a time when language becomes increasingly technical and a *lingua franca* is being developed from the media, it may become more and more necessary for teachers to create the kinds of speech situations in which and through which learners can open themselves to their lived worlds, to one another and to themselves (Greene, 1986). Today's talented students are likely to be leaders of the future and on the cutting edge in their fields of specialization. Throughout their careers, they will frequently need to present to others their findings and their insights. It is therefore essential that they receive instruction in oral communication so that they will be equipped with the skills necessary to deal with diverse audiences.

Oral skills also provide the foundation for acquiring the related language arts skills of writing and reading (Lundsteen, 1979). There is a close relationship between verbalization and knowledge acquisition. Through oral interaction in the classroom, students discover and develop new knowledge (Tough, 1977). The syntax of language also enables students to join and transform concepts. Numerous studies have found that verbalization—oral performance—can reinforce learning about concepts and their relations (DiVesta, 1974). Oral communication helps improve students' writing because it enables them to develop fluency, effectiveness, and breadth of expression (Mallet & Newsome, 1977).

Furthermore, oral communication activities create a positive learning environment. Learning is student centered, and students work in collaborative settings and learn from one another. Skills of oral communication enhance self-confidence and social adjustment.

In the teaching of oral communication, students' critical thinking skills will also be developed. The widespread use of radio, sound recordings, telephone, television, and film gives rise to the need to develop skills of listening to understand aural messages (Hade, 1982). In this age of information explosion, students must learn to be more discerning recipients of informative and persuasive messages. They must know how to distinguish fact from fiction and myth from truth. To develop persuasive arguments, students will be required to develop "proof" and supply the best evidence. These abilities are crucial for success—not only in school but also for participation in the working world.

Key Features of the Unit

Oral communication requires thinking skills, argumentation and debate, persuasion in public speaking and interpersonal communication, critical reception of persuasive messages, and participation in group problem solving. As part of the National Language Arts Curriculum Project for High Ability Learners at the College of William and Mary, six units were piloted for high-ability students in grades K–8. Each featured a strand of oral communication outcomes as part of the integrated language arts curriculum.

A sixth-grade unit, *Changing Ideas and Perspectives through Persuasion*, was designed to emphasize oral communication and persuasion. The unit used literature to develop critical thinking skills through discussions. Literature selections included poetry by Robert Frost; "The Pied Piper of Hamelin" by Robert Browning; *The Valiant*, a play by Holworthy Hall and Robert Middlemass; a chapter from *The Adventures of Tom Sawyer* by Mark Twain; various essays; and a number of novels that were read independently by students in preparation for class discussion. The literature served as the catalyst for many of the activities of the unit.

Paul's (1992) elements of reasoning were used as a basis for many discussion questions. Examples of the questions include the following:

- *Evidence*: What facts does Jefferson provide to support his case?
- *Assumptions*: What assumptions were made by the Pied Piper and the Town Council?
- *Issue*: What issues did Martin Luther King Jr. talk about in his speech?
- *Purpose*: What purpose does the author have in using a particular cultural group as the context of the story?
- *Inferences*: What inferences might you make about the life of the main character after the story ends?
- *Point of view*: What point of view does the American Library Association take on the issue of censorship?
- *Implications*: What are the implications of these problems for us/you today?

See the Unit Teaching Models at the end of this section for a discussion of Paul's Reasoning Model and the Wheel of Reasoning.

The *Changing Ideas and Perspectives through Persuasion* unit also provided for the development of skills of persuasion. This unit focused on the development of strong patterns in reasoning, and included the exploration of basic reasoning patterns such as deductive, causal, and analogical reasoning. Students learn how to develop "proof" to strengthen their persuasive writing/speech and to construct a rational argument to defend their opinions. They are also taught how to shape their message to suit the audience and the occasion.

The teaching of persuasion skills also increases the perspective-taking abilities of the students as they will have to expand their views to include the opposite positions (Johnson & Johnson, 1988). By encouraging students to view problems from multiple perspectives and reformulating the problem in different ways to allow new orientations to emerge, students develop creative insights and offer more imaginative solutions.

To create, one must be able to manipulate the medium of speech. Through speech, one can win respect and influence as a person, offer knowledge and information, present opinions that are well reasoned and grounded on evidence, and report the interests of a given audience (Bryant, Wallace, & McGee, 1982). Ample opportunities are provided in the unit for students to make oral presentations and speeches.

To teach students the critical reception of persuasive messages, listening is taught as an active rather than a passive process. The unit focuses on two types of listening skills:

1. *Discriminative listening* refers to listening to instructive or informative oral communication with the goal being to gather information to understand the material and learn something from it so that it will be of use.
2. *Evaluative listening* refers to listening to persuasive oral communication with the goal being to participate in the two-way process of persuasion in a responsible manner by learning to evaluate the merits of a persuasive message.

The following description of sample activities in the unit illustrate how these features are put into practice in the classroom.

Activity One

The teacher will select any paired speeches from this list:

"First Inaugural Address" by Thomas Jefferson **and** "First Inaugural Address" by Abraham Lincoln

"A Century of Dishonor" by Helen Hunt Jackson **and** "Silent Spring" by Rachel Carson

"Address to the Broadcasting Industry" by Newton Minnow **and** "The Case for Public Schools" by Horace Mann

In small groups, students will discuss the persuasive elements of these speeches. Questions they will be asked to answer include:

- Why is this speech memorable?
- Compare and contrast Speech #1 with Speech #2. How are they similar/different?
- What is the issue of significance? Is this an issue in today's world? Cite examples.
- What is the argument advanced by the author? What claims does he or she make? What data does he or she provide? What conclusions are drawn?
- How credible is the argument? Why?

For homework, students are asked to read the speeches that are not discussed in class, and write their reactions to each one in their response journals. They are also asked to include comments on how credible they think the argument is.

Activity Two

Students are given a handout on examples of propaganda techniques. They are then divided into groups of three or four. For homework, they are to collect different types of advertisements from different media (advertisements on food, clothes, cars, books, etc., from magazines, newspapers, television, movies) and bring these to class. In their groups, they are to discuss the persuasive advertisement techniques used in the advertisements they have collected. Each group will then share their findings with the class.

The class is then introduced to the Model for Persuasive Writing and Speaking (see page 331). This is to prepare them to give a one-minute speech to persuade us to want something that they possess. To help students in their preparation, the teacher can ask them to recall items in the "Glorious White-washer" that Tom Sawyer asked the children to give up. Have students decide on criteria they would use to determine the value of the items and discuss the types of questions they would ask someone to find out what is valued by them.

In the next lesson, each student will make a one-minute presentation. To help students evaluate one another's presentations, a Persuasive Speech Evaluation Form (see page 326) will be given to each student. The teacher will discuss the criteria used before the students make their speeches.

The culminating activity will be the student's presentation on his or her research topic on book banning. As each student makes his or her speech, the class will use the Persuasive Speaking Evaluation Form to assess the speeches. In addition, after each speech, the following questions will be discussed:

- What was the thesis statement of the speech?
- In what ways did the presenter persuade you?
- What did you like about the speech?

Activity Three

Students will be given a handout on debate. The following questions will be discussed:

- What is the difference between a debate and a discussion?
- What is the traditional set speaking order for a debate?
- How do you prepare for a debate?
- How are debates judged?

Students will do a practice debate using their literature reading "Pied Piper of Hamelin" as the topic source. They will debate on this topic: *The mayor should have/should not have paid the Piper.*

Students will be grouped into teams for/against the resolution. They will be given time to plan their arguments. Each time, two teams will debate and the other teams score and mark the argumentative points made. This encourages active listening and enhances critical listening skills. The Persuasive Speaking Evaluation Form will be used by students to critique the debates.

For homework, students will be given a week to prepare a debate on the issue: *Resolved: That warning labels should be placed on music CDs and cassettes that contain objectionable lyrics.* The same format for the practice debate is recommended for use. The debates should be scored and discussed.

Implementation Issues

The teaching of this unit focused strongly on the development of oral communication skills. The four main oral communication outcomes for the unit were:

- Discriminate between informative and persuasive messages.
- Evaluate an oral persuasive message according to argument pattern, key strategies of persuasion, decision making, and credibility of speaker.
- Develop skills of argument formulation (claim, data, and warrant).
- Organize oral presentations using logical ordering techniques, adequately supporting material, and structured arguments.

Activities in the unit included a one-minute persuasive speech, whole and small group discussion and questioning, debates; the unit culminated with a three- to five-minute persuasive speech: "It's OK/Not OK to Ban Books." Writing skills were developed through the writing of the speeches or through writing thoughts before discussions, and using journals for their thoughts. Assessments employed were structured observation forms, journals, and videos.

The unit, *Changing Ideas and Perspectives through Persuasion,* was taught during the regular reading class for a group of 17 high-ability sixth-graders. The literature selections of the unit increased the skills of discussion, debate, persuasion, and speech making. The students were very engaged and interested in the lessons. This was indicated by their enthusiasm and participation in discussions. They brought in extra materials and books to enhance the study. Debates were held and many topics pertaining to the literature were suggested to be debated. The students involved in the implementation of the unit did not want it to end. Some were heard to say they wished the reading class lasted all day. It was clearly their favorite class.

The students gained confidence in their abilities and learned to discuss, share, and analyze their own thoughts as well as the thoughts of others. The results of the pilot indicated that students can be taught the skills of persuasion and use them effectively in both oral and written form. Exemplary shared literature gave them a common element for discussions and debates.

In implementing this unit of study, several issues may be important to emphasize for other teachers.

1. Cultivating oral communication skills through studying literature can and should be an important emphasis of the curriculum for the verbally talented. Literature allows for a common ground for students to interact and develop important skills. Students using this unit developed significant skills in oral persuasion as a result of 30 hours of instructional emphasis.

2. Questions that permit the student to inquire and probe for answers are highly recommended in the teaching of oral communication skills. Students are required to expand their own thoughts and communicate and give support for complex ideas. With this type of questioning, the students also learn to give consideration to the ideas of others, to weigh the opposing arguments, and to modify initial opinions as the evidence demands. Such rigorous practice in thinking was a strong motivation for students using this unit.

3. Studying debate offers training for life situations of cooperative deliberation and advocacy. Teaching debate also enhances student growth in studying a self-selected topic, clarifying thinking, and organizing ideas in written and oral contexts. Students in the pilot study found such activities very challenging since it required in-depth work not experienced in other classes.

4. Too often, listening skills are not included as part of the oral communication curriculum. Yet such a curricular emphasis helps students differentiate the types of listening required in different communication situations. Learning listening skills can also enhance learning for students in all the disciplines. Students using this unit of study began to practice what they were learning in other classes as well, thus promoting interdisciplinary connections.

Conclusion

Oral communication instruction increases discussion and thinking to enable students to gain a better understanding of their own ideas and put them in control of their thought (Close, 1990). The students gain confidence in their abilities and learn to share ideas in a structured context.

Literature comes to life in a study using oral communication skills. Many topics pertaining to the literature lead to debates, discussions, research, and speeches. For the students in the pilot, reading became exciting and enhancing communication became the favorite class activity.

Key Points Summary

- Oral communication enhances the development of listening and speaking skills as well as indirectly addressing the development of reading and writing skills.
- Verbally talented learners are motivated and challenged by engaging in debate activities.
- Debate skills require students to engage in the act of research on a significant topic.
- Teaching debate allows for interdisciplinary connections to all areas of the curriculum.
- Underlying the teaching of oral communication is an emphasis on students' use of reasoning to carry out activities.
- Evaluative listening sharpens students' perceptions about others' thinking in relationship to their own.

Sample Lessons

Sample Lessons from Changing Ideas and Perspectives through Persuasion

Lesson 11

Curriculum Alignment Code					
Goal #1	Goal #2	Goal #3	Goal #4	Goal #5	Goal #6
	✕		✕		✕

Instructional Purpose:
- To introduce the Model for Persuasive Writing and Speaking (at end of chapter).
- To prepare students to give a one-minute persuasive speech.

Materials Used:
1. "Need to Know" Board (see page 332)
2. Notecards
3. Research Model (see page 367)

4. Model for Persuasive Writing and Speaking (page 331)
5. Magazine articles
6. Examples of propaganda techniques adapted from N. Pollette's *The Research Book for Gifted Programs* (O'Fallon, MO: Book Lures, Inc., 1984).

Activities:
1. Begin the class by sharing the research proposals that students developed in Lesson 10. Discuss with the class how they could use their proposals to prepare for their speech on censorship.
2. Introduce the Model for Persuasive Writing and Speaking (page 331):

   a. Distribute the Model for Persuasive Writing and Speaking and discuss each of the steps.
   b. Compare the Model for Persuasive Writing and Speaking (page 331) with the Research Model (page 367). Help students to see the similarities and to understand how their censorship research correlates with their writing and speaking.

3. Close the session by going to the "Need to Know" Board (page 332) to add information about censorship by asking students:

   • What do we know?
   • What do we need to know?
   • How can we find out?

4. Ask students to recall items in the "Glorious Whitewasher" (read in Lesson 11) that Tom asked the children to give up. On paper have students do the following:

   a. For one minute have students brainstorm things that are valuable to them.
   b. Discuss the list.
   c. Have students evaluate their list to decide what criteria they have used to classify value.
   d. Write three questions to ask someone to enable you to find out what is valued by them.

5. Assign students to prepare a one-minute speech that persuades us to want something that they possess. The speech will be delivered at the next class session. Give the following directions as guidelines for preparing for the speech:

   a. Formulate the argument statement.
   b. Develop each main point to some extent.
   c. Deliver the speech from an outline on note cards.

Writing Assignment:
1. Have students write in their Response Journals the answers to these questions:

   - What changes took place in the Tom Sawyer story?
   - How do these changes support or refute the generalizations about change?
   - Would there be any reason or reasons to ban this book? Explain.

Homework:
1. Prepare the assigned speech for the next lesson.

Extensions:
1. Read the last paragraph of the "Glorious Whitewasher." Write how you would have felt had you been Tom when Aunt Polly gave you the treat "along with an improving lecture upon the added value and flavor a treat took to itself when it came without sin through virtuous effort." Include answers to the following questions:

   - Would Aunt Polly's lecture change you? Why or why not?
   - How do you think the lecture affected Tom?
   - What changes took place in this story?

2. Have students work in groups of 3 or 4 to discuss persuasive advertisement techniques. Give each group different types of advertisements (examples: advertisements from magazines and newspapers for clothes, foods, drinks, movies, books). Allow 10 minutes for the groups to discuss and list what persuasion techniques have been used in the ads. Have each group share with the class the persuasion techniques they listed (examples: color to attract us, use of words, logos, celebrity endorsement, acceptance by others).

Lesson 13

Curriculum Alignment Code					
Goal #1	Goal #2	Goal #3	Goal #4	Goal #5	Goal #6
			✕	✕	

Instructional Purpose:
- To present research on the issue of censorship.

Materials Used:
1. Camcorder
2. Speakers' stand equipment required by students for their presentation
3. Persuasive Speech Evaluation Form (see page 326)

Activities:
1. Review with the class the skills of oral communication.
2. Review the Persuasive Speech Evaluation Form (page 326), which will be used to assess the speeches.
3. Students present their speeches on book banning. Videotape students as they present their speeches.
4. Ask the following questions after each speech:
   - What was the thesis statement of the speech?
   - In what ways did the presenter persuade you?
   - What did you like about the speech?

Persuasive Speech Evaluation Form

Name _____

Exercise _____

Directions: Use the following rating scale to evaluate each quality.

3 = Excellent   2 = Satisfactory   1 = Needs Improvement

	Needs Improvement	Satisfactory	Excellent
1. The purpose of the speech was clear.	1	2	3
2. The speaker's reasoning was clear and logical.	1	2	3
3. The basic components of the argument were evident.	1	2	3
4. The speaker showed knowledge of the subject.	1	2	3
5. The speaker addressed opposing points of view.	1	2	3
6. The speaker was audible, maintained eye contact and spoke with expression.	1	2	3
7. The speaker held the interest of the audience.	1	2	3

The best part of this speech was:

A suggestion for improvement is:

Lesson 15

Curriculum Alignment Code					
Goal #1	Goal #2	Goal #3	Goal #4	Goal #5	Goal #6
			✕		

Instructional Purpose:
- To teach debate skills.

Materials Used:
1. "The Pied Piper of Hamelin" by Robert Browning in *Poems of Robert Browning* (London: Oxford University Press, 1949)
2. Debate Format (see page 329)
3. Persuasive Speech Evaluation Form (page 326)
4. "Need to Know" Board (page 332)

Activities:
1. Hand out the worksheet on Debate Format (page 329) and use it to teach the skill of debating to students. Ask the following questions:

   - What is the difference between a debate and a discussion?
   - What is the traditional set speaking order for a debate?
   - How do you prepare for a debate?
   - How are debates judged?

2. Students will debate the following issue:

   Resolved: That warning labels should be placed on music CDs and cassettes that contain objectionable lyrics.

3. Students will do a practice debate using the "Pied Piper of Hamelin" for the topic source. The debate topic is: *The mayor should have/should not have paid the Piper.*
4. Assign the teams to be for or against the resolution. Allow students time to plan their arguments.
5. Using the procedure outlined in Handout 15A, have the teams debate. One team debates and the other team scores and marks the argumentative points made. Reverse the roles. (Teachers may want to refer to the following article for more information on debate: Swicord, B. (1984, Summer). Debating with gifted fifth and sixth graders—Telling it like it was, is, and could be. *Gifted Child Quarterly, 28*(3), pp. 127–129.)
6. Discuss the debate, using the Persuasive Speech Evaluation Form (page 326).

7. Close the lesson by having students write in their Response Journals reactions to the poem "Pied Piper of Hamelin" and discuss whether there are any reasons to ban the poem.
8. Refer to the "Need to Know" Board (page 332) and add information.

Homework:
1. Students will prepare for a debate on the issue:

   Resolved: That warning labels should be placed on music CDs and cassettes that contain objectionable lyrics.

2. Allow a week to prepare for the debate.
3. Read *The Valiant* by Holworthy Hall and Robert Middlemass.

Debate Format

What Is a Debate?

A debate is a series of formal spoken arguments for and against a definite proposal. The best solution is approved and adopted.

A debate is a special type of argument in which two or more speakers present opposing propositions in an attempt to win the audience to their sides. The teams are not concerned with convincing each other. The purpose is to try to alter the audience thinking by presenting the issues honestly with reliable evidence.

Why Debate?

Debate helps you:

1. Analyze problems
2. Reinforce statements with proof
3. Express your ideas clearly
4. Gain confidence
5. Think quickly

What Are the Rules of Debating?

Debates begin with a proposed solution to a problem. The proposal should begin with the word *resolved*. Examples:

> Resolved that the United States should abolish the electoral college and elect the President by popular vote.

> Resolved that television has beneficial effects on listeners.

1. The same number of persons speak on each opposing side.
2. Begin with careful analysis by both teams on the subject to be debated. All members should know as much about the opponent's arguments as they do their own position.
3. Decide which arguments are closely related and worthy of being included and which are irrelevant and should be excluded.
4. Chief points of differences between the affirmative and negative sides are the main issues.
5. List the main issues for each side.
6. Find evidence that will prove the issue true and false (facts, examples, statistics, testimony).
7. Be prepared to answer the arguments of the other team's issues, called a *rebuttal*.

What Is the Format for a Debate?

The suggested procedure is as follows:

> First Affirmative—Affirmative speech—5 minutes
> First Negative—Rebuttal—2 minutes
> Second Negative—Negative speech—5 minutes
> Second Affirmative—Rebuttal—2 minutes

Continue this pattern.

The debate always begins and ends with the affirmative team.

Scoring will be done by giving one point for an argument and two points for an argument with proof.

Model for Persuasive Writing and Speaking

Paragraph #1
State your issue or problem. Give illustrations and examples of it.

Paragraph #2
Present and develop an argument for dealing with your issue or problem in a particular way. Cite *reasons* for your position. Use sources you have read or interviewed to *support* your argument.

Paragraph #3
Develop a conclusion for your argument that restates your problem and resolves it.

Note: Organize your argument so that it is clear, specific, accurate, and logically consistent.

"Need to Know" Board

What Do We Know?	What Do We Need to Know?	How Can We Find Out?

References

Bryant, D. C., Wallace, K. R., & McGee, M. C. (1982). *Oral communications: A short course in speaking.* Englewood Cliffs, NJ: Prentice-Hall.

Chaney, A. (1992). *Issues in contemporary oral communication instruction, Topics papers.* Williamsburg, VA: The College of William & Mary, Center for Gifted Education

Close, E. E. (1990). Seventh graders sharing literature: How did we get here? *Language Arts, 67,* 817–823.

DiVesta, F. J. (1974). *Language, learning, and cognitive processes.* Monterey, CA: Brooks/Cole.

Frith, G. H., & Mims, A. A. (1984). Teaching gifted children to make verbal presentations. *Gifted Child Quarterly, 28*(1), 35–40.

Greene, M. (1986). Philosophy and teaching. *Handbook of research on teaching* (3rd ed.). New York. Macmillan.

Hade, D. D. (1982, August). Literacy in an information society. *Educational Technology, 22*(8), 7–12.

Johnson D. W., & Johnson, R. T. (1988). Critical thinking through structured controversy. *Educational Leadership, 45*(8), 58–64.

Lundsteen, S. (1979). *Listening: Its impact on reading and the other language arts* (rev. ed.) Urbana, IL: National Council of Teachers of English.

Mallet, M., & Newsome, V. (1977). *Talking, writing and learning 8–13.* London: Evans/Methuen Educational.

Paul, R. W. (1992). *Critical thinking: What every person needs to survive in a rapidly changing world.* Rohnert Park, CA: Foundation for Critical Thinking.

Tough, J. (1977). *Talking and learning: A guide to fostering communication skills in nursery and infant schools.* London: Ward Lock Educational.

18

Constructing Meaning
through Shared Inquiry

CAROL CAWLEY
Teacher of Gifted,
Hampton, Virginia

JAN CORBETT
Classroom Teacher,
Hampton, Virginia

Current research in the area of reading indicates that the historical emphasis on skill development has not improved the literary standards in the United States. The State of California Framework (1987) and the National Assessment Governing Board (NAGB) (1992) reports on reading both stress the need for a student-centered reading curriculum that accentuates shared inquiry discussion techniques of authentic and worthy literature (VanTassel-Baska, 1992a). Segmented instruction in language arts has not produced a society of individuals skilled in reading, writing, listening, or speaking; therefore, we should seek an alternative solution.

Talented learners need opportunities for active participation in their education and in taking responsibility and ownership for their learning. Language study for these students should be multicultural and holistic, enabling the development of creative and critical thinking at accelerated levels. The instruction should address real-world problems of concern to the students, incorporating all disciplines in an interactive fashion. Rather than the traditional skills-bound language arts program, gifted students need to experience language arts from an investigatory approach, questioning and seeking meaning to issues of significance through exploration of quality literature.

Books are a major avenue to the world of ideas. Quality literature stimulates thought and establishes the knowledge base necessary for creative thinking and problem solving (VanTassel-Baska, 1992a). Traditionally, the use of literature in educating talented learners has been similar to the approach used with other learners. This approach ignores several significant issues worthy of consideration in understanding how such students learn.

The verbally talented student reads voraciously, loves to ask questions and solve problems, and has a capacity for divergent as well as convergent thinking. With these factors in mind, educators should redirect literature study for such students toward a more transactional-inquiry approach. This method places the student in control of the learning situation through his own search for meaning through the medium of literature.

Moreover, recent national reports on education have called for a reconstruction of the language arts curriculum that uses high-powered materials and inquiry-based approaches to instruction (Suhor, 1984). The State of California Framework (1987) and the National Assessment of Educational Progress (NAEP) Reading Framework (1992) both stress the need for student-centered reading curriculum that focuses on shared inquiry techniques of authentic and worthy texts. Feldhusen, VanTassel-Baska, and Seeley (1989) have recommended inquiry instruction for use with gifted students because it implies achievement of a deeper understanding through search, investigation, and use of critical thinking skills. Kaplan (1977) has considered observing, experimenting, criticizing, and evaluating as critical components of an inquiry model that develops thinking skills at high cognitive operational levels. Although inquiry can bring to mind a variety of concepts, VanTassel-Baska (1992b) characterized it as:

- Creating a climate of mutual investigation into a problem, issue, or idea worthy of attention
- structuring a situation or activity in a way to elicit high-level thinking
- asking open-ended and suggestive questions to lead the student to think through a problem issue or idea in a deliberate manner

Models of Inquiry

Several important approaches to teaching inquiry are available for language arts classrooms. These models will be described briefly in the next section.

Junior Great Books

The Junior Great Books (Great Books Foundation, 1990) series is designed for use with advanced readers. It encourages a seriousness of purpose in reading and offers a structured discussion format that renders it highly successful in programs interested in developing student inquiry skills. Students read short classical literature selections followed by a reflective discussion (Halsted, 1988).

The goal of the Junior Great Books program is to instill through literary study the habits of mind that characterize a self-reliant reader, learner, and thinker. The instructional approach, referred to as *shared inquiry*, is a method in which students search for answers to the fundamental questions each story raises. This active search involves taking ideas and information the author supplies, and trying to grasp the story's full meaning. Students then interpret or reach an understanding of the text while taking their own experiences into consideration. The questions and the pattern of discussion fall into these categories:

- Opening or introduction of the topic (What type of story is this?)
- Core or examination of central points (According to the text, is it better to act or not to act in this stiuation?)
- Closing or relationship to the world (How does this story relate to real world issues?)

The Junior Great Books inquiry approach focuses more on interpretative questions and less on factual or evaluative questions. The model encourages the use of question clusters that direct the discussion along specific lines (Sanders, 1966; Barth & Shermis, 1981). In shared inquiry, students learn to give full consideration to the ideas of others, to weigh opposing viewpoints, and to make modification in initial opinions when appropriate (Great Books Foundation, 1990). Even though the program is beneficial for all students, its open-ended use of inquiry allows verbally talented students to respond in divergent ways.

The instructor of Junior Great Books establishes a special relationship with students. She guides the students in reaching their own interpretations of the story without imposing personal opinion or imparting information. The leader poses thought-provoking questions and follows up in a purposeful manner on what students say.

Use of Bloom's Taxonomy

Hunkins (1976) and Sanders (1966) emphasized that quality questioning techniques can be developed around Bloom's taxonomy of educational objectives: knowledge, comprehension, application, analysis, synthesis, and evaluation. Bloom's objectives share some of the elements of the shared-inquiry approach in Junior Great Books and include the fundamental questioning techniques needed to direct students' inquiry in two stages: (1) analysis of data from the standpoint of logical accuracy, consistency, and other internal criteria; and (2) analysis of data in terms of external criteria requiring the student to apply a known standard to judge situations, conclusions, or objectives that she has encountered or developed. This is the most critical aspect of questioning because it directs the students to consider their perceptions and conclusions critically.

Socratic Questioning

The application of Socratic-style questioning requires the student to think more deeply about the core of an issue and to explore it from various sides. Adler (1983) used the seminar as the Socratic method of teaching in which a director or moderator provides students with experiences in problem solving through critical/analytical thinking. In the seminar, the teacher does not lecture but asks leading questions about what the students have read or experienced. The tasks of the moderator in a seminar experience are to:

- Ask a series of questions that give direction and control the discussion.
- Examine the answers and probe further to clarify students' thinking.
- Engage the participants in two-way talk with one another.
- Summarize the key points of the discussion.

This method of inquiry is highly dependent on a skilled leader to control the dynamics of the discussion.

Creative Problem Solving

Another highly successful model of inquiry often used with gifted students is Parnes' Creative Problem Solving (1975). In this model, the instructor presents students with a problematic situation of real-world significance (Feldhusen & Treffinger, 1979). Students work through identification of the problem and the related pertinent facts through a questioning approach. They then develop a self-generated highly structured plan of action that alternates between divergent and convergent inquiry with the goal of generating a worthwhile solution.

During a questioning/discussion period, there should be few literal questions and more emphasis placed on inferential questions. Questioning may encourage students to predict outcomes. This helps set a purpose for the reading, maintain student focus on the passage, and aid overall comprehension. The goal of a questioning/discussion session should be to have the students actively participate in using available evidence to generate thoughtful responses—not correct answers. The teacher should encourage students to offer predictions and interpretations based on background information, prior knowledge, and the storyline (Routman, 1988).

Kamii (1989), Maker (1982), Polette (1982), and Taba (1975) concur that inquiry, discovery, and problem-solving approaches are characterized by involving the learner in the process of creating new knowledge, not merely accumulating knowledge. The teacher's role in inquiry instruction is critical and requires consideration of several key points. The teacher should serve as stimulator, questioner, listener, and positive reinforcer, but not as the source of knowledge (Cushenberry & Howell, 1974).

According to VanTassel-Baska (1992b), when a teacher is guiding a discussion with students, there are several relevant issues to consider:

- *Level of difficulty:* How suitable is the passage for the gifted student at various ages?
- *Selection of passages:* Consider key elements such as outstanding authors, classical works, genre, and topic.
- *Length of passages:* Short passages are advantageous because they allow for the development and comparison of ideas, permit the student to "grapple" with meaning, show the development of analytical skills, and allow an appreciation of structural issues such as word choice and usage.
- *Questions as motivators for extended work:* Group or class discussions of a short passage may inspire the gifted student to read the complete work, more books by that author, more on the topic, or more on the ideas engendered.
- *Interaction of question types with the topic:* Clustering of questions encourages the movement toward key ideas and understandings, helps fulfill instructional purposes, and ensures the use of a variety of question types.

This review of inquiry-based approaches provides a set of alternatives for teachers to employ in language arts instruction. In each approach, instructors need to guide students to question and probe the concept under investigation, collect and analyze data, and formulate conclusions and principles based on their findings. They also should encourage students to examine a problem situation from various viewpoints and accept more than one right answer to a question. Ultimately, the use of inquiry models such as those described in this chapter should develop in the learner a deep appreciation for reflective and critical thought.

Inquiry Instruction: Classroom Examples

The inquiry-based language arts unit for high-ability third-graders, *Journeys and Destinations: The Challenge of Change,* was developed as part of the National Javits Language Arts Curriculum Development Project. This unit provides opportunities for gifted students to explore quality literature in an interdisciplinary, multicultural curriculum. The primary focus of the unit is to engage students in an in-depth inquiry experience that emphasizes an open-ended approach to the discussion process. This curriculum incorporates the key elements of general inquiry models that have been developed for use with students of varying ability levels in the core subjects. Along with an inquiry approach in the examination of exemplary literature, the unit addresses critical factors pertinent in curriculum designed specifically for high-ability students, defined as the top 20 percent of the school-age population. Throughout the unit, students experience many opportunities for divergent as well as convergent thought. From the reading level of the selected literature, to the advanced level of the questions applied in discussions, lessons are presented at an accelerated level to expose the students to concepts not normally introduced to third-graders. As students move through the lessons, they search for solutions to problems and questions, generate new knowledge and understandings, and work in numerous teaming experiences.

The teacher serves as facilitator in the classroom, assisting students in activities, providing a stimulus for questioning and thinking, and establishing a safe environment for exploration and risk taking. The literature lessons are intradisciplinary (reading, speaking, writing, and listening) and interdisciplinary in nature. The inclusion of science, math, social studies, and fine arts experiences enable the verbally talented student to attach greater meaning to the learning experience by addressing real-world issues from various perspectives.

In the piloting phase, the unit was taught during a three-hour period, one day a week for eight consecutive weeks. The students met in a classroom at a center for primary gifted instruction in an urban community. Twelve identified gifted students from two elementary schools participated in the pilot study. In terms of the ethnic composition, the group comprised Caucasian, African American and Asian American students. They were from average and above-average socioeconomic backgrounds.

Key Components of a Language Arts Unit

The unit used to instruct third-grade students contains important components that run parallel to the other units developed in the National Language Arts Curriculum Project. These components are selection of exemplary literature, holistic treatment of curriculum, brainstorming, problem solving, research, literary discussion, response journals, and vocabulary development.

Selection of Exemplary Literature

One of the most advantageous vehicles to accomplish the goal of lifelong learning is to expose students to quality literature early. Verbally talented students typically are avid readers who respond well to complex literature that addresses the problems of humanity. These young readers love to delve into a thorough analysis of a text, examining key aspects from multiple perspectives. Hans Christian Anderson's classic tale *The Ugly Duckling*, for example, lends itself nicely to an analysis of fictional text as a mirror of the author's life. Prior to analysis of the story, students read a biographical sketch of Hans Christian Anderson's life, noting pertinent details. Although many students may be familiar with *The Ugly Duckling* story, the teacher guides the reading of the story with a different purpose in mind—that of how the story compares and contrasts with the author's life. Following the readings of the biographical sketch and *The Ugly Duckling*, the teacher facilitates a thorough class analysis of the text in relation to the author's life. In the art of literary analysis it is critical to recognize that one of the important qualities of exemplary literature is that it lends itself to divergent interpretation. (See the sample lesson at the end of this chapter.)

Holistic Curriculum

Verbally talented students are highly successful in holistic learning experiences because of their exceptional ability to recognize connections. Curriculum for them should provide *intra*disciplinary opportunities (reading, writing, listening, and speaking) that provide language arts experiences as well as *inter*disciplinary connections with other academic disciplines. Through the establishment of learning connections, students recognize connections as a natural component of life experiences. In the unit piloted, there are specific traits of scientific thinking that correlate well with literary habits of mind: inferring, hypothesizing, and evaluating. These ways of thinking are emphasized in the learning activities of the unit. Learning centers provide experiences that integrate other disciplines; for example, students write stories in response to works of art. The artwork of M. C. Escher is used in the unit to encourage students to study tessellations, observe their application to book illustrations, and make inferences about change based on their observations. The activities include discussions, response journal writing, and students' own creation of tessellations. (See the sample lesson at the end of this chapter.)

Brainstorming

In teaching a shared inquiry approach to literature, an important focus is to enhance the opportunities for oral expression. Brainstorming provides an ideal opportunity for students to express their ideas, use convergent and divergent thinking, and establish a focus on the literature (Parnes, 1975). Brainstorming provides a risk-free environment for oral expression in which judgment is withheld and all answers are taken and recorded. It is a technique for generating information with any size group. When students are reluctant to interpret, discuss, or write about what they have read, brainstorming often helps stimulate thinking. A method often used in getting students to initiate original ideas is concept mapping or webbing. This is done by creating a web (often called *a sun with rays*) and recording student responses around a key word. Students can then target a concept, make associations, and extend their ideas about the topic. For instance, they can easily explore the theme in literature selections of the unit by analyzing: How does each character change in the story? How do relationships among characters change? and What events changed a story's outcome? Brainstorming offers gifted students the opportunity for creative thinking, collecting and categorizing ideas, and making connections in their interpretation of literature. Literature webs are used throughout the unit to aid student expression of ideas about their reading.

Problem Solving

Questioning, exploring, analyzing, debating, and finding solutions for problems will increase students' abilities to solve problems. Creative problem solving not only will expand their intellectual growth but will also improve their discussion skills and oral and written responses to questions. In inquiry-based instruction, creative problem solving is a valuable strategy for students to interpret literature using an investigatory approach. This method also helps students recognize and accept other ideas and interpretations of the literature. For example in this unit, after completing prereading activities (i.e., introducing key vocabulary words and locating Kenya, Africa, on a world map), the teacher reads aloud the African folktale, *Bringing the Rain to Kapiti Plain*, by Verna Aardema. Students then discuss the role of Kipat as problem solver. (See the sample lesson at the end of this chapter.)

Research

Quite often, exemplary literature will spark in a thirsty young reader the desire to learn more about a specific topic. As students read in the unit about real world issues such as Alzheimer's disease in *Sachiko Means Happiness* by Kimiko Sakai or dysfunctional families in "The Shell" by Cynthia Rylant, issues of worldly significance provide a natural springboard for research opportunities. Through research, students make a valuable connection with an important issue in the literature selection.

A productive way to involve gifted students in literary inquiry and research is through organizing investigative teams. Each team is assigned a literary selection to read either in several parts (each followed by a group analysis) or in a one session reading followed by group analysis. A brief assessment of what students know about the topic, what they need to learn about the topic, and how to find the needed information extends learning into a research mode. Students tap numerous and varied primary and secondary sources. Once the teams have collected sufficient background data, the teacher guides them through a thorough examination of possible product vehicles to develop one that would reflect what they learned through their research. Sample products from the research of the pilot class included an interview with a woman whose mother has Alzheimer's disease and an oral presentation about the benefits of a community-supported animal shelter.

Literary Discussion

Traditionally, the reading and discussion of literary selections has been driven by teacher-generated questions that focus student thinking toward the identification of the right answer. A more productive approach lies in the application of literary discussion groups that involve students in a "read-around" format (Kennedy, 1992). In this format, students compose their own questions in response to a literary selection and discuss them one at a time in a small discussion group. This "read-around" model establishes an open-ended, risk-taking environment conducive to interpretative discussion. As the group progresses through its story chats, posing questions and discussing possible answers, students decide on one or two questions they feel are significant in the story. They then share these questions in a whole class discussion. Initial experiences in student-driven literary inquiry typically result in lower-level questioning of who, when, and where (called "skinny questions" in this unit). Students can be methodically guided to develop more "fat questions" that elicit divergent answers rather than a yes, no, or one-word answer (Fogarty & Opeka, 1988). The literary discussion/story chat experiences place the student at the center of the inquiry process and thereby expand opportunities for involvement and engagement with the literature. (See the sample read-around lesson at the end of this chapter.)

Response Journals

It is imperative that students become immersed in the literary work they study. A variety of opportunities for students to respond to literature allows students to develop skills in both verbal and written expression. Response journals encourage reflective thought, nurture confidence in personal written expression, and provide opportunities for responding to literature in a nonthreatening manner (Routman, 1988). In introducing response journals to students, the expectations should be informal at first. The teacher should explain that this is an individual activity and that each student will interpret and respond in writing differently. It may be helpful if the teacher does an example on an overhead transparency. First, he or she displays a brief passage or a question related to the piece of literature. Then the teacher writes a response on a blank transparency; this models thinking aloud and writing while the students observe the process.

During the pilot of this language arts unit, students used the response journal to write responses to inquiry questions. At other times, students were asked to write their interpretation of a significant passage. Following the journal writing, students engaged in group discussion that encouraged responses to the posed question or passage. Assessment and evaluation was an informal process. The teacher read the journals and wrote comments to each student.

Vocabulary Development

A characteristic of verbally talented students is advanced vocabulary development. In analyzing literature, students need to study the rich vocabulary used. The unit implemented in the classroom focused on words from each selection in relation to origin, meaning and part of speech. Students were encouraged to demonstrate use of new vocabulary in original writings. While working in groups, each student selects three words (round-robin style) and writes the definition, part of speech, and word origin for those words. In the following lesson, students take turns (within their group) teaching their words to teammates. This jigsaw vocabulary activity was repeated for each new list of words introduced during the literature unit. Students appreciate the literature more fully once they investigate key vocabulary words. This method, employed through the use of vocabulary webs in the unit, expands knowledge of vocabulary in the context of literature and assists students in developing a broader understanding of literary interpretation.

Issues of Implementation

In setting the climate for inquiry-based instruction, the facilitator must consider the format most conducive for student learning and responsive interaction. An instructional format such as Readers' Workshop offers teachers a consistent approach to intradisciplinary teaching of a literature-based curriculum (Hagerty, 1991). The principles of the reading workshop are: *time* (to select books, read, reflect, and interact with others), *choice* (choose books, engage in open-ended activities and individual interpretation), *response* (react, record, share, and confer), *community* (work cooperatively, assume roles, help others, and become active listeners), and *structure* (teacher as the facilitator, management and quality reading time). These principles provide a supportive framework for teaching the key components of shared inquiry instruction and mesh well with the William and Mary unit developed and piloted.

Inquiry-based language arts instruction can be successfully implemented in a full-day program, in a pullout program, or through enrichment programming. If programming is on a weekly or bimonthly basis, reasonably brief literature selections such as those found in the *Junior Great Books* are advantageous since the timing allows for a thorough examination of the literature and an appropriate debriefing within one lesson. Share time activities may be done in small groups or as a whole class. Students should be encouraged to examine and discuss their own interpretations of the literature selection.

As the teacher is preparing for inquiry-based literary instruction, it is essential that he or she establish an open and nonjudgmental learning environment. If we are to foster positive risk-taking behaviors, students and teachers must feel their ideas are welcome and respected. As a result of more traditional language arts instructional methods, it is reasonable to expect that it may take some time for students to grow in understanding that the "one right answer" is not what is sought in the inquiry classroom. Divergent thinkers should be encouraged to experiment with ideas and to reflect on what prompts them to think in a specific manner. The examination of one's own thinking as it is influenced by personal experiences is a richly rewarding component of inquiry instruction.

Respecting the individuality of each student, the teacher in the inquiry classroom should provide various opportunities for personal choice in topics of study, assignment/products, and presentation methods. The teacher should plan experiences that provide for individual, paired, and group learning. The assessment of student learning is based on authentic approaches such as student products, class performance, and individual student/teacher conferences rather than on traditional forms of assessment. The student is a key participant in the evaluation component in an inquiry-based language arts program.

Inquiry instruction results in a change in classroom focus. Student questioning and interaction, rather than the teacher's knowledge base, drives the learning experience. Using the story chat format, students conduct an interpretive discussion related to the literature. Because the teacher has traditionally been expected to be limitless in knowledge, this new focus may present some adjustments for both the teacher and the students. This shift in role empowers students as generators of new ideas and masters of their own learning. A reflection of this new student role is evident in the vocabulary jigsaw activity in which students are responsible for assisting their teammates in developing an understanding and application of the vocabulary words.

A critical consideration in implementing inquiry-based instruction at the elementary level is a conscious awareness of the developmental stages of young students because of how such development affects curriculum delivery. The pacing in an inquiry-based literature curriculum must respect the attention span and learning style of the young student. Teacher sensitivity to the length of inquiry sessions and student need for a change of pace greatly enhances its effectiveness.

In implementing a shared inquiry program, the teacher must model a love for reading and literature, be knowledgeable about the subject matter, and especially know the individual needs of her gifted students. If he or she creates an open and accepting classroom climate that promotes risk taking and creative thinking, students will become active participants in their own learning.

Conclusion

The shared inquiry approach employed in this project incorporated important considerations for use in language arts classrooms nationally. Instruction of students through shared inquiry empowers students to plan and carry out research and establish criteria for evaluating their own products. Students learn to take a lead in literary discussions through development of the key questions and personal interpretations from the literature they have read. These key literary habits enable gifted students to examine their own thinking and to develop skills in defending a point of view—important skills for developing self-confidence for tackling future academic challenges.

Key Points Summary

- The use of inquiry-based techniques in teaching literature to young children promotes positive learning behaviors, including thinking skills, risk taking, and questioning attitudes.
- Use of specific techniques, such as Junior Great Books shared inquiry model, can allow teachers to enhance any discussion.
- Questioning strategies based on Bloom's taxonomy, Socratic modes, or creative problem solving all offer varied instructional approaches found to be effective in language arts classrooms.
- Use of carefully selected rich, complex, and short reading passages works best for employing inquiry techniques to literary discussion in the classroom.

- Implementation of inquiry techniques in specific units of study requires specific considerations as delineated in the chapter.
- Applications in language arts for inquiry-based work include literary discussions, research projects, vocabulary development, and writing in response journals.
- Sample lessons from the unit reinforce chapter commentary about the effective use of inquiry.

Sample Lessons

Sample Lessons from Journeys and Destinations: The Challenge of Change

Lesson 5

Curriculum Alignment Code					
Goal #1	Goal #2	Goal #3	Goal #4	Goal #5	Goal #6
×	×	×		×	×

Instructional Purpose:
- To develop reasoning skills in literature through discussion of *The Green Book.*
- To promote vocabulary understanding.

Materials Used:
1. Classroom set of *The Green Book.*
2. Literature Web (see page 361).
3. Vocabulary Web (see page 360).
4. Read-Around Activity (see page 347).
5. Venn Diagram (see page 365).

Activities:
1. Have students complete a literature web on their reading of Chapters 1–2 in *The Green Book.*
2. Introduce the Read-Around Activity (see page 347).
3. Begin discussion of the book using the following questions:

Literary Response and Interpretation Questions

- Why are these people leaving the Earth?
- Why doesn't the author give a name to the new planet?
- On page 11, what does Joe mean when he says, "Oh, Pattie! You're a fine one to talk about choosing!"

- What surprises do the travelers find on the new planet?

Reasoning Questions

- What issues are raised by the children about their new home on page 11? (i.e., Can the planet support life? Should each person be allowed to decide about taking the pills?)
- What do you know about who the people are on the spaceship? What evidence tells you that?
- What assumptions did the children make about the grass and flowers before they ran forward (on page 15)?

Change Questions

- What does the paragraph about games on page 7 tell us about change?

4. Have students work in groups to complete a vocabulary web for the following words that are taken from *The Green Book: rations* (p. 3), *perishable* (p. 3), *wistfully* (p. 4), *treacle* (p. 4), *allocated* (p. 8), *runnel* (p. 14), *rivulet* (p. 17), and *flagons* (p. 18). A cumulative list of words should be kept for review at the end of the unit.
5. Imagine that you are going on the voyage to the new planet. Decide what book you would choose to take along. Write about it in your Response Journal and give reasons for your choice.
6. Make a Venn Diagram showing how the environments of the Earth and the new planet are the same and different.
7. The remaining time should be used for activities in the Learning Centers.

Homework:
1. Read Chapters 3–4 in *The Green Book.*

Extensions:
1. On page 19, Joe sets up a calendar. How does it work? What determines a day on the new planet? Do you think it is the same length as a day on Earth? Explain. Find out more about the lengths of days and years on planets in our solar system. Why are they different from each other?
2. It took four years for the spacecraft to travel to the new planet. How far away from Earth might that be? How can you find out?
3. Scientific aspects of the story provide an excellent opportunity for interdisciplinary instruction. The following unit is also available from the Center for Gifted Education at the College of William and Mary:

Small Ecosystems: Planet X—This unit poses a problem for the students to resolve which will enable them to approach the study of ecosystems through the eyes of apprentice scientists. In order to resolve the problem, students will have to build a model ecosystem and understand the global systems (weather, planetary), which are the bases for the model. The ill-structured problem gives the students a real issue of significance to solve, which serves as a vehicle for student involvement and enables them to see the complexity of one system in relation to the systems it depends on.

Read-Around Activity

This activity offers students an opportunity to ask authentic questions and to answer the questions of their classmates. Divide the class into groups of five. Ask students to think of something about *The Green Book* that puzzles them. For instance, they might ask about something they don't understand or find confusing; something they want to know more about; or question something with which they disagree or find disturbing. These questions are not intended as recall questions or "stump the expert" factual questions, but as honest inquiry.

After they have written their questions, each student should pass his or hers to the left. Now each student will answer the questions in two to four sentences, writing immediately under the question. When students are finished answering, they pass the question once more to the left. The next student reads the question and the answer, then writes a different answer or explains why he or she agrees with the first student's answer. The questions are then returned to their authors. Each student reads the question and the two answers.

After students have read their original questions and the answers they received, share the questions and answers. Discuss how the process changed the students' understanding of the story.

Lesson 11

Curriculum Alignment Code					
Goal #1	Goal #2	Goal #3	Goal #4	Goal #5	Goal #6
					×

Instructional Purpose:
- To expand the concept of change through interdisciplinary study of Escher art.
- To use symmetry and tessellations to create an image of change.
- To link art and literature through the works of Escher and Wiesner.

Materials Used:
1. *The Graphic Work of M. C. Escher* by M. C. Escher (New York: Ballantine, 1967)
2. *Free Fall* by David Wiesner (New York: Lothrop, Lee & Shepard, 1988)
3. Pattern blocks (available from Dale Seymour or Creative Publications)
4. Student Response Journals

Tessellations Resources for Teachers:
Available from Dale Seymour Publications, P. O. Box 10888, Palo Alto, CA 94303-0879 or (800) 872-1100 or FAX (415) 324-3424:

Introductions to Tessellation by Dale Seymour and Jill Britton
Teaching Tessellating Ar, by Jill Britton and Walter Britton

Available from Creative Publications, 5005 West 110th Street, Oaklawn, IL 60453 or (800) 624-0822 or in Illinois (800) 435-5843:

Creating Escher-Type Drawings by E. R. Ranucci and J. L. Teeters *Tessellations : The Geometry of Patterns* by S. Bezuska, M. Kenney, and L. Silvey

Activities:
1. Have students do the following activity on tessellations, symmetry, and art.
2. Distribute individual copies or display a poster of M. C. Escher's "Night and Day." (This woodcut features images of white and black birds flying over fields, towns, and rivers. Symmetry and tessellations are used in unique ways to create a remarkable effect.)
3. Have students write in their Response Journals an answer to the following question:

   • What do you see in the picture?

4. In small groups have students share their reactions.
5. As a whole class activity, discuss the picture, focusing on these questions:

   • How is this picture similar to a diamante poem?
   • The "mirror images" represent symmetry. How does symmetry contribute to the effect of the picture?
   • The bird images alternate between light and dark with no blank space between them. This kind of pattern is called a *tessellation*. How does the tessellation create the effect of the picture?
   • The artist called this woodcut "Night and Day." Create another title for it and justify your title.
   • What does this picture tell us about change?

6. Show and discuss other examples of Escher's prints, especially "Metamorphose." Answer these questions:

   • What examples of symmetry do you see? What do they contribute to the artwork?
   • Where are tessellations used? How do they affect the quality of the artwork?

- What do these works illustrate about change?

7. Invite students to explore the book, *Free Fall,* by David Wiesner. In this wordless picture book, a boy's dream transforms ordinary objects into an adventure. Wiesner has used ideas and images that are similar to Escher's work. Ask the following questions:

   - How are the images in Free Fall similar to Escher's "Night and Day" and "Metamorphose"?
   - How are the generalizations about change reflected in *Free Fall?* (Have students in small groups use the Change Model [page 358] to work through this question.)

   Note to Teacher: The pictures in *Free Fall* were created end to end as one continuous mural. Encourage students to note the continuity of the pictures in order to observe change from the beginning to the end of the book.

8. 8. Have students use pattern blocks to create their own tessellations. Share in small groups.

Homework:
1. Create a tessellation using an interesting pattern. Write a diamante poem about it.

Extensions:
1. Examine other works by Escher and other "pattern" artists like Vaserely and Mondrian. How are their works alike and different?

Lesson 13

Curriculum Alignment Code					
Goal #1	Goal #2	Goal #3	Goal #4	Goal #5	Goal #6
×				×	×

Instructional Purpose:
- To discuss change in the life of an author (H. C. Andersen) as well as in the character of his story (*The Ugly Duckling*).

Materials Used:
1. Venn Diagram (see page 365).
2. Biographical Sketch of Hans Christian Andersen (Handout 13A, pages 350–351)

Activities:
1. Introduce the following Compare/Contrast Activity.
2. Lead students in a brainstorming session on how authors get ideas for their writings. Explain that this activity will focus on how the life of Hans Christian Andersen, author of *The Ugly Duckling*, paralleled the life of the duckling.
3. Students will use a Venn Diagram (page 365) to compare and contrast *The Ugly Duckling* and the life of H. C. Andersen. Explain that as they read the biographical sketch of Hans Christian Andersen (Handout 13A), they should look for ways his life is similar to (compare) and different (contrast) from his story.
4. Distribute copies of the biographical sketch and the Venn Diagram. Allow approximately 30 minutes for students to read the biographical sketch and work in small groups to complete the Venn Diagram activity. Monitor and assist students as they work. Debrief the lesson at closure by compiling a class Venn Diagram.

Homework:
1. Interview your parents about major changes in their lives. Write a one-page paper telling about those changes.

Extensions:
1. Read another story about being different. Choose from the following list:
   Cooney, B. (1982). *Miss Rumphius.* New York: Viking.
   Jarrell, R. (1963). *The bat-poet.* New York: Macmillan.
   Pinkwater, D. M. (1977). *The big orange splot.* New York: Hastings.
   Tolan, S. (1983). *A time to fly free.* New York: Scribner.

2. Create a poster showing how the main character changed throughout the story. Compare the character to the ugly duckling. Make a list of the ways they are alike and different.

Biographical Sketch of Hans Christian Andersen (Handout 13A)

Hans Christian Anderson is famous for writing many enchanting fairy tales, among them *The Ugly Duckling* and *The Emperor's New Clothes.* In 1805, he was born in Odense, on the island of Fyn in Denmark, as an only child to a poor family. His father, a cobbler, died when Hans was 11 years old. His mother took a job as a washer woman, leaving Hans to dream and fantasize alone.

In school, the other children made fun of Andersen's awkwardness and large hands and feet. After his father's death, he stopped going to school.

While at home, he read as many books as he could find and spent time creating puppets and paper cut-outs. His make-believe, combined with the fantastic stories his mother told him as a child, laid the foundation for the fairy tales he wrote as an adult.

At the age of 14, Andersen left home for Copenhagen in hopes of becoming an opera singer and dancer. Because of his poor voice and lanky, awkward body, his musical dream was never fulfilled. However, during his attempt at it, he met several friends who encouraged his writing and education and eventually made it possible for him to go to a university. He did not like the university where he studied for six years. Even though he towered over the younger students, both the students and teachers bullied him.

As an adult, Andersen earned his living by writing. In 1829, he wrote his first successful book. It earned him enough money to travel around Europe. He then wrote about his travels in a novel. In 1835, he published a book of fairy tales. He continued to write novels, plays, and travel sketches but he began a second and third series of fairy tales. His stories were translated into English and Andersen became a celebrity wherever he traveled. He was more understood by children who accepted and loved him when grown-ups did not. He never married. He continued to write fairy tales until he died in 1875 at the age of 70. During his lifetime, he wrote 186 fairy tales.

Lesson 14

Curriculum Alignment Code					
Goal #1	Goal #2	Goal #3	Goal #4	Goal #5	Goal #6
×		×			×

Instructional Purpose:
- To develop reasoning about literature through using the African folk tale *Bringing the Rain to Kapiti Plain.*

Materials Used:
1. Globe and individual maps of Africa.
2. *Bringing the Rain to Kapiti Plain* by Verna Aardema (New York: The Dial Press, 1981)
3. Vocabulary Web (see page 360)
4. Literature Web (see page 361)
5. *Rain Player* by D. Wisniewski (New York: Clarion, 1991)
6. Student Response Journal
7. Change Matrix (see page 355)

Activities:

1. Open the lesson using a classroom globe to locate Kenya, Africa. Explain that the story that will be read is a folk tale from Kenya.
2. Have students do a Literature Web for *Bringing the Rain to Kapiti Plain.*
3. Guide a discussion based on the following questions:

   Literary Response and Interpretation Questions

   - What caused the grass to turn brown?
   - What are some of the other things that happened as a result of no rain?
   - What did Kipat do to solve the problem of no rain?
   - What important qualities did Kipat have?
   - Why did Kipat think of using a feather?
   - How does this story show the relationship of cause and effect in nature?
   - Why did the author end the story with Kipat's son tending the herds?
   - How might the story have been different if the cows had died?
   - Why do you think Kipat waited as long as he did to get married?
   - In your opinion, what is the best part of the story? Why?

   Change Questions

   - How are ideas about change (related to time, everywhere, positive/ negative and orderly) Brought out in this folk tale?

4. Have students write in their Response Journal about one of the following questions:

   a. The drought in Africa was a terrible problem for Kipat in the story. It also is a terrible problem in the world today, along with famine. Develop an argument supporting the need for global assistance to Africa and other places in the world experiencing these problems. (To the teacher: Introduce UNICEF and other world help organizations here.)

   OR

   b. Write a letter to the President of the United States supporting an airlift of food and medical supplies to a country under siege.

5. As a whole class activity, complete a Vocabulary Web for the word *migrated* from the story *Bringing the Rain to Kapiti Plain.*
6. As a whole class activity, complete the column of the Change Matrix (see page 355) that applies to this reading. Have students complete their copy of the matrix as well as filling in the butcher paper or posterboard copy. The completed grid will serve as the basis for a discussion in later lessons about change.

Homework:
1. Read *Rain Player*. How is this book similar to and different from *Kapiti Plain*? Write about it in your response journal.

Extensions:
1. How widespread is drought and famine in Africa? Research causes and effects of these problems. Prepare a chart or graph to show how Africa as a continent is affected.
2. If you enjoyed reading *Bringing the Rain to Kapiti Plain*, you may enjoy reading these other books by Verna Aardema:

Aardema, V. (1985). *Bimiwili and the Zimwi*. New York: The Dial Press.

Aardema, V. (1984). *Oh, Kojo! How could you!* New York: The Dial Press.

Aardema, V. (1960). *What's so funny, Ketu? A Nuer tale*. New York: The Dial Press.

Aardema, V. (1984). *Who's in Rabbit's House?* New York: The Dial Press.

Aardema, V. (1984). *Why mosquitoes buzz in people's ears*. New York: The Dial Press.

What are some common characteristics of her books? Identify three characteristics and describe them.

Lesson 21

Curriculum Alignment Code					
Goal #1	Goal #2	Goal #3	Goal #4	Goal #5	Goal #6
	✕				✕

Instructional Purpose:
- To assess student understanding of the generalizations about change.
- To discuss the unit-guiding question: How does change help us grow?

Materials Used:
1. Change Matrix (see page 355)
2. Student Response Journals

Activities:
1. Students were asked to come to class prepared to share a change in their own lives or a change in the life of someone else.
2. Have students share their stories in small groups. (The stories were assigned as homework in Lesson 19.)

3. While they are in their small groups, have students complete the Change Matrix (see page 355) on the literature used in the unit and their own story.
4. As a whole group activity, discuss the ways in which the literature helped students to grow and change. Put butcher paper or other large paper on the wall for summarizing the responses. Emphasize the guiding question: How does change help us grow?
5. Revisit the five generalizations on change:

   - Change is linked to time. (How is change linked to time?)
   - Change may be positive or negative. (Does change always represent progress?)
   - Change may be perceived as orderly or random. (Can we predict change?)
   - Change is everywhere. (Does change apply to all areas of our world?)
   - Change may happen naturally or may be caused by people. (What causes change?)

6. Divide students into five small groups. Assign each group one of the change generalizations. Allow 10 to 15 minutes of discussion within the groups to address the following question as it relates to that generalization. Students should take notes on the discussion.

   - How have the experiences of this unit supported the generalization?

7. Have students share their findings with the whole class.
8. Have students reread all products in their portfolios and Response Journals and write a response to the following question:

   - How have your written products changed during this unit?

9. Any remaining time should be used for activities in the Learning Centers.

Change Matrix

Literature	Changes in Characters	Changes in Setting	Changes in Relationships	Change in You as a Result of Reading
"Shells"				
The Green Book				
Poems				
The Ugly Duckling				
Bringing the Rain to Kapiti Plain				
Sachiko Means Happiness				
"The Green Man"				
Your Own Story				

References

Adler, M. J. (1983). *How to speak. How to listen.* New York: Macmillan.

Barth, J. L., & Shermis, S. S. (1981). *Teaching social studies to the gifted and talented.* Indianapolis, IN: State Department of Public Instruction.

California Department of Education. (1987). *State of California language arts framework.* Sacramento, CA: Author.

Cushenberry, D. C., & Howell, H. (1974). *Reading in the gifted child: A guide for teachers.* Springfield, IL: Thomas.

Feldhusen, J., & Treffinger, D. (1979). *Creative thinking and problem solving.* Dubuque, IA: Kendall-Hunt.

Feldhusen, J., VanTassel-Baska, J., & Seeley, K. (1989). *Excellence in educating the gifted.* Denver, CO: Love.

Fogarty, R., & Opeka, K. (1988). *Start them thinking : A handbook of classroom strategies for the early years.* Palatine, IL: IRI Group.

Great Books Foundation. (1990). *Junior Great Books teachers' edition.* Chicago, IL: Author.

Hagerty, P. J. (1991). *Mini-lessons in readers' workshop: Learning about reading.* Greeley, CO: Colorado Reading Council Journal.

Halsted, J. W. (1988). *Guiding gifted readers—From preschool through high school.* Columbus, OH: Ohio Psychology Publishing.

Hunkins, F. (1976). *Involving students in questioning.* Boston, MA: Allyn and Bacon.

Kamii, C. K. (1989). *Young children continue to reinvent arithmetic—Second grade.* New York: Teachers College Press.

Kaplan, S. (1977). *Providing programs for the gifted and talented.* Reston, VA: The Council for Exceptional Children.

Kennedy, C. (1992). *Teaching with writing: The state of the art.* Williamsburg, VA: The College of William and Mary.

Maker, C. J. (1982). *Teaching models in the education of the gifted.* Rockville, MD: Aspen Systems.

National Assessment Governing Board. (1992). *Reading framework for the 1992 National Assessment of Education Progress.* Washington, DC: US Department of Education.

Parnes, S. (1975). *Aha! Insight into creative behavior.* Buffalo, NY: DOK Publishing.

Polette, N. (1982). *Three R's for the gifted.* Littleton, CO: Libraries Unlimited.

Routman, R. (1988). *Transitions from literature to literacy.* Portsmouth, NH: Heineman.

Sanders, N. M. (1966). *Classroom questions: What kinds?* New York: Harper and Row.

Suhor, C. (1984). *1984 Report on trends and issues in English: A summary of reports from the NCTE commissions.* (ERIC Document Reproduction Service ED 239290).

Taba, H. (1975). Learning by discovery: Psychological educational rationale. In W. B. Barbe & J. S. Renzulli (Eds.), *Psychology and education of the gifted* (2nd ed., pp. 346–354). New York: Irvington.

VanTassel-Baska, J. (1992a). *Creating a new language arts curriculum for high ability learners.* Williamsburg, VA: Center for Gifted Education, The College of William and Mary.

VanTassel-Baska, J. (1992b). *Planning effective curriculum for gifted learners.* Denver, CO: Love.

Unit Teaching
Models for Part IV

Teaching models used consistently throughout the units described are included in this portion of the book. These models were used in the creation of student activities and questions for discussion. They represent major organizers for specific lessons. The models employed include teaching concepts, vocabulary web, literature web, reasoning, graphic organizers, writing process, research, and metacognition.

Teaching Concepts[*]

1. Students must focus on several examples of the concept.
2. Students must gather and verify information as to the concept-relevant characteristics of each individual example and nonexample.
3. Students must note how the examples vary and yet are still examples of the concepts.
4. Students must note what is alike about all the examples of the concept.
5. Students must generalize that what is alike about all the examples they've examined is also true of all other examples of the concept.
6. Students must know how the nonexamples resemble examples, but, particularly, how they differ from them.
7. Students must generalize about the characteristics that distinguish all examples of the concepts from any item that might resemble them in some way.

*Source: From S. Seiger-Ehrenberg, "Concept Development" from Costa, Art. *Developing Minds: A Resource Book for Teaching Thinking*. Alexandria, VA: Association for Supervision and Curriculum Development. Copyright 1991 by ASCD. Used with permission.

The Change Model

Develop a list of three to five examples for each of the following statements (generalizations) about change.

Change is linked to time.

Examples: _____
_____
_____

Change is everywhere.

Examples: _____
_____
_____

Change

Change may be positive:

Examples: _____
_____
_____

...or negative
_____
_____
_____

Change may be
perceived as orderly:

Examples: _____
_____
_____

...or random
_____
_____
_____

Change may happen
naturally: _____
_____

or may be caused
by people: _____
_____

The Vocabulary Web Model

The purpose of the vocabulary web is to enable students to grasp an in-depth understanding of interesting words. Rather than promote superficial vocabulary development, the web approach allows for deep student processing of challenging and interesting words.

The following is an example of a vocabulary web. The teacher should introduce the activity by doing the first one with the whole class. Subsequently, students should work in groups to complete worksheets for other assigned words that are found in the literature selections. Students may add any number of extensions to the main circles if they identify additional information about the word.

Once students become familiar with this activity, they should use a streamlined version to accommodate new words that they meet in their independent reading. A vocabulary section should be kept in a separate place in students' notebooks for this purpose. They need only list the word, definition, and sentence where the word was encountered. *The American Heritage Dictionary* (third edition) is recommended for this activity.

Vocabulary Web Model

Directions: Place a new vocabulary word in the center circle. With your group, complete as much information in the other shapes as you can. Be sure to consult a dictionary.

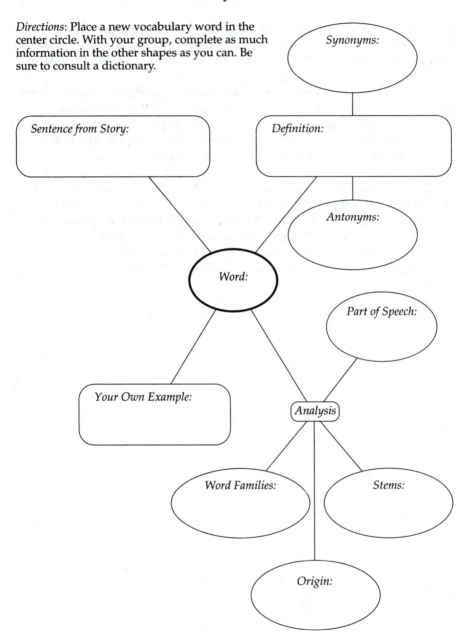

The Literature Web

The literature web encourages students to consider five aspects of a selection they are reading: key words, ideas, feelings, structure of writing, and images (or symbols). The web helps students to organize their initial responses and provides them a platform for discussing the piece in small or large groups. Whenever possible, students should be allowed to underline and to make marginal notes as they read and reread. After marking the text, they then organize their notes into the web.

After students have completed their webs individually, they should compare their webs in small groups. This initial discussion will enable them to consider the ideas of others and to understand that individuals interpret literature differently. These small groups may compile a composite web that includes the ideas of all members.

Following the small group work, teachers have several options for using the webs. For instance, they may ask each group to report to the class, they may ask groups to post their composite webs, or they may develop a new web with the class based on the small group work. However, each web serves to prepare students to consider various issues the teacher will raise in whole group discussion.

The Literature Web

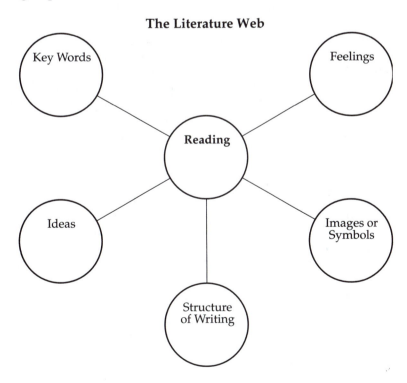

*The Reasoning Model**

The reasoning model used throughout the unit focuses on eight elements. It is embedded in all lessons of the unit through questions, writing assignments, and research work.

1. *Purpose, Goal, or End in View:* Whenever we reason, we reason to some end, to achieve some purpose, to satisfy some desire or fulfill some need. One source of problems in reasoning is traceable to "defects" at the level of goal, purpose, or end. If our goal itself is unrealistic, contradictory to other goals we have, or confused or muddled in some way, then the reasoning we use to achieve it is problematic. The goal, purpose, or end of our thinking is something our mind must actively create.

2. *Question at Issue (or Problem to Be Solved):* Whenever we attempt to reason something out, there is at least one question at issue, at least one problem to be solved. One area of concern for the reasoner should therefore be the very formulation of the question to be answered or problem to be solved. If we are not clear about the question we are asking, or how the question related to our basic purpose or goal, then it is unlikely that we will be able to find a reasonable answer to it, or one that will serve our purpose. The question at issue in our thinking is something our mind must actively create.

3. *Points of View or Frame of Reference:* Whenever we reason, we must reason within some point of view or frame of reference. Any defect in our point of view or frame of reference is a possible source of problems in our reasoning. Our point of view may be too narrow or too parochial, may be based on false or misleading analogies or metaphors, may not be precise enough, may contain contradictions, and so forth. The point of view that shapes and organizes our thinking is something our mind must actively create.

4. *The Empirical Dimension of Our Reasoning:* Whenever we reason, there is some "stuff, " some phenomena about which we are reasoning. Any defect, then, in the experiences, data, evidence, or raw material upon which our reasoning is based is a possible source of problems. We must actively decide which of a myriad of possible experiences, data, evidence, and so on we will use.

5. *The Conceptual Dimension of Our Reasoning:* All reasoning uses some ideas or concepts and not others. Any defect in the concepts or ideas (including the theories, principles, axioms, or rules) with which we reason is a

---

*Source: From *Critical Thinking: What Every Person Needs to Survive in a Rapidly Changing World* by R. Paul, 1992, Rohnert Park, CA: Foundation for Critical Thinking. Copyright 1992 The Foundation for Critical Thinking. Reprinted by permission.

possible source of problems. The concepts and ideas that shape and organize our thinking must be actively created by us.

6. *Assumptions (The Starting Points of Reasoning):* All reasoning must begin somewhere; some things must be taken for granted. Any defect in the starting points of our reasoning, any problem in what we have taken for granted, is a possible source of problems. Only we can create the assumptions on the basis of which we will reason.

7. *Inferences:* Reasoning proceeds by steps called inferences. To make an inference is to think as follows: "Because this is so, that also is so (or probably so). " Any defect in the inferences we make while we reason is a possible problem in our reasoning. Information, data, and situations do not determine what we shall deduce from them; we create inferences through the concepts and assumptions that we bring to situations.

8. *Implications and Consequences (Where Our Reasoning Takes Us):* All reasoning begins somewhere and proceeds somewhere else. No reasoning is static. Reasoning is a sequence of inferences that begin somewhere and take us somewhere else. Thus, all reasoning comes to an end, yet could have been taken further. All reasoning has implications or consequences beyond those the reasoner has considered. Any problem with these (implications that are false, undesirable consequences) implies a problem in the reasoning. The implications of our reasoning are an implicit creation of our reasoning.

The Wheel of Reasoning Worksheet should be used to probe different avenues of student reasoning about what they read. Teachers may select a few of the questions or develop the complete Wheel of Reasoning through story-based questions. (Some types of questions will work better with certain pieces of literature.) The purpose of using the Wheel is to enhance reasoning qualities of mind in students as they engage in written and oral communication.

Wheel of Reasoning

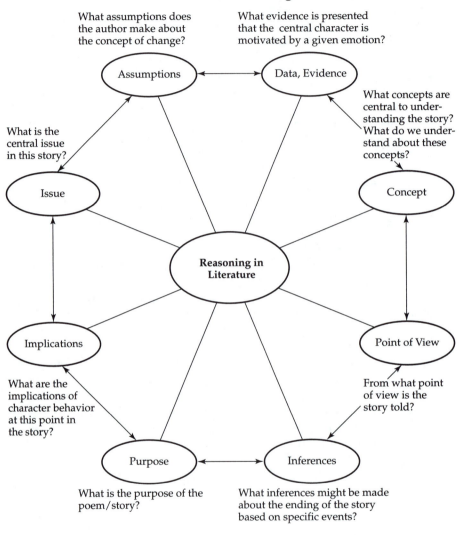

What assumptions does the author make about the concept of change?

What evidence is presented that the central character is motivated by a given emotion?

What concepts are central to under-standing the story? What do we under-stand about these concepts?

What is the central issue in this story?

Assumptions

Data, Evidence

Concept

Issue

Reasoning in Literature

Implications

Point of View

What are the implications of character behavior at this point in the story?

Purpose

Inferences

From what point of view is the story told?

What is the purpose of the poem/story?

What inferences might be made about the ending of the story based on specific events?

Models for Graphic Organizers

Graphic organizers help students to organize their thinking and to develop strategies for studying and communicating. Various types of organizers provide different patterns for thinking. The patterns used in the units for this project include:

Webs to Show Relationships

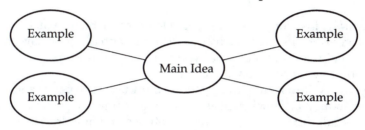

Venn Diagrams for Comparison and Contrast

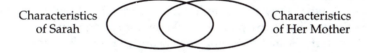

Concept Maps to Define Concepts and to Show Cause/Effect Links

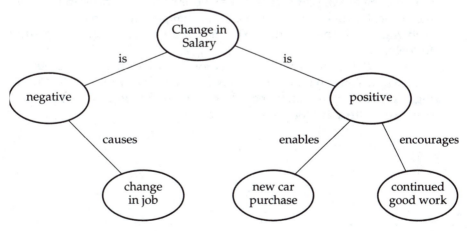

The Writing Process Model

The writing process shows the stages that writers use to work on a piece. The stages are not separate parts that writers go through from step 1 to step 5. Rather, writers move back and forth among the stages and use them to construct, clarify, and polish their writing. The writing process model is used throughout the unit to encourage students to engage in actively improving their own writing.

1. *Prewriting:* List your ideas and begin to organize them. You may want to use a graphic organizer such as a web or a Venn diagram. Graphic organizers help you to "see" what you will write about. As you write, you can add to your diagram or change it.
2. *Drafting:* Write a rough draft getting your ideas onto paper and not worrying about mechanics such as spelling, grammar, or punctuation. Some writers call this stage *composing*. Sometimes, the first draft is a "messing around" stage where your drafting or composing helps you to "hear" what you want to say.
3. *Revising:* Conferencing is an essential step in the revising stage. Ask people (friends, family, teachers) to listen to your work and to tell you what they like, what they don't understand, and what they'd like to know more about. This is the place to make major changes in your "composition" or draft. Sometimes, you may want to go back to the prewriting stage and redo your organizer so that your paper has a new structure. Beware of skipping this step and jumping directly to Step 4.
4. *Editing:* After you have revised your paper, look for the small changes that will make a big difference. Check your choice of words and identify mechanical errors. After you make the changes and corrections, proofread your work one final time. You may want to ask a friend or an adult for help.
5. *Sharing or Publishing:* There are numerous ways to share and to publish your work. You can bind it into a book, recopy it in your best handwriting and post it on a bulletin board, read it aloud to your class or family, or make it into a gift for someone special.

The Research Model

The research model provides students a way to approach an issue of significance and work it through individually and in small groups. Its organization follows major elements of reasoning.

1. Identify your issue or problem.
- What is the issue or problem?
- Who are the stakeholders and what are their positions?
- What is *your* position on this issue?

2. Read about your issue and identify points of view or arguments through information sources.
   - What are my print sources?
   - What are my media sources?
   - What are my people sources?
   - What are my preliminary findings based on a review of existing sources?

3. *Form a set of questions that can be answered by a specific set of data.* (For example: (1) What would the results be of _____? (2) Who would benefit and by how much? (3) Who would be harmed and by how much?)
   - My Questions?

4. *Gather evidence through research techniques such as surveys, interviews, or experiments.*
   - What survey questions should I ask?
   - What interview questions should I ask?
   - What experiments should I do?

5. *Manipulate and transform data so that it can be interpreted.*
   - How can I summarize what I found out?
   - Should I develop charts, diagrams, or ghraphs to represent my data?

6. Draw conclusions and inferences.
   - What do the data mean? How can I interpret what I found out?
   - What conclusions and inferences can be drawn from my results?

7. *Determine implications and consequences.*
   - What are the implications and consequences of my results in light of the initial problem?
   - Do I know enough or are there now new questions to be answered?

8. *Communicate results.*
   - Have I used Sections 1–7 above to organize a written report?
   - Have I used Sections 1–7 above to organize an oral presentation?

The Metacognition Model

Metacognition Steps	Research Process	Writing
I. Task Analysis and Planning		
• Set Goals	• Identify Problem or Issue	• Prewriting
• Deternine Steps to Reach Goals	• Identify Points of View on Arguments	
• What More Do I Need to Know?		
• What Obstacles Must Be Overcome? How Can Potential Errors Be Fixed?		
• What Will the Solution Look Like?		
II. Monitoring Progress		
• Is Progress Being Made?	• Gather Evidence	• Composing
• What Are the Next Steps?	• Manipulate and Transform Data for Interpretationn	• Revising
• Are Strategies Working?		
• What Are Other Strategies?		
• Identify Mistakes and Fix Them		
III. Assessing Progress		
• Was Goal Researched?	• Draw Conclusions and Inferences	• Editing
• Were Mistakes Fixed?	• Determine Implications and Consequences	• Publishing
• Does Solution Fit Prediction?	• Communicate Results	
• Was Time Used Well?		
• What Could Be Improved?		

Appendices

Appendix A:
The Concept of Change: Interdisciplinary Inquiry and Meaning
by Linda Neal Boyce

What Is Change?

Because change is a complex concept that inspires fear as well as hope, the idea of change has engaged thinkers throughout the ages and across disciplines. Therefore, change is best studied as an interdisciplinary concept for several reasons. First, an understanding of change in one discipline informs the study of change in another discipline and results in important connections. Second, an interdisciplinary study of change provides insights into the structure of each discipline. Equally important, the increasing rate of global change resulting in social, political, and environmental upheaval, an information explosion, and a technological revolution creates an urgent need to understand the dynamics of change.

To provide a basis for understanding change as a concept, this Appendix explores change in several disciplines. While exploring the concept, it identifies resources for teachers and for students that focus on change. Finally, it examines the way the concept of change was applied in the National Language Arts Project for High Ability Learners.

Religion and Philosophy

The *Encyclopedia of Philosophy* (Capek, 1967) and the *Encyclopedia of Religion and Ethics* (Hyslop, 1910) provide overviews of change from the perspectives of religion and philosophy. Both sources agree that change is one of the most basic and pervasive features of our experience. Hyslop goes so far as to say that change is difficult to define and that it is easier to discuss the types of change. He identifies four types of change: (1) *qualitative* change, a change in the qualities or properties of a subject such as chemical reaction; (2) *quantitative* change, which includes expansion, contraction, detrition, and accretion; (3) *local* change, or a change in the subject's position in space; and (4) *formal* change, a change of shape. Hyslop adds that all changes involve time, which is an essential condition of change.

Historically, philosophers and theologians have not always acknowledged the existence of change (Capek, 1967; Hyslop, 1910). Ideas of God, Being, and One that are based on eternal order and perfection of nature regard time and change as illusions of finite experience. Hyslop points out that acknowledging change is crucial to inquiry; that change represents the dynamic as the source of all investigations into causes. He states, "Curiosity regarding causal agency begins with the discovery of change and terminates in explanation" (p. 357). Capek's and Hyslop's essays offer an important backdrop to our understanding of the current controversies, the intense emotion, and the values that surround the concept of change.

Social Studies

In his outline of "Social Studies within a Global Education," Kniep (1991/1989) identifies change as one of the conceptual themes for social studies and asserts, "The process of movement from one state of being to another is a universal aspect of the planet and is an inevitable part of life and living" (p. 121). He lists adaption, cause and effect, development, evolution, growth, revolution, and time as related concepts. Kniep's comprehensive scope and sequence for social studies includes: (1) essential elements (systems, human values, persistent issues and problems, and global history), (2) conceptual themes (interdependence, change, culture, scarcity, and conflict), (3) phenomenological themes (people, places, and events), and (4) persistent problem themes (peace and security, national/international development, environmental problems, and human rights). Change is both a concept to understand and an agent to consider in all social studies ideas and themes.

In discussing social change, Daniel Chirot (1985) views social change as pervasive. He states that most societies, however, delude themselves into believing that stability prevails and that unchanging norms can be a reality.

Chirot identifies demographic change, technological change, and political change as the most important causes of general social change. In his discussion of how and why critical changes have occurred, Chirot considers three transformations in social structure among the most important:

- *The technological revolution produced by the adoption of sedentary agriculture*
- *The organizational revolution that accompanied the rise of states*
- *The current "modernization" that encompasses major changes in thought, technology, and politics (p. 761)*

Chirot (1985) points out that studying current major changes such as the increasing power of the state and the proletarianization of labor helps us understand smaller changes such as those in family structure, local political organizations, types of protest, and work habits. Because change impacts on our lives in large and small ways, we must understand and confront it.

Vogt's (1968) analysis of cultural change echoes Chirot's discussion of social change: "It can now be demonstrated from our accumulated archeological and historical data that a culture is never static, but rather that one of its most fundamental properties is change" (p. 556). Vogt cites three factors that influence change in a given culture:

- Any change in the ecological niche as a result of natural environmental changes or the migration of a society, such as when the Anasazi Indians left Mesa Verde to find new homes and lost their cultural identity in the process
- Any contact between two societies with different cultural patterns, such as when Hispanic and Native American cultures converged in New Mexico

- Any evolutionary change occurring within a society, such as when a food-gathering society domesticates its plants and animals or incorporates technology to effect lifestyle changes

In his discussion of cultural adaptation, Carneiro (1968) distinguishes between cultural adaptation (the adjustment of a society to its external and internal conditions) and cultural evolution (change by which a society grows complex and better integrated). Adaptation may include simplification and loss resulting from a deteriorating environment. Thus, adaptation may signal negative as well as positive changes for a cultural group.

History—the social sciences discipline that chronicles change—provides insight into specific changes from a range of perspectives. For instance, resources such as *The Timetables of History* (Grun, 1991) and the *Smithsonian Timelines of the Ancient World* (Scarre, 1993) record changes by significant annual events in the areas of history and politics; literature and theater; religion, philosophy, and learning; the visual arts; music; science and technology; and daily life. These tools allow readers to see at a glance the simultaneous events and significant people involved in changes occurring throughout the world or in a specific area.

Various scholars chronicle ideas about change on an interdisciplinary canvas. Boorstin (1983) focuses on man's need to know and the courage of those who challenged dogma at various times in history. He provides an in-depth look at the causes of change, considering such questions as why the Chinese did not "discover" Europe and America and why the Egyptians and not the Greeks invented the calendar. Tamplin (1991) demonstrates the interrelationship of personal, cultural, and societal change with discussions and illustrations of literature, visual arts, architecture, music, and the performing arts. Petroski (1992) chronicles change and investigates its origins through technology. He argues that shortcomings are the driving force for change and sees inventors as critics who have a compelling urge to tinker with things and to improve them.

Science

Echoing the call for curriculum reform that centers on an indepth study of broad concepts, Rutherford and Ahlgren (1989), in *Science for All Americans* state, "Some important themes pervade science, mathematics, and technology and appear over and over again, whether we are looking at an ancient civilization, the human body, or a comet. They are ideas that transcend disciplinary boundaries and prove fruitful in explanation, in theory, in observation, and in design. " Rutherford and Ahlgren proceed to recommend six themes: systems, models, constancy, patterns of change, evolution, and scale. Of the six themes, three of them—constancy, patterns of change, and evolution—focus on change or its inverse. In discussing patterns of change, Rutherford and Ahlgren identify three general categories, all of which have applicability in other disciplines: (1) changes that are steady trends, (2) changes that occur in cycles, and (3) changes that are irregular.

Sher (1993) identifies and discusses four general patterns of change: (1) steady changes—those that occur at a characteristic rate; (2) cyclic changes—those changes that repeat in cycles; (3) random changes—those changes that occur irregularly, unpredictably, and in a way that is mathematically random; and (4) chaotic change—change that appears random and irregular on the surface, but is in fact or principle predictable. Sher considers the understanding of chaotic change as one of the most exciting developments in recent science.

As in the other disciplines, change in science can be studied as a concept and as a specific application or type of change. For example, our view of the earth over the last 40 years has changed from a static globe model to a dynamic plate tectonics model, affecting our understanding of earthquakes, volcanoes, and other seismic events (NASA, 1988, 1990).

Language—Creative and Changing

In *Language in Thought and Action*, Hayakawa and Hayakawa (1990) state categorically, "Language…makes progress possible" (p. 7). They argue that reading and writing make it possible to pool experience and that "cultural and intellectual cooperation is, or should be, the great principle of human life" (p. 8). They then examine the relationships among language, thought, and behavior and how language changes thinking and behavior. For instance, they discuss how judgments stop thought, thereby leading to unfounded and dangerous generalizations. They explore the changing meanings of words and point out "no word ever has exactly the same meaning twice" (p. 39). For the Hayakawas, dictionaries are not authoritative statements about words but rather historical records of the meanings of words. Finally, the Hayakawas discuss the paralyzing effects of fear of change and the anger that accompanies it. They propose that the debate around issues facing society should center on specific questions such as What will be the results? Who would benefit, and by how much? and Who would be harmed, and to what degree? rather than questions of "right" or "wrong. " They contend that this way of thinking reflects a scientific attitude and harnesses language to accurately "map" social and individual problems, thereby enabling change.

While *Language in Thought and Action* is an eloquent manifesto about the possibilities of language, the anthology *Language Awareness* (Eschholz, Rosa, & Clark, 1982) provides a resource on specific topics. The essays cover the history of language; language in politics and propaganda; the language of advertising; media and language; jargon; names; prejudice and language; taboos and euphemisms; language play; and the responsible use of language. Each essay examines either changes in language or how language changes thinking and action. For example, in her outline of the devices of propaganda that include name calling, generalities, "plain folks" appeal, stroking, personal attacks, guilt or glory by association, bandwagon appeals, faulty cause and effect, false analogy, and testimonials, Cross (1982) examines the manipulative power of language.

The powers of language range from strident manipulation to the quiet heightening of awareness. Response to language involves a change—a change of perspective, a new understanding, an insight in the search for meaning. Coles (1989) speaks of the power of literature to give direction to life and to awaken moral sensibilities. He states, "Novels and stories are renderings of life; they can not only keep us company, but admonish us, point us in new directions, or give us the courage to stay a given course" (p. 159).

While Coles discusses the impact of literature on private lives, Downs (1978) discusses revolutionary books throughout history in his *Books That Changed the World*. Examining such books as *The Bible*, Machiavelli's *The Prince*, Beecher's *Uncle Tom's Cabin*, Darwin's *Origin of Species*, and Freud's *The Interpretation of Dreams*, Downs attempts to discover and to analyze two categories of writings: works that were direct, immediate instruments in determining the course of events and works that molded minds over centuries. He concludes that, "Omitting the scientists in the group, for whom these comments are less pertinent, the books [which changed the world] printed since 1500 were written by nonconformists, radicals, fanatics, revolutionists, and agitators" (p. 25).

The reading process that enables readers to search for information and meaning is an active, recursive process that includes choosing a book, reading, discussing from the reader's point of view, listening to another's point of view, reflecting and responding, and rereading or making a new choice (Bailey, Boyce, & VanTassel-Baska, 1990). Effective reading includes revising an interpretation or changing ideas, a step which is mirrored in the writing process and in speaking and listening. Kennedy (1993) sees all of the language processes—reading, writing, speaking, listening, and thinking—as complex, interrelated activities that result in a dynamic, changing discourse.

Censorship reflects the public's acknowledgment and fear of the power of language to change thinking, behavior, and society at large. The debate over censorship and freedom of expression has raged for centuries and ranges from the use of racist and sexist language in literature to the effects of violence on television. Plato, one may remember, argued against allowing children to listen to imaginative stories and banned the poets from his ideal society. The continuing controversy regarding the burning of the American flag is one of several censorship issues widely debated in our society that illustrates the linkage of symbols, language, and freedom of expression (Bradbury & Quinn, 1991).

Telecommunications in a Changing World

Telecommunications has dramatically changed our capacity to access information. Electronic mail, known as e-mail, is a telecommunications system that links computers around the world through telephone lines and satellites. It has created significant changes in scientific and business communities, such as increased flexibility for team members working in various locations across time zones, an end to isolation of researchers around the world, and the restructuring of organizations by eliminating corporate hierarchies (Perry, 1992a). Perry also cites the role of e-mail in the Russian coup of Boris Yeltsin and the use of faxes during the Tiananmen uprising. E-mail and fax machines provided sources of information that were difficult to control and allowed dissenters to communicate with one another and with the outside world (Perry, 1992b).

Video, television, cable, compact discs, and computers and the Internet are transforming not only access to information but also the content of information as well. In a recent *U.S. News and World Report* article John Leo (March 8, 1993) discusses the new standard of television news that blends information and entertainment. He contends that images, story line, and emotional impact are replacing a commitment to evidence,

TABLE A–1   Generalizations and Outcomes about Change

Generalizations	Outcomes
1. Change is pervasive.	Understand that change permeates our lives and our universe.
2. Change is linked to time.	Illustrate the variability of change based on time.
3. Change may be perceived as systematic or random.	Categorize types of change, given several examples. Demonstrate the change process at work in a piece of literature.
4. Change may represent growth and development or regression and decay.	Interpret change in selected works as progressive or regressive.
5. Change may occur according to natural order or be imposed by individuals or groups.	Analyze social and individual change in a given piece of literature.

ethics, and truth. In another development, compact discs and computers are combining sound tracks, animation, photography, and print information that replace standard multivolume encyclopedias and that enable users to combine information in new ways. The Grolier Multimedia Encyclopedia (1994) on CD-ROM, for example, supplements its text with features such as animated multimedia maps that show the growth and development of U.S. railroads, the women's suffrage movement, and other topics. This changing information technology demands new standards for the evaluation of information and new consideration of how technology can limit or expand thinking.

The Concept of Change and Language Arts Unit Development

For the purposes of teaching the concept of change for the National Javits Language Arts Project for High Ability Learners, five generalizations about change were drawn from the literature of various disciplines. Table A–1 illustrates those generalizations and their accompanying outcomes. Examples of how the generalizations were addressed in the units through language study, language processes, and literature follow the table.

Language Study

Throughout the units, word study and vocabulary served as a primary source for studying change. Students constructed vocabulary webs that mapped words by (1) the definition, (2) a sentence that used the word from the literature being studied, (3) an example of the word, and (4) an analysis of the word that identified stems (roots, prefixes, and suffixes), word families, and word history. To build on the verbal talent of high-ability learners, resources such as *Sumer Is Icumen In: Our Ever-Changing Language* by Greenfeld (1978) and *Oxford Guide to Word Games* by Augarde (1984) were included in the units to encourage students to explore language changes and to play with the possibilities of inventing it themselves.

Each unit included a grammar packet developed by Michael Thompson and based on his work, *The Magic Lens: A Spiral Tour through the Human Ideas of Grammar* (1991). Thompson's packets were designed to help students learn why some ideas are clear and others are confusing; to understand the power of grammar to reveal deep thinking and deep meaning. Implicit in this study was the idea that changing the grammar of a sentence or paragraph meant changing its meaning. Literature selections on which the units were built and the students' own writing provided the context for studying grammar.

Language Processes

The processes of reading, writing, listening, and speaking were studied as change processes. Literature discussions were based on the premise that each person's interpretation and understanding of meaning would be different from another person's interpretation. Through listening to one another, students were encouraged to seek new meaning and to examine how their interpretations changed during the discussion. In like manner, students studied the writing process as a way to explore ideas and to generate their own thinking and learning. The revision stage of writing emphasized seeking feedback and listening to responses from teachers and peers. Considering another's perspective often led to changes in the understanding of one's own work and to subsequent changes in the structure and clarity of the writing.

Oral communications in these units centered on persuasive speaking and critical listening. Students studied how to change their audience's opinion and actions through argument formulation and strategies of persuasion. As students listened to persuasive speeches, they analyzed the arguments and evaluated their effectiveness. Resources for the speaking and listening components included videotapes of master persuaders such as Franklin D. Roosevelt, Martin Luther King Jr., and Adloph Hitler that provided students with opportunities to consider the role of persuasion in social and historical contexts. Other resources, such as *The American Reader: Words That Moved a Nation* (Ravitch, 1990), documented the persuasive role of oral communications such as orations, Congressional hearings, and songs in the process of change.

Literature

Each of the units centered on literature selections with vocabulary and language study emerging from the selections. The development of the concept of change also emerged from the literature discussions and activities. Typically, each literary piece was examined for evidence of character changes, both physical and psychological, as well as social, political, and economic changes. For instance, in "The Power of Light" by I. B. Singer (1962), students discussed the issue of whether characters change themselves or are changed by events outside of their control.

In addition to the literature selections that were discussed with the total group, additional resources embedded in each unit illustrated the generalizations about change and addressed the social, cultural, and environmental implications of change.

For instance, *Commodore Perry in the Land of the Shogun* (Blumberg, 1985) documents the dramatic social and cultural changes created by Perry's visits to Japan in 1853 and 1854. Illustrated with reproductions of primary sources, the account presents misconceptions, hostilities, and humorous episodes encountered from multiple points of view. Change is palpable while reading the book. A very different book, *Letting Swift River Go* by Yolen (1992), tells of the drowning of a Swift River town for the building of the Quabbin Reservoir, a water supply for Boston and now a wilderness area. The open-ended story alludes to necessary tradeoffs and provides opportunities to discuss changes linked to time as well as the positive and negative aspects of change.

Conclusion

The idea of change crosses all disciplines and offers learners an opportunity to construct a concept that will inform their lives in meaningful ways. Because of the accelerating rate of change in our world, students need to understand the concept and to acquire effective tools for meeting its challenges. Language with its powers of inquiry, persuasion, and critique provides a powerful tool for meeting the challenges of change.

Literature, in particular, offers students and teachers a rich content arena for analyzing change and for considering the issues that surround it. Literature captures the voices, the emotions, and the concerns of thinkers through the ages and across cultures. It demonstrates types of change, responses to change, the causes and agents of change, as well as the effects of change. In a time of dizzying change, literature also offers continuity and a welcomed opportunity for reflection.

References

Augarde, T. (1984). *The Oxford guide to word games*. Oxford: Oxford University Press.

Bailey, J. M., Boyce, L. N., & VanTassel-Baska, J. (1990). The writing, reading, and counseling connection: A framework for serving the gifted. In J. VanTassel-Baska (Ed.), *A practical guide to counseling the gifted in a school setting* (2nd ed., pp. 72–89). Reston, VA: The Council for Exceptional Children.

Blumberg, R. (1985). *Commodore Perry in the land of the Shogun*. New York: Lothrop.

Boorstin, D. J. (1983). *The Discoverers: A history of man's search to know his world and himself*. New York: Random.

Bradbury, N. M., & Quinn, A. (1991). *Audiences and intentions: A book of arguments*. New York: Macmillan.

Capek, M. (1967). Change. In P. Edwards (Ed.), *The encyclopedia of philosophy* (Vol. 1, pp. 75–79). New York: Macmillan.

Carneiro, R. L. (1968). Cultural adaptation. In D. L. Sills (Ed.), *International encyclopedia of the social sciences* (Vol. 3, pp. 551–554). New York: Macmillan & The Free Press.

Chirot, D. (1985). Social change. In A. Kuper & J. Kuper (Eds.), *The social science encyclopedia* (pp. 760–763). Boston: Routledge & Kegan Paul.

Coles, R. (1989). *The call of stories: Teaching and the moral imagination*. Boston: Houghton Mifflin.

Cross, D. W. (1982). Propaganda: How not to be bamboozled. In P. Eschholz, A. Rosa, & V. Clark (Eds.), *Language awareness* (pp. 70–81). New York: St. Martin's.

Downs, R. B. (1978). *Books that changed the world* (2nd ed). Chicago: American Library Association.

Eschholz, P., Rosa, A., & Clark, V. (1982). *Language awareness* (3rd ed.). New York: St. Martin's.

Greenfeld, H. (1978). *Sumer is icumen in: Our ever-changing language*. New York: Crown.

Grolier multimedia encyclopedia. (1994). Danbury, CT: Grolier.

Grun, B. (1991). *The timetables of history: A horizontal linkage of people and events.* New York: Simon & Schuster.

Hayakawa, S. I., & Hayakawa, A. R. (1990). *Language in thought and action* (5th ed.). Fort Worth, TX: Harcourt Brace Jovanovich.

Hyslop, J. H. (1910). Change. In J. Hastings (Ed.), *Encyclopaedia of religion and ethics* (Vol. 3, pp. 357–358). New York: Charles Scribner.

Kennedy, C. (1993). Teaching with writing: The state of the art. In *Language arts topics papers.* Williamsburg, VA: College of William and Mary, Center for Gifted Education.

Kniep, W. M. (1991). Appendix 3: Social studies within a global education. In W. C. Parker (Ed.), *Renewing the social studies curriculum* (pp. 119–123). Alexandria, VA: Association for Supervision and Curriculum Development. (Reprinted from *Social Education,* 1989, pp. 399–403.)

Leo, J. (1993, March 8). Spicing up the (ho-hum) truth. *U. S. News & World Report, 14*(9), 24.

National Aeronautics and Space Administration. (1988). *Earth system science: A program for global change.* Washington, D. C: NASA.

National Aeronautics and Space Administration. (1990). *The earth observing system: A mission to planet earth.* Washington, DC: NASA.

Newmann, F. M., & Wehlage, G. G. (1993). Five standards of authentic instruction. *Educational Leadership, 50*(7), 8–12.

Perry, T. S. (1992a, October). E-mail at work. *IEEE Spectrum, 29*(10), 24–28.

Perry, T. S. (1992b, October). Forces for social change. *IEEE Spectrum, 29*(10), 30–32.

Petroski, H. (1992). *The evolution of useful things.* New York: Knopf.

Ravitch, D. (1990). *The American reader: Words that moved a nation.* New York: HarperCollins.

Rutherford, F. J., & Ahlgren, A. (1989). *Science for all Americans: Scientific literacy.* New York: American Association for the Advancement of Science.

Scarre, C. (Ed.). (1993). *Smithsonian timelines of the ancient world: A visual chronology from the origins of life to AD1500.* New York: Dorling.

Seiger-Ehrenberg, S. (1991). Concept development. In A. L. Costa (Ed.), *Developing minds* (Rev. ed., Vol. 1, pp. 290–294). Alexandria, VA: Association for Supervision and Curriculum Development.

Sher, B. T. (1993). *Guide to science concepts: Developing science curriculum for high ability learners K-8.* Williamsburg, VA: College of William and Mary, School of Education, Center for Gifted Education.

Singer, I. B. (1962). *Stories for children.* New York: Farrar, Straus, and Giroux.

Tamplin, R. (Ed.). (1991). *The arts: A history of expression in the 20th century.* New York: Free Press.

Thompson, M. C. (1991). *The magic lens: A spiral tour through the human ideas of grammar.* Unionville, NY: Trillium.

Vogt, E. Z. (1968). Culture change. In D. L. Sills (Ed.), *International encyclopedia of the social sciences,* (Vol. 3, pp. 554–558). New York: Macmillan & The Free Press.

Yolen, J. (1992). *Letting Swift River go.* Boston: Little, Brown.

Appendix B:
Curriculum Framework Goals and Objectives

The following goals and objectives guide the language arts units developed under the National Language Arts Curriculum Project for High Ability Learners.

GOAL #1: To develop analytical and interpretive skills in literature.
Students will be able to:
  a. Describe what a selected literary passage means.
  b. Cite similarities and differences in meaning among selected works of literature.
  c. Make inferences based on information in given passages.
  d. Create a title for a reading selection and provide a rationale for the creation to justify it.

GOAL #2: To develop persuasive writing skills.
Students will be able to:
  a. Develop a written persuasive essay (thesis statement, supporting reasons, and conclusion), given a topic.
  b. Complete various pieces of writing using a three-phase revision process based on peer review, teacher feedback, and self-evaluation.

GOAL #3: To develop linguistic competency.
Students will be able to:
  a. Analyze the form and function of words in a given context.
  b. Develop vocabulary power commensurate with reading.
  c. Apply standard English usage in written and oral contexts.
  d. Evaluate effective use of words, sentences, and paragraphs in context.

GOAL #4: To develop listening/oral communication skills.
Students will be able to:
  a. Discriminate between informative and persuasive messages.
  b. Evaluate an oral persuasive message according to main idea and arguments cited to support it.
  c. Develop skills of argument formulation.
  d. Organize oral presentations, using elements of reasoning as the basis.

GOAL #5: To develop reasoning skills in the language arts.
Students will be able to:
  a. State a purpose for all modes of communication, their own as well as others.
  b. Define a problem, given ill-structured, complex, or technical information.
  c. Formulate multiple perspectives (at least two) on a given issue.
  d. State assumptions behind a line of reasoning in oral or written form.
  e. Apply linguistic and literary concepts appropriately.
  f. Provide evidence and data to support a claim, issue, or thesis statement.
  g. Make inferences, based on evidence.
  h. Draw implications for policy development or enactment based on the available data.

GOAL #6: To understand the concept of change in the language arts.
Students will be able to:
  a. Understand that change is pervasive.
  b. Illustrate the variability of change based on time.
  c. Categorize types of change, given several examples.
  d. Interpret change as progressive or regressive in selected works.
  e. Demonstrate the change process at work in a piece of literature.
  f. Analyze social and individual change in a given piece of literature.

Appendix C:
Description of Curriculum
Materials: National Language Arts Curriculum
Project for High Ability Learners

A Curriculum Framework in Language
Arts for High Ability Learners (K–8)

The purpose of this curriculum framework is to provide a model for developing appropriate and meaningful language arts curricula for high-ability learners at K–8 levels. It is intended as a guide to making decisions about traditional curricular emphases within the language arts areas of reading, writing, speaking, and listening, as well as nontraditional emphases in areas such as thinking, multiculturalism, and technology. The target audience of the guide is teachers, administrators, and curriculum specialists who have responsibility for shaping appropriate curriculum experiences for these students in language arts.

Journeys and Destinations:
The Challenge of Change (Grades 2–3)

This unit uses an inquiry-based approach to investigate literature in an inter-disciplinary, multicultural curriculum. The guiding theme of the unit is the recognition of change as a concept that affects people and their relationships to the world around them. An open-ended approach to the discussion process is emphasized in the search for meaning in literature selections such as *The Green Book*, *Bringing the Rain to Kapiti Plain*, and *The Ugly Duckling*. Vocabulary development and writing activities support the readings.

Autobiographies: Personal Odysseys
of Change (Grades 4–6)

In this unit, students study the concept of change by reading autobiographies of writers and by looking at change in selected lives. They examine life stories and self portraits through literature and works of art from various cultures. They read selected stories from Junior Great Books to probe issues of identity. Discussions, reflective writing, the development of a research project, and a presentation provide insights into talent development and encourage students to explore their own identities as talented learners.

Literary Reflections on Personal and Social Change (Grades 4–6)

Even though all four language arts strands of literature, writing, language study, and oral communication are integrated into this unit, the core of the unit involves students interacting with literature while enhancing reading comprehension and textual analysis skills. By reading the literature and engaging in shared inquiry, students should develop an awareness about the nature and importance of change, particularly as it affects people in various circumstances, times, and cultures. The literature selections, including *The Secret Garden* and world-class short stories by such authors as Tolstoy and Singer, serve as a basis for discussion. Students engage in writing activities not only by responding to the literature but also by using persuasive writing to express opinions on issues of significance that arise from the literature.

Changing Ideas and Perspectives through Persuasion (Grades 5–6)

This unit highlights persuasion, especially as it relates to oral communication. Emphasis is placed on providing evidence for opinions. Students must cite passages from literature to defend their points of view in discussion as well as in written arguments. Literature such as *The Valiant* and Junior Great Books stories frame the basis for exploring the reasoning process through analysis and interpretation. Opportunities are presented for impromptu speeches, informative speeches, and persuasive speeches, debate, both small and large group discussion, and critical listening skills. Throughout the unit, students work independently on the issue of censorship and make an oral presentation of their opinions and supporting evidence at the end of the unit.

Literature of the 1940s: A Decade of Change (Grades 7–9)

This unit looks at the historical events and social issues of the 1940s through the literature of the decade, including novels, short stories, poetry, essays, letters, and newspapers. Numerous opportunities for reading, writing, listening, and speaking are incorporated into the unit. Each student is required to pose a hypothesis and conduct research concerning some issue of significance that arises out of the literature that is studied. Students make both a written and oral presentation of their research. The unit is rich in materials that highlight the concept of change, including works like Hersey's *Hiroshima*, Frank's *The Diary of Anne Frank*, and McCuller's *Member of the Wedding*.

Threads of Change in 19th-Century American Literature (Grades 7–9)

This unit explores five themes in nineteenth-century American history through literature of the times: romanticism, transcendentalism, abolitionism, industrialism, and feminism. Each of the five "isms" has its own Literature Box that contains appropriate documents to serve as a resource for small investigative teams of students. The "isms" are investigated as change agents in American life through the study of key writings of the period, including Hawthorne, Melville, Thoreau, and Emerson. Students produce both written and oral presentations of their findings and ideas. Literary works discussed in the unit include *The Adventures of Huckleberry Finn*, *Billy Budd, Sailor*, and Hawthorne and Poe short stories.

Index

This page constitutes a continuation of the copyright page.